Sixties Radicalism and Social Movement Activism

Sixties Radicalism and Social Movement Activism

Retreat or Resurgence?

Edited by
Bryn Jones and Mike O'Donnell

ANTHEM PRESS
LONDON · NEW YORK · DELHI

Anthem Press
An imprint of Wimbledon Publishing Company
www.anthempress.com

This edition first published in UK and USA 2012
by ANTHEM PRESS
75-76 Blackfriars Road, London SE1 8HA, UK
or PO Box 9779, London SW19 7ZG, UK
and
244 Madison Ave. #116, New York, NY 10016, USA

First published in hardback by Anthem Press in 2010

© 2012 Bryn Jones and Mike O'Donnell editorial matter and selection;
individual chapters © individual contributors

The moral right of the authors has been asserted.

All rights reserved. Without limiting the rights under copyright reserved above,
no part of this publication may be reproduced, stored or introduced into
a retrieval system, or transmitted, in any form or by any means
(electronic, mechanical, photocopying, recording or otherwise),
without the prior written permission of both the copyright
owner and the above publisher of this book.

British Library Cataloguing in Publication Data
A catalogue record for this book is available from the British Library.

Library of Congress Cataloging in Publication Data
A catalog record for this book has been requested.

ISBN-13: 978 0 85728 573 7 (Pbk)
ISBN-10: 0 85728 573 4 (Pbk)

This title is also available as an eBook.

For: Asa, Leah, Michael, Tara and Saisha
– inheritors of the Sixties

PREFACE AND ACKNOWLEDGEMENTS

In December 2009 a campaign, begun by an unaffiliated British couple Jon and Tracy Morter, made the 17 year-old 'Killing in the Name' recording by anarchistic US band *Rage Against the Machine* the UK's best-selling popular music track. This success kept a heavily promoted, mass-market ballad from the coveted first place in the UK's Christmas pop music chart. Instead of a sentimental jingle hymning individual struggle and fortitude, the Christmas theme was *Rage*'s profane, heavy rock polemic, which denounces racism and exploitation of violence by the 'system'. This outcome stymied the previously successful joint operation of recording companies and mass-audience TV show *The X-Factor* in delivering 'Britain's top Christmas single'. The campaign against excess business monopolisation of chart music used the new power of the internet, but in the tradition of sixties protest against Establishment hegemony, it arose from an ethic of activism discussed throughout this book.

The timely manifestation of this spirit of the sixties, as we completed the manuscript, further vindicated our original motivation in compiling it. As the *Introduction* and *Conclusion* contend, many values, sentiments and practices of sixties radicalism have not, as some argue, been extinguished in the recent, seemingly more conformist and conservative climate. Sixties survivals and legacies retain a significant social, cultural and political influence. Indeed, please note that the book uses the term 'sixties' to refer to the continuance of inter-related, politically and socially radical phenomena which writers, such as Arthur Marwick and Gerd-Rainer Horn, describe as the 'long sixties'. The designation '1960s' or '60s' is reserved for the chronological period 1960–1969 from which the broader 'sixties' social patterns began.

The book's scope owes much to its contributors' varied backgrounds and fresh perspectives: a multi-national mix of young and older scholars, whom we thank for providing patience and a diverse range of accounts of sixties radicalism; with common themes further explored in the *Introduction* and *Conclusion*. Most chapters originated at the British Sociological Association conference *1968: Impact and Implications*, so we thank two of its organisers, Gurminder Bhambra and Ipek Demir, for their early cooperation. Thanks also to Asa Desouza-Jones for alerting us to Foucault's lecture on utopia and heterotopias, utilised in the *Conclusion*; and to Dori and Phil for their emotional support. Anthem's Tej Sood, plus Janka Romero's editorial advice, gave timely and efficient assistance. For surviving errors and shortcomings, we accept only partial responsibility. We blame these on the intoxicating, disconcerting and bedazzling impressions of a remarkable epoch which – despite its undoubted excesses, fantasies and self-indulgences – continues to exert a powerful effect, even on mature imaginations.

Bryn Jones and Mike O'Donnell
Bath and London 2010

CONTENTS

Introduction

Sixties Radicalism: Creating Spaces and Leaving Legacies   vii
Bryn Jones and Mike O'Donnell

PART I. Radical Movements Around the World   1

1. All Along the Watershed: Sixties Values as Defence of Community Lifeworlds in Britain 1968–2008   3
Bryn Jones
2. May's Tensions Today: France, Then and Now   23
Kevin McDonald
3. The War Against the War: Violence and Anticolonialism in the Final Years of the Estado Novo   39
Miguel Cardina
4. From Sartre to Stevedores: The Connections between the Paris Barricades and the Re-emergence of Black Trade Unions in South Africa   59
Helen Lunn
5. 1968 – Was it Really a Year of Social Change in Pakistan?   73
Riaz Ahmed Shaikh

PART II. Theoretical & Cultural Significance   89

6. Nineteen Sixties Radicalism in the United States: Its Rise, Decline and Legacy   91
Mike O'Donnell
7. Students, Artists and the ICA: The Revolution Within   111
Ben Cranfield
8. The Situationist Legacy: Revolution as Celebration   133
Eloise Harding

9. Habermas on Sixties Student Protests: Reflections on Collective Action and Communicative Potential   149
James Driver

PART III. Social Movement Legacies   **167**

10. Sixties Movements, Educational Expansion and Cognitive Mobilisation: Postmaterialist Values and Unconventional Political Participation in West Germany   169
Andreas Hadjar and Florian Schlapbach
11. Carrying the Flame Forward: Activist Legacies of 1968 in Life Story Reflections   189
Barbara Körner and Rosemary McKechnie
12. When the Personal Became Political: A Reappraisal of the Women's Liberation Movement's Radical Idea   211
Maureen Freely

Conclusion

Resurgence? The Legacy of the Sixties to Contemporary Social Movements   225
Bryn Jones and Mike O'Donnell

Notes on Contributors   241

Author Index   245

Subject Index   251

Introduction

SIXTIES RADICALISM: CREATING SPACES AND LEAVING LEGACIES

Bryn Jones and Mike O'Donnell

> I'm talking to the 60s group ... that survived the war, the drugs the politics the violence on the streets, the whole shebang. We've survived it and we're here.
>
> (John Lennon, 1980. 12 hours before his murder outside his New York home)

Introduction

The title of this collection may prompt two types of reaction. For some, it is inappropriate to talk about the resurgence of phenomena that have become established and 'mainstream'. Personal freedoms in sexual relations, artistic expression and ongoing campaigns for equal rights have all become institutionalised in the past 40 years. However for other readers, familiar with the extravagant mission of the counter-culture and the shrivelling of revolutionary – or pseudo-revolutionary – politicking, the 'spirit of the 60s' may be thought of as beyond resuscitation. As one seasoned political journalist recently opined: '1968 was not a beginning – it was humanity's last rage against the dying of the light, the last, great street festival before darkness closed in.' (Wilby 2008) Or, as a music expert wrote of the cultural upsurge of the period, it is 'our former way of life, far away from us on the other side of the sun-flooded chasm of the Sixties' (MacDonald 1995, 34).

The contributions in this book however demonstrate that continuity and 'resurgence', exceeding the liberalisation of personal freedoms, exist in two key respects: as spaces and as active legacies. Resurgence is possible because the radical movements of the sixties opened up a series of previously non-existent, or only embryonic, social *spaces* (Touraine 2004, 225). The most prominent of which are those established by the struggles for equal rights by women and minorities, for sexual freedoms and the legitimacy of environmental protest. Several of our contributors clarify how the scope of such spaces was won or expanded, and in other cases lost, by sixties' movements. The *legacies* passed on to the present day consist, as the chapter by Freely suggests, and that from Körner and McKechnie shows, mainly in a kind of ethic. A psycho-cultural disposition, which may be expressed in articulated values, or in political practices which are still active across the generations (see Andreas Hadjar and Florian Schlapbach, chapter 6). These ideas are conceptualised more fully in the Conclusion to this volume. We suggest below, that current socio-political conditions may now be re-energising this ethic.

Yet 1960s radicalism was a diverse and virtually unprecedented complex of protest and transformative campaigns, whose many facets it is impossible to scrutinise in one volume. Moreover, most of these have already been analysed from a variety of angles: its politics, cultural innovations, life-style changes and social movement campaigns, sexual and ideological conflicts, media and artistic transformations (Sayres et al 1984; Collier and Horowitz 1989; Brick 1998; Grunenburg and Harris (eds.) 2005; Weeks 2007). On the other hand, assessment of the causes and longer-term implications of the decade is, necessarily and justifiably, open to continuous revision as contemporary developments stimulate different perspectives, while continuing research and scholarship produces new evidence. Broader judgements tend to polarise verdicts: sixties radicalism as either a combination of political failure and cultural introversion (Marwick 1999; Sandbrook 2007; DeGroot 2008), or the sixties as an epochal socio-cultural transformation that moulded today's institutional structures (Horn 2007).

The present collection aims to provide more forensic analyses of the spaces and legacies of radical causes and movements through detailed investigations of both the more celebrated cases, such as France 1968, and less well-known instances: South Africa, Portugal, Pakistan. These cases further illustrate diversity of activity within common themes and also the ways in which the 'explosion' had international, almost global dimensions. In these latter societies uneven economic development and authoritarian regimes were factors which, in turn, affected the roles and tactics of both campaigners and repressive forces, such as the army. The associated use of violence as a repressive or emancipatory tactic emerges as an important theme in several chapters: McDonald chapter 2; O'Donnell chapter 6; Driver chapter 9. The collection also examines underlying but significant causal factors: the role of artistic protest (Cranfield chapter 7; Harding chapter 8), and the phenomenon of generational identity (O'Donnell chapter 6; Hadjar and Schlapbach chapter 10).

Collectively, the various contributions also provide new material and perspectives on the longer-term consequences and implications of sixties radicalism for contemporary movements and institutions. These include: political attitudes and practices, civil society organisations and the ideational perspectives used by both activists and theorists in defining current concerns. The rest of this Introduction relates these themes to key points in the contributors' chapters – on socio-political movements, the political implications of artistic and cultural activity, and the social theory prisms reflecting and interpreting these developments – through a general overview of sixties radicalism. It goes on to identify the legacies and continuities identified throughout the book, before providing a succinct guide to the individual chapters.

Making Waves or Creating Spaces?

Part of the problem in identifying both the original significance of the sixties phenomenon is its multidimensionality. As Varon, Foley and McMillian aptly put it:

> ... so many people in so many settings devoted themselves so ardently to the work of transformation... change ranged widely, affecting governance, legal and political rights, and the distribution of wealth and power among and within regions, nations, races, ethnicities, and classes... also to more intimate and abstract realms... the meaning and identity of the family, education, sex and sexuality, adolescence and adulthood, work, pleasure, art, nature, divinity, the psyche, and the cognitive and sensory frames by which we apprehend "reality." (Varon et al 2008, 1)

The various contributions that follow seek to make sense of this efflorescence by examining its socio-political dynamics. While the gamut of cultural dimensions is given due weight, the micro- and macro-political thrust and uniqueness of the central social movements is here taken as the central dynamic and one with long-lasting and contemporary relevance.

One transversal focus is the social tectonics between cultural and normative upsurges and political activity. At this conjunction, accumulations of popular dissent and rebellion coalesce into movements for institutional change. For many former radicals and sceptical social historians the cultural-political phenomenon a identified as 'the Sixties' ran out of steam long ago and has had little surviving political impact. From the point of view of disillusioned radicalism (Collier and Horowitz 1989; Frank 1997; Debray 2007) market capitalism subverted sixties radicalism, commoditising and sanitising its formerly revolutionary icons and ideas. Similarly, social history sceptics play down the longer-term consequences because they conceptualise sixties radicalism as hubris: egoist and utopian posturing by a self-important minority (Marwick 1999; Sandbrook 2007; DeGroot 2008).

Post-sixties developments lend some credence to these relativising characterisations. Commentators tend to refer to the 'long 1960s' as the period of radicalism which began in that decade but which continued well into the 1970s; until mainstream politics shifted markedly to the right and economic recession set in. In this later phase, as libertarian left politics splintered into more doctrinaire forms of Marxism, or even self-destructive terroristic sects, left-radicalism was eclipsed by the ascendancy of doctrines eventually defined as Thatcherism and Reaganism. The rebellious epicentres of France and US campuses and political arenas returned to conformity and orthodox party politics. Sixties political radicalism was deemed to have failed.

> The end of the social movement arc is more approximate. In the US context, President Nixon's demise in 1974 through the Watergate scandal signaled the end of a certain quality of conflict that had defined American life for years. The world over, the early and mid-Seventies witnessed the palpable decline in the classic social movements of the Sixties – civil rights, Black Power, anti-war, student and youth. (Varon et al. 2008, 5)

Yet Varon and his colleagues go on to say that the post-sixties period saw; '…the maturation of newer movements, such as feminism, gay liberation, and New Right activism, which far transcended their 1960s roots.' Varon et al 2008, 5). It is plausible thus to say that the Sixties' movements created the spaces within which the successor campaigns flourished.

For a significant section of American opinion, radical content – in the form of the hedonistic counter-culture – was simply absorbed, transmogrified or co-opted into the more adventurous elements of corporate consumer culture (Heath and Potter 2006). But commentators have, perhaps, always been too quick to bury its radicalism after the dissipation of the first tidal wave. It is true that North American protest failed to halt its main target in the Vietnam War and was upstaged by mainstream conservatism in the Nixon years. And, in France, the semi-authoritarian structures of the Fifth Republic survived both 1968 and its founder Charles DeGaulle. More recently, as the 40th anniversary of the emblematic '68' was celebrated and debated, a swathe of opinions arose to indict the decade of rebellion, radicalism and irreverence for its infantilism, utopianism and narcissistic hedonism.

Leaving Legacies

And yet…in many respects, and beyond the formal procedures of political bureaucracies, sixties' social spaces have expanded and been filled by dynamic movements. A key question addressed by several of the contributions is whether the radical values which helped to create the social spaces have continued (Jones chapter 1; O'Donnell chapter 6)? Or, whether they have mutated within new forms of discourse (McDonald chapter 2; Hadjar and Schlapbach chapter 10)? After the fading of initial Sixties' expressions of radicalism, the world did not return to the social and cultural conservatism of the early Cold War period. Although the institutions of conventional politics may, in many respects remain largely unaltered, social movement and policy agendas and reference points still reflect key sixties causes: gender and sexual rights, localism vs. 'gigantism', and ethical vs. materialistic life styles. In some respects the popular terrain of United States politics could be said to be continuing the cultural and life-style controversies initiated by sixties radicals: the axiomatic political cleavage of the USA electorate into either socially-conservative and religiously-defined voters, or those favouring sexual rights and tolerance and the defence of 'minorities' (Frank 2005).

Europe is a more complex mosaic, but despite the electoral ascendancy of centre-right parties, a highly active plethora of campaigns, civil society organisations and civil rights' networks influence political agendas and constrain right-oriented politicians. So governments are less able to extend their ascendancy in the economic sphere to social and cultural conservatism. Embedded in civil society, seeking to avoid the sirens of state and business, NGOs and many other civil society organisations, may be regarded as quintessential sixties' institutions. These civil society organisations are not of course immune to the pressures and blandishments of dominant institutions. NGOs have been criticised from both the Left, for their dependence on state resources and agendas (Morris-Suzuki 2000; Short 2009), for a trend towards business characteristics (Jones 2007), and from the Right, for inadequate accountability to civil society (Johns 2002). NGOs have, nevertheless, inherited and utilised much sixties activism. Their institutionalisation is a longer-term and multi-faceted phenomenon, but it was the 1960s and early 1970s which saw quantum increases in NGOs; particularly with the injection of more radical discourses and activities (Rootes 2007; Jamison 1998).

Broader political-economy circumstances also inflect our sociological senses with an almost eerie sense of déjà vu. A young, apparently liberal, U.S. President captures the imagination of the world's youth. Like the cusp between sixties' affluence and seventies' 'stagflation', a long period of relatively stable prosperity in the economic order is faltering. An increasingly unpopular war against recalcitrant enemies to westernise a seemingly, indifferent or hostile population fuels mass resentment and protest in Europe and North America. France has experienced student strikes and university closures unparalleled since 1968; although this time the cause is government rationalisation proposals rather than intrinsic student grievance. Consumer capitalism may, as some allege, have outflanked, hegemonised and incorporated counter-cultural radicalism on one dimension. But, on others, it retreats and concedes ground to the descendants of sixties protest. Despite questioning of NGOs' independence and *bona fides*, many retain radical edges. They also provide the more organised and strategic elements to campaigns for: corporate social responsibility (and a more genuine accountability than businesses' financial duties prescribe), environmental sustainability, and human rights that are not otherwise guaranteed or monitored by official bodies.

Indeed as several of our chapters explain – Jones on the UK, O'Donnell on the USA, McDonald on France – the spaces created by the amorphous, over-confident, multi-faceted 'Movement' of the sixties provide, at the very least lessons, templates and warnings for its successors in the present century. Varon et al may be correct to say that the retreat from the high point of '68 means that 'a sense of having tried to do too much, too soon, and in the wrong way thus hovers over so many of the era's signal movements and experiments' (2008, 4). Yet, idealism and utopianism have certainly not vanished. The slogans of the anti-globalisation and alterglobalisation movements (see McDonald chapter 3) – 'another world is possible', 'the people, united, can never be defeated' – echo the optimistic defiance of sixties sentiments. While the tactics of parody, street theatre – inherited, as Harding's chapter 8, shows from 60s' Situationists – and occupations persist. Moreover, despite their unorganised fluidity, today's campaign protests are anchored by the more 'professional' and efficient expertise of some NGOs and institutionalised campaigns. And are not the anti-globalisers' international Social Forums a more organised reprise on the 24/7 debates in the Odeon of Paris '68? Occupying some of the sixties social spaces and adapting their ethics, contemporary movements' mixture of idealism and organisational potency – aided by vastly superior communication technologies – seems able to exert longer-term and more, well-rooted pressures on Establishment power; even in an otherwise conservative political culture.

It should also be remembered that the harbinger of today's global solidarity amongst social movements was the international awareness and inter-connectedness of its anti-war and anti-capitalist predecessors in the late sixties:

> What was remarkable about 1968 was the geographical breadth of the global revolt. It was as if a single spark had set the entire field on fire.
> (Ali 2008, 2)

Several of the contributions in this volume, on France, Portugal and its colonies, on South Africa and Pakistan both substantiate and qualify this incendiary explanation. The core institutions of northern Europe and North America may remain unaltered, but offshoots of sixties radicalism catalysed social movements in these 'peripheral' countries playing significant roles in toppling authentically authoritarian and racist regimes. The conflagration had multiple sources and its trajectories were uneven and even unpredictable in their outcomes. Riaz Ahmed Shaikh's chapter describes the outcome of the student-initiated revolt against the Ayub Khan dictatorship in Pakistan in the first general election in the country's history. But this turning point also meant that:

> Bengali nationalists in East Pakistan won a majority that the elite and key politicians refused to accept. Bloody civil war led to Indian military intervention and ended the old Pakistan. (Ali 2008, 4)

More fundamentally, key conditions which provoked the counter-cultural and self-styled 'revolutionary' movements that connect the sixties to the present have not disappeared. Analysing the socio-political factors which triggered the upsurge in voluntary and campaigning organisations of forty years ago Crowson, Hilton, and McKay identify familiar causal conditions.

- Relative inability of established political parties, to articulate 'post-industrial' concerns through existing ideologies and policy preferences
- Rigid electoral systems perpetuating the dominance of established parties, structurally biasing dissent towards absorption and dilution
- Decline of trade union movements as forums of mass socio-political engagement
- New social/individual identities, and associated political beliefs
- Affluence, welfarism and mass education of the post-war decades, engendered an increasingly critical and empowered citizenry

(Crowson, Hilton, and McKay 2007)

Such conditions still prevail today. The parties and official institutions of the political systems of several countries, notably the UK and – the Obama epiphenomenon notwithstanding – the USA continue to provoke social movement opposition, by still remaining relatively impervious to radical demands from civil society. Although sections of the trade union movement have embraced the 'Green' and minority rights platforms, stemming from sixties' social radicalism, unions as a whole have less political influence than forty years ago. Moreover these constraining structures have been accompanied in recent decades by an institutionalisation of plural, assertive, social identities and, for the middle strata at least, greater educational and material resources. In these respects the basic fault-lines which gave rise to radical social movements in the sixties have become, if anything, more permanent.

However, one final, and more sinister, comparison between the 1960s and today's more focussed radicalism needs to be made. Despite surviving the post-sixties conservatism and repressive tendencies of Thatcherism and Reaganism (Varon et al 2008, 5) and the intervening efflorescence of sexual, political and economic liberalism, political authoritarianism seems to be once again moving to defuse and curtail radical protest. From the proliferation of surveillance technologies in urban areas to the strengthening of police powers in the 'War on Terror', state security apparatuses have gained a panoply of repressive techniques. As the intimidation of 'green' associations in the USA (Hardisty and Furdon 2004), to the policing of environmental protesters and anti-globalism demonstrations in Britain and Italy have shown, these are readily used against non-violent campaigns (Lyon 2001). Even the internet – which might be considered a social space extended and colonised by sixties' libertarianism – is on some reports being tamed and regulated by official regulation ('A Walk on the Dark Side' *Guardian*, G2, 26/11/2009). This narrowing of the bands of tolerance by social control agencies recalls particularly the vindictive suppression of dissidence and non-conformity which led in the 1960s to events like the Oz trial in the UK and the FBI's destruction of organic food literature (Sams 2005). Will the resentment caused by these and more subtle incursions into the 'lifeworld' of civil society (see Jones chapter 1) fuel some wider recrudescence of sixties rebellion? Or will there be a more successful coercion of the kind that flourished alongside that rebellion on both sides of the Atlantic. In the USA, this was a repressive force that has been credited with administering the *coup de grace* to sixties' radicalism through quasi-martial law suppression and covert 'anti-subversion' operations (Churchill and Vander Wall 2002, 208–30).

While various contributions to this book evidence the survival and expansion of spaces and legacies from the sixties this initial overview would not be complete without also acknowledging the period's extinctions and disappearances. Of these – student radicalism, subversive youth cultures, participative democracy apart – perhaps the most significant has been the transmogrification of radical discourse. To use a popular aphorism of the 60s from Karl Marx: 'the ideological forms in which men [sic] become conscious of … conflict and fight it out'. Echoing the sentiments of the radicals interviewed by Körner and McKechnie (chapter 11), McDonald observes in his chapter, that new types of action in the 1960s came to be 'couched within an old language' of alienation, revolutionary violence and, increasingly, class conflict. Especially, in countries like France and Portugal, as Cardina explains, struggles against authoritarianism at home and Cold War conflicts abroad pressured radicals towards the rhetoric and concepts of the 'Third World' Marxism of Cuban and Chinese discourse. The initial decline of sixties radicalism can be partly ascribed to the working out of the inadequacies of these discursive vehicles. As McDonald also explains, this alter-Marxism took up 'the imaginary of the front and the army' then the 'community and collective', before replacement by a discourse based, as European social movement theorists would argue, on 'expressions of identity' in the 1970s and 1980s. Now, with the near-exhaustion of these constructs, social movements must look for new forms of discourse to respond to the unfolding political crises of war, recession, and environmental disaster. If nothing else, social movements may be able to avoid the mistakes of their sixties' predecessors: a possibility which we explore in the Conclusion to this book.

The Sections and Chapters

The contributions in section I describe comparable and contrasting developments in the European metropoles of Britain and France and former colonial regions in Africa and the Indian sub-continent: Pakistan and South Africa. In addition, Miguel Cardina's analysis of the build-up of a revolutionary movement in 1960s' and early 70s' Portugal (chapter 3) shows how northern Europe's radicalism influenced the struggles against dictatorship at home and colonialism and militarism in Africa. To extend a metaphor of the British-based, Pakistani activist, Tariq Ali: sparks from the largely student-centred, European and North American protest movements travelled the expanding routes of air transport and telecommunications to ignite different fires in Asia and southern Africa. Shaikh's account of the protest movements that eventually toppled the dictatorship of Ayub Khan (chapter 5) identifies some of these links. But it also illustrates how the combustion process drew in, and then embedded, indigenous ideas and practices which, in Pakistan's case, spread far beyond the intellectual and middle-class activism of Europe and North America. However, the potency of those 'Northern' political cultures must not be underestimated. Black activists' sacrifice and perseverance may have been the basic force that eventually thwarted apartheid in South Africa. But, as Helen Lunn's subtle narrative in chapter 4 shows, links with, and examples from European libertarian Marxist ideas inspired some more privileged, white students there to make decisive contributions to the organisation of black workers' economic resistance to their exploitation by the South African regime.

Jones and McDonald, in chapters 1 and 2 respectively, explore the cases of students in France and community activists in Britain probe both the roots of radicalism and their contrasting dynamics and outcomes. Though Paris 1968 is widely recognised as the episode, *par excellence*, of sixties' youth-led, political rebellion, it is also regarded as the classic case of the ultimate political irrelevance and failure of such movements. However, McDonald shows not only how the '*evenements*' had deeper roots and implications than the emblematic two months of insurrection and carnival. He also identifies a profound and continuing disjunction between the heterodox and evolving discourses of protest and the grievances and contradictions they sought to express. France, he suggests, is still dogged by the issues manifested in the events of 1968. While France's political establishment seeks to bury them, the underlying tensions and frustrations continue to arise in new and, perhaps, more effective discursive forms. As such, 'May 1968' has become a more potent and irrepressible force than its brief, pubescent but volcanic impact indicates.

Though France's sixties radicalism is widely depicted as a spectacular if largely unsuccessful novelty, its British counterpart tends to be more dismissively regarded. With a smaller, more restrained student movement and a less advanced intellectual radicalism, it is easy to pigeon-hole the British sixties as a largely apolitical efflorescence of musical and youth culture of little wider political significance. But these kinds of characterisation depend on a narrow conception of socio-political dynamics. Jones's chapter draws on Habermas's classic theorisation of new social movements – examined in more detail by Driver (chapter 9) – as normative reactions to the colonisation of the civil society's 'lifeworld' by the instrumental and bureaucratic rationalities of states and corporations. This analysis advances beyond Horn's (2007) verdict on the role of the British sixties movements as primarily contributing cross-class youth and musical sub-cultures to wider radical social movements. Through an examination of the rise and persistence of a radical community activist movement in Britain, it substantiates Bordieu's appreciation (p. 207 below) of the self-defined, 'personal is political' ethos of radical movements such as feminism, as one expression of a broader shift in sentiments. Paralleling McDonald's thesis, Jones argues that, while those period-specific sentiments may have faded, the ethics to which this shift gave rise have persisted in different cultural and practical forms.

Chapters in section II offer analytical accounts both of key theoretical contributions and of 'iconic moments' of sixties radicalism in the various contexts of activism and contestation in which they arose. The widest ranging of these is Mike O'Donnell's chapter 6, on the radical sixties in the United States. This provides an historical account of 'the Movement' that treats the ideological debate of the period as intellectual history – as part of 'the story' – rather than as detached and objective commentary. In particular, the crucial but ultimately unresolved clash of the new radicalism and liberalism is highlighted. This chapter continues the theme of the interplay of personal values and political identity explored in the previous section that was also central to the American Movement. Ben Cranfield's chapter 7, *Students, Artists and the ICA: The Revolution Within*, describes the emergence of intense and searching rebellion and debate about the meaning and wider application of art and art education at the British Institute of Contemporary Arts and Hornsey School of Art including links between the two locations. In a sharply focused micro-level analysis, Cranfield draws primarily on two contemporary sources: Michael Kustow's *TANK: An Autobiographical Fiction* (1975), an account of his eventful stewardship at the ICA, and *The Hornsey Affair* (1969) written by the students and staff of Hornsey Art College about their six-week long sit-in. Cranfield concedes nothing to easy generalisation but his dramatic case studies are valuable not only for highlighting the extent of cultural ferment within the 'arts'. They also illuminate several themes that were preoccupying the wider constituency of radical youth, including: the social impact of technology and the new media; how to engage with the public through culture; and the implementation of institutional democracy as a means of minimising and humanising bureaucracy.

Eloise Harding's notably lively and committed contribution to this collection in chapter 8, focuses on the French Situationists, mainly Guy Debord and Raoul Vaneigem. Like Cranfield she revisits key contemporary texts, including Debord and Vaneigem, and goes on to illustrate Situationism in action. Like the American *Yippies* (Youth International People's Party) of the late 1960s the Situationists attempted to undermine, by means of mockery and farce, taken-for-granted notions of 'reality' and the self-interested nature of power structures. They regarded any devolution of decision making from the individual to another, and particularly to institutions, as a derogation of personal choice. Their emphasis on personal choice and responsibility was perhaps the most uncompromising example of sixties individualism based not, as is arguably the case with much twenty first century individualism, on consumerism, but on a scepticism of hierarchy and rejection of authoritarianism. Their problem was and remains how to persuade the powerful to agree with them and to act accordingly. Although he did not view the issue in quite the same way as the Situationists, it is one that the seminal figure of the American New Left, Charles Wright Mills, would readily have recognised.

James Driver's (chapter 9) is one of two contributions to this volume that draw heavily on the work of the German social scientist, Jurgen Habermas. However while the author of the first chapter, Bryn Jones, borrows from Habermas' work to inform his own theoretical perspective and analysis, Driver offers a critical account of Habermas' engagement with the main German radical student organisation of the 1960s the Socialist German Students (SDS). This analysis is important because, although Habermas's position-taking is well-known, his politics are less familiar to English speaking countries than his theoretical work. It is, therefore, particularly interesting to read of his principled clash in 1967 with the student leader Rudi Dutschke about the ethical propriety and practical limits of revolutionary action at that time. While highly critical of aspects of both the academy and German society, Habermas argued that violent revolutionary action was not justified or prudent in a functioning democracy, despite its flaws. A position that Driver goes on to link to Habermas' later reflections on radical politics and their relevance to the 'new social movements' for which his theorising is more widely known.

The third and final section of this collection focuses more specifically on contemporary legacies of key strands of sixties radicalism. In a meticulous statistical analysis of generational attitudes and practices in the Federal Republic of Germany, Andreas Hadjar and Florian Schlapbach (chapter 10) show how core sixties political norms have been carried on into today's Germany. The generation that was active in the 1960s have modified their views only slightly with aging. More significantly, subsequent generations, even the most recent adult cohorts, display similar proclivities with regards to both political values and what were once, unorthodox political activities. Though Barbara Körner and Rosemary McKechnie's analysis, in chapter 11, is based on completely contrasting methodology it reveals some analogous patterns amongst former British activists. Korner and McKechnie's life story approach, using qualitative interviews, identifies individuals from a range of former activists and fellow travellers' in sixties movements who, by and large, *'ne regrettent rien'* and in some instances see themselves, in Körner and McKechnie's words, as 'carrying the flame forward' to new causes and later generations. The final chapter, 12, by novelist and feminist Maureen Freely, broadens and highlights such reflections in relation to the women's movement. Her account offers a re-interpretation of the feminism that came out of sixties radicalism, in the light of its more recent successors. Freely both diagnoses and celebrates the accumulating and tenacious diffusion of multitudes of informal women's forums. A 'quiet revolution' which has maintained an ethic of piecemeal resistance and personal commitment. An under-estimated but insistent profusion of practices has spread out from the pioneer groups of the sixties, even as, in the intervening decades, celebrity and media debate and controversy on feminism has waxed and waned.

All in all, these various chapters justify and corroborate our contention that the upsurge of radicalism in the 1960s was significant for more than the transformations in life-style and popular cultural institutions to which some historians try to restrict it. The image of conflagrations and incendiary sparks spreading rebellion and anti-conformity occurs in several reflections on the widening impact of late-60s radicalism. But fires eventually die out. A more appropriate metaphor might be that borrowed from astrophysics' 'Big Bang' in Jones's chapter: to convey both the force and scale of the upsurges and their multifarious, and still-unfolding, consequences. In this view of the socio-political universe the dead matter and black holes of spent revolts co-exist with the still-blazing suns of successful social movements. In this Introduction we have outlined some of the diverse and far-flung 'explosions' of political, cultural and institutional developments identified by our contributors. In the Conclusion we return to the complex and, arguably, more contentious issue of the relevance of these various developments to social movement radicalism in the 21st century.

References

Ali, T. 2008. Where has all the rage gone? *The Guardian*, Saturday 22 March

Brick, H. 1998. *Age of Contradiction: American Thought and Culture in the 1960s*. (Twayne's American Thought and Culture Series.) New York: Twayne of Macmillan.

Churchill, W. and Vander Wall, J. 2002. *The CoIntelPro Papers*. Cambridge Ma.: South End Press

Collier, P. and Horowitz D. 1989. *Second Thoughts: Former Radicals Look Back at the Sixties*. Lanham, MD: Madison Books

Crowson, N., Hilton, M., McKay, J. 2007. Discussion Points for *DANGO Conference*. 5–6 July 2007. Birmingham: University of Birmingham Centre for Contemporary History

Debray, R. 2007. *Praised Be Our Lords: The Autobiography*. Translated by John Howe. London: Verso

Frank, T. 2004. *What's the Matter with Kansas? How Conservatives Won the Heart of America*. New York: Metropolitan/Holt

Grunenburg, C. and Harris, J. eds., 2005. *Summer of Love: Psychedelic Art, Social Crisis and Counter-Culture in the 1960s* – Tate Liverpool Critical Forum No. 8. Liverpool: Liverpool University Press

Hardisty, J. and Furdon, E. 2004. Policing Civil Society: NGO Watch *From The Public Eye*. 18, 1. Spring. http://www.publiceye.org/magazine/v18n1/hardisty_ngo.html (accessed 9th December 2009)

Heath, J. and Potter, A. 2006. *The Rebel Sell: How the Counterculture became Consumer Culture*. Chichester: Capstone

Horn, G-R. 2007. *The Spirit of '68: Rebellion in Western Europe and North America, 1956–1976*. Oxford: Oxford University Press

Jamison, A. 1998. The Shaping of the Global Environmental Agenda: The Role of NGOs. In Lash, S., Szerszynski B. and Wynne, B. eds. *Risk, Environment and Modernity*. London: Sage

Johns, G. 2002. Protocols with NGOs: The Need to Know. *IPA Backgrounder*. 13, 1.

Jones, B. 2007. Citizens, Partners or Patrons? Corporate Power and Patronage Capitalism. *Journal of Civil Society*. 3, 159–177

Lyon, D. 2001. Surveillance after September 11. *Sociological Research Online*. 6, 3. http://www.socresonline.org.uk/6/3/lyon.html

MacDonald, I. 1995. *Revolution in the Head: The Beatles' Records and the Sixties*. London: Pimlico

Morris-Suzuki, T. 2000. For and Against NGOs, the Politics of the Lived World. *New Left Review*, Mar–Apr 63

Rootes, C. 2007. NGOs, Environmental Movement Organizations and the Environmental Movement in England. Paper to the *DANGO Conference*. Birmingham: University of Birmingham Centre for Contemporary History

Sams, C. 2005. The Craig Sams Story. http://macrobiotics.co.uk/thecraigsamsstory.htm. Accessed January 20th 2010
Sayres, S. Stephanson, A., Aronowitz, S. and Jameson, F. eds., *The Sixties Without Apology*. Minneapolis: University of Minnesota Press, 1984
Short, C. 2009. The Forces Shaping Radical Politics Today. In *What Is Radical Politics Today?* J. Pugh (ed.) London: Palgrave Macmillan
Touraine, A. 2004. On the Frontier of Social Movements. *Current Sociology*. 52, 4: 717–725
Varon, J., Foley, M.S. and McMillian, J. 2008. Time is an Ocean: the Past and Future of the Sixties. *The Sixties*. 1: 1–7
Wilby, P. 2008. Humanity's last rage. *New Statesman*, 8th May

Part I

RADICAL MOVEMENTS AROUND THE WORLD

Chapter 1

ALL ALONG THE WATERSHED: SIXTIES VALUES AS DEFENCE OF COMMUNITY LIFEWORLDS IN BRITAIN 1968–2008

Bryn Jones

'The new left worked to give life to politics as community...rejected the criteria of narrow efficiency, efficacy, compromise, discipline, of the "rules of the game", as they are played in politics today.' (Breines 1989, 151)

Introduction

There is an influential historical consensus that 1960s radicalism in Britain had no significant or lasting impact on the social and political order. In this view, the longer-term effects of the ideas and movements, often associated with the climactic year of 1968, have been confined to popular culture, lifestyles and inter-personal relations. It is said that political institutions remained unperturbed and almost unaffected by the intellectual and ideological ferment occurring in the arts, media, universities, street politics and youth cultures. From this historical-empiricist perspective the significance of '68 in Britain was apolitical and confined to the personal and cultural sphere (Marwick 1998, 15–20; Sandbrook 2007, 543–5). Proponents of a revolution in society ended up changing little but their own life styles.

The present analysis examines sixties radicalism in Britain –and potentially more widely – as the fusion of counter-cultural and radical political ideas and movements that came together in the late 1960s to challenge the ruling socio-political order. It will critique 'culturalist' interpretations of this radical upsurge – as confined principally to life styles and sub-cultural institutions – on two grounds. Firstly, that the critical feature of the cultural upheavals of the high 60s, acknowledged by virtually all commentators, was not the immediate establishment of distinct and operational values. Rather, an amorphous and inchoate, but very widespread complex of radical sentiments or sensibilities dominated. Secondly, it will be argued that, despite contemporary rhetoric, the logic of much of sixties radicalism was a defence and reformation of civil society institutions, rather than a transformation of the political sphere. The implication of the first point is that the legacy of the sixties in social values is one that has been continuously unfolding in different spheres rather than something that crystallised forty years ago and was soon superseded. The second point, on the scope of the upheavals, is important because it provides a different set of criteria with which to assess the persistence and success of late 60s' radicalism. If, as will be argued, the essence of that upsurge was to defend or expand those aspects of civil society that Habermas refers to as the 'lifeworld', then the legacy today must be judged in relation to this sphere; and not to change or stasis in the wider political system.

Contrary to a corollary of the cultural impact view, that the main political outcome of sixties cultural disaffection and protest was statist neo-liberalism (Cockett 1999; MacDonald 1995), I argue that one outcome has been a more libertarian micro-politics. This politics is much more deeply rooted in the institutional complexes of civil society and is therefore still consistent with the underlying sixties ethos. The analytical and empirical focus therefore becomes the changing frontier between civil society and the state over the past 40 years. Habermas's theory of new social movements is applied critically to this focus for two reasons. One is that for Habermas the main concern of social movements is establishing rights and institutions for personal politics and identities; rather than, like older social movements rooted in economic interests, with capturing or adapting state power. The second reason is that the contours of Habermas's 'lifeworld', which social movements seek to defend, can be mapped fairly directly, though not completely, onto the social sphere conventionally known as civil society.

Across a variety of viewpoints there is a similar acknowledgement that it is both the personal networks of the lifeworld and its morals, and the broader civil society in which they are nested, that are the areas most affected by sixties 'revolution' (Hobsbawm 1995, 320–343; Marwick 1998; Cockett 1999; Sandbrook 2007; Cohn-Bendit 2008) But it is along the watershed between state and civil society communities that these changes have transformed, and continue to change institutions and micro-politics. British governments have increasingly changed their *governance* processes to engage with, and work through a range of civil society entities: community and campaign groups, charities, non-governmental organisations and leisure and residents associations; within which core sixties values and legacies persist. The analysis firstly details prevailing verdicts on the nature of the value changes of that period. Then in the second and third sections it explores the socio-political crisis affecting British society during the 1960s and its relationship to Habermas's thesis of lifeworld colonisation and rebellion. In the fourth section the value clashes and shifts accompanying these changes are related to the contemporaneous crisis of community and the rise of urban activism affecting the lifeworld. The final, fifth, section focuses on the resurgence of both state and civil society involvement in community regeneration and the question of whether the sixties ethos and its aspirations still influence an age of renewed state paternalism.

Cultural Change: The Problem of Sixties Values

In the historical-empiricist perspective of observers such as Sandbrook and Marwick the 1968 'Revolution never happened in Britain'. Its long term significance was acceleration of prior cultural changes, particularly in the arts, popular culture, life-styles and personal relationships (Marwick 1998, 15–20; Sandbrook 2006, 545). This containment effect is attributed by Marwick *et al* to the low numbers involved in either 'counter-cultural' activities, or more overtly political acts of protest and rebellion. It is claimed that these were confined to specific and minority strata. Two propositions point towards a rejection of this rationale for restricting long-term impacts to apolitical fields. Firstly those most directly involved in the developments and events symbolised by '1968' were indeed minorities. But they were from social groups best equipped to practice and propagate new values in later years; so their impact could be wide: for example, and *inter alia*, higher education graduates and those in, or entering professional fields such as arts, media, politics, education and welfare. An outcome recorded for the USA by O'Donnell in his chapter. However, research evidence on value formation in general is confused, contradictory and eclectic (Hitlin and Piliavin 2004).[1] On the other hand, because much value formation takes place during the years of secondary socialisation, it was particularly important for the younger cohorts of the 1960s. As McDonald points out in his chapter, these young people were not only experiencing value socialisation in conditions of material change but also whilst the discourses and institutions propagating values were themselves in transition or turmoil.

The second contradictory proposition, on which this chapter concentrates, is that precisely because the cultural changes were diffuse and initially low-impact in nature, new sentiments and beliefs could be shared in partial or tacit ways by much wider groups; especially amongst the young. A university place wasn't necessary to sing along to Lennon or Dylan protest songs or the Rolling Stones' ambiguously worded, *Street Fighting Man*. A song explicitly rejoicing in an imminent armed 'revolution' – Thunderclap Newman's *Something in the Air* – couldn't top the record sales charts for three weeks without its many buyers sharing some of the lyrics' sentiments. Evaluation of the relationship between these new outlooks and their long-term consequences first requires theoretical clarification of the nature of such cultural changes.

Sentiments, Values and Anti-System Radicalism

The most prominent description and analysis of the post-World War II schism in Western popular political cultures comes in Inglehart's large-scale, cross-national surveys of an alleged dichotomy between materialist and post-materialist beliefs. But these dichotomous clusters have been criticised on the grounds that individuals' socio-political values are both more diverse and multi-dimensional; e.g. comprising different combinations of conformist, rebellious, individualist and collectivist attitudes (Majima and Savage 2007). Though indicative, Inglehart's distinction between values stressing material and personal security versus those prioritising ideas, democracy and environmental improvement (Inglehart 1990,130–43) fails to capture the distinctiveness of the sixties watershed in sentiments. Some components of the latter were significantly materialistic; not only in an emphasis on personal hedonism for example, but also egalitarian beliefs in wealth sharing. Moreover, the distinctive late '60s ideals fluctuated both in their range of adherents and specific meanings; albeit within a generalised bedrock of underlying sentiments.[2]

'Sentiments' are important because historiographers are now recognising that periods of fundamental socio-cultural change arise less from the conscious and articulate propagation and pursuit of clearly defined values than from shifts in a more general and deeper set of emotional and cognitive 'sensibilities'; instanced in Huizinga's *Waning of the Middle Ages*. Wickberg advocates a history of sensibilities which:

> 'focuses on the primacy of the various modes of perception and feeling, the terms and forms in which objects were conceived, experienced, and represented...rather than the objects of representation themselves....' (Wickberg 2007, 662)

An analogous value-changing shift in sensibilities was the transformation in outlooks shaping the humanitarian movements, such as the anti-slavery campaigns, at the start of the 19th century (Wickberg 2007, 665; Wilson 2008, 78-83). This approach suggests it is pointless to presume that what Inglehart refers to as cognitive values – articulate, internally-coherent beliefs – were the decisive keystones of sixties culture. Rather we should focus on the underlying sentiments, or 'sensibilities' to use Wickberg's term, from which more coherent values may form into specific ideas and contexts.

The New Sensibilities of the 1960s

Perhaps the key change in sensibility from the mid-60s was a widely acknowledged basic belief, an omnipresent 'leitmotiv' of 'personal emancipation, or liberation'. Adherents applied this sentiment to 'the entire variety of human life, economic, social, physical and moral' (Cockett 1999, 89). The ensuing 'decompartmentalising' of conventional categories and restrictions – also reflected in the holistic perspectives of the Gestalt psychology of the self-styled Counter-Culture (Roszak 1970, 186–9) – logically entailed removal of lateral social barriers, of ethnicity, gender and class and vertical barriers of social, political and cultural hierarchy. These interlocking dimensions of liberation through decompartmentalisation of social barriers entailed a belief that personal emancipation was dependent on *social* liberation, often of less fortunate others.

This sensibility was undoubtedly influenced by overseas developments. However, the British anti-war and student protests of 1967–68 were less connected than the interlinked American anti-war movement and campus rebellions. The British anti-war demonstrations peaked and dwindled by the end of 1968 (Young 1972 222–6; Sandbrook 2007, 540–1). Such movements and their beliefs therefore functioned as temporary conduits feeding international ideas and causes into the more general groundswell of libertarian and anti-authoritarian sentiments. The more generalised, fluid libertarian *lebensphilsophie* could sustain and encompass both lifestyle-cultural and quasi-political movements. The new 'sensibilities' were most widely expressed in a non-sectarian, populist, loosely ideological and tacit counter-culture. Informing yet exceeding the burgeoning lifestyle cults, intellectual and artistic innovations and political sects, new sensibilities towards sex, leisure, creativity, authority and sociability were adopted across swaths of Britain's younger generations.

Horn, in his detailed comparative analysis, specifically singles out this phenomenon as the distinctive English-speaking contribution to the sixties political culture (Horn 2007, 32–5). A counter-cultural sensibility, fostered through the anti-war, anti-nuclear protests and the mushrooming arts and popular music scenes became precariously institutionalised in rock festivals, communal living experiments and the 'underground' press (Nelson 1989, 6–7). However, this contrary, sub-culture was broader than, and extended beyond the self-professed Counter-Culture. Its libertarian and solidaristic ethos was sufficiently general and flexible to include anyone from office-working festival goers and week-end drug trippers to anarchistic artists and radical welfare professionals.

Many, perhaps most of these participants, did not espouse, may never even have considered the credos of personal and collective liberation articulated by Counter-Culture intellectuals and radicals. However they connected to and shared the underlying sensibilities. In some senses the cultural and chronological phenomena of '1968' can be compared to an astrophysical Big Bang. As early as 1968 the general counter-consensus of basic libertarian values of social equality, democracy and cooperation (Wainwright 1990) – to which, following Horn, we should add 'participation' – began to differentiate. Life-style libertarians sought to build alternative institutions. Looking for more organisationally effective and intellectually rigorous politics, other campaigners moved towards more doctrinal forms of Marxist theory and practice. By the end of the decade ideas in these latter trends were even influencing the underground press and cultural figures such as former Beatle John Lennon (Nelson 1989; McDonald 1995, 288).

The Peculiarities of the British '68: Politics or Values?

Britain seems the one major country, whose political system was least affected by the protests, political campaigns and disorder centred on 1968. Britain differed from developments in France and Italy, which destabilised governments or industrial relations; or Germany where political party alignments changed; or even the USA where black civil rights activism was boosted, and the Vietnam War and party politics partly de-legitimised (Jarausch 1998; Horn 2007, 151–2). Historians' downbeat verdicts on the British case seem justified. Minor public order problems apart, the explosion of radical ideas, acts of deviance and spectacle, protests and cultural and sub-cultural ferment in higher education and urban centres had little or no direct impact on establishment politics and policy-making. Indeed by 1970 any prospect of direct socio-political transformations seemed to have evaporated (Young 1972, 226).

However, if we apply Wickberg's 'sensibilities' perspective then some of the widely acknowledged lifestyle value transformations can be seen as connected to socio-political ideals and attitudes; instanced by radical and manifestly utopian discourses across the broader counter-culture. Moreover there is evidence of substantial volatility in organised and personal beliefs in the cultural hothouse of the late '60s. Some disillusioned, or pseudo-radicals may have retreated into the more hedonic pleasures of drugs, travel or consumerism. But others moved in opposite directions: the gradual move towards socialist politics in the last years of the underground press (Nelson 1989); or John Lennon's progression from contrarian rejection of revolutionism as a Beatle, to songs about class, equality and pacificism in his solo career. The shift to a libertarian sensibility entailed a wide-ranging and shifting mosaic of overlapping beliefs, attitudes and sentiments rather than well-defined, cultural silos. But what was the nature of the 'oppressive' culture and institutions which they were countering?

Establishment Culture, 'Stagnation' and Modernisation

If there was a lot of protest in British society in the 1960s, that was because, at the start of the decade, there was a lot to protest about: reformed but still restrictive sexual laws and mores, the declining and uncompetitive industrial economy, the still-censored, stilted and traditionalist arts such as theatre, the elitist political and cultural establishment and a stalled social reformism in welfare, education and the urban environment. The nature of this pervasive 'stagnation' – attacked on various fronts by technocrats, managerialists and liberals – was succinctly and boldly captured by Perry Anderson's seminal 1964 tract in *New Left Review*. From a theoretical standpoint of the, then largely unknown, Gramscian concept of hegemony, Anderson diagnosed the 'English' 'power structure' as: 'an immensely elastic and all-embracing hegemonic order.' The decisive feature of the ruling bloc's hegemony, he argued, lay not necessarily in the undoubted possession of economic and political power, but in an overwhelming *cultural* superiority over multiple aspects of social life: 'not articulated in any systematic major ideology, but ... diffused in a miasma of commonplace prejudices and taboos' The result of this dominance was cultural stagnation as:

> 'A comprehensive, coagulated conservatism ... covering the whole of society with a thick pall of simultaneous philistinism (towards ideas) and mystagogy (towards institutions).' (Anderson 1964, 39–40)

With classical Marxist logic, Anderson identified the antithesis of stagnation in 'a profound, pervasive but cryptic crisis' with 'ubiquitous' 'reverberations' (Anderson 1964, 34). Recognising a grudging acknowledgement of the need for technocratic social and economic planning, even amongst members of the governing elite, Anderson predicted that:

> 'to preserve its hegemony' the dominant bloc'... must... undergo yet another metamorphosis... the class ... realizes that it must change itself once again. The ...pressures of contemporary capitalism require a radical adaptation.' (Anderson 1964, 52)

A wider range of critics of stagnation pinned their hopes on a Labour government. Anderson and his NLR collaborator Tom Nairn saw a Labour General Election victory, which happened later that year, as an indirect catalyst for some sort of political breakthrough. But the Wilson regimes of 1964–1970 did not achieve successful economic revitalisation. Nor did they attempt the levels of social transformation which radicals increasingly expected. Though important rights-based innovations, in gender inequalities and race relations were begun by the second Wilson government. Perhaps more importantly, these Labour administrations did not seem directly to dismantle Anderson's 'miasma' of cultural traditionalism, nor the conservatism attacked by numerous other radical critics. Moreover, some of the technocratic initiatives, which Wilson administrations did pursue, had the perverse consequences of antagonising other sensitivities and sharpening oppositional sentiments.

60s Modernisation: System and Lifeworld Clashes

From New Left perspectives the modernising changes were confined to technical efficiencies in business and economic management which failed to budge underlying social and welfare inequalities (Williams et al 1968, 44–6). Attempts at modernising and expanding educational opportunities were, as student radicals from the mid-sixties recognised, leading to unsatisfactory compromises between meritocratic and technocratic policies and the liberal-elitist institutions of the educational establishment (Adelstein 1970, 78–79). Habermas's theory of the 'colonisation of the lifeworld', as precipitating anti-system rebellion, provides an effective complement to the Anderson thesis for understanding the broader, negative impacts of such modernisation programmes. Habermas's fuller significance for sixties social movements is explained in Driver's chapter in this volume.

Identifying a profound distortion of the cultural and discursive practices of bourgeois civil society – the social sphere between the state and markets – Habermas argues that civil society's once free-standing institutions, their ethical and humanistic practices and 'open' discourses, are increasingly constrained and undermined by the instrumental rationalities and closed discourses of states and markets. Civil society, once a flourishing alternative and complement to these narrow and potentially dehumanising institutions, risks being subjugated to their expansion. The bureaucratic enlargement of state welfare activity and the exploitative demands of capitalist business invade and subvert the cultural and practical autonomy of the local and personal complexes of family and particularistic associations. These complexes represent the relational basis of the 'lifeworld'; which is said to lie, in turn, at the core of civil society.

Habermas attributes the 'colonisation' of this lifeworld to the instrumental-rationalities of interlocking state and market logics. With a felicitous similarity to contemporaneous counter-culture terminology Habermas calls these economic and political spheres the *system*. Experience of this colonisation then allegedly provokes dissenting and rebellious reactions: threats to identities, values and social and natural environments stimulate the formation of new and revived lifeworld constituencies. In the German case Habermas cites such movements as 'anti-nuclear and environmental movement; the peace movement; single issue and local movements; the alternative movement ... squatters and alternative projects... rural communes; the minorities...; the elderly, gay, handicapped etc; ... the women's movement' (Habermas 1987, 393). Despite important criticisms (*cf* Kellner n.d; Cohen 1996, 188–95) of the theory, its key insight – a clash between the 'colonising' instrumental rationalities of the dominant politico-economic spheres and the values and discursive norms of lifeworld domains of personal-associative relationships – helps explain specifics of sixties protest and rebellion in Britain.

Anderson's cultural hegemony of the 'dominant bloc' should have pre-empted or stunted conscious challenges from below. However, it can be argued that it failed in this respect because its attempts to modernise and reform, without changing its basic structures, also fostered disruptive forces. Indeed, moves toward economic and civic planning were started under Macmillan's final, 1959, Conservative government. Bureaucratic state initiatives and other socio-economic trends at the base of British society, while liberating aspects of ordinary lives, were disrupting the popular attitudes on which that hegemony rested; provoking emotional reactions within the lifeworld against the effects of such 'solutions'.

As Marwick insists, rising real wages and the spread of mass produced goods throughout the 1950s and early 60s finally brought North American consumerism within reach of a majority (Akhtar and Humphries 2001; Bocock 1993, 21–7; Smith Wilson 2006; Marwick 1998); widening car ownership, reducing domestic labour, saving and enhancing leisure-time. But the leisure and lifestyle spaces created by this affluence widened expectations for greater personal freedoms; even if only initially in the hedonistic spheres of entertainments, drugs and sexual liberties (Horn 191–2; McDonald 2005, 27–37). Heightened consumer expectations of personal economic freedom could be, partly, met through markets. However, the accompanying economic, technological, and welfare state modernisations gathering pace from the mid-1960s could also be presented as threatening and disruptive. From the later 1950s various media depicted technological changes as sinister with alien forces threatening dystopian 'take-overs' or dehumanisation of familiar lifeworlds; often as tools of authoritarian elites. Kneale's TV drama *Year of the Sex Olympics* depicted a totalitarian-consumerist version of Orwell's 1984. Michael Frayn's book *Holovision* presciently portrayed a future virtual reality world of depersonalised communications. Kubrick's much vaunted film *2001: A Space Odyssey* predicted omnipotent computers which could disobey and try to subjugate their human creators. While from 1967 millions of UK viewers watched a TV series, *The Prisoner*, in which the identities of rebellious misfits were reshaped under remote surveillance controls in bland, socially engineered communities.[3]

Moreover, such media fictions resonated with recurrent, real-life episodes of technological 'take-over' and industrial disaster. The prescribed drug thalidomide led to the births of thousands of deformed children. In 1967 a pit heap avalanche killed 116 children at Aberfan, South Wales and the wreck of the oil tanker *Torrey Canyon* with 100,000 tons of oil off the Scilly Isles symbolised chemical pollution. Industrialised construction of alienating and socially disruptive tower-block flats had reached 41% of new housing by 1968. When, apocalyptically, an accidental explosion collapsed the Ronan Point tower block in East London. Elsewhere, there were concerns about the impacts of the new road traffic systems on traditional urban areas and communities (McKie 1972, 205–9). These, and other, techno-industrial disasters and disruptions provided a continuing thematic punctuation of the credibility of technocratic modernisation. They contributed to a growing mistrust, not only of the Establishment hegemony attacked by Anderson and Nairn, but also of the top-down, and technocratic panaceas for that order's social and economic stagnation. Community activism, linked to participatory-libertarian ideas, began challenging the planners' penchant for tower block solutions – 'budgie-boxes in the sky' – for run-down localities (Gosling 1970; Rosetti interview 2008). In line with Habermas's diagnosis, the state's attempts to remedy poverty, family and health crises in the lifeworld simultaneously antagonised sensitivities about the autonomy and integrity of families and communities (*cf* O'Malley 1970; Radford 1970).

Much of the higher spending on social services through the 1960s (Lapping 1972, 149) entailed an impersonal bureaucratization. Instead of acting as supplementary safety nets to an ever-expanding scheme of insurance-based benefits, as envisaged in Beveridge's plans, the needs-based National Assistance and, later, Supplementary Benefits brought more means-testing inquisition of poor people and deprived communities. Well-meaning attempts to improve service delivery by centralising and integrating social workers in local authority social service departments associated them, in the eyes of clients and critics, with the burgeoning bureaucracies of local councils. When these, in their turn, were rationalised and formalised through the adoption of business-derived 'corporate management' systems it was unsurprising that the 'growing power of the social service sector' (Lapping 1972, 164) linked with nascent anxieties over computerisation of personal data and mistrust of police powers to feed: 'an increasing fear of the State as Big Brother' (McKie 1972, 204).

The Search for 'Community' and Urban Activism

Part of the reaction against modernising remedies for Britain's social stagnation centred on an apparent indifference by the 'system' to the welfare, and disrupted social integrity of local communities. Diverse social actors identified this crisis-of-community syndrome as another aspect of the national malaise. Academic community studies in East London, Nottingham, Birmingham and Liverpool had drawn attention to defects in state-directed urban modernisation programmes. Young and Willmott, in particular, contrasted the social sterility of the new council estates in Essex with the formerly dense and vital social networks and support relationships in the old slum communities (Young and Willmott 1957; 1960; Coates and Silburn 1967; Rex and Moore 1967; Vereker, Mays et al 1961). Undergraduate courses in the universities' newly expanding sociology and social policy departments, highlighted classical sociology's dichotomy between *Gemeinschaft* and *Gessellschaft*: between traditional community and industrial society's impersonality. The social policy apparatus also recognised the importance of community disintegration. The Seebohm Committee, which advocated centralised, integrated social services functions, wanted to complement these with a community dimension; to help combat delinquency by 'the fostering of positive community values…' (Loney 1983, 23). More dramatically, an independent Gulbenkian study group saw 'community work' as a dynamic antidote to the wider structural problems.

> 'It is part of a protest against apathy and complacency [*the stagnation theme again: BJ*] and against distant and anonymous authority [*Habermas's 'system: BJ.*] … part of the whole dilemma of how to reconcile the 'revolution of human dissent' with the large scale organisation and planning … inseparably interwoven with the parallel revolution of rising expectations…. community work is a means of giving life to local democracy.' (Calouste Gulbenkian Foundation 1968, 4–5; cited in Loney 1983, 21)

On another wing of the fast waxing sensibility towards community solidarity, the underground press was voicing counter-cultural arguments for local activism. At first, unimpressed but then intrigued by activities spawned by the May *evenements* in France, magazines such as *Friends* were calling for alliances with working-class populations to open a new front in the struggle for 'community control' (Nelson 1989, 107). Community activists had already begun concerted squatting campaigns in London and Kent in 1968 to help homeless groups and challenge inadequate local authority services (Radford 1969, O'Malley 1970). A new category of officially-recognised 'community workers' was emerging. These consisted of ex-voluntary workers, activists and new-style social workers, including many social science graduates fresh from courses covering theories of community decline (Loney 1983; Green 1992, 170).

The 1970–1978 Community Development Project warrants particular analysis because of its subsequent influence on urban activism movements and the light its discourse and ideologies shed on the dynamics of sixties values. CDP was an official acknowledgement, and half-hearted effort, by central government to accommodate and respond to many of these concerns and to the participatory and anti-authoritarian strands in the new sensibility. A prime mover was Derek Morrell, a senior civil servant at the Home Office. Allegedly an adherent of proto- New Age philosophies, opposed to increasing bureaucratisation, and partly inspired by the US federal Community Action Programme, Morrell, reportedly wanted a project that would 'kick the system' (Loney 1983, 44–45). The initiative consisted of a chain of twelve community projects, each combining action and research teams, in deprived urban areas in Scotland, Wales and England. Their brief was to improve links between local residents and their councils and help coordinate implementation of local housing, education and social services. Central Whitehall control and interest in the programme soon waned. Partly as a result of this vacuum, and in line with the hardening, sharpening and splintering of post-60s counter-cultures, many community workers and researchers became more radical in their ideological assumptions. A Marxist current increasingly focussed its concerns on the economic forces shaping local deprivation, promoted alliances with local trade union organisations; and critiqued local councils for their dependent status as branches of the capitalist state (*cf* Cockburn, 1977). Ideological schisms became apparent between technocratic and 'pluralist' strands and this, increasingly radical, 'structural conflict' (Marxist) faction constituted itself as a 'Political Economy Collective'.

The pluralist strand overlapped this PEC perspective but had a more libertarian activist ethos, influenced by US practitioners and advocates; ranging from the radical direct action approach of Saul Alinsky[4], to more conventional local pressure group politics (Gilbert and Specht 1975). These latter were linked to the US civil rights movements' campaigning and mobilisation tactics amongst poor communities (Alinsky 1972, 98–125). Despite some CDPs' successes in issues such as housing provision, the local focuses were criticised by the more ideologically *marxisant* element (the Political Economy Collective) for the lack of structural economic and class solidarity perspectives (Loney 1983, Craig *et al* 1982, 3). The PEC clamour for broader alliances with a wider working class movement may also have weakened the development of viable local organisations to pressurise local government policies and services (Miller and Bryant 1990, 317,321). On the other hand the CDP experience and concurrent upsurge of local campaigning and action groups (Baldock 1977; Miller and Bryant 1990) refined and passed on sixties' ideological sentiments to later cohorts of activists and community workers. In the early 1970s, for example, the nascent Association of Community Workers eschewed the conventional professional organisational model, adopted by the recently formed British Association of Social Workers. It rejected a centre-and-branches organisational model for one based on a federation of networks, more consistent with an anti-elitism ethos of equality and participatory democracy (Baldock 1979). Indeed these two latter ideals persisted into the 1990s as twin principles of voluntary and community organisations (Leat 1993, 38).

Rebellious isolation began to give way to more expansive and pragmatic perspectives in the 1980s. Many sixties radicals redirected their political energies into the Labour Party and local Labour councils became self-professed bastions of resistance to Thatcherism. Community workers and activists began finding common cause with the 'local state'; particularly within the big metropolitan authorities such as Manchester and the GLC (Miller and Bryant 1990). Then as Thatcherism began to be complemented by first Tory and New Labour forms of communitarianism, central government also helped to integrate community groups and projects into local authority programmes. Major government programmes, such as the Single Regeneration Budgets, made funding conditional upon involvement with grassroots organisations. By the 1990s, there was talk of councils and community networks interpenetrating and mutually supporting each others' activities and initiatives (Miller and Bryant 1990, 318, 324).

Apotheosis in the New Millennium? Participation and Communities

Local government has become the main State tier with which Third Sector organisations interact (Kendall and Knapp 1996). The question is whether the increasing isomorphism in organisational character between the civil society organisations (CSOs) and their governmental protagonists/patrons (Hood 1998, 202; Morison 2000, 109–10) is realising or neutralising the legacy of sixties values. Since the 1980s, Government initiatives – from City Challenge through the Single Regeneration Budget scheme to the New Deal for Communities – have increasingly stipulated that local authorities responsible for detailed planning and implementation of scheme budgets must include relevant local bodies, representative of communities, in the administration of the schemes. Government promulgation of Local Strategic Partnerships, in 2001, stipulated an 'important role for intermediate, community and voluntary organisations' (ODPM 2005:125).

Many doubt the authenticity of this participatory democracy. Participation by voluntary and community organisations may be cosmetic, manipulative and divisive through '[state] control of the conditions under which networks operates' (Marinetto 2003: 599-600; *cf* also: Morgan 1999; Skelcher 2000). By imposing organisational and resource costs on them, state policy may muffle or stifle spontaneous articulation of needs and values. Smaller, more informal and less organised groups and associations – those closest to the 'lifeworld' core of civil society – may not be included (Fyfe 2005). Other critics highlight the use of central and state incentives, directives and controls to channel, control and sometimes even manufacture civil society organisations (Newman 2001, Hodgson 2004). Moreover, the cooption of CSOs to revitalise a democratically deficient hierarchy of central-local government may distract from more urgent needs for internal reform of that system (Cento-Bull and Jones 2006). More broadly, critics see what a sixties radical would represent as Marcuse's 'repressive tolerance'.

But these criticisms may be missing a broader point. Inclusion may involve encroachment of some 'system' characteristics, such as professionalisation of organisational roles and bureaucratisation of external relations. But, in appropriate conditions, it may also revalidate and renew older interpretations of democratic participation, which voluntary and community organisations and associations have sustained and nurtured since the late '60s and the CDP experiments. On Merseyside an EU/UK government regeneration programme. 'Pathways to Integration' set up 'area boards' to link community groups to the planning of specific local schemes. Despite some negative experiences, over time a majority of the boards became chaired by community representatives rather than council officials. Many of the policy-making arrangements met local community representatives' expectations about consultation and participation:

> ' … the power base has changed. Whereas we had to beg for every little bit we have now realised that without the community involvement they [council and agencies] can't go forward.' (Jones 2003, 594)

Reviewing the entire programme covering five local authorities and 38 Area Partnerships, the investigator, Perris Jones, concluded:

> 'For all the difficulties, participants are able to play an increasingly important role in the 'spaces of participation' that are regenerating cities and neighbourhoods and recharging governance.' (Jones 2003, 598)

Here the 'top down' determination of community-participation provisions for centrally-funded projects seems to have catalysed latent beliefs in participatory activism. Elsewhere, local networks of voluntary and community associations and groups had already institutionalised such values before the new participatory partnerships arrived. Like the trajectory of community work activism, described in the Miller and Bryant forum above, local groups and associations in Bristol moved from opposition and conflict with the city council (*cf* Basset *et al* 2002) to overlapping roles and cooperation. Crucially however, this process was conditioned by the previous, autonomous construction of a mutually supportive bloc of over 700 independent, community and voluntary organisations which gave these groups, collectively, more visible influence, if not power, in civic activities. Moreover, this network organisation VOSCUR (Voluntary Organisations Council for Urban Regeneration) was developed with a consciously solidaristic, egalitarian and democratic ethos that would be instantly recognisable to sixties radicals. VOSCUR's stated core values are: *equality, sustainability, democratic accountability, equality, co-operative partnership*, and *community development and self organisation* ('direction and action at grass roots level.'). While aware of the dangers of cooptation, regulation and manipulation by the state systems, representatives in Bristol also reported satisfaction in promoting their own goals and values through increased participation in council-coordinated, regeneration programmes (Jones and Bull 2006).

A more direct, if provisional piece of evidence for the persistence of sixties values is emerging from a current survey of workers in voluntary and community sector organisations. In light of tacit state regulation, mentioned by critics of participatory-partnership governance above, and media reporting of increasing hierarchical professionalism in the third sector (Bubb 2007, Dearden-Phillips 2008), it might be supposed that these workers would now adhere more to a business-like and bureaucratic ethos of organisation and practice. However, similar to the antipathies stated by the professionals interviewed by O'Donnell (see Conclusion chapter), pilot results from a current survey show only weak support for such principles compared to values like the VOSCUR ones, resonant of the spirit of the sixties. Significantly, a specific question about the *'relevance of 60s' values such as solidarity, political activism and personal politics'*, produced unequivocal support.[5]

Conclusion

The peculiarities of the British socio-political explosion associated with 'the Sixties' and its progeny were indeed that its main location, at least initially, was in the cultural sphere. A phenomenon characterised here as a shift in sensibilities. But the long-term outcome was not 'only' a personal-cultural change – 'a revolution in the head'. The range and depth of the cultural storm was, as in other countries, linked to the nature of the perceived oppressiveness of the political regime: here Nairn and Anderson's ossified but hegemonic bloc. In a context of constrained economic modernisation and burgeoning consumerism, the mores and controls of this political and cultural Establishment were increasingly resented by vocal segments of the 'educated' middle classes and indirectly within the cross-class youth cultures. Attempts were being made to modernise British society within this traditional institutional framework, via the Post-War Settlement of Keynesian economic growth and centralised state welfarism. But these modernisations further antagonised a broad oppositional counter-culture; one that extended beyond the self-professed Counter-Culture and into the sensibilities of the lifeworld.

Contemporary resentment of the first excesses of technocratic-bureaucratic welfarism, expanded Fordist industrialism and urban modernisation, can be viewed as sources of civil society reactions to the colonisation of the lifeworld by state and market processes. These reactions were reinforced by the emerging sentiments in the counter-cultures and shaped by critical and dystopian themes within mass culture and media. This cultural shift was initially more akin to a pervasive transformation of underlying sensibilities than coherent value sets such as post-materialism: which developed to complement those sentiments. But such sentiments fuelled aspirations for a transformation of the politico-cultural institutions and alternatives to technocratic modernisation by industrialism and welfarism. The counter-cultural Big Bang of radical and libertarian sentiments of the late 1960s fragmented but spread widely and in at least one of the resultant spiral nebulae – the sphere of urban deprivation, activism and 'community' re-development – they cohered and in some cases developed institutional roots.

From the conflicting discourses of participants in the CDP initiative and the subsequent fortunes of its successors in community activism, key sixties values of egalitarianism, solidarity, and participative democracy have survived and institutionalised; sometimes with significant effects on the politics of urban development and regeneration. Nearing the end of another political era, with the evident decline of New Labour, it is questionable whether its communitarian ideology, of governance through officially sponsored participation, will survive and, if it does, whether it will renew or finally absorb and hollow out, the ethos founded on late sixties values. However, what can be affirmed now is that their role in the continuing struggle, to defend the lifeworld from the system, has been one of the more persistent legacies of sixties radicalism.

Notes

1 'A temporal dimension about values is virtually absent from the literature. What values do individuals hold across different points of the lifecourse? To what extent are values stable and to what extent do they shift with individual and societal changes?' (Hitlin and Piliavin 2004, 384)
2 Though Inglehart himself partly recognises this difference by distinguishing between the emotive and cognitive dimensions of the generalised 'values' identified (1990, 372).
3 BBC Radio 4, 7th June 2008; Sandbrook 2007, 611–9.
4 Later to influence a young Barack Obama: 'Reading Hillary Clinton's hidden thesis', Bill Dedman Investigative reporter MSNBC (updated 11:20 a.m. ET May 9, 2007) http://www.msnbc.msn.com/id/17388372/page/3/print/1/displaymode/1098/
5 Preparatory survey from University of Bath on values of voluntary and community workers in the south-west. A 'snowball technique' for the pilot stage produced responses from seven current community workers in various occupational levels and age groups.

References

Adelstein, D. 1969. Origins of the British Crisis. In *Student Power*, eds. R. Blackburn and A. Cockburn. Harmondsworth: Penguin Books

Akhtar, M. and Humphries, S. 2001. *The Fifties and Sixties: A Lifestyle Revolution*. London, Boxtree

Alinsky, S. 1972. *Rules for Radicals: a practical primer for realistic radicals*. New York: Random House

Anderson, P. 1964. Origins of the Present Crisis. *New Left Review* 23

Andrews, G., Cocket, R., Hooper, A., Williams, M. (eds). *New Left, New Right and Beyond. Taking the Sixties Seriously.* London: Palgrave-Macmillan

Baldock, P. 1979. An Historical Review of Community Work 1968–78. *Community Development Journal* 14: 72 –181

Baldock, P. 1977. Why community action? The historical origins of the radical trend in British community work. *Community Development Journal* 12, 2

Bassett, K., Griffiths, R. & Smith, I. 2002. Testing governance: partnerships, planning and conflict in waterfront regeneration. *Urban Studies* 39, 10: 1757–75

Bocock, R. 1993. *Consumption*. London: Routledge1993

Breines, W. 1989. *Community and organization in the New Left, 1962–1968: the great refusal.* New Brunswick: Rutgers University Press

Bubb, S. 2007. No Longer the Hippy Sector. *Society Guardian.* 7th November

Calouste Gulbenkian Foundation. 1968. *Community Work and Social Change. A report on training.* London: Longman

Cento-Bull, A. and Jones, B. 2006. Governance and Social Capital in Urban Regeneration: A Comparison between Bristol and Naples. *Urban Studies*, 43, 4: 767–786

Coates, K. and Silburn, R. 1967. *Poverty, Deprivation and Morale in a Nottingham Community: St Anns.* Nottingham University

Cockburn, C. 1977. *The Local State. Management of Cities and People*. London: Pluto Press

Cockett, R. 1999. The New Right and the 1960s: The Dialectics of Liberation. In G. Andrews *et al.* (eds) *New Left, New Right and Beyond*

Cohen, J.L. 1997. Mobilization, Politics and Civil Society: Alain Touraine and Social Movements. In J.Clark and M. Diani (eds). *Alain Touraine.* London: Falmer Press

Cohn-Bendit, D. 2008. 1968 French Revolution left an elusive legacy. *The Japan Times Online.* http://search.japantimes.co.jp/cgi-bin/eo20080511a1.html Accessed 10th January 2010

Craig, G., Derricourt, N. and Loney, M.1982. *Community Work and the State. Towards a Radical Practice. Community Work 8*. London: Routledge and Kegan Paul

Dearden-Phillips, C. 2008. Our CEOs must inspire passion, not envy. *Society Guardian*: 25th June

Fyfe N. R. 2005. Making Space for 'Neocommunitarianism'? The Third Sector, State and Civil Society in the UK. *Antipode* 37, 3: 536–557

Gilbert, N. and Specht, G. 1975. Socio-Political Correlates of Community Action and Anti-Community Action. In P. Leonard. (ed.) *The Sociology of Community Action*. Keele: Sociological Review Monograph

Gosling, R. 1970. St. Ann's Nottingham. In A. Lapping (ed.). *Community Action*. Fabian Society Tract 400

Green, J. 1992. The community development project revisited. In P. Carter, T. Jeffs and M. Smith. (eds) *Changing Social Work and Welfare*. Buckingham: Open University Press

Habermas, J. 1987. *The Theory of Communicative Action: vol 2, Lifeworld and System, a Critique of Functionalist Reason*. Cambridge: Polity Press

Hitlin, S. and Piliavin, J.A. 2004. Values: Reviving a Dormant Concept. *Annual Review of Sociology*. 30: 359–393

Hobsbawm, E.J. 1994. *The Age of Extremes: The Short Twentieth Century 1914–1991*. London: Penguin

Hodgson, L. 2004. Manufactured Civil Society: Counting the Cost. *Critical Social Policy*. 24, 2: 139–164

Hood, C. 1998. *The Art of the State*. Oxford: Clarendon Press

Horn, G-R. 2007. *The Spirit of '68: Rebellion in Western Europe and North America, 1956–1976*. Oxford: Oxford University Press

Inglehart, R. 1990. *Culture Shift in Advanced Industrial Society*. Princeton, New Jersey: Princeton University Press

Jarausch, K.H. 1998. 1968 and 1989: Caesuras, Comparisons, and Connections. In C. Fink. (ed.) *1968: The World Transformed*. Cambridge: Cambridge University Press

Jones, B. and Cento-Bull, A. 2006. Governance through Civil Society? An Anglo-Italian Comparison of Democratic Renewal and Local Regeneration'. *Journal of Civil Society* 2:2

Jones, P. S. 2003. Urban Regeneration's Poisoned Chalice: Is There an Impasse in (Community) Participation-based Policy? *Urban Studies* 40, 3

Kellner, D. (n.d.) *Habermas, the Public Sphere, and Democracy: A Critical Intervention*: http://www.gseis.ucla.edu/faculty/kellner/kellner.html; accessed 30th June 2008

Kendall, J. and Knapp, M. 1996. *The Voluntary Sector in the United Kingdom*. Manchester: Manchester University Press

Lapping, A. 1970. *Community Action*. Fabian Society Tract 400

Lapping, A. 1972. Social Welfare and Housing. In D. McKie and C. Cook (eds) *The Decade of Disillusion*. London: MacMillan

Leat, D. 1993. *Managing across Sectors*. London: Centre for Voluntary Sector and Not-for-Profit Management

Loney, M. 1983. *Community Against Government. The British Community Development Project 1968–78: a study of government incompetence*. London: Heinemann

MacDonald, I. 1995. *Revolution in the Head. The Beatles Records and the Sixties*. 2nd revised edition. London: Pimlico

Majima, S and Savage, M. 2007. Have There Been Culture Shifts in Britain? A Critical Encounter with Ronald Inglehart. *Cultural Sociology* 1,3: 293–315

Marinetto, M. 2003. Governing Beyond the Centre: a Critique of the Anglo-Governance School. *Political Studies* 51: 592–608

Marwick, A. 1999. *The Sixties: Cultural Revolution in Britain, France, Italy, and the United States, 1958–1974*. Oxford: Oxford University Press
McKie. D. 1972. The Quality of Life. In D. McKie and C. Cook (eds.) *The Decade of Disillusion: British Politics in the Sixties*. London: Macmillan
Miller, C. and Bryant, R. 1990. Community Work in the UK: Reflections on the 1980s. *Community Development Journal* 25, 4: 316–325
Morgan K, Rees G, and Garmise S. 1999. Networking for Local Economic Development. In G. Stoker (ed.). *The New Management of British Local Government*. Basingstoke: Macmillan
Morison, J. 2000. The Government-Voluntary Sector Compacts: Governance, Governmentality and Civil Society. *Journal of Law and Society* 27, 1: 98–132
Nelson, E. 1989. *The British Counter-Culture, 1966–73: A Study of the Underground Press*. London: Palgrave Macmillan
Newman, J. 2001. *Modernising Governance: New Labour, Policy and Society*. London: Sage
Office of the Deputy Prime Minister (ODPM). 2005. *New Localism – Citizen Engagement, Neighbourhoods and Public Services Evidence from Local Government*. ODPM, Local and Regional Government Research Unit
O'Malley, J. 1970. Community Action in Notting Hill. In A. Lapping (ed.) *Community Action*. Fabian Society Tract 400
Radford, J. 1970. From King Hill to the Squatting Association. In A. Lapping (ed.). *Community Action*. Fabian Society Tract 400
Rex, J. and Moore, R. 1967. *Race, Community, and Conflict: A Study of Sparkbrook*. Oxford: Oxford University Press
Rosetti, F. 2008. Interview with Florence Rosetti former director of Southwark CDP. 16th July 2008
Roszak, T. 1970. *The Making of a Counter Culture: Reflections on the Technocratic Society and Its Youthful Opposition*. London : Faber
Sandbrook, D. 2007. *White Heat: A History of Britain in the Swinging Sixties*, London: Abacus
Skelcher, C. 2000. Changing Images of the State: Overloaded, Hollowed-out, Congested. *Public Policy and Administration* 15. 3: 3–19.
Smith Wilson, D. 2006. A New Look at the Affluent Worker: The Good Working Mother in Post-War Britain *Twentieth Century British History* Advance Access published April 5. http://tcbh.oxfordjournals.org/cgi/rapidpdf/hwl008v1.pdf
Vereker, C., Mays, J. B., Broady, M., Gittus, E. 1961. *Urban Redevelopment and Social Change*. Liverpool: Liverpool University Press
Wainwright, H. 1999.1968's Unfinished Business – Cultural Equality and the Renewal of the Left. In G. Andrews et al. (eds) *New Left, New Right and Beyond: Taking the Sixties Seriously*. Macmillan, London
Wickberg, D. 2007. What Is the History of Sensibilities? On Cultural Histories Old and New. *American History Review* 112: 661–684
Williams, R. *et al.* 1968. *May Day Manifesto*. Harmondsworth: Penguin
Wilson, B. 2008, *Decency & Disorder 1789–1837*. London: Faber & Faber
Young, H. 1972. Politics Outside the System, in D. McKie and C. Cook (eds). *The Decade of Disillusion*. London: MacMillan
Young, M. and Willmott, P. 1962. *Family and Kinship in East London*. London: Pelican
Young, M. and Willmott, P. 1968. *Family and Class in a London Suburb*. London: Routledge and Kegan Paul

Chapter 2

MAY'S TENSIONS TODAY: FRANCE, THEN AND NOW

Kevin McDonald

Introduction: Contested Legacies

On 15 March 1968 France's most important newspaper, *Le Monde*, published an editorial by Pierre Viansson-Ponté, its chief political writer, entitled 'France is bored' (Viansson-Ponté 1968). The author, a former member of the Resistance and one of the country's most respected political commentators, bemoaned the fact that France was 'removed from the convulsions reshaping the world', a place where 'nothing is happening'. He observed in passing that a few students were demonstrating at Nanterre University for the right of female students to enter the male dormitories, dismissing this as 'despite everything, a limited conception of human rights'. Anyone familiar with French political culture can understand why he would attach so little importance to what was happening at Nanterre. This was at a new university, poorly resourced (the buildings were not even completed), on the edge of Paris' suburbs, not even serviced by the Metro system. France's intellectual life was centred on the Sorbonne and the Ecole Normale, the cafés of the Latin Quarter, not a new campus on the edge of town. And in France, politics was organized by political parties; its language was political ideologies. Complaints about dormitories were hardly the thing that 'convulsions reshaping the world' are made of. Yet a week after Viansson-Ponte's article those same students would occupy Nanterre's administration building, creating what they called the 'Movement of 22 March'. This movement, involving people such as the second-year sociology student Daniel Cohn-Bendit (who would soon be called 'Danny the Red' by a fearful press), set in motion the events that we now refer to as May '68: a month of riots and street confrontations, closure and occupation of universities, and the largest workers' strike in France since the Popular Front of 1936.

In the immediate aftermath it was not at all obvious what these events meant. The demonstrations, the occupations of buildings, the barricades, the closure of university campuses, the strikes, the sense that the world had been turned upside down was experienced as a shock that many people, including the actors involved, struggled to understand and articulate. A month later the conservative government was re-elected in a landslide, and it seemed that France would return to being a country where nothing happens. And indeed, the years following appeared to give the impression that May 1968 was not of lasting significance: the first anniversary of May's events came and went without any particular commemoration, as did the fifth.

Ten years later, however, it was clear that something very important had happened. Books were published, conferences and seminars marked the anniversary in a context of renewed awareness of social conflicts within France. The student movement of 1976 had involved wider action than had occurred in 1968. Anti-nuclear mobilizations were contesting the French nuclear state, and had reached a peak with the occupation of the proposed site for a super-reactor at Malville by some 20,000 people in July 1977. Regional movements affirming the cultural integrity of the Occitan language and way of life were contesting the domination of the French state. Conflicts around women's autonomy had led to the legalisation of abortion in 1975. There were signs of renewal of the labour movement, evident in an increasing importance of 'autogestion' (self-management) linked to the CFDT, the main non-communist trade union federation. Interpreting 1968 had become central to political and cultural debates in 1978.

Four decades after May 1968, the debate is still going on, both in France and beyond. In France itself the 40th anniversary year saw over 50 books published on the 'events of May', countless hours of television, hundreds of newspaper articles and columns. Much of this was charged with nostalgia, most obviously in the raft of reminiscences published by intellectual and political figures who had participated in the events. A more argued text was published by Daniel Cohn-Bendit, who in *Forget 68* (2008) contends that social and cultural life had been so profoundly transformed by May 1968 that the type of critique it addressed towards an authoritarian French society is no longer relevant today. The events figured in the Presidential elections of the year earlier, with the then candidate Sarkozy declaring that the heirs of May had 'weakened the idea of citizenship', accusing them of 'denigrating the law, the state, the nation'; and arguing that the movement had encouraged 'the rise of individualism' by inciting people to: 'rely only on themselves, and not to feel concerned by the problems of others'. Such debates were not restricted to France, with events and commemorations being held in many countries. While Sarkozy called for the legacy of 1968 to be 'liquidated', many others looked back to May 68 to see if there was any link between it and the rise of movements and conflicts increasingly evident in the new millennium, from the alterglobalization movement to the urban violence that had seen thousands of cars burnt in French suburbs during the summer of 2005.

Interpretations of May 1968 involve claims about the nature of social life and social transformation. At the time influential figures of the French political left opposed the events – most famously, of course, the French Communist Party whose leader Georges Marchais described the students from Nanterre as 'mostly sons of the grand bourgeoisie' who would soon become 'directors in papa's business'. Louis Althusser, the Marxist philosopher who would become extremely influential in the period after (in particular among university students in English-speaking countries), described May's events as 'infantile leftism'; while one of his former students, Regis Debray, described the events as a 'successful counter revolution' that opened out the way for a new type of liberal capitalism and a world of ferocious competition (2008). A more stimulating and much less polemic analysis, proposed by Luc Boltanski and Eve Chiapello (2006), argues that the movements of May played a key role in sweeping away paternalist and bureaucratic capitalism, opening out the way for new forms of capitalism celebrating personal freedom and autonomy through consumption and personal mobility through labour. Francis Fukuyama describes the students in Paris as 'for the most part pampered offspring of one of the most freest and most prosperous societies on earth'; the explanation for their involvement in protest being 'the absence of struggle and sacrifice in their middle class lives' (1994). The historian Eric Hobsbawm offers a more nuanced opinion, embracing an influential Tocquevillian account of contemporary social life, arguing that the movement of May is best understood in terms of the increasing autonomy of youth culture in modern societies, locating May 1968 as part of a 'cultural revolution… best understood as the triumph of the individual over society' (1994 334).

As we can see, there is a tendency among both supporters and opponents of May to reduce the events to a single narrative (social crisis, product or pathology of individualism, heroic struggle for freedom, transition to new capitalism etc), in the process losing sight of the actors involved and the tensions they confronted. This effaces uncertainties and silences, and above all it masks the extent to which actors themselves lacked categories and language to make sense of their experience. Movement supporters and ideologists naturally emphasize the correspondence between action and the language actors use to describe themselves and their struggle. But what is striking in the events of May 1968 is the distance between the discourses and slogans of the time, often framed within a language of the 'old left', and forms of action that appear radically different. In memorialisation just as much as condemnation, this gap between the experience of actors and their discourse disappears. But it is precisely in this space that we encounter creativity, often more associated with tensions, uncertainties and silences than programs and clearly articulated discourses. And this above all is important to us today, in a period shaped by new conflicts and movement.

Between Student Life and Revolution

> 'It was on the evening of 20th March 1967, the weather was fine. As we were coming out of the campus cinema-club, someone said 'how about occupying the girls' building?' and everyone joined in. The next morning, the cops arrived. It was a completely spontaneous event, it came about completely independently of the political groups. It was not a thought-out initiative, like the occupation that would take place the year after.'
> (Duteuil 1988)

The historian Michael Seidman notes that the conflicts that broke out on the Nanterre campus in 1968 were part of on ongoing dispute around student residencies that had begun in 1962 at Anthony, in Paris's southern suburbs, where students had destroyed a concierge's lodge used to control access to a female students' residence. Students from that same residence initiated a rent strike in 1964, demanding meeting places and day-care facilities for children, an action prefiguring the emerging women's movement. In 1965, students from male and female residencies pulled down a wall that had been built to separate male and female students, occupying the site to prevent its reconstruction. Student leaflets decried regulations that 'oppose freedom' and 'against any real life at the residence' (Seidman 2004, 128–131).

In March 1967 this conflict spilled over to Nanterre, with students occupying the female residential building. The significance of Nanterre as place and experience looms large in these events. The campus was difficult to access by public transport, and at a time when most students did not have cars, it was not only a place for study, it was their social world. The student union offices were a place where students 'hung out', not a centre for professional activists. Nanterre was meant to be experimental and innovative, created as a new campus for social sciences like sociology that were often marginal in the older universities. Yet the reality was an increasing opposition between student life and culture on the one hand and what was experienced as the brutalism and irrationality of the university on the other (soulless architecture, overcrowding and inadequate facilities, and an educational model that required high rates of student failure so that massive first-year enrolments would lead to manageable final year courses). An expression of French modernization, the campus seemed to embody tensions in the student life. Experienced in terms of confinement, isolation, and segregation, it was cut off from its immediate neighbourhood, a suburb that was not only poor but with a very significant North African population.

It is not surprising that accounts of participants in the first occupation at Nanterre locate its origins in student life and sociability. Jean-Pierre Duteuil's autobiographic account of his student days at Nanterre (1988) describes how the decision to undertake the first occupation of the student residence in 1967 was not the product of an organization, but came from a group of friends leaving the campus cinema club. This world of friends was opposed to the cold brutalism of the university, manifest not only in its architecture but by the way the University looked to security guards and increasingly the police to manage student conflicts. This was in part the result of the lack of autonomy of French universities at the time, which saw government ministers assuming direct control of the response to student actions. It was widely believed that following the occupation of 1967 a blacklist of students had been prepared at the instructions of the government identifying student agitators who were to be failed out of the university – one of those being the Franco-German student, Daniel Cohn-Bendit (born in France to German Jewish refugees). Cohn-Bendit had been at the centre of a strike held by sociology students at Nanterre in November 1967, which had organized a series of debates around the content of the discipline and the way it was being taught. Students opposed passive learning and the importance given to exams, objecting to teaching methods that reduced them to passive receptacles of standardised knowledge. These debates led to the production of a collective text, *Pourquoi des sociologues?* (Why Sociologists?) that was circulated at Nanterre in April and reprinted the month after by the influential journal *Esprit* (Cohn-Bendit, Duteuil, Gérard and Granautier 1968). The authors argued that as sociology was being increasingly integrated into modern management and production control systems, sociology students were having their critical abilities destroyed as they were trained to become the servants of the exploiters.

The conflict around residencies underlined the issue of sexual autonomy, with the students at Nanterre initiating seminars on the work of Wilhelm Reich, particularly his writings exploring the relationship between sexual repression and social repression. This was central to the campaign around student residencies. Late in 1967 a government attempt at compromise ruled that women would be allowed to enter men's residence buildings, but did not allow women to receive men in their residence. This restriction on the freedom of female students was opposed as paternalism. The Minister for Youth and Sports visited Nanterre in early January 1968 for the opening of a swimming pool, an event at which he found himself confronted by demonstrating students. During the dialogue that followed Cohn-Bendit accused the Minister of following a Nazi-influenced policy of attempting to shape youth through sport, in order to distract them from more real and pressing issues such as sexuality. On Valentine's Day, 14 February 1968, male and female students occupied the female residence. The conflict continued during the month of March, involving student meetings and disruption of classes.

Despite this action, there was no mention of sexuality in *Pourquoi des sociologues* co-authored by Cohn-Bendit and three others, the document focusing uniquely on the relationship between sociology and modernizing capitalism understood as a system of production.

How did a conflict around student residencies transform in such a short time so as to generalise and provoke a political crisis that led to early elections for the national government? In part, because this conflict grounded in student life and culture had an ambiguous convergence with a revolutionary imaginary, one where students' action in France came to be seen for a short period as part of a wider struggle against imperialism, where the struggle of workers and students in France was the same struggle as that of the 'heroic people' of Vietnam. And as Isabelle Sommier (2008) argues, the revolutionary imaginary of this time was deeply indebted to the idea of 'revolutionary war', associated with Lin Piao's theory of revolution, Che Guevara's call for 'a thousand Vietnams', and solidarity with the struggle of the National Liberation Front in Vietnam.

The interpenetration between student action and campaigns against imperialism is a complex story of convergence and opposition, beyond the scope of this chapter. The campaign against imperialism, focusing on the war in Vietnam, was present in the student world through two opposed organizations, one linked to Trotskyists and socialists (the Comité Vietnam National) and the other linked to Maoists (the Comité Vietnam de Base), each in turn linked to different political organizations: the first to the Jeunesse Communiste Révolutionnaire (Revolutionary Communist Youth), the second to the Union de la Jeunesse Communiste (Marxiste-Léniniste). A number of Trotskyist students were involved in the action at Nanterre, but the cultural difference between them and the students of the Movement of 22 March was enormous: while those students celebrated a culture of freedom and experimentation, the culture of the members of the JCR was one that emphasised loyalty to the organization and sacrifice. The student Maoists, grouped in particular around Louis Althusser at the elite Ecole Normale, rejected in principle the very the idea of student action.

Actions against the Vietnam War were intensifying in the period leading up to May. Formal peace talks between the United States and North Vietnam were scheduled to begin in Paris on 11 May, in the context of a massive escalation of US bombing of North Vietnam. On the night of 17 March between 3.00 and 4.00 am, three small bombs exploded outside the offices of prominent American corporations, with no claim of responsibility made. No injuries were caused, but these explosions amplified a sense of tension and immanent crisis. Four days later, on 21 March, the Comité National Vietnam held a demonstration against the war, and as it wound down a group of demonstrators split off and attacked the offices of American Express, using iron bars to smash reinforced windows. A prominent Nanterre student, Xavier Langlade, was arrested at a nearby metro entrance. Langlade was well versed in martial arts and a member of the Nanterre students' 'security service' (street fighters who would defend students against attack by the neo-fascist group Occident that periodically attacked student events). Langlade was a member of the JCR and active in the Nanterre campaigns, and it was his arrest in the ongoing climate of confrontation at Nanterre that led students the next day to occupy the 8th floor of the administration building, demanding his release without charge. The occupation carried on until 2.00 a.m., the occupiers debating how to transform protests against police repression into wider action (Charrière 1968).

To continue their action the students called themselves the 'Movement of 22 March', and issued a leaflet calling for a boycott of classes and university wide debates on the following Friday, around four key themes: capitalism in 1968 and workers' struggles; the university and the critical university; the anti-imperialist struggle; worker and student struggles in Eastern Europe. These themes point to a desire to engage with and transform the university – the 'critical university' – while attempting to link this with struggles both in the Third World and Eastern Europe and with worker action in France. Whether it is possible to combine these is another question, but the themes chosen indicate clearly what these students were attempting.

Reactions to the occupation and to the call for a boycott of classes for a day of debate are significant. The Maoist Union de la Jeunesse Communiste (Marxiste-Léniniste) called the idea 'reactionary' and asserted 'intellectual youth could play a progressive role, but only through placing themselves under the authority of the workers, and in the form of a movement supporting the workers' struggle against capitalist exploitation'. Students aligned to the Communist Party equally opposed the call, the Communist newspaper *l'Humanité* describing it as 'a diversion'. However the student residents' association came out in support of the day. The University administration decided to block any potential boycott by cancelling classes and brought in private security guards to prevent students accessing buildings. The campus was eventually reopened, but as the conflict continued courses were suspended and the university was closed on 2 May. Finding themselves expelled from the campus, these students decided to continue their action with their colleagues at the Sorbonne.

The Anti-Student and the Imaginary of Revolutionary Violence

The following day the Sorbonne was also closed in response to a Paris-wide student meeting being held on the campus, with police sent in to forcibly expel students, a violent action provoking arrests and injuries. Locked out of Nanterre and excluded from the Sorbonne, the streets became the focus of action. The next day a number of student leaders were convicted of public order offences, several being sentenced to prison terms, and this brutal response set in motion the dynamic of street fighting and building barricades that would continue through the rest of the month, with the Sorbonne campus being occupied by students from 5 May. As Sommier (2008, 38) observes, this new type of action, in particular the practice of barricading streets, evoked the Paris Commune, drawing students into the revolutionary imaginary. Activating the myth of the 'revolutionary people', barricading streets was a way of producing continuity between the student action and Paris' revolutionary history, and in the process, the students become part of the world revolutionary movement. This was evident in the new kinds of leaflets that began to appear, their language referring to 'heroic students', a term paralleling the 'heroic people' of Vietnam.

What is striking is the extent that the students of the 22 March Movement became rapidly absorbed into this revolutionary imaginary. In an article published on 8 May Cohn-Bendit had underlined that the starting point for the action that was now a major confrontation was 'the condition imposed upon us at the university'. However in a leaflet distributed on 17 May by the 22 March Movement, themes of student life had almost completely disappeared, the leaflet calling upon supporters to continue the street combat, declaring that workers, students, lecturers and the unemployed were at the barricades not to defend 'the university serving the unique interests of the bourgeoisie'. The leaflet goes on to affirm that 'an entire generation of future *cadres* (managers) is refusing to serve as planners for the needs of the bourgeoisie and as agents of exploitation and repression of workers. Rather than about 'student amusement in defence of student interests', the 'profound sense' of the barricades was a 'direct struggle against the bourgeois state and its police'. Arguing 'the struggle we are engaging in against the police apparatus is the struggle of all the workers', the pamphlet concludes in block letters:

'IT IS NOW, IN THE STREET AND IN THE FACTORIES, THAT THE STRUGGLE AGAINST REPRESSION AND BOURGEOIS OPPRESSION IS BEING CARRIED OUT.' (in Perrot et al 1968)

The themes of the 'critical university', the content of academic disciplines, student autonomy and experience such as sexuality were eclipsed. The next day the Movement joined calls for the constitution of Revolutionary Action Committees to 'organize the revolutionary struggle'.

The sociologist Edgar Morin, sympathetic to the movement, suggests that what is at stake here is best understood as a 'simulated revolution'. He underlines the place of 'the tragic' in this action, without which the movement would be reduced to a celebration of liberation. Morin underlines in particular the dramatisation of repression in slogans such as CRS=SS, or 'A New Charonne in Paris' (referring events of 1962 where demonstrators, mainly members of the Communist Party opposing the war in Algeria, became trapped in the stairway of Charonne Metro station while fleeing from charging riot police, an event leading to death by asphyxiation of eight people). Isabelle Sommier (2008) points to similar dramatisations, noting one pamphlet entitled *War Gas!*, which describes students as 'guinea pigs for the sadistic experiments of police', referring to them being 'bled white' and having 'limbs torn off and amputated'. Another argues the gas being used on the streets of Paris was the same being used against the people of Vietnam.

This type of dramatisation is not a key dimension of other types of mobilization, such as those of the labour movement. Arguably it points to a dimension of youth culture underlined by Hobsbawm (1994), who perceptively notes the importance of tragic figures who die young, from James Dean to Janis Joplin. Morin developed a similar analysis in the period immediately following May 68, also underlining the place of the tragic in youth culture and forms of youth revolt that had occurred before May 68. He suggests that a dimension of this can be understood in terms of 'hysteria' that may point to what he calls 'a desire for being'. Such a 'desire for being' may be in continuity with the earlier period of action that responded to the emptiness of courses, campuses and consumer society, and which would later emerge in the theme of 'identity' in the post-1968 period.

If a 'desire for being' gave rise to the tragic form that revolution took in this period, what is striking is the extent to which the theme of revolution set out to devour its parent. Revolutionary discourse increasingly came to understand the state as the agent of imperialism, its principal medium of action being violence. A language of civil war and people's war became increasingly important at the blockades, popularised by Maoists through references to Lin Piao (the Chinese military leader and theorist of 'people's war'). The theme of war also drew on national cultures and histories. This was evoked by the barricades in France, while in Italy this was even more pronounced in the post-1969 period, when a large number of groups came to understand themselves as 'brigades', the term used for the armed resistance to Mussolini and the fascist government. The question of the violence, that emerged out of the post-1968 period, also raised in Cardina's chapter in this book, is beyond the scope of this chapter. However, it clearly emerges out of a context where a social conflict becomes transformed into a conflict against a state, understood as an instrument of violence.

What we might call the 'anti-student' was particularly important among Maoist groups for whom violence exercised the most direct fascination. Serge July (who would later become editor of the left-wing newspaper *Libération*, created with the support of Jean-Paul Sartre) had been active at Nanterre, and in August 1968 travelled to Cuba to a hero's welcome, returning to France to create the Maoist group *Gauche Prolétarienne*, co-authoring a book entitled *Towards Civil War* (Geismar, July and Morane 1969). This revolutionary ideology denied any autonomy and creativity to social conflicts, regarding them uniquely as 'fronts' in the construction of the revolutionary organization and its project. We encounter this logic starkly in April 1969, in the *Cahiers* published by the Gauche Prolétarienne: 'All militants know that the ideas they had in their heads during the May combats came for the most part from the practice of the Vietnamese people' (*La cause du peuple*, 5, 24). This revolutionary discourse became increasingly narrow and mechanical as the events of May progressed. Alain Krivine, leader of the Jeunesse Communiste Révolutionnaire (and who would remain its leader for the next 30 years), defined revolution in the narrowest Leninist terms, where 'those above' are no longer able to govern, 'those on the bottom' no longer are prepared to accept the status quo, and those 'in the middle' join with the proletariat (Krivine cited in Sommier 2008). For Krivine, May had failed because it had not produced a revolution, and this was because the Communist Party had failed to offer the necessary leadership. For the JCR, priority was to be given to constructing a revolutionary party, one which would be capable of 'educating the workers' in the direction of revolution (Krivine 1973, 150). Krivine stood in the Presidential election of 1969, gaining 1.05% of the votes cast.

This 'anti-student' imaginary also played a key role in the cultural Marxism that developed in this movement, and which is today widely regarded as an expression of the counter culture. This is evident among the Situationists, a movement examined in detail in Harding's chapter 8, a moment with its origins in avant-garde European art, which set out to create cultural events or 'situations' that appeared out of place, both in terms of content and method: creating humorous events in serious contexts, preaching the 'death of God' in churches. This group was absent at Nanterre, but played an important role in the Sorbonne occupation, amplifying themes of derision and 'detournement' that had become increasingly important earlier at Nanterre. It is important to recognize the extent to which the Situationist political program was based in Marxist orthodoxy: the key to social transformation lay in the creation of Workers Councils and direct democracy in factories. Seidman notes that the Situationists condemned the isolated individual: 'the realization of the personal had to be collective. Workers councils would be the foundation of a truly libertarian communist society' (Seidman 2004, 28). The Situationists, just as much as the Maoists, insisted that the sources of social utopia were only to be found in the working class: 'Without a doubt, the proletariat brings forth the project of human fulfilment and *complete existence*' (cited in Seidman 2004 28, emphasis added).

The Situationists understood the student condition as one of alienation, a view emphasised in the Situationist pamphlet *The Misery of Student Life* (1964), printed by the national student union, its circulation reaching an extraordinary 250,000 copies. There we read:

> 'The student is a product of modern society, the same as Godard or Coca-Cola. The only way to contest the student's alienation is by contesting society in its entirety. There is no way at all that this critique can be developed through the student world (*sur le terrain étudiant*); students as such possesses only a pseudo-value that prevents them from becoming conscious of the reality of their dispossession, and as such, are the peak of false consciousness. But everywhere modern society is beginning to be contested there is a youth revolt that corresponds immediately to a total critique of student behaviour.' (Union Nationale des Etudiants de France 1966/1976, 19)

As Touraine notes (1972, 224), this understood the student condition as one of alienation and submission to domination; to that extent action becomes directed towards escaping the student condition rather than transforming it. However refusing to think about transforming the university and education proved difficult to combine with the Situationists' strategy, which centred on occupying the university (the Situationists were in a majority during the Sorbonne occupation). This strategy was not based on a claim that the university was a key institution to transform; rather it was modelled on the Situationist commitment to workers councils taking physical control of the factories. As a result, these students found themselves occupying an institution that they asserted had no role in building a movement for change.

Some of these dilemmas were evident in the United States at the same time. As O'Donnell explains in chapter 6, the Revolutionary Youth Movement succeeded in taking control of the SDS (Students for a Democratic Society) and later transformed itself into the Weather Underground. Even as it was taking control of the SDS, RYM leaders were arguing that they had to 'destudentize' the struggle, making a break with an earlier period where 'student power' had been modelled on 'black power'. One of those making this call, Mark Rudd, went from leading student action at Columbia in April 1968 to being elected President of the Students for a Democratic Society to becoming a founder of the Weather Underground. There are certain parallels between the period of the Weathermen (before going underground) and the Gauche Proletarienne: both emphasised the importance of smashing sexual norms and constraints. In the case of the Weathermen, group sex sessions were organized as part of its campaign called 'Smash Monogamy'. In this case, a culture emphasising group sex explicitly opposed forming one-to-one relationships that might potentially come to rival the loyalty of the individual to the group, and the group had the power to split couples apart if it was deemed that these relationships were 'possessive' or 'selfish' (Varon 2004, 58).

Movements, Post-1968 and Today

A dominant approach in the English-language sociology of social movements regards movements as non-institutionalised political actors that emerge to represent and advance the interests of groups who are inadequately represented by political parties or who find themselves excluded from access to what is termed the 'political process' (McAdam et al 2001). Charles Tilly, one of the most influential American scholars in the study of movements, argues that they proceed through making claims based on their unity, size and commitment. Others argue in terms of a 'protest cycle', suggesting a rise and decline of social movements fundamentally shaped by the extent that their demands are institutionalised, in a model that moves from 'protest to reform to consolidation to retreat' (Tarrow 1998, 35).

The events we have briefly recounted here are much more structured around tensions and creativity, about producing experiences rather than representing a group or being part of a somewhat linear transition (welcomed or decried) from bureaucratic to network capitalism. Certain transformations remain of major importance. The shift from a 'student' movement to a 'youth' movement is clear, but this is not simply a movement of individualism in the way Hobsbawm suggests. This transition is in fact much more charged with risk and much more unstable than evolutionary models of the rise of individualism suggest. Sexuality was central to the birth of this movement, at the heart of the conflicts around student residences. It was central to collective and personal experiences being constructed against a world experienced as bureaucratic, brutal and increasingly a reality of 'non-sense' (Touraine 1968, 118). The risk in this is evident in particular in the experiences where radicalised expressions of the movement collapse the category of personal experience, which had played such an important role in what Seidman calls the 'love wars', into types of fusion experiences: either into sex, into an imaginary of violence, or into a mystical proletarian experience that would render the student 'complete'.

While the theme of the tragic played an important role in May's action, this was in constant tension with humour and ridicule, with forms of action that combined mockery with appropriation and exaggeration of bourgeois disapproval. Such forms of 'detournement' transformed 'a discourse of shame into a badge of honour' (Atack 1999, 44), and clearly prefigure forms of action that would later be evident in queer action and other forms of action seeking to amplify and reverse stigma. For Touraine, the strategy of derision was a response to a world that was experienced as absurd, while the strategy of shock and irony had the effect of creating as a social reality the dimension of social life to be denounced. Humour, derision, parody and irony became a medium of communication that highlighted the 'absurd presented as logic' (Atack 1999, 44). In the process a moralizing order claiming to be rational was unmasked as immoral and irrational.

The period following May was not one of 'consolidation and retreat'. Instead actors found themselves profoundly changed and part of a world that before they had not even imagined. This transformation of subjectivities and social realities was evident in events that followed soon after. The first 'women only' meetings of activists involved in May were held from October of that year. Convened by Monique Wittig and Antoinette Fouque, they set in motion a process that would lead to the creation in spring 1970 of the Mouvement de Libération des Femmes. The question of homosexuality had been briefly posed, then suppressed, during the Sorbonne occupation. A small group involved in the occupation had called itself the Comité d'Action Pédérastique Révolutionnaire (Revolutionary Pederast Action Committee), and had posted eight hand written notices on the walls of the occupied Sorbonne denouncing the repression of homosexuals, their shattered careers as well as their own defeatism. These notices had been hastily torn down by the leaders of the occupation who declared that they did not want their revolution 'soiled' (Martel 1999 16). Three years later, however, the Front Homosexuel d'Action Révolutionaire was born when a group of women stormed the platform of one of France's highest rating live radio talk shows that was earnestly discussing the unnatural condition of homosexuality and the suffering involved. This direct action had been inspired by Stonewall uprising in New York 1969, but the slogans the women shouted as they took control of the stage were the product of the May movement: 'We are a social scourge!', 'Down with the heterocops!', and 'Homosexuals are sick of being a painful problem!' (Martel 1999, 19). The radio transmission was cut, but not before the public birth of a new movement.

When we look back at May 1968, what we see are new types of action couched within an old language. This is evident not only in the expressions denying the creativity of action, but the constant use of images where the totality acts through the person, whether this be class, party or proletariat. This borrowing is also shown in the importance of the imaginary of the term 'front'. A front is the creation or instrument of a revolutionary party that uses it to penetrate or mobilize populations. It denies the creativity of social actors, understanding them as the product of another actor. The theme of 'people's war' extended beyond France. Not only was it evident in the final days of the American student movement, it had an important role in the early imaginary of the Gay Liberation

Front in Britain, which called in its first manifesto in 1971 for the 'full participation of gays in the people's revolutionary army', modelled on a demand coming from the United States. The imaginary of fronts and armies was completely absent in the early mobilizations at Nanterre, where students demanding new freedoms did not in the least consider themselves to be a 'front' for some other organization working through them. During the May mobilization however, as the movement increasingly became defined by a revolutionary imaginary, these became more important, and carried on in the period after.

It was after the events of May that new themes and ways of acting present in the mobilization started to produce a new language. It was in this period that new types of action emerged that increasingly came to understand themselves as what came to be called 'new social movements' (Touraine 1982). In the process actors freed themselves from the revolutionary imaginary, and from its conception of organization in terms of fronts, and began to construct new grammars of action around what would come to be known, from a term created in the United States, 'identity' (Gleason 1983). For a time 'identity' promised a new relationship between individual and collective, as actors shifted from building organizations and fronts to constructing communities (in the United States and Britain in particular) and 'collectives' (in France). The key to these forms of action was the construction of collective identity through mobilizations seeking to name and contest forms of power.

For observers of the 1980s and 1990s such as the influential sociologist Manuel Castells, the very basis of these new movements lay in their 'powerful expressions of collective identity' (Castells 2004, 2). Arguably today we are at the end of this period. This appears very clear in the patterns of action and culture of contemporary movements that emphasise convergence rather than fusion, an encounter with 'the other' rather than the creation of an 'us' (McDonald 2006). Many observers would agree with French anti-globalization compaigner José Bové when he described the protests at Seattle in December 1999 as 'just like May 1968' (cited in Bleiker 2002). There are significant parallels between forms of action emerging in the alterglobalisation movement, in attempts to develop new types of public presence and experience, and the action of May. This is most evident in the use of humour and detournement, from the 'radical cheerleaders' in the United States to protesters dressed as bankers at the G20 action in London in 2009, or in attempts to explore the relationship between art and politics evident in the role of puppets in mobilisations.

Conclusion

These contemporary actions suggest a break with the paradigm that emerged in the 1970s and consolidated itself in the 1980s, where movements came to be understood as 'expressions of identity'. Today, as in May 1968, we encounter attempts to construct new types of public experience, and a renewed awareness of the place of culture and art in protest and action. The model of community and collective that replaced the party and the imaginary of the front and the army is itself giving way to new types of action grounded in a culture of convergence and encounter rather than celebration of 'us'. As 40 years ago, it is not yet clear what form of organization that these themes might give rise to, but it does seem clear today that we are witnessing a similarly important transformation in forms of culture, action and organization. The challenge actors and intellectuals face today is just as urgent as that faced 40 years ago: to find a language to make sense of forms of social activism that do not yet have words to describe them. And here we have much to learn from the movements of 1968.

References

Atack, M. 1999. *May 68 in French fiction and film: rethinking society, rethinking representation*. Oxford: Oxford University Press

Bleiker, R. 2002. 'Politics after Seattle: Dilemmas of the anti-globalisation movement'. *Cultures and Conflicts*, http://www.conflits.org/index1057.html (accessed 8 October 2009)

Boltanski, L. and Chiapello, E. 2006. *The New Spirit of Captialism*. London: Verso

Castells, M. 2004. *The Power of identity*. Oxford: Blackwell

Charrière, C. 1968. *Le Printemps des Enragés*. Paris: Fayard

Cohn-Bendit, D. 2008. *Forget 68*. Paris: Editions de l'Aube

Cohn-Bendit, D., Duteuil, J-P., Gerard, B. and Granautier, B. 1968. 'Pourquoi des sociologues?'. *Esprit*. May, pp. 877–882

Debray, R. 2008. *Mai 68: Une contre-révolution réussie*. Paris: Mille et une nuits

Duteuil, J.-P. 1988. *Nanterre 1965–1968: Vers le mouvement du 22 mars*. Paris: Acratie

Fukuyama, F. 1994. *The End of History and the Last Man*. New York: Free Press

Giesmar, A., July, S. and Morane, E. 1969. *Vers la guerre civile*. Paris: Lattes

Gleason, P. 1983. 'Identifying identity: a semantic history'. *The Journal of American History*. 69, 4, pp. 910–931

Hobsbawm, E. 1994. *Age of Extremes*. London: Penguin

Krivine, A. 1973. *Questions sur la Révolution*. Paris: Stock

Lancelin, A. 2008. 'Liquider le merchandising 68?'. *Le Nouvel Observateur*, issue 2270. Online: http://hebdo.nouvelobs.com/hebdo/parution/p2270/articles/a374309-.html (accessed 8 October 2009)

Martel, F. 1999. *The Pink and the Black: Homosexuals in France since 1968*. Stanford: Stanford University Press

McAdam, D., Tarrow, S. and Tilly, C. 2001. *Dynamics of Contention*. Cambridge: Cambridge University Press

McDonald, K. 2002. 'From solidarity to fluidity: social movements after collective identity – the case of globalization conflicts'. *Social Movement Studies*. 1, 2, 109-128

McDonald, K. 2006. *Global Movements: Action and Culture*. Oxford: Blackwell

Morin, E. 1970. 'Remarques sur la commutation des traits sociaux' in Georges Balandier (ed) *Sociologie des mutations*. Paris: Anthropos

Perrot, J-C., Perrot, M., Rebérioux, M. and Maitron, J. (eds). 1968. *La Sorbonne par elle-même: mai-juin 1968*. Paris: Les Editions Ouvrières

Seidman, M. 2004. *The Imaginary Revolution: Parisian students and workers in 1968*. New York: Berghahn

Sommier, I. 2008. *La violence politique et son deuil*. Rennes: Presses Universitaires de Rennes

Tarrow, S. 1998. 'Social protest and policy reform', in Marco Giugni, Doug McAdam and Charles Tilly (eds) *From Contention to Democracy*. New York: Rowan and Littlefield

Touraine, A. 1968. *Le communisme utopique*. Paris: Seuil

Touraine, A. 1972. *Université et société aux Etats-Unis*. Paris: Seuil

Touraine, A. 1982. *The Voice and the Eye*. Cambridge: Cambridge University Press

Union Nationale des Etudiants de France (Strasbourg). 1966/1976. *De la misère en milieu étudiant*. Paris: Champ Libre

Varon, J. 2004. *Bringing the War Home: The Weather Underground, the Red Army Faction, and Revolutionary Violence in the Sixties and Seventies*. Berkeley: University of California Press

Viansson-Ponté, P. (1968) 'Quand la France s'ennuie...', *Le Monde* 15 March. Internet: http://www.lemonde.fr/le-monde-2/article/2008/04/30/quand-la-france-s-ennuie_1036662_1004868.html (accessed 8 October 2009)

Chapter 3

THE WAR AGAINST THE WAR: VIOLENCE AND ANTICOLONIALISM IN THE FINAL YEARS OF THE ESTADO NOVO

Miguel Cardina

If the slogan 'make love, not war' became a constantly evoked symbol of the kind of protest generated in the 'long sixties' (Jameson 1984; Marwick 1998, 16–20), the fact is that the attitudes and discourses that originated in this period have not always corresponded to this pacifist image, at times understood retrospectively as parodic, individualistic and carefree. In different times and places, at a gradually more intense pace, the new youth culture introduced profound changes in the fields of customs, taste and morality, and set in motion modes of daring and resistance which often evolved towards open confrontation with bourgeois social codes. The sixties experience, namely in its radical and politicized strand, promoted a new kind of fracturing and transgressive conflictuality, which, rather than rejecting violence, questioned its meaning and sought to redefine its application.

In Portugal, despite socio-cultural and political obstacles, some sectors, primarily originating in student settings, showed their openness to the influence of a certain 'space 68' (Frank 2000). This phenomenon intersected with the emergence of a new type of protest against the colonial war, in which philo-Maoist activism had a relevant role. Condemning the bellicose and nationalistic rhetoric of the Estado Novo [New State], these groups nevertheless saw violence as an indispensable means to achieve a desired classless society. This text seeks to analyse the question of violence in the new left radicalism, to contextualize the specificity of the Maoist experience throughout the sixties, and to characterize the practice and discourse of this multifaceted political field during the decline of the Portuguese dictatorship.

Violence in the Sixties Narratives

The question of violence has often been raised in what concerns the interpretation of the content and legacy of the sixties. Some of the more conservative readings even tend to associate the period with a whirlwind of destruction of the established order. In his influential *The Conflict of Generations*, Lewis Feuer talks about the 'irrationalities and self-destructive components of all student movements' (1969, 102). Using also the idea of a Nihilism stemming from this period, Allan Bloom (1987) criticizes the devaluation of the 'Great Books' that had its origin in sixties radical thought. Referring more specifically to the events of 'May of 68' in Paris, Raymond Aron mentions a carnival-like delirium brought about by 'barbarians unaware of their barbarity' (1968, 13). This deprecating discourse was actually revived during the 2007 French presidential campaign by Nicolas Sarkozy, who accused 'May of 68' of having created a society in which hierarchy, authority and social peace are frequently challenged. According to Alain Badiou (2008), this is a result of the fact that the events of that period were one of the last real expressions of the 'communist specter'.

In a different manner, the American Todd Gitlin (1993), associating the decade to a multifarious field of hope and rage, suggests the existence of the 'good' sixties – constituted by the opposition to the Vietnam War and the civil rights struggle – clearly distinct from the 'bad' sixties, which were filled with struggles that had destructive effects and frequently no long-term goals. On the contrary, for Max Elbaum (2002), the days of rage of the late sixties signaled a step up in protests and do not correspond merely to a period of hangover or loss of faith. According to this former activist, the periods of 1960–4 and 1968–73 not only demanded different kinds of commitment – meaning that one cannot analyze the period outside of the larger political context from which it stemmed – but also the so-called 'bad sixties' were, as a matter of fact, a time of systemic critique of the political structures that enthusiastically involved significant social segments of the population.

Others, such as Arthur Marwick, highlight the coexistence of contrasting though complementary streams, integrated into a set of changes directed at calling into question the existing establishment. In his monumental book on the period, this British historian dedicates a whole chapter to the issue of violence, noting that 'it is pointless to divide the sixties into a peaceful, optimistic first half and a violent, pessimistic second half', given that, more often than not, the violence of the second phase stemmed precisely from movements that emerged in the first phase (Marwick 1998, 533–83).

In a comparative study of the urban guerilla carried out by the American Weather Underground and the German RAF (Rote Armee Fraktion), Jeremy Varon (2004, 3) points to the existence of relatively widespread debates within the New Left on the issue of violence, both in defensive terms, against police repression, and in offensive terms, as a tool for needed social change. In his turn, Paul Berman (2005, 40–1) considers that the debates within the New Left focused essentially on the question of crypto-Nazism in modern life and on the means to offset it. Frequently mixed up with the concrete context of activism, the question of violence/non-violence was supposedly a tactical matter, and it emerged more vigorously from 1969 because the Vietnam War was escalating, the anticolonial movement seemed to be taking a more radical path, and the actual experience of confrontations with the police was leading to fits of rage.

New Left Radicalism

The radicalism of the decade was characterized by the adoption of an imaginary of rebelliousness based on new ethical, aesthetic and political references with internationalist and combative traits. This trend was not based on a unified body of theses, but rather on multiple, and often conflicting, contributions. Be that as it may, it is still possible to identify some common features. First, the fight against alienation, not only in economic terms of renewal, but also in psychological, sexual, cultural and ideological terms. Second, the critique of traditional forms of authority which, in some cases, extended to the very notion of authority itself. Third, the critique of everyday life, and the insistence on a model of socialism that was intimately connected to a necessary and radical change in customs and mentalities, and not just based on social and political revolution. Finally, the enhancement of the role of youth as an agent of change, replacing or going side by side with the proletariat in the historical mission of social transformation that Marxism had attributed to it (Katsiaficas 1987, 23–7).

Especially in English-speaking countries, this strange mixture was widely dubbed the 'New Left', although many segments remained faithful to the 'old' Marxist left and to its principle of the organization of industrial workers as the basis of societal transformation. This movement had three currents: the first consisted in a return to 'old fashioned sectarian Marxism', through the organization of 'disciplined, Leninist structures based on obedience, dedication, and self-sacrifice'. The second was made up of the 'Marxism of Ho, Mao, Che, and Fidel, mixed with a few doctrines of the Frankfurt School philosophers', and its organizational framework was often undefined. The third was based on the libertarian drive of Kropotkin, Bakunin, the Dutch council communists and the French situationists, as well as 'on a breeze blowing through the university neighborhoods and on rumors from the California counterculture' (Berman 2005, 42–4).

Despite relevant differences among these groups, it is possible to find a point of intersection among the pieces of this emerging kaleidoscope, which consisted in their equally distant positioning regarding both modern western consumer societies, from which the movement by and large emerged, and Soviet bureaucratism. The new insurgent groups were united in their defense of participatory democracy and of internationalism, in their use of daring forms of protest, and in the proclamation of their common dream of bringing about a revolution that would put an end both to western imperialism, symbolized by the USA, and to eastern European bureaucratic communism.

Thus, Moscow-type socialism was rejected by a variety of groups which, despite significant differences, concurred on the same condemnation of formal bourgeois democracy and the political apparatchik and reformism of the pro-Soviet Left. In other words, all of them frequently expressed an interest in Marx, showed a revolutionary posture, and considered themselves to be on the left of traditional communist parties, which they attacked with different degrees of virulence. In fact, after the mid-fifties, a series of events helped call into question the exemplary image of the Soviet regime. Among these, we should mention the questioning of Stalinism at the 20th Congress of the KPSS (Communist Party of the Soviet Union), the uprisings in Poland and Hungary in 1956, the Sino-Soviet conflict, and the invasion of Czechoslovakia in August of 1968. At the same time, the struggles of Third World independence movements, the informal image of the Cuban revolution, and the elated – and often truncated and flawed – reading of the Chinese phenomenon, seemed to show that the revolutionary transformation of society was possible following apparently new models, which, precisely because of their newness, had an obvious appeal.

International Maoism

The Maoist experience underway in several places throughout the world in the sixties and seventies was based on an inflexible and bipolar theory of class struggle and on the defense of revolutionary war as a means of achieving power. Thus, it promoted the idea that the flaws of the world can only be eliminated by the force of arms, something which was illustrated with a few quotations by 'Chairman Mao', such as the one that expressed the conviction that 'political power grows out of the barrel of a gun'. This belligerent image generated a lot of support from militants. For instance, when questioned about the reason why he had a poster of Mao Zedong on the wall, Eldridge Cleaver, a key member of the American Black Panthers, answered: '[B]ecause he is the baddest motherfucker on the planet earth' (Avakian 2005, 167). Sinophilia was also fed by the laudatory readings of intellectuals that visited China, such as Maria Antonietta Macchiocchi, Charles Bettheleim, K.S. Carol, Julia Kristeva and Alberto Moravia, who helped to transplant to the West the myth of the 'Great Helmsman' and of an ever-evolving revolution.

After the anarchist split at the 1st International, and the Trotskyite dissent from the 1930s, Maoism represented the third great schism in the international communist movement. Stalin's death in 1953, and Krushchev's denunciation of 'the cult of personality' during the 20th Congress of the KPSS in 1956, initiated a new stage in the history of this movement. From then onwards, the divergences between China and the Soviet Union became increasingly more pronounced until their final rupture in the early seventies. For the Chinese, the Soviet thesis of 'peaceful coexistence' meant the effective abandonment of the fight between communism and imperialism, and this led Mao Zedong to support the establishment of 'Maoist' organizations throughout the world.

The sole communist party in power that supported Chinese dissent was the Albanian communist party in 1961. At an early stage, among the emerging groups in Europe, we can highlight the one led by Jacques Grippa, which arose from an important split in the Belgian Communist Party. It became an international center of 'Marxist-Leninist' (M-L) regrouping until the late sixties, when China stopped endorsing it. If in Europe Maoist groups rapidly appeared in eighteen countries, it was in areas of the so-called 'Third World' – namely in Latin America and Asia – that Maoism achieved the greatest success (Alexander 1999; 2001).

While the rupture between the Soviet Union and China, in the early sixties, nourished splits within the communist parties of different countries, a second Maoist wave gained ground in the late sixties, induced in particular by the impact of the Chinese cultural revolution, and the resulting conviction that the transformation of the world was a process that was nurtured by the permanent challenge to established hierarchical structures, even if they had a socialist format. This second wave was especially felt in radical youth milieus, and among sectors which, as a rule, had never been affiliated to traditional communist parties and which, despite their staunchly Leninist discourse, had deep ties to the voluntarist activism of a certain type of historical anarchism.

This double affiliation led Marxist-Leninist militants to waver between disciplinary and antidisciplinary protest which characterized sixties radicalism (Stephens 1998). Within various groups, and sometimes within militants themselves, the imaginary of rebellion as a 'party' struggled with the refusal of the hedonistic dimension of protest; personal experimentation and openness confronted puritanism and 'proletarian morality'; the reception of theoretical heterodoxies faced up to dogmatism and the ideological vulgate; the seduction of arms conflicted with the need to develop painstaking work with 'the masses'.

In truth, we need to be aware of the danger of treating this political field as a homogeneous reality. In a comparative study on Maoism and Trotskyism in France and the United States, Belden Fields talks about the existence of a 'hierarchical Maoism' and an 'anti-hierarchical Maoism' in the French context

(1998, 87 and 226). Along the same lines, Marnix Dressen divides organizations into 'Maoist-Leninist' – which includes the old Union des Jeunesses Communiste marxiste-leniniste (UJCml) and the Parti Communiste Marxiste-Leniniste de France (PCMLF), officially recognized by China – and 'Maoist-Anarchist' – the case of Gauche Prolétarienne and its short-lived offshoot Vive la Revolution!. In broad strokes, the first strand was influenced by the Sino-Soviet conflict and the Bolshevik concept of the proletarian vanguard, whereas the second was characterized by a greater spontaneity in attitudes and practices, and seduced by the imaginary of the Cultural Revolution (Dressen 1999, 21).

Portuguese Oppositions: Between Colonialism and Anticolonialism

The geopolitical context that emerged from World War II had a strong impact on the anticolonial movement of the ensuing years. Seen as a struggle against Germanic expansionism, the Allied victory served to affirm the principles that would be established in the United Nations Charter, namely in chapter XI, compelling countries with colonies to encourage the progressive development of free political institutions. Later on, the UN would even advocate that colonial powers had the duty to prepare the territories under their administration for independence. In April of 1955, at the Bandung Conference (Indonesia), twenty-nine African and Asian countries met, including the USSR, China and India, and condemned colonialism, calling for the unity of all peoples against it.

In Portugal, the 1951 constitutional revision transformed the colonies into 'overseas territories', a cosmetic change that in fact aimed at neutralizing the above-mentioned chapter XI of the UN Charter. This ploy was intended to assert that the country indeed had no colonies, but only national provinces that had the remarkable characteristic of being located on different continents, although the so-called 'Indigenous Statute' in force excluded the vast majority of the native inhabitants of those territories from the rights of Portuguese citizenship.

Colonialism and the cult of the Empire were, as a matter of fact, the mainstays of the ideological discourse of the Estado Novo (1933–1974). At the same time that the regime extolled rural life – the dictator Salazar defined himself as a Catholic 'peasant, son of peasants, poor, son of poor people' (Salazar 1951, 351) – it based itself on a strong imperial mystique that identified the country with an inescapable civilizing mission overseas. The sacralization of the Empire is intimately connected, in Portugal, both to the idea of maintaining its independence from Spain within the Iberian Peninsula, and to the need of preserving the image of a nation associated to the 'sacred legacy' of the golden period of the 'Discoveries'.

Also because of that, the post-war decolonizing winds reached the opposition in a very indirect manner. Like the supporters of the regime, a significant part of the old republicans believed that the Empire provided an opportunity to recover the nation's 'lost glory'. Prominent opposition figures were open supporters of Portuguese colonialism, and so the issue was marginalized in the forums of political debate that the dictatorship allowed to take place from time to time. The subject is not raised in either the Programme for the Democratization of the Republic in 1961, or in Humberto Delgado's electoral manifesto in 1958 – whose candidacy galvanized the opposition and alarmed the regime to such an extent that it trumped the results and prohibited the holding of presidential elections from then on.

The Socialists themselves, gathered in 1964 around the ASP (Portuguese Socialist Action), maintained an ambiguous position during the sixties: they condemned the colonial policy, but only declared the right of colonized peoples to independence at a later stage. By the time the war started in Angola, in early February 1961, only the PCP (Portuguese Communist Party) had recognized the right of the colonies to self-determination and independence. During its 5th Congress, in 1957, it had shifted from its previous position, based on the establishment of local party sections in the colonies, to one which consisted in encouraging parties formed of essentially indigenous bases and leaders to fight for independence (Pereira 2005, 502–72).

An 'Evolving Dualistic Society'

In the late sixties, Portugal saw the intensification of the tendency towards the concentration and modernization of industry that had been noticeable since the beginning of the decade. Portuguese society, primarily rural and dominated by the peasantry, could now begin to be defined as an 'evolving dualist society', influenced by the conflicting coexistence of both traditional and modern values, attitudes and behaviors (Nunes 2000, 25–84). For the first time ever, there seemed to be 'an industrial alternative to agricultural employment, and this implied a new organization of work, higher wages, and longer periods of employment throughout the year'. Thus, the years between 1960 and 1973 registered 'the greatest rate of economic growth in the history of the country' (Barreto 2000, 70). This spurt of industrialization was attended by a set of changes that contributed to a shift in mentalities.

In the first place, one should note the growing influx of foreigners to Portugal, especially to the coastal areas. Whereas, in 1959, foreign visitors barely reached 300,000 [three hundred thousand], in 1973 this number jumped to over four million (Telo 1989, 86). The Portuguese population, traditionally isolated from outside influences, now had direct contact with the British, French or Germans that visited the country, especially in the summer. Additionally, this period also saw a growing number of Portuguese departing from their homeland. Emigration fluxes, usually to Africa or the Americas, shifted rapidly to Europe, particularly to France. If until the late fifties the numbers remained stable at around thirty thousand, between 1958 and 1974 one and a half million people emigrated, an impressive figure if we bear in mind that the country had just over eight million inhabitants at the time. We should also note that this figure is somewhat underestimated, since, besides legal emigration, it only takes into account illegal emigration to France. Between 1969 and 1971, about 350,000 Portuguese left the country for France, and 90 per cent of them did it illegally (Freitas 1989, 191–200).

We should also mention the new lease on life given to the media. Television had a fundamental role in this process. Whereas in 1960, three years after RTP (Portuguese Radio-Television) began its regular broadcasts, there were 31,256 TV sets in Portugal, by 1974 this number had increased twenty-four times, reaching 722,315. All of a sudden, images of 'Vietnam, of Hollywood, of May of 68 or of the mass in Saint Peter's Basilica, entered Portuguese homes, changing forever their view of the world, which until then had been confined to barely more than their town or village' (Telo 1989, 87). However much the regime sought to resist this tendency, prohibiting public demonstrations, censuring the media and carefully inspecting their boundaries, it was practically impossible to control the influx of new means of mass consumption which were undoubtedly helping to shape young people.

Thus, music, cinema, literature, comics, the theater and clothing styles served as means of questioning the *status quo*, and explicitly showed that things were beginning to change: the urban schooled youth – and people in close contact with them – no longer saw themselves as an amalgam of subjects in an unfinished process of social integration, but started to act, think and feel according to their own models, more often than not out of sync with the isolationist rhetoric of the regime and the dominant features of moral conservatism.

Even so, in Portugal it was primarily the combative version of the sixties culture that prevailed. For some, unlike what happened in other countries, 'the mystic hippy movement' was never an object of symbolic construction (Resende and Vieira 1992, 134). Rui Bebiano (2003), however, points to localized spaces where this symbolic construction began to take shape, although it had no practical expression and was clearly subordinated to the urgency of politicized discourse. The reason for this is surely related to the persistence of the specter of the colonial war, political repression, the reach of a conservative Catholic morality over several domains, and the country's weak urban development. In the multifaceted field of the opposition itself, hedonistic and anti-hierarchical behaviors were seen as irreconcilable with the abnegation required by the 'antifascist' cause and with the conspirational cautions that the political situation demanded from all those who wanted to join the organized fight against the regime.

Marcelism, the Last Station

In August of 1968, the 79 year-old António de Oliveira Salazar fell from a chair in his vacation residence, at the Fort of São João do Estoril, and become unable to lead the government. Marcello Caetano, seventeen years younger than Salazar, and with connections to the Estado Novo since its foundation, was appointed to his place. Despite these connections, Caetano had acquired the reputation of being a liberal in the fifties and sixties, particularly after his resignation from the position of rector at the University of Lisbon in 1962, in the aftermath of the invasion of the student union premises by the police. Withdrawn from active politics since then, Caetano had led from the wings a sort of 'informal party', seeking to 'make a difference; to gather strength and influence within the regime; to wait for the right moment for succession' (Rosas 1994, 507).

Marcello Caetano's political project consisted in a 'program of opening up and decompression of the regime, with technocratic and developmentalist undertones' (Rosas and Oliveira 2004, 11–2). Bent on uniting the ultraconservative and liberalizing sectors of society, Marcello Caetano summed up his program in the expression 'renewal in continuity'. If 'continuity' meant abiding by the legal-institutional line of the Estado Novo, as well as maintaining the overseas territories as a national, and even civilizational, issue of the utmost importance, the 'renewal' was reflected in a series of measures of political decompression that would take shape in the so-called 'Marcellist Spring'. Among these were the return from exile of the Socialist Mário Soares in October of 1968, and of the Bishop of Oporto, António Ferreira Gomes, in July of 1969; the limitation of certain powers of the political police and its transformation from the International Police for the Defense of the State (PIDE) to General Security Directorate (DGS) in November of 1969; the passing of new labor union laws in April of 1969, which no longer required elected union directorates to be officially approved; the change of the National Union party into the Popular National Action party in February of 1970, and its opening to new currents, of which the most significant example is the integration of the so-called 'liberal wing' into its lists for the 1969 general elections.

In the early seventies, keeping up the military effort in Africa led to the sacrifice of liberalization and ultimately of the regime itself. The political police returned to its repressive role, not only against the Communist Party and the extreme left, but also against more moderate ideological sectors. The intensification of repression against Catholic oppositional fringes would culminate, in 1973, in the imprisonment and compulsive resignation of individuals from public service after a vigil for peace that took place at the Rato Chapel in Lisbon. Inside the government, a bill on the freedom of the press presented to Parliament by representatives of the liberal wing was rejected, a fact which signaled the tendency of the regime towards closure. This tendency was also visible in the constitutional revision of 1971, where all liberal proposals were rejected.

This process of hardening went hand in hand with the consolidation of the oppositional dynamic. From 1970, strikes, protests and social unrest increased. Intersindical was established, gathering together several unions that did not support the regime. Specific Catholic fringe groups that were particularly active in their denunciation of the war expressed their opposition to the regime. Armed opposition against the Estado Novo began, organized by civilian groups of a political-military character intent on wearing down the regime – namely, ARA (Armed Revolutionary Action), connected to the PCP, LUAR (Revolutionary Unity and Action League) and the BR (Revolutionary Brigades). A large variety of small leftist groups appeared and challenged the Communist Party's hegemony in the universities and, in some cases, in the unions and working-class milieus. As a rule, these new groups were the offspring of the fragmentation of Portuguese Marxist-Leninist founding organizations, namely FAP (Popular Action Front) and CMLP (Portuguese Marxist-Leninist Committee), which were established after Francisco Martins Rodrigues left the PCP, in August 1963. At about this time, at a meeting of the Central Committee that took place in Moscow, Martins Rodrigues presented his criticisms of the party, which would later be summarized in the document entitled *Luta Pacífica e Luta Armada no nosso Movimento (Peaceful Struggle and Armed Struggle in our Movement)*. In it, he proposed an armed proletarian revolution rather than the prevailing party line, based on 'cross-class alliance' and on the thesis of the 'national democratic revolution', which Martins Rodrigues considered a 'pacifist distortion of Leninism' (1970, 18). After leaving the PCP, he and a small group of people created the FAP, directed towards the armed struggle, and, in April of 1964, the CMLP, the embryo of a "true" future communist party. Both organizations, indistinguishable in practical terms, would be hit hard by the police in 1965 and 1966, and their principal leaders condemned to heavy prison sentences.

An increasing and intricate divisiveness would lead to the splitting of FAP/CMLP into a set of new groups. Accusing the PCP of being 'revisionist' and 'reformist', all of them claimed to represent the 'pure' Marxist-Leninist principles, which meanwhile had shifted from the Soviet Union to countries like China or Albania. Despite their small size, most of these structures had their 'mass' and 'theoretical' newspapers, and devoted themselves to intensive work of agitation. One part of activist work was developed abroad, among emigrants – especially in France – by former members of the CMLP, whose constant infighting led to bitter splits. At home, two groups stood out: the MRPP (Reorganizing Movement of the Party of the Proletariat), founded in September of 1970 from a Lisbon student structure; and the OCMLP (Portuguese Marxist-Leninist Communist Organization), established at the end of 1972 from the merger of O Comunista [The Communist], active among emigrants, and O Grito do Povo [The People's Shout], based especially in the North.

These organizations had a number of features that came to revamp the oppositionist *modus operandi*. In the first place, they chose as their major banners the struggle against the colonial war and the defense of the proletarian revolution, using a radical and voluntarist discourse. Second, they elected new political icons, such as Ho Chi Minh, Mao Zedong and Che Guevara, characterized by a 'fundamentally antirealist voluntarism' which, in the case of Mao and Che, extended to the ideological, political and cultural questioning of the Soviet norm (Frank 2000, 36). Third, and as a consequence, they introduced a different style of confrontation of power, bolder and more direct, which included daring demonstrations, the distribution of pamphlets in broad daylight and the stoning of banks. Primarily located in student and young workers milieus, this new kind of activism spilled over into adjoining social spaces, a phenomenon confirmed by the fact that the police began to pay more attention to it.

The Colonial Wars

Beginning in February of 1961 in Angola, and gradually extending to other territories – Guinea in January of 1963, and Mozambique in August of 1964 – the wars that the Portuguese state waged against the African independence movements directly affected the young college students. Most young men knew that they had to serve in the military for a period of at least three years, far away from their homes and communities, and facing severe physical and psychological risks. Even so, the issue of war was rarely raised in a critical and open manner. A veil of silence covered 'a misinformed and controlled public opinion, distant from the African problems, but educated within an intense imperial mystique' (Ribeiro 2004, 174). The reasons for this are also to be found in cultural norms – of honor, pride, masculinity –, as Fernando Dacosta writes in *Nascido no Estado Novo [Born in the Estado Novo]*:

> Not to serve in the army, to be exempted, had become a sign of inferiority, a blemish. To be released from this was even shameful – there were young men who lost their girlfriends and reputations because of this. (Dacosta 2001, 265)

Little by little, the colonial war led to a clear distancing between the interests of the Estado Novo and the aspirations of young people. Between 1961 and 1974, about 200,000 young men missed conscription. Between 1970 and 1972, the percentage of draft evaders was already over 20 per cent, corresponding to more than 50,000 in these 3 years (*Resenha*... 1988, 258). We should take into account the fact that, in percentage terms, Portugal had more men in the army than any other western country, excepting Israel. Mobilization would have been equivalent to the United States sending two and a half million men to Vietnam rather than the 500,000 that actually served there (Fernandes 2002).

In contrast to the compliant attitude of the Catholic Church hierarchy in general, some Catholic groups developed a pacifist action, essentially consisting in attempts to defy censorship and report on the war. Opposition to the conflict was, however, restricted to a few critical circles. In February of 1968, a demonstration against the Vietnam War in front of the US Embassy organized by sectors of the emerging extreme left, had already indirectly brought the subject into the public arena. However, the colonial war was still absent from the explicit list of demands made during an important student incident that took place in Coimbra in 1969, although soon after it became the central issue of activism in the universities.

In contrast to the cautious way in which the PCP approached the issue, the M-L groups placed the colonial war at the top of their agenda of demands. Advising desertion (with arms, if possible), the Maoists distanced themselves from the PCP's proposal of sending its militants to the frontlines. The stance taken in relation to the colonial war – to desert or to keep serving in the army – was often crucial when choosing political sides. Hélder Costa, one of the main leaders of O Comunista, talks about the way he confronted this question in an interview:

> Those guys [PCP] were after me for over a year. Then I went on holidays, for months, bought the Communist Party Manifesto in Paris, the history of socialism, I learned a lot, read the thing during my holidays, and when I got back I met with the guy and said, 'Hey, I want in. I looked at it, read some stuff, and since this is a decision for life...' 'For life?' he said. And I said, 'Yes, it is, it is up to one to choose, it's for that'. The guy was very impressed, and I said immediately, 'the colonial war'. 'Hey man, we have to go and such', he answered. 'But why? Hell, my comrades are over there, and then how is it going to be? We all meet in the jungle and such, hey, Long live the Prá-Kys-Tão!?' [a college fraternity in Coimbra where he had lived and socialized with African students]. It's out of the question [laughter]! The guy starts looking at me: 'Well, it's got to be, to make the

war more human'. 'Hey, we're wrong, there is no problem, but I won't join'. It was like this, it was easy. For me it was a key issue.

(Costa 2007)

For the PCP (M-L) [the Marxist-Leninist Communist Party of Portugal], born in France in the early seventies from the former CMLP, the watchword was 'to join the army' in order to 'learn how to deal with guns' and make 'agitation and anticolonialist propaganda amongst the soldiers who were about to leave for the war'. However, the question was whether 'to desert before boarding the ship or to sail to the colonies'. Bearing in mind the unorganized situation of the proletariat, which precluded 'true revolutionary work among the expeditionary units', their proposal was to desert. On the other hand, and unlike the cases in which the communists were told they should take part in imperialist wars in order to take advantage of the arming of the working classes, in this case 'the bourgeoisie established in S. Bento [the seat of Parliament] never loses control of the armed masses, because they are unarmed when they return to Portugal'. Thus, 'in the end, to desert is the lesser evil' (*Estrela Vermelha* 1972, n.13).

Desertion did not always imply having to emigrate illegally. A less obvious alternative was to go underground 'inside', with the goal of assuming leadership assignments or becoming proletarian under a false identity. Many processes of 'embedding' in factories took place within the OCMLP, involving mostly students who chose of their own free will to follow a path of downward social mobility. Pedro Bacelar de Vasconcelos was someone who did this. As he reports,

In September of 1973 I deserted with all the war equipment I could stuff into my bag ... Of my own will I went undercover and went to work at a factory in the area of Covilhã. I formally joined the OCMLP only then, when I decided to 'go to the factory'.

(Vasconcelos 2008)

Nevertheless, these groups did not uniformly encourage desertion. We should highlight the dissonant position of the URML (Marxist-Leninist Revolutionary Unit), for which desertion represented an 'individualistic and opportunistic attitude' that led 'necessarily to the loss of elements on whom the Proletarian Revolution might count' (*Folha Comunista* 1971, n.2). It should also be noted that some groups inhibited the leading militants from deserting, opting instead for their staying in the country underground. Vidaúl Ferreira, one of the MRPP founders, states:

A person like me would not go to France. Certain people of ours who deserted from the war did indeed. But if I went, we would all go. One of our criticisms of the PCP was precisely that: 'Well, Cunhal is the leader of the PCP and he is in Paris, in Russia, etc.' For us it was important to stay here.

(Ferreira 2007)

The MRPP was, indeed, the group that achieved the greatest visibility in the field of anticolonial activism. Resorting to a triumphalist language copied from posters of the Cultural Revolution, the first issue of the party newspaper *Luta Popular [Popular Struggle]*, dated February 1971, has this headline on its front page: 'Long Live the Great, Glorious and Just Revolutionary Fight for the National Liberation of the Oppressed Peoples of the Colonies' (*Luta Popular* 1971, n.1). Furthermore, MRPP militants were clearly hostile towards the PCP, and were, at one point, the only Maoist group that did not propose to 'reconstruct' this party, but rather 'to found it', since they held that no communist party had ever existed in Portugal. The murder of their militant Ribeiro dos Santos by the DGS would contribute to an even greater escalation of this sectarian rift, with accusations of communist involvement in this homicide. Neither was the remainder of the extreme-left groups spared, being dubbed as a 'neo-revisionist brotherhood' (*Que Viva Estaline!* 1972).

Most groups created structures that dealt specifically with the anticolonial struggle. The CRML (Marxist-Leninist Revolutionary Committee) was practically indistinct from the Popular War Committees that were active in some Lisbon schools, and which were their sole visible face, since this group viewed the colonial war as 'the main contradiction in the Portuguese social formation' (*Guerra Popular* 1972, n.4). In the early seventies, several Anticolonial Struggle Committees emerged, driven by militants of different M-L groups, although with a strong informal and decentralized component. In addition to these structures based in student milieus, which showed a more aggressive and strident activism, the different Maoist organizations also established units in barracks and in some working-class clusters.

Among political emigrants, namely in France, the M-L extreme left kept putting out papers such as *A Voz do Povo* [The People's Voice] (1968–75), *O Salto* [The Leap] (1970–4), *O Alarme!* [The Alarm!] (1972–5), *Ergue-te e Luta* [Rise and Fight] (1972–3), *Alavanca* [The Lever] (1972–4) and *A Voz do Desertor* [The Deserter's Voice] (1973), which focused on denouncing colonialism and supporting African liberation movements. Many of these publications, although short-lived, were sponsored by important French intellectuals: Marguerite Duras was director of *Camarada*, François Chatelet was in charge of *Les luttes de classe au Portugal*, and Jean-Paul Sartre supported *O Alarme!*, due to the connections between the OCMLP, which published the paper, and the Gauche Proletariènne. At the same time, the cultural work carried out in emigrant associations, namely through theatre groups, literacy courses and social events with politically engaged music, deepened the connections between deserters and economic emigrants, which constituted the great majority of the Portuguese community in France (Clímaco 1992).

Rhetorics of Violence

The practices and discourses originating in the M-L area were based on exercises of legitimation of violence, which was viewed simultaneously as a way of resisting tyranny and of achieving power. As one of the URML newspapers stated, 'the essence of the capitalist State lies in the counter-revolutionary violence of the exploiting classes, and can only be destroyed by the revolutionary violence of the oppressed and exploited' (*Revolução Proletária* 1973, n.2). Thus, for the Maoist-based groups, the point was not to condemn the violence of war, but to show that its iniquity lay in its imperialist character. The watchword 'War of the people against the colonial war', introduced in the anticolonialist demonstrations of February 1973, served precisely to encapsulate this idea (*Luta Popular* 1973, n.11–12).

The idea of revolution as a process carried out by armed popular masses, led by a disciplined party under the rule of democratic centralism, naturally appeared as an indisputable dogma in the theoretical production of these groups. The model of the 'people in arms' and the need for a type of disciplined and selfless militant, following Lenin's statements in *What Is To Be Done?*, was asserted in the following manner by the CCR (M-L) (Marxist-Leninist Revolutionary Committees):

> The bourgeoisie will never give up power in a peaceful manner; therefore, we have no illusions about the possibility of a smooth and peaceful transformation of the dictatorship of the bourgeoisie into the dictatorship of the proletariat. In the second place, we want the armed struggle to be a true popular struggle... In this we distance ourselves from the Castrists, who want to replace the armed struggle of the working masses with the violent action of a fistful of lone heroes.
> (*Viva o Comunismo!* 1970, n.2–3).

However, the problematic relationship that developed with the Cuban phenomenon allows us to qualify this idea and also to point to the existence of other ways of understanding violence in this political field. Indeed, right at the beginning of the sixties, Cuba was regarded with fondness in some sectors, both inside and outside the PCP, which contested its policy of alliances. Francisco Martins Rodrigues, then in the process of breaking away from the PCP and on the verge of creating the FAP and the CMLP, recalls that the Cuban appeal was 'actually at the base of the party', since it illustrated an unprecedented 'revolutionary transformation in favor of the workers, which opted for the armed struggle', and which showed that it was possible to take an insurrectionary route that was distant from the putschist anticommunism of the republicans (Rodrigues 2008).

Although defending the thesis of 'armed popular uprising' in the early years of Portuguese Maoism (1964–6), there are indications of a certain sympathy for the Cuban revolutionary eagerness. This would reappear within the CMLP in the years that followed, giving rise to internal protests, self-criticism and splits. O Comunista, a federation gathering different committees throughout Europe, was one of the collectives in which these ideas found extensive expression. Hélder Costa, one of its major figures, underlines the issue in the following way:

> I also had great admiration for the Cuban revolution. Because they started a revolution there, on their own, on an island, the boycotts, the invasion, and those guys resisting... And the question of Cuba, of Che Guevara, began to create a certain kind of friction. I had a position that was not theoretical, it was more at the level of sensitivity, how one feels things... I never supported the focus theory, but I always admired the guys that wanted to get into a fight.
>
> (Costa 2007)

As a matter of fact, only the PRP/BR (Revolutionary Party of the Proletariat/Revolutionary Brigades), founded in 1973, proclaimed its support of Guevarism. A couple of years earlier, in 1971, another organization that emerged outside the strict Maoist circle, ARCO (Communist Revolutionary Action), had shown its support of Marighela's theories of armed struggle, but it was rapidly dismantled by the PIDE/DGS before it had been able to carry out any action. Nevertheless, even an openly Maoist structure like the OCMLP witnessed an attempt to impose guerilla tactics at the beginning of 1974. One of the leaders that did not go along with the new strategy, and as a consequence was arrested by militants of the emerging faction, was José Queirós. He describes how it happened in the following manner:

> It was basically a conflict between what we called a 'mass line' (or, in the language of the period, the 'reconstruction of the party in the mass struggle') and a guerilla line, which wanted to arm the Workers Committees and set off violence... But none of this was yet very clearly assumed, and it came wrapped in an ideological discourse that mixed up radical swaggering and slogans inspired by the Chinese Cultural Revolution.
>
> (Queirós 2008)

Whether or not they gave in to the temptation of armed struggle, Portuguese Maoist groups were marked by a yearning for rupture that led them to believe that arms were necessary for the overthrow of the dictatorship and the establishment of a classless society. In contrast to the PCP, which defined itself around a notion of 'national identity' (Neves 2008), these collectives put the accent on an insurrectionary internationalism and anti-imperialism that is quite visible in their magazine and newspaper articles, in the texts of their communiqués and in the watchwords used in their demonstrations.

Even the dates celebrated by the political prisoners illustrate this issue. According to the group *A Vanguarda [The Vanguard]*, the 'revisionists' – as the PCP militants were called – commemorated, at the Peniche Prison, the 5th of October of 1910, the day of the establishment of the Republic, a day when 'the liberal bourgeoisie triumphed over the monarchy'. They also celebrated the 1st of December [of 1640], marking the restoration of independence, when 'the Portuguese monarchy overthrew the rule of the Spanish monarchy'. In contrast, the M-L militants celebrated, among other events, the anniversary of the Chinese Revolution, the October Revolution, the beginning of the armed struggle in Angola, the centenary of Lenin's birth, and paid homage to Ho Chi Minh on the day of his death (*As lutas…*, n.d.).

On April 25th 1974, when a military coup led by middle-ranking army officers, tired of an endless war fought on three fronts (Angola, Mozambique and Guinea-Bissau), put an end to the longest dictatorship in Europe, the immediate flooding of the streets by the population showed that there was a 'fourth front', non-aligned with the regime. Although not unique, the action and rhetoric of the constellation of M-L groups and organizations were the most boisterous, clearly exceeding the restricted militant circles and promoting an extreme politicization of some social sectors. This is a process that needs to be taken into account in order to understand the agitated process of decolonization in those African places and the turbulent revolutionary period that occurred in Portugal after the Carnation Revolution, between 1974 and 1975.

References

Contemporary Publications and Documents

As lutas dos revolucionários portugueses no interior das prisões. (Grupo de Base "A Vanguarda" do Comité Marxista-Leninista Português) (n.d.).
Estrela Vermelha. (Partido Comunista de Portugal Marxista-Leninista) (1972).
Folha Comunista. (Unidade Revolucionária Marxista-Leninista) (1971).
Guerra Popular (Comité Revolucionário Marxista-Leninista) (1972).
Que Viva Estaline! – Resolução do Comité Lenine a propósito do grande Estaline. (Movimento Reorganizativo do Partido do Proletariado) (1972).
Luta Popular. (Movimento Reorganizativo do Partido do Proletariado) (1971–3).

Revolução Proletária. (Unidade Revolucionária Marxista-Leninista) (1973).
Viva o Comunismo! (Comités Comunistas Revolucionários Marxistas-Leninistas) (1970).

Interviews

Costa, Hélder. 2007. Interview by M.Cardina. Tape recording. Lisbon, October 5.
Ferreira, Vidaúl. 2007. Interview by M.Cardina. Tape recording. Paio Pires, October 5.
Queirós, José. 2008. Interview by M.Cardina. Tape recording. Oporto, February 7.
Rodrigues, F.Martins. 2008. Interview by M.Cardina. Tape recording. Lisbon, January 29.
Vasconcelos, P.Bacelar. 2008. Interview by M.Cardina. Tape recording. Oporto, February 7.

Bibliography

Alexander, R. J. 1999. *International Maoism in the Developing World.* Westport, CT: Praeger.
Alexander, R. J. 2001. *Maoism in the Developed World.* Westport, CT: Praeger.
Aron, R. 1968. *La Révolution introuvable.* Paris: Fayard.
Avakian, B. 2005. *From Ike to Mao and beyond. My journey from mainstream America to revolutionary communist.* Chicago: Insight Press.
Badiou, A. 2008. Communist Hypothesis. *New Left Review* 49: 29–42.
Barreto, A. ed. 2000. *A Situação Social em Portugal, 1960–1999.* Lisboa: Imprensa de Ciências Sociais.
Bebiano, R. 2003. *O Poder da Imaginação. Juventude, Rebeldia e Resistência nos anos 60.* Coimbra: Angelus Novus.
Bebiano, R. 2005. Contestação do regime e tentação da luta armada sob o marcelismo. *Revista Portuguesa de História* 37: 65–104.
Berman, P. 2005. *Power and the Idealists.* Brooklyn, NY: Soft Skull Press.
Bloom, A. 1987. *The Closing of the American Mind.* New York: Simon & Schuster.
Clímaco, C. 1992. *La presse de l'émigration politique portugaise en France – analyse du journal O Salto. 1970–1974.* Paris: Université de Paris VII, Mémoire de DEA.
Dacosta, F. 2001. *Nascido no Estado Novo.* Lisboa: Editorial Notícias.
Dressen, M. 1999. *De l'amphi à l'établi. Les étudiants maoïstes à l'usine (1967–1989).* Paris: Belin.
Elbaum, M. 2002. *Revolution in the Air. Sixties Radicals turn to Lenin, Mao and Che.* London/New York: Verso.
Fernandes, Á. (2002), Uma Guerra de baixa intensidade e longa duração. *História* 51: 48–53.
Feuer, L. 1969. *The Conflict of Generations: The Character and Significance of Student Movements.* New York: Basic Books.
Fields, A. B. 1988. *Trotskyism and Maoism. Theory and practice in France and the United States.* New York: Autonomedia.
Frank, R. 2000. Imaginaire politique et figures symboliques internationales: Castro, Hô, Mao et le Che. In *Les Années 68. Le temps de la contestation,* eds. G. Dreyfus-Armand, R. Frank, M.-F. Lévy, M. Zancarini-Fournel, 31–47. Paris: Complexe.
Freitas, E. 1989. O fenómeno emigratório: a diáspora europeia. In *Portugal Contemporâneo, vol. V (1958–1974),* ed. A. Reis, 191–200. Lisboa: Alfa.
Gitlin, T. 1987. *The Sixties. Years of Hope, Days of Rage.* New York: Bantam Books.
Jameson, F. 1984. Periodizing the Sixties. In *The Sixties without Apology,* eds. S. Sayres and A. Stephanson, 178–209. Minneapolis: University of Minnesota Press.

Katsiaficas, G. 1987. *The Imagination of the New Left: a Global Analysis of 1968*. Boston: South End Press.
Marwick, A. 1998. *The Sixties. Cultural Revolution in Britain, France, Italy and the United States, c.1958–1974*. Oxford: Oxford University Press.
Neves, J. 2008. *Comunismo e Nacionalismo em Portugal. Política, Cultura e História no Século XX*. Lisboa: Tinta-da-China.
Nunes, A. S. 2000. *Antologia Sociológica*. Lisboa: Imprensa de Ciências Sociais.
Pereira, J. P. 2005. *Álvaro Cunhal. Uma Biografia Política. Volume 3: O Prisioneiro (1949–1960)*. Lisboa: Temas e Debates.
Pietrocolla, L. G. 1996. Anos 60/70. Do sonho revolucionário ao amargo retorno. *Tempo Social* 8 (2): 119–145.
Raby, D. L. 1988. *Fascism and resistance in Portugal. Communists, liberals and military dissidents in the opposition to Salazar, 1941–1974*. Manchester / New York: Manchester University Press.
Resende, J. and M. M. Vieira. 1992. Subculturas Juvenis nas Sociedades Modernas: Os Hippies e os Yuppies. *Revista Crítica de Ciências Sociais* 35: 131–147.
Resenha Histórico-Militar das Campanhas de África (1961–1974). 1º Volume. Enquadramento Geral (1998). Lisboa: Estado-Maior do Exército.
Ribeiro, M. C. 2004. *Uma História de Regressos. Império, Guerra Colonial e Pós-Colonialismo*. Porto: Afrontamento.
Anon [Rodrigues, F. M. 1970 (1963)]. *Luta Pacífica e Luta Armada no nosso Movimento*. S.l.: Edições do Partido.
Rosas, F. 1994. *O Estado Novo (1926–1974)*, Lisboa: Círculo de Leitores / Editorial Estampa.
Rosas, F. and P. A. Oliveira, eds. 2004. *A Transição Falhada. O Marcelismo e o Fim do Estado Novo (1968–1974)*. Lisboa: Editorial Notícias.
Salazar, A. O. 1951. *Discursos e Notas Políticas. 1943–1950*. Coimbra: Coimbra Editora.
Stephens, J. 1998. *Anti-Disciplinary Protest: Sixties Radicalism and Post-Modernism*. Cambridge: Cambridge University Press.
Telo, A. J. 1989. Portugal, 1958–1974: sociedade em mudança. In *Portugal y España en el cambio político (1958–1978)*, ed. Hipólito de la Torre, 73–88. Mérida: UNED, Centro Regional de Extremadura.
Varon, J. 2004. *Bringing the War Home. The Weather Underground, The Red Army Faction, and Revolutionary Violence in the Sixties and Seventies*. Berkeley/Los Angeles/London: University of California Press.

Chapter 4

FROM SARTRE TO STEVEDORES: THE CONNECTIONS BETWEEN THE PARIS BARRICADES AND THE RE-EMERGENCE OF BLACK TRADE UNIONS IN SOUTH AFRICA

Helen Lunn

Introduction

Two major discourses of change in the 1960s, student revolt and black consciousness, were introduced to South Africa primarily through, literature, music, and individual agency. The knowledge transfer helped to define and transform resistance to apartheid from liberal expressions and values to ideologically informed New Left activism. The impact of this shift and the forms it took had highly significant long term outcomes for South Africa, but the perception of South Africa as an isolated place disconnected from early forms of globalization has become a self reflective trope and the significance of links with global changes are not recognized.

In this chapter I will not examine the links between black consciousness (BC) and developments in the USA. There are intimate connections between BC and Anglophone students, but it is rather, the narrative of the shifts, influences and changes represented by the events of 1968 and their impact on mainly Anglophone students on which this chapter focuses. It will look particularly at the linkages between radical ideas and movements in Europe and North America and the role of radicalized white students in assisting black workers struggles against the apartheid regime. Academically the transition from liberal to class based historiography was to have a profound impact on students and future leaders in the post 1994 South African government. At a practical level the value of the transition into class based analyses of South Africa, assisted in the formulation of internal worker resistance to apartheid as the largely black working class evolved into a more coherent and self-consciously aware class embracing a political agenda. The foundations of these discourses at Anglophone universities and their roots in the New Left of the 1960s are important in describing the way in which educational institutions and research came to have political and practical applications in South Africa.

South Africa in the '60s: The Politico-Cultural Background

Student resistance was not imported into virgin territory. In 1959, the Nationalist led government passed the University Education Act, which effectively closed white universities to black students and proscribed university autonomy. Anglophone universities responded within the liberal paradigm of well-mannered protest marches and letters to the press and parliament. The inadequacy of such responses was highlighted by the massacre of 69 blacks at Sharpeville on March 21, 1960. The Pan African Congress (PAC) had organised a protest against the pass laws which obliged all black South Africans to carry an officially stamped document permitting them to be in a 'white' area.

The event became a transitional milestone between passive resistance and the development of militant opposition. State reaction forced this response through its growing intransigence and intensification of apartheid laws. Throughout the 1960s resistance remained more reactive rather than proactive. What was also notable in this period was the uneasy racially bounded nature of radical opposition. Following Sharpeville the declaration of both the African National Congress (ANC) and PAC as illegal organizations forced them into exile. Within South Africa a group of mainly white academics and students formed the National Committee for Liberation (NCL). It was composed of 'a heterogeneous conglomeration of people who in retrospect seemed united only in their hatred and defiance of apartheid – ex-communists, liberals, members of the ANC Youth League, Trotskyites.' (Claire 2006,196) This group became ARM (African Resistance Movement) after 1963, and performed random acts of sabotage. They were easily penetrated by the Security Police aided by the testimony of a University of Cape Town (UCT) student, Adrian Leftwich, following his arrest in June 1964.

Leftwich, a former leader of the National Union of South African Students, (NUSAS) together with other students in ARM left a legacy for NUSAS of being branded as a 'communist' and 'left wing movement' by the government long before it achieved an ideological framework that reflected anything other than liberal values. They also guaranteed a high level of scrutiny of student movements by the security police. The real legacy, however, was one of a temporary vacuum in leadership as well as a loss of direction and focus. 'The whole episode made a profound impact on me, as it did to many others of my generation, serving as a sober warning of the consequences of badly conceived political strategies.' (Webster 2005, 100). Many students chose to go into exile abroad with only a few choosing the option of joining the ANC in armed struggle.

The importance of this period of pause in this narrative was that it coincided with the growth in student movements abroad. The expansion of youth-based culture and the emergence of the New Left provided a form of continuity. At the same period as students overseas were mounting their most sustained challenge to authority, South African students were seeking new directions, leadership and continuity. It was the latter that was most critical, and one of the forms in which it came was of South African academics who had gone abroad to pursue postgraduate study. They brought back new discourses and perspectives to students.

The reason direct contact was so important was because of the controls exercised by the apartheid state over all media. There was no TV and the censorship board, whose powers were extended in 1963, was extremely active in banning anything that was seen as a threat to the State. Despite these controls there was a tradition in both English-speaking schools and tertiary institutions of critical responses to the State. The effect of this outlook was to increase curiosity as to what was being banned. Webster (ibid: 105) describes how upon arriving at Balliol in 1968: 'I immediately threw myself into reading any banned book on South Africa I could lay my hands on.'

At an academic level it meant that: 'young South Africans who went abroad to study in the 1960s not only found in Britain and America a strong anti-racist climate, but also a new freedom to consider ideas taboo in their repressive country. Marxism, as a coherent body of theory, attracted émigré intellectuals searching for a way to understand South Africa.'(Saunders1988, 178) The work of these academics and those upon whom they based their work, started to be introduced in the late 1960s. The effect was radical and was reflected in the changing analyses of the role of white students being explored by student ideologues. By 1969 words such as 'proletariat', 'working class', and 'conscientisation' were beginning to find their way into texts written by South African student leaders. More importantly academics were starting to investigate the history of the working class and particularly the neglected history of black workers.

The Seeds of Activism

Whereas events in Europe, UK and the States peaked in 1968, in South Africa they were only starting. This time gap underlines the fact that South African Anglophone youth at that stage took their lead from abroad. Despite and because of their own sense of isolation they were outward looking and anything that came from 'overseas' held disproportionate cultural significance. As news of student events abroad appeared and were analysed in the pages of student magazines and other liberal journals, the potential of students to influence change became apparent. The catalysts for these ideas were individuals who could help students interpret and reformulate the ideas in a South African context. Within the narrative of the time one particular academic emerged as a unique translator of new discourses.

Richard (Rick) Turner was a South African who went to the Sorbonne in 1964 to write his doctorate on the philosophy of Jean Paul Sartre. He returned to SA in 1966 missing the immediate build up to the events of 1968 in France, but his contacts and interest in the country, meant that he maintained a close watch on events unfolding there. His first wife, Barbara Follett has written:

'Although we were no longer living in Paris when the events of May 1968 unfolded, he was very excited by the idea that real change could be on the way. He was particularly excited about the relationships being forged between student activists and workers in France ... his desire to see things change in South Africa increased at this time.'(Follett 2008)

The highly politicized nature of French society affected him profoundly. In France, a radical language was already encoded in the minds of those to whom discourse was addressed. 'In addition to this radical culture, there were radical institutional forms, political parties and trade unions, that served to universalize the individual experience.' (Greaves 1984, 43) Turner was aware that the repressive nature of the South African Government had prevented the emergence of widespread radicalism. However within the universities there were small groups of student leaders and individuals who were becoming highly politicized and he made contact with them after his return.

In 1968 the rescinding of an offer of employment to a black researcher, Archie Mafeje, by University of Cape Town (UCT) caused countrywide protests. Students returning from the July vacation challenged the university administration with a sit-in if it failed to change its decision. A nine day sit-in started at UCT on August 14, 1968 with students at the University of the Witwatersrand (Wits) acting in solidarity by staging a teach-in following the banning of a protest march. South African Anglophone students were echoing what they had learnt from student activists abroad. Even though student leadership failed to exploit student enthusiasm, both the sit-in and teach-in marked the beginning of a change in student activism. Jeremy Cronin, who subsequently became an important ideologue in the South African Communist Party, (and currently holds the position of deputy minister of transport in the Government) but had barely been introduced to such ideas in 1968, described Turner at the UCT sit-in 'as the key seducer...He was a fantastic teacher.' (Turner 2003)

Turner fell into the category of someone who was under the magical age of 30 (he was born in 1941). His physical style appealed to students. It represented disdain for the commercially minded world of conformists and drew considerable reaction. For Ralph Lawrence a student at University of Natal, Durban, Turner:

> 'embodied the spirit of 1968…The wild red locks, periodically a ferocious Castro like beard. He marked such a radical departure from the prevailing norm. Most academics stuck to dowdy formalism, looking like retreaded FBI agents…Turner appeared the rebel incarnate: I loved it.' (Lawrence 1990, 101)

Anglophone students were keen to be seen as no different from youth in America or the UK. Metropole-based culture was unchallenged and dominant and anyone who bought the most radical expression of it to SA was a leader by default.

Turner's lectures and writing reflect the thinking of the 1960s with a symmetry that helps explain why his ideas struck such a chord with Anglophone students. Turner was the one lecturer in the period who openly used the world 'love' and talked of the freedom one had to change one's consciousness. He quoted Herbert Marcuse and Jean Paul Sartre. 'He encouraged students to stretch their minds in a way I seldom encountered at a University. Reading there was aplenty, the more eclectic the better.'(Lawrence1990, 102) Turner was interested in the question of anteriority and the manner in which one could escape and transcend the historical limitations of one's environment. For students who grew up under the ideology of apartheid, this question was particularly challenging and relevant. His interest in Sartre, as with so many other others at that time, partly lay in the fact that Sartre dealt with the awareness that individuals could and did transcend their environments. In a decade when students were self-consciously aware of not wanting to be part of the society they were born into, Sartre provided a way of balancing an interest in the left without having to concede that individuals could not escape their historically determined positions.

Sartrean philosophy dealt with the concepts of alienation, group responsibility and interaction. Alienation in particular, was a powerful and widely explored concept as it gave a structure to the feeling of anomie and disconnectedness felt by students who neither supported nor wanted to be part of wars based on economic and ideological concerns. Part of the appeal of the New Left in the decade was derived from the fact that Western governments were so opposed to Marxism and the countries that had adopted the ideology. The critique of capitalism was fundamental to Marxist-based ideologies and clinched the interest in theorists who could balance a concern with the individual with Marxism.

Turner's criticism of capitalists and his inability to understand them is tellingly referred to in his thesis where he comments on the illogic of capitalists who rather than retire to a cottage at the sea once they have made more than enough to retire on, perversely carry on as capitalists (Turner 1966). This incomprehension encapsulates one of the motifs prevalent amongst youth in the decade, namely the desirability of opting out of society and living close to the land in a like-minded community. This was something Turner had tried at his mother's farm outside of Stellenbosch, and continued to explore once he moved to Durban, both in his own living arrangements and at the Phoenix settlement established initially by Gandhi. These sentiments were extraordinarily novel in a lecturer at that time. In his undated lecture notes Turner wrote: 'The most interesting question I think to ask about any society, or about societies, is why they in fact hang together. What is it that keeps societies in place?' His related question was what ensures stability in unequal societies? (Turner, R. The Present as History. Turner Papers)

This was a question of central interest to South African Anglophone students who were faced with a complex set of choices and questions. Within the essays and writings of student leaders of the time these questions recur in one form or another. There are some mechanistic arguments based on what are clearly first readings of Marx and Marcuse, but there are also emotional statements that testify to the deep sense of guilt and despair that was not uncommon amongst liberal and radical students at the time.

The significance of the shift from largely liberal historiography, which had informed liberal reaction to apartheid, to class-based analysis was the way in which it became the foundation for new responses in theory and praxis. It not only shifted the focus of academic study but also influenced student interpretations of the role of whites and ultimately the way in which resistance to apartheid was conceptualized and organized. This could be seen in the more advanced and radical ideas beginning to circulate amongst students in 1970.

From Theory to Praxis: Engagement with Black Workers' Struggles

Anglophone students who had started to analyse South Africa in terms of class rather than race, were exploring the role they could potentially have in bringing about change. They did not see themselves as liberals and they were not prepared to accept the role outlined for them by Steve Biko. Turner, who was friends with Biko, supported Biko's suggestion that Anglophone students should focus on changing the way whites thought. He, however, believed that they should extend themselves and be involved in literacy and educational campaigns. (*Dome*, 1970) A few of his students, however, were developing more radical ideas. Two political science students, David Davis and Halton Cheadle, were seeking ways of connecting with black workers. They sought the advice of a former UND political science student David Hemson, who was developing a Marxist-based analysis of SA. Hemson was a postgraduate scholar who was researching the 1969 Durban dockworkers strike. He was critically influential in the discussions around the formation of the first Wages and Economics Commission in 1971. The idea of a student led research commission emerged following hours of discussion between Turner, D. Hemson, H. Cheadle, D. Davis, K. Tip and C. Nupen.

As early as 1969, Rob Davies had suggested a potential role for white students proposing that 'much useful work could be done encouraging, discussing issues, strategies and tactics, present to the proletariat ideas from abroad, attempting to organize workers.' He argued that because of the white students 'greater awareness of events abroad, of SDS and overseas thinkers and philosophers e.g.. Marcuse and Sartre...the white student has a role – indirect and elitist though it may seem, in raising the political consciousness of the proletariat.' (Schlebusch 1974, 466) The need to redefine a role for white students became more urgent following the 1969 breakaway led by Biko of black students from NUSAS. The resulting formation of the South African Students Organisation (SASO) guided by the ideas of Black Consciousness led to explicit rejection of white involvement. It was not an accident that SASO's leadership was based at UND which had the largest number of black medical students attached to a 'white' University in South Africa. The relative freedom that such students experienced compared to those on exclusively black campuses in the 'homelands', was the space within which they developed a more radical philosophy. The philosophy of Black Consciousness and the rejection of white students did not go uncontested, if anything it helped the latter to focus their efforts on finding practical ways to be involved in bringing about change. The Wages and Economics Commission was the first practical expression of this intention:

> 'For the first time, white students were moving beyond the politics of reactive protest, away from the marches and the endless public meetings... Now they were out there in the real South Africa, on the docks, in the abattoirs and the union halls. Rick Turner inspired all this, although he did not specifically encourage students to get involved in the worker's movement.' (Boynton 1997, 95)

Student activism coincided with the first sustained labour resistance in decades. 'The 1970s began for South African employers early on the morning of January 9, 1973, when 2,000 workers at the Coronation Brick and Tile Works on the outskirts of Durban gathered at a football field and demanded a pay rise.'(Friedman 1987, 37) By Wednesday 7th March 1973, 30,000 workers were on strike in Natal and the unrest had begun to spread to other cities and smaller towns in Natal. It was also the day that the strikes started to subside and workers began to accept small wage increases. However by the end of the year 90,000 workers had struck throughout the year and the seeds of the rebirth of the African trades unions had been planted.

The questions surrounding these events are many but the most debated and prominent one is why did labour strike first and massively in Durban and not in the Witwatersrand, the industrial heartland of South Africa? The 1960s, although a time of great economic prosperity and growth, had been a decade in which harsher pass laws had been enacted. This had limited the rights of blacks to live in urban areas as well as to seek work. Job reservation had been tightened and workers who had jobs could not afford to lose them because their rights to live in an urban area could be lost. South Africa had been facing a skills shortage throughout the decade, but the government persisted in its view that 'Non-whites should ... be trained to use their skills in the services of their own people.' (Horrell 1965, 241) The government was expanding and consolidating the 'homelands' and using restrictive labour laws to prevent the numbers of black South Africans from increasing within 'white areas'. The limitations placed on black workers were the same in all major centres in South Africa, and there were sporadic individual strikes in all these areas throughout the country in the 1960s, but not one of them managed to spark off a series of strikes as did the Coronation strike. The question then is what was the critical difference between the Coronation strike and all the strikes of a similar nature in the previous decade?

The Wages Commissions and the Intensification of the Workers Struggle

A small part of the answer has to lie in the activities of the Wages Commission and their link with Harriet Bolton, a trade unionist who was then secretary of the Garment Workers Union. Students had been put in touch with Bolton through Rick Turner. They had been collecting data on wages directly from workers and their research revealed that most wages were well below the poverty datum line (PDL). Based on this information the next phase of their activity was to make workers aware of their low wages. It was the first example of the use of academic research to mobilize political opposition.

From June 1971, students began their campaign of publishing and distributing pamphlets explaining to workers that wages were below the poverty datum line of R16.30 per week (*Dome* 1972). The Commission invited workers to a meeting at Bolton Hall. It was filled to capacity and all present signed an objection to the Wage Boards determination, which had set the minimum wage at half of the PDL figure. (NUSAS Newsletter 1971) They unanimously agreed to inform the Minister of Labour they were demanding R20 a week.

(*Natal Mercury* 1971) A day after the meeting, workers at the McWillaw Iron and Steel Foundry in Isipingo, south of Durban, stopped work. They held up Wages Commission pamphlets in support of their demands for an increase, underscoring the value of the information provided by the students.

Following the advice of experienced unionists, the Wages Commission and workers agreed to work within the structures of existing wage negotiation to effect change. The mechanism they could exploit was the Wage Board, which had been established under the Wage Act of 1924. It provided a loophole that allowed for the negotiation of wages in industries not covered by the Industrial Conciliation Act. The first Wages Board meeting where students presented evidence was for the cement products industry on 25 June 1971. It was the beginning of a strategy that produced results throughout the decade.

In publications distributed on campus members of the Wages Commission suggested to students that:

> 'Students may feel that wages as such are peripheral to student concern, but in a capitalist society wages are the key to food, shelter, health, education etc…The function of students is to redress the imbalance by using the facilities provided by a university: Information gathering, correlation and dissemination and undertaking social action to make people aware of the situation of poverty wages'. (SRC 1971, 2)

In 1971 this call was adopted at other universities in South Africa and UCT, Wits, Rhodes and Pietermaritzburg took up the challenge. As the other campuses created their own Wages Commissions, Cheadle and Hemson at UND were moving on from the collection of data to the question of how labour could be organized. They were considering how white students could use their status as students, to represent workers at Wage Board meetings and somehow activate the collective strength of labour. The new, mainly Marxist historiography was central to the thinking that underpinned this development. Anglophone universities were becoming the site of a translation of theory into praxis. It was a critical step beyond their liberal foundations and research agendas.

Despite the radical theory that guided the new directions, it was the experienced advice of Bolton that helped to keep the momentum rolling whilst sidestepping the complex and punitive legislation in existence. It should be mentioned that all of the activities described so far were done against a backdrop of fear and intimidation. The presence of Security Branch spies on campuses was widely known and acted as a powerful deterrent to many students. Harriet Bolton suggested that instead of attempting to establish an illegal union a fund should be set up that would collect subscriptions from workers and pay out funeral benefits. This was Bolton's pragmatic response to a meeting addressed by Rick

Turner where he spoke to workers and suggested that they should organize themselves. This led to the creation of the General Factory Workers Benefit Fund, which was launched in Durban in 1972. Shortly after this the Durban stevedores attended a meeting of the Wage Board on 18 July 1972. Workers were happy to have allies and support 'on those things which we do not see or understand.' (SRC 1971) Alec Erwin who attended the stevedores' wage board meeting commented 'it was very easy for people who were prepared to do some work with black workers to be accepted, because there was just such a hunger for support and assistance.'(Frederickse 1979–1990)

There was some confusion about the wages agreed upon by the wages board. Workers thought they had been granted R18.00 per week, however they had not. The failure of the Wages Board to come to a decision on the demands of the stevedores resulted in a strike in October 1972 in both Durban and Cape Town. It ended when striking workers were threatened with retrenchment (redundancies). In December they were still waiting for their R18.00 and 2,000 stevedores went out on strike again. 20 were dismissed. The UCT economics commission suggested that the stevedores form a trades union and sent them a list of five steps to forming a trades union ending with the line, 'Write to us and tell us if you need help forming a trade union.' (FOSATU 1972)

At the end of the Christmas holidays and the beginning of 1973, the Coronation Brick workers strike started. It was the spark that led to continued action and change in responses to workers, which culminated six years later in the formal recognition of black trades unions and the formation of the Federation of South African Trades Unions (FOSATU). An unexpected outcome of the research carried out by students from Pietermaritzburg University on wattle farms in the Natal Mist belt was the publication of their findings in UK-based *Guardian* newspaper. The estates were owned by a subsidiary of Slater Walker a British company. The outcome of the publicity on aspects of British investment in SA was the establishment of a British parliamentary enquiry, which resulted in the establishment of new employment codes for British firms operating in South Africa. (Dubois 1973)

None of these events escaped the scrutiny of the security police. B.J. Vorster the Prime Minister set up a Commission of Enquiry to investigate four anti-apartheid organizations, including NUSAS. In February 1973, as a result of the findings of the Commission, the Government banned 16 NUSAS and SASO leaders as well as Rick Turner who was the only lecturer in this group. A banning order prevented individuals from engaging in their profession or acting within society. They were confined to a magisterial district and were not allowed ever to be in the presence of more than one other person at any time. The loss of determined and committed leadership had an impact on students and caused a period of reassessment and restructuring, but the lessons of the Wages Commission were applied and the restructuring was more focused and informed. The Wages Commissions did not halt, and the numbers of students joining the nascent workers movement escalated throughout the seventies. Their involvement was an example of the more practical and committed path onto which the Commission had steered student opposition. The significance of academic research and Anglophone universities in assisting the nascent worker movement was further evident in their involvement in worker education.

Harriet Bolton (Institute of Labour Education 1973) observed that: 'During the strikes the trade unions and other interested bodies were appalled by the lack of knowledge displayed by the workers, the employers and the general public, about the rights of workers'. The response to this was the founding of the Institute of Labour Education (ILE). It was an off campus, educational cum research body set up in 1973 in Durban largely by academics from the University of Natal. The key ideas were contained in six study books in English and Zulu produced largely by Richard Turner.

> 'These booklets introduced union activists to the key ideas of accountability and mandate among worker representatives-concepts that were to percolate into the movement and over time were to help shape the political culture of shop floor democracy that was to emerge in the eighties.' (Webster1992, 90)

The founders of the ILE also produced a newsletter, which became the South African Labour Bulletin. 'The ILE initially operated as a relatively autonomous body, although it was linked with the trade union movement…However the tension between freelance intellectuals,'(Webster, ibid) and the unions manifested in changes which ultimately resulted in the unions taking greater control over the Institute and the Labour Bulletin becoming more independent of the Institute.

Turner's influence continued in both the individuals involved in these organizations as well as in a new student activism that saw students' countrywide move into trades unions on a full time basis. The commissions also had a direct impact on strategies adopted by students from 1973 and encouraged student leaders to state: 'We *do* have a role to play, an important one, in hitting at the real power in our society.' (*Wits Student* 1973) The commission was seen as a useful guide forward:

> 'We must realise that traditional platform protest is an impotent expression of opposition. The powerless worker who strikes as his only method of bargaining power against an all powerful employer, shows the way to the relatively powerless student who is up against the massive forces of repression.' (Nupen 1973)

At the time of his arrival at UND, Turner had noted that 'white students come from the most privileged class and by protesting vociferously they endanger this privileged position.' (*Dome* 1970) Through his engagement with new discourses many students stepped out of their privilege. In Turner's case it resulted in his assassination in 1978 whilst for many of the students it resulted in their banning. For students who became involved with labour the work was gratifying, based as it was on their theoretical knowledge of the potential role of workers in bringing about change. Turner in his book *Eye of the Needle* wrote about this potential power. It was to remain a focus for both students and colleagues such as Eddie Webster who, following Turner's banning in 1973, became an active force amongst students at UND. The focus on black workers was to inform the new historiography but it always retained a practical emphasis and never returned to a purely academic consideration.

Conclusion: Replacing Race with Class

The importance of New Left theory lay in the framework it provided for a recontextualising of South African history. The move beyond the foregrounding of race was critical to a broad understanding of how an engagement with the economy could challenge racial politics. The irony of this recognition growing partially out of a response to the formulation of BC added a layer of complexity that has remained evident within the debates around these events. There has been a direct link between this period and individuals who have risen to prominence in the Governments since 1994. Alec Erwin became the Minister of Trade and Industry in the first freely elected Government and subsequently became Minister of Public Enterprises from 2004–2008. Robert Davies, who was one of the earliest to posit a role for white students within the New Left framework, is currently Minister of Trade and Industry. Other members of the Wages Commission are prominent academics, researchers in government-funded organizations as well as lawyers both writing and interpreting South Africa's laws and mediating labour disputes.

The South African framing of the role of students in effecting political change continued well beyond the decade of greatest student activism. It helped to shape and inform political change primarily within an economic context. The translation of theory into praxis was the work of many and indicated that the central theme of the period of changing consciousness when married to New Left theory offered a practical way in which students could translate the privilege of their education into praxis. In that sense it was one of the most remarkable and enduring incidences of the impact of the activism of the 1960s on South Africa.

References

Boynton, G. 1997. *Last Days in Cloud Cuckooland*. Johannesburg: Jonathan Ball
Claire, H. 2006. *The Song Remembers When*. Cape Town: Double Storey
Dome. 17 June 1972. Special issue on the Wages Commission
Dome. 17 September 1970
Dubois, M. 1973. The role of the Wages Commission. *Reality* Sept, 5, 4: 4–8
Friedman, S. 1987. *Building Tomorrow Today*. Johannesburg: Ravan Press
Greaves, D. 1984. Pessimism of the Mind but Optimism of the Will: Richard Turner's Politics 1968–1973. *Southern African Studies Seminar*. UND. PMB
Horrell, M. 1965. *A Survey of Race Relations in South Africa 1964*. Johannesburg: Institute of Race Relations
Lawrence, R. 1990. Democracy in a Future South Africa. *Theoria*, 76, (October): 101–114
Nupen, C. 1973. State of the Nation. *Wits Student* 21 September
Schlebusch Commission. Republic of South Africa. 1974. Fourth Interim Report of the Commission of Inquiry into Certain Organizations. Pretoria: Government Printers
Saunders, C.C. 1988. *The Making of the South African Past*. Cape Town: David Philip
Webster, E.1992. The impact of Intellectuals on the Labour Movement. *Transformation* 18: 88–92
Webster, E. 2005. Rebels with a cause of their own. *Transformation* 59: 98–108
Wits Student, 1973. The New Issue- Labour. 30 March

Archival Sources

Frederickse, J. 1979–1990 AL2460. Historical Papers. UWL
Follett, B.RE: Questions on Rick Turner. E-mail to H.Lunn (25 February 2008)
_____1973. Minutes of Inaugural meeting, 30 May in FOSATU papers AL2457(ORIG) M4.3 Historical Papers. UWL
FOSATU Papers *Workers in the Stevedoring Trade* AL2457(ORIG) M4.3 Historical Papers. UWL
Morphet,T. Brushing History against the Grain. *The Richard Turner Memorial lecture*, Durban 27 September 1990. Malherbe Library. UKZN
NUSAS Newsletter May 18, 1971. NUSAS Papers AL2457 (ORIG) N8.1;AL3137f. Historical Papers. UWL
SRC UND 1971. Proposed Establishment of Wages Committee under the Students Representative Council. In FOSATU Papers. AL2457(ORIG) M4.3 Historical Papers. UWL
Turner, J. 2003. *My Father Rick Turner*. Available from: http://www.barbara-follett.org.uk/richard_turner/index.html (Accessed March 2008)
Turner, R. *Sartre's Political Theory*. Undated D 72/107 Turner Papers. Malherbe Library. UKZN
Turner, R. undated. *Lecture series on the Present as History*. Turner Papers. Malherbe library. UKZN
UND SRC, Izincwadi/letters 1971. Bulletin of the Wages Commission. In FOSATU Papers. Al 2457 (0RIG) M4.3 Historical Papers. UWL

Chapter 5

1968 – WAS IT REALLY A YEAR OF SOCIAL CHANGE IN PAKISTAN?

Riaz Ahmed Shaikh

Introduction

In 1968 on the completion of ten years of autocratic rule, Pakistan's first military dictator, General Ayub Khan decided to celebrate 'the decade of development'. The Ayub regime had achieved the fastest economic growth in Pakistan's history and was lauded in the West as a dynamic model for Third World capitalism. Despite this, inequality and the percentage of the population living below the poverty line had increased. Wealth was concentrated in few hands and the country's twenty-two richest families controlled approximately 90 percent of the assets of financial institutions. In 1968 disillusioned students, workers and peasants, as well as members of the military and the professions mounted public protests against the dictator.

At the start of 1968 the military dictatorship of Ayub Khan appeared as one of the most stable regimes of the time. His confidence could be judged from the fact that he arrested the country's most popular political leader Shaikh Mujeeb-ur-Rehman (later founder of Bangladesh), with twenty-eight civil servants, politicians and members of the armed forces on charges of being implicated in an Indian government supported conspiracy to separate the province of East Pakistan from the rest of the country. Ayub had posed as the country's saviour and in 1968, the tenth year of his presidency, he advised his close associates to begin a one-year celebration labeling it the 'Decade of Development'. The achievements of the military dictatorship would be highlighted through the government-controlled media. Meanwhile resistance against the regime was gathering momentum (Dobell 1969).

The government's professed rationale behind its policy of high economic growth was to bring about a real improvement in the living standard of groups living below the poverty line. However the outcome was rather different as from the early 1960s real wages steadily declined. The share of wages in value-added manufacturing industry which was 45 percent in 1959, dropped from the start of the 'Decade of Development' to 25 percent in 1967. The increasing concentration of wealth in the hands of a minority was realized at the expense of an industrial workforce suffering an alarming degree of exploitation (Hussain 1999).

The government supported the Pakistan bourgeoisie with a range of policies including investment in infrastructure, financial support and favourable tariff barriers. The list of state reforms is a very long one but the Khan government failed on several crucial counts. It failed to reform the basically feudal structure of agrarian production; to create a genuinely modern nation state; to resolve the national question through equitable socio-economic integration; to give a secular character to the state; or to establish a genuine parliamentary democracy through adult franchise (Jahan 1972). The whole pattern of industrial and social development, during this 'decade of reforms' was strikingly uneven and the government increasingly appeared weak and corrupt (Ahmed 1971). The bourgeoisie's inability to develop into a progressive class was evident in its need to forge an alliance with feudal remnants and parts of the religious establishment, and also in its dependence on imperial powers. Unsurprisingly the Pakistan bourgeoisie was a major target of the 1968–69 uprising (Ziring 1971).

Major public unrest sometimes occurs in the aftermath of war. In the case of Pakistan, the mass chauvinism fomented by the 1965 conflict with India was short lived and the toll taken by the war was a significant factor underlying the 1968–69 public protests. The war further aggravated the burgeoning gap between rapid economic growth and sluggish social development. The strong economic growth and industrial and infrastructural development under Ayub Khan's regime and its failure simultaneously to achieve social progress demonstrated the inability of the postcolonial bourgeoisie to complete the tasks of the National Democratic Revolution (Feldman 1967). The burden of war devastation was borne by the working class and the impoverished masses. However, social and political opposition and resistance initially started to emerge among unemployed graduates and students. Frustrated at their unemployment and social deprivation in a time of economic expansion, some burnt their degree certificates (Siddiqui 1972). This chapter analyses the emergence and explosion of public anger against the Ayub Khan regime started by student protests, partly linked to and inspired by student rebellions in the advanced capitalist countries. It also suggests why, despite huge sacrifices and society-wide protest movements, no fundamental change flowed from a rebellion that far exceeded contemporaneous revolts elsewhere.

Ayub's Industrialization Policy and Economic Growth

An aspect of industrial development under Ayub Khan was the migration of rural peasantry that fed into the proletariat in the country's newly emerging urban industrial zones. Thrown out of work by the crisis in rural farming partly the result of the mechanisation of the agricultural sector, these migrant workers were sucked in by rapid industrialization. Importantly, however, the government had controlled the development of trade unionism and the established trade unions were routinely characterized by corruption and opportunism (Shaheed 1983). The absence of strong, representative trade unions hampered the development of proletarian interests. However, the experience of industry and advanced technology gave them new insight and brought out the innovative skills of their trade union and political leaders. Their consciousness was rising and as more concluded that the way forward was collective action for collective gains. This plunged them into the struggle for their rights in November 1968 along with other groups of Pakistanis (Zaidi 2000).

This new section of the proletariat was, then, the product of relatively rapid industrial and economic development of Ayub's era. Karl Marx said in his epic work on the 1857 Indian War of Independence:

'by laying every mile of railway track and telegraph the British imperialism was digging its own grave'. (Marx quoted in Hasan ed., 2008, 27)

The same observation could equally be applied to industrial development under the Ayub Khan regime. The contradiction generated by the lag between social and economic development exploded into the 1968–69 public uprising that certain intellectuals and political commentators have termed a revolution (Khan 2008; Ali 1987).

The rate of economic development under Ayub Khan's regime was unprecedented. In the years of the public uprising (1968–69) economic growth was 9.1%, the highest Pakistan has ever experienced. However, the high growth rate and accompanying industrialization were not due to the miracles of military rule. A number of different factors were involved. Mainly growth coincided with the boom in the West and the spin-off effects of the upswing of world capitalism, which gave the Pakistani rulers room to maneuver. At this time they adopted Keynesian strategies and state intervention in the economy was quite significant (Hussain 1999). Pakistan's growth was to become a reference point for US economists 'advising' other neo-colonial regimes, serving as a 'model' for the rest of the third world and 'a shining example' of free enterprise (Banuri et al. 1997).

Yet there was nothing 'free' about this enterprise, it was state subsidies and protection that enabled capitalism to be established. Having first established industrial units, the state offered them to private capitalists at 'reasonable prices'. This process was labelled 'Harvard's Development Advisory Services'. Although Papanek referred to Pakistan's fledging bourgeoisie as 'robber barons' he defended their growing exploitation on grounds of necessity. In his words:

> 'The problem of inequity exists, but its importance must be put in perspective. First of all, the inequalities in income contribute to the growth of economy, which makes possible a real improvement for the lower-income groups.' (Papanek 1967, 242)

But such Harvard advisers seriously underestimated the damage being done to Pakistani agriculture during the Ayub regime and the extent of the diversion of funds into industry. Moreover, two-thirds of capital investment in West Pakistan came from outside the country, as a stable military regime induced foreign investors to support the growth of indigenous capital (Burki 1988).

The economic policies of the military dictator, Ayub Khan, also led to the concentration of the county's wealth in very few hands. Revelations by the regime's own chief economist, Dr. Mahbub ul Haq, about the hugely unequal distribution of wealth startled the nation. He calculated that 66% of the country's industrial capital was concentrated in the hands of 22 families. Economic expansion and growth in national income had occurred simultaneously with deterioration in the living standard of the majority of the population, whose food consumption had actually declined over the preceding five years (Mazari 1999). In urban areas, the army and government bureaucracy had helped to create an exploitative millionaire elite, while in rural areas they promoted the interests of feudal landlords and capitalist farmers at the expense of peasants and landless labourers (Inayatullah 1970).

Any attempt to challenge this state of affairs was met by state repression. In the urban areas, all trade-union activity was kept firmly under control: all strikes were banned and several union leaders were put on the regime's payroll. Under Ayub Khan's regime, it became nearly impossible for workers to receive equitable treatment in an industrial relations system increasingly dominated by state adjudication procedures (Shaheed 2007).

Student Movements Sparking the Protest of 1968

In 1968 when Ayub Khan decided to celebrate his 'Decade of Development', the Marxist oriented National Student Federation (NSF), despite its ideological diversity, united to condemn it and announced it would celebrate a 'Decade of Decadence' and organised a 'week of demands'. The NSF emerged as the most active student organisation in the sometimes violent 1968–69 anti-Ayub student protests in Karachi, Rawalpindi and Peshawar (Sayeed 1980).

The wider context of the protests was the deepening Sino-Soviet schism over the leadership of the international socialist movement that split many leftist parties around the world, creating separate Chinese and Soviet camps. These ideological divisions also affected the highly volatile progressive student groups in Pakistan. One fraction of the progressive student organisation, the Democratic Student Federation (DSF), supported the pro-Soviet fraction of Pakistani communists, whereas the NSF emerged as a pro-Chinese (Maoist) organization. The main pro-Chinese fractions of NSF became respectively NSF (Meraj) and NSF (Kazmi). NSF (Meraj) moved close to mainstream politician Zulfiqar Ali Bhutto and its leader Meraj Muhammad Khan became a founding member of Bhutto's Pakistan Peoples Party (PPP) in December 1967. Meraj, along with veteran leftist politicians, J. A. Rahim and Dr. Mubashir Hassan became an important member of PPP's 'socialist wing'. In addition to Meraj, other major NSF leaders of the anti-Ayub movement included Saeed Hassan, Tarek Fathe, Fatehyab Ali Khan, Ameer Ahmed Kazmi, Dr. Rashid Hassan Khan, Nawaz Butt and Sibghatullah Qadri (Haroon and Saleem 2008).

In an incident in Rawalpindi on 7 November 1968, the police opened fire on a student rally killing three students. This triggered major student protest as well as nationwide protests condemning the Ayub regime and urging a change of system. A rent-strike occurred and many shops and passengers refused to pay bus and railway fares. It seemed that a substantial section of the Pakistani nation was heading towards civil disobedience and a challenge to the writ of the state perceived as safeguarding the privileges of capital, the feudal establishment and the civil and military bureaucracy while seriously neglecting the needs of the majority (Ahmed 1973).

After the initial protests, it was decided to establish a Student Action Committee (SAC) to increase the effectiveness of student action. Shaikh Abdul Rasheed was selected as the coordinator of the SAC. He was arrested with other students while leading a student rally from Gordon College, Rawalpindi. Due to police brutality, a number of students were injured and arrested. The next day student activists called for a shut down and 'wheel jam' strike. Foreign media, including BBC radio, covered the protests comprehensively, noting their effectiveness in paralyzing the entire Pakistani capital for the whole day (Choudhry 1974). In the view of Meraj Muhammad Khan, the prominent and charismatic activist, the incident of 7 November, in which the NSF students were killed, sparked the 1968-69 movement. The scale of the protests was entirely unanticipated (Khan 2008).

Shahid Mahmood Nadeem, another student leader, played a key role in student protest in the Punjab, helping to organize the student protest in Lahore. In October 1968, the government selected the Fortress Stadium in Lahore, as a venue for week-long celebrations of the achievements of the military dictator. Parades, exhibitions and demonstrations were organised to pay tribute to General Ayub Khan. Punjab University was directed by the military authorities to ensure the attendance of students in order to fill the stadium. The university sent students from different departments on a rotation basis. Students of NSF secretly prepared a song 'The Decade of Sadness', condemning the dictator, Ayub Khan. When the parade started and tributes were underway to the military dictator, students suddenly started singing their own song. The audience, including ministers and senior civil and military officials were shocked, embarrassed and angry. This event resulted in serious crackdown against student leaders, but the police were unable to stop the students' actions particularly as they gained inspiration from radical protests taking place in other countries (Khan 2008).

The anti-Vietnam war movement had caught the imagination of young peace campaigners. Major protests had occurred in the US, UK, France and Germany. The dream of world revolution seemed realisable. Students in Pakistan followed events in Europe and their own clashes with the authorities, including the police increased. Tariq Ali, a former student leader of a progressive student organization in Lahore, who had moved to London a few years previously and was prominent in the anti-war protests in England, provided guidance to student activists in Pakistan. He initially communicated from London and later, in December 1968, visited Pakistan for several weeks providing new momentum to the student protests. He was later selected as a member of Bertrand Russell's international war crime tribunal. Ali's powerful personality and personal presence in Pakistan invigorated student action. Meanwhile, the police put pressure on some students by arresting family members, including parents, and keeping them in prison until the students agreed to stop their activities.

An earlier action in Hyderabad particularly illustrates the reactionary role of religion in supporting the Ayub regime. Student leader, Jam Saqi who later became Secretary General of the Communist Party of Pakistan, was prominent in organising the March 4 1967 movement of workers, peasants, students which started at Hyderabad. Among the demands of the protestors were the end of the dictatorship and the implementation of radical social and economic reforms. To counter the students' revolutionary and radical slogans, the state decided to harness the forces of religious fundamentalism notably Jamiat-i-Islami and its student wing Jamiat Tulba-e-Islam (JIT – Organization of Islamic Students). JIT engaged in anti revolutionary activities and tried to gain popular sympathy in the name of religion. In one such instance, JIT organised a demonstration to counter progressive student agitation. It planned a march from the 'Talak Incline' to 'Gehri Khata' area of Hyderabad city to burn the pictures of Jamal Abdul Nasser the President of Egypt, who had successfully crushed attacks by Islamic fundamentalists on the Egyptian left. JIT extremists extended this treatment to Nasser, despite his opposition to Israel's repression of the Palestinian people (Qureshi 2003).

Industrial Workers Join the Protest Against Ayub Khan

The 1965 Indo-Pakistan war had exacerbated existing poverty in the country and the most affected group was the industrial workers. Due to rising inflation and increasing unemployment workers had little option but to join students and other activists. This was a crucial period of development for the labour movement during which important structural realignments were effected. In the process of united action, various groups worked together to organize workers against the Ayub regime. A major and well-organized railways strike lasting 13 days was mounted and this became the precursor of the 1968–69 public uprising. In response, the government attempted to run the trains with the army's support. In turn, workers at various stations lay on the track to block the railway traffic. This movement gained such popular support that the police and army hesitated to move against individuals. Soon another influential union, the Water and Power Development Authority (WAPDA), responsible for the management of electricity and irrigation systems, joined the action. Both these striking unions had the support of the Communist Party of Pakistan (CPP) (Feldman 1971). An important labour leader emerging during this period was Kaniz Fatima who came from a family of renowned trade unionists and communists. Her father was a veteran member of the Communist Party of India (CPI). She enjoyed huge respect and influence among the workers of the country's biggest shipyard as well as Karachi Municipal Corporation (KMC) whose workers routinely responded to her calls for industrial action (Khan 2008).

Agitation started by the industrial workers in 1968 soon acquired a more radical shape and workers adopted a range of tactics including *gherao* (encirclement) of factories and mills. This tactic was not new: communists of Indian Bengal, Bihar and East Pakistan had been using it since 1954. Previously militant workers had encircled a number of factories including Mohini Textile Mill and People's Jute Mills in Khulna, for twelve days in 1964. In April 1965, workers encircled Amin Jute Mills in Chitagong and a huge *gherao* occurred in Tongi industrial area the same year. In most of these actions the state used police and paramilitary forces on the demand of industrialists, resulting in many killings (Ahmed 1978).

However, the *gherao* agitation of 1968–9 was distinctive from and notably more radical than earlier agitation. In particular, it was not confined to any specific mill, or area, but spread over all the major industrial zones of East Pakistan. Workers succeeded in getting their demands fulfilled. The most important characteristic of the 1968–69 gherao was that it was it was a part of a wider political struggle rather than concerned with the immediate interests of workers. This *gherao* derived its strength from an ongoing mass movement.

Crucially this *gherao* involved not only employees, but also students and other workers and peasants who took part in encircling mills and factories. This joint action reflected the involvement and support of student bodies, political parties and the trade unions leadership attached to the East Pakistan Communist Party (Marxist-Leninist) and Bhashani for the *gherao* movement (Ahmed 1975).

Intellectuals, Journalists and Professionals Join the Agitation

After imposing martial law on the country, General Ayub Khan came under severe criticism from leftist and progressive publications in Pakistan and responded by taking steps to curtail the freedom of press. The regime introduced the draconian *The Press and Publication (Amendment) Ordinance-1963*. The military took control of independent newspapers including *Daily Pakistan Times*, *Imroze* and the weekly *Lail-o-Nahar* belonging to the Pakistan Progressive Papers Ltd. These were owned by the renowned communist leader Mian Iftikharuddin and edited by well-known intellectuals Faiz Ahmed Faiz, Ahmed Nadeem Qasimi and Mazhar Ali. They were highly critical of the military government's economic policies. Shortly afterwards, the government took direct control of a further fourteen newspapers and periodicals. The military regime established a 'National Press Trust' (NPT) clearly aimed at coercing the press including using it as a platform for presenting pro-government unions as a model for others (Ahmed 1971).

The Pakistan Federal Union of Journalists (PFUJ), an organization of working journalists, opposed these measures and many PFUJ members and other journalists joined the public protests shortly after they had started in November. The government took further aggressive action against the press including banning weeklies *Chataan* Lahore and *Purban*i Dhaka, and the daily *Ittfaq* Decca. Advertisements in various newspapers including dailies *Pakistan Observer*, *Nawa-e-Waqt*, *Ibrat*, *Azad* and *Sangbad* were immediately curtailed for contravening state policies. The government also introduced the nefarious system of 'press advice' requiring all news items to be cleared by the government's information and propaganda department. Several journalists who refused to accede to this were arrested. In response to these pressure tactics, the PFUJ met in Karachi from December 15 to 17, 1968 to review the situation. The meeting concluded that in recent months the functioning of the national press as a constructive and democratic instrument of public opinion had become almost impossible. It alleged that the situation had deteriorated to such an extent that people had lost faith in the print media and that the role of journalists as watchdogs of the society had been completely compromised. Journalists argued that the situation was the cumulative result of a series of repressive measures adopted over the previous decade to stifle the press (Salauddin 2008). Restoration of press freedom was seen as imperative.

Many working journalists broke the government's restrictions on press freedom and protest rallies were held in different cities. Rawalpindi – the capital of Pakistan – emerged as an important venue of this agitation where journalists regularly held public meeting in Liaquat Park. At one rally of journalists, writers and poets held in Lahore in December 1968, the general public, industrial workers and students also joined in creating a huge public procession. The entire Mall Road became 'red'. Journalists and industrial workers wore red turbans and women red shawls. To counter the rising socialist and communist trend, the military government tried to give it a religious character. When this rally reached the Ichra area of Lahore, Jamat-i-Islami supporters, holding bread in one hand and the Holy Quran in the other, inquired of the agitating workers: 'Do you want *Roti* (bread) or *Koran*. People replied: 'We have the *Koran* in our homes, but we don't have bread' (Niazi 1998).

Many Pakistani intellectuals also attempted to resist Ayub's repression. Political theatre was put on in various cities to motivate members of the public. One important drama by Munno Bhai was *Jaloos* ('Political Rally'). This was inspired by a sit-in of female students of Rawalpindi in front of the entrance of the Rawalpindi cantonment. The drama contained a number of revolutionary lyrics and was later repeated in many other cities. Another example was the film *'Zarqa'* released in 1968 by the prominent progressive writer Riaz Shahid. The film was apparently about the struggle of Palestinians against-Israeli occupation of their homeland but carried a message to the audience to rise against the military dictator. A further example of protest writing is the lyrics of a song by the revolutionary poet Habib Jalib and sung by Mehdi Hasan: *'Raqs zanjeer pehn kar bhi kiya jata hai* (one has also to dance while wearing chains and fetters). This broke all popularity records and emerged as a symbolic reflection of common people's desire to resist military dogma. Other revolutionary poets including Faiz Ahmed Faiz, Ahmed Nadeem Qasmi, Baba Najmi, Shaikh Ayaz, Ustad Bukhari, and many others. One of Faiz's poems became a public icon:

Speak
Speak, your lips are free
Speak, it is your own tongue
Speak, it is your own body
Speak, your life is still yours.

See how in the blacksmith's shop
The flame burns wild, the iron glows red,
The locks open their jaws
And every chain begins to break.

Speak, this brief hour is long enough
Before the death of body and tongue,
Speak, 'cause the truth is not dead yet,
Speak, speak, whatever you must speak.

Peasant Revolts Against Oppression

The most serious threat to Ayub Khan's military was still to come. Following the radicalization at university campuses and industrial units, peasants of rural Pakistan joined the protest movement. Abdul Hamid Bhashani, a member of Communist-Party of Pakistan (CPP) (pro-Chinese) who had for long been engaged in organizing the peasantry played a leading role. At same time the political line of the Communist Party of India (Marxist-Leninist) led by Charu Majumdar, popularly known as the Naxalbari line, began to influence the pro-Chinese faction of communists in Indian Bengal and East Pakistan. Their agenda was more radical and anti-constitutional (Umar 2006).

For Bhashani the mere change of one military dictator for another was not the solution of Pakistan's socio-economic problems. He saw the real problem of the country as the exploitative feudal and capitalist control of its economy. For the communists the full re-distribution of land to the peasants and the complete nationalization of industry was the only answer. Towards the end of December 1968 Bhashani announced a *gherao* (encirclement) programme for the peasants and asked them to encircle the village *hats* (weekly rural markets), police stations, and government offices. This was intended to be a rural substitute for urban strikes. He also declared that programmes of encirclement would start throughout East Pakistan on 29th December 1968. Accordingly, in a number of rural areas, including Hatirdia near Narsingdi in the district of Dhaka, encirclement took place. While gheraoing the local *hat* the villagers clashed with the police who opened fire, killing several people (Umar 1974).

The initial uprising, then, started in the urban and industrial areas soon spread to the rural areas. The situation in the rural areas had been deteriorating for the previous three to four years due to the exploitative tactics of *jotadrs* (land owners) and *mahajans* (money lenders). From the mid-60s incidents in which land owners and money lenders were killed by the peasants increased significantly. It was therefore unsurprising that in a countrywide uprising the peasantry would become involved. Thus in late 1968 and early 1969 peasants and other working people from rural areas began to attack their oppressors and the state officials who supported them. Major conflict occurred in many areas including Chandpur, Tangail, Jamalpur and even Chittagong and peasants came out in thousands joining the protests and encircled police stations and local administrative offices.

The killing of large numbers of land owners, money lenders, cattle rustlers and police officials was reported (Khan 1999).

In many villages the peasants, following communist commune principles, elected their own village committees, established local courts and began to try land owners, money lenders, cattle rustlers and police officials, and to settle local disputes and punish criminals. Although this peasant uprising was very much part of the general uprising of 1968–69, the peasant association (Krishak Samity) under Bhashani and particularly the pro-Peking communists played an active role in shaping its political character. Everywhere the peasants adopted the slogan: 'land to the tillers, establish the rule of peasants and workers' (Umar 2006).

In my view, the main reason for peasants' actions was the failure of Ayub Khan's regime to implement fundamental change in class relations in rural areas, although it did begin to inject government subsidies to raise agricultural output. Capitalist farming was encouraged and the area under cultivation grew. However, small farmers were virtually ignored. The main beneficiaries of Ayub Khan's 'green revolution' were in fact the large feudal lords who were the major recipients of subsidies and loans and were exempted from any taxes. Hardly any money remained for building schools and hospitals or to improve sanitation facilities in rural areas. The poor peasantry, who comprised the overwhelming majority of the population, received few benefits from Ayub Khan's well-publicised 'green revolution' (Wilcox 1970).

During the entire decade of his rule, Ayub Khan instead of directly approaching the peasant class used the intermediary of 'Basic Democrats'. In fact, these 'Basic Democrats' were government-patronized feudal lords or their nominee members of the petty bourgeoisie, who were supporters of Ayub Khan's martial law regime and thoroughly anti-peasant. The Basic Democrats constituted the electorate for the provincial and the National Assembly elections as well as for the presidency. Their political importance underpinned their economic power. Large amounts of money and other resources were placed at their disposal for development programmes and their expenditures were virtually unaccountable (Sobhan 1969). This created an unprecedented opportunity for the concentration of wealth, not only in the hands of land owners and money lenders but also for a new generation of business people. This was because the Basic Democrats helped to fund many development activities including construction, earthwork, and education and health programmes but in a way that fostered the growth of a rural bourgeoisie more than the development of rural infrastructure or the welfare of the people (Islam 1990). These developments established the rural bourgeoisie as a powerful factor in the rural areas and they continued to exploit the peasants, artisans, landless labourers and all sections of the rural poor with impunity (Burki 1972).

In Sindh province the Sindh Hari (Peasant) Committee led by Comrade Hyder Baksh Jatoi put up stiff resistance to the feudal lords who had turned them into bonded labourers. Sindhi feudalists set up their own private jails where peasants existed in inhuman conditions. Incidents occurred in which feudal lords and police officials raped female peasants. The districts of Sanghar, Nawabshah, Tharparkar, Hyderabad and Khairpur were the worst affected areas. The Sindh Hari Committee organized various conferences to express their anger and indignation at this situation (Ahmed 1985). The Hari Committees' activities resulted in an upsurge of peasant activities in Sindh province with Haris forcing the feudal landlords to discontinue *Baigar* (wageless labour) and unnecessary ejections of the peasants.

The peasants' organisations within North West Frontier Province (NFWP) were also active in holding meetings and protests against feudal lords throughout the province. The wave of urban protest of 1968–69 was the main factor behind the rise of the peasant movement in NWFP. The movement soon extended to Charsadda, Malakand, Swat and the Rustam area of Mardan. Feudal landlords tried to convert what was basically a class struggle into a tribal clash. Reactionary forces succeeded in containing this movement due to which it was unable to integrate with other revolutionary risings in the country. Although brief, several conflicts between peasants and feudal lords were fierce and bloody (Naseem 1981).

The 1968–69's people movement reverberated in some of the most primitive regions of NWFP. In Dera Ismail Khan region, the NSF with the support of a local organization *Dehqan Qalam* (Peasant's Pen) started campaigning against the feudal lords. Haq Nawaz Gandapur, Shaista Baloch and Hameed Khakwani emerged as some of the new names that created awareness of class struggle among the peasantry of the area. At the invitation of the local leadership of NSF, PPP leader Bhutto addressed a public meeting on 31 October 1968 in Jalal Park. A workers' and peasants' convention was also scheduled for the next day. The state used brutal means to disrupt this public gathering in this highly feudal tribal area of NWFP. The police employed violent baton charges and, for the first time, tear gas was used to disperse the meeting. For the first time in these feudal strongholds slogans of *'Asia Shurk Hai'*, (Asia Is Red) resounded as well as in other parts of the country (Waseem 1994).

Impact of the Revolts on the Khan Regime: Success and Failure

The development of this widespread public resistance movement forced General Ayub Khan to announce his decision not to contest the next presidential election and agree to hold a general election. When it became clear he had lost control and that radical forces might take over, the army decided to intervene and demanded Ayub Khan's resignation in March, 1969. He readily handed over powers to the army chief, General Yahya Khan. On 25 March, 1969 Yahya Khan announced a general election on an adult franchise to be held in August 1970. These were the first elections to be held in Pakistan since independence in 1947 (Cohen 2005).

However, as the major political parties started preparing for the general election, Pakistan's communist fractions under the radical leadership of Maulana Bhashani adopted a resolution on 4th January 1969 stating that under the existing system it was not possible to secure the rights of the people to participate in an election. Therefore entering into any electoral process would be futile. The communists decided to boycott all elections and to organise a united mass movement to realize the basic political and economic rights of the people. The pro-Peking group of the communist party soon came up with the radical slogan of *'Parchi naheen Barchi'* (Spear, not Ballot) (Khan 2008).

There is a long-running debate in Pakistan about whether this strategy of Communist Party was justified, given that the communists might have secured at least 50 seats had they participated in the general election. Many student leaders and trade unionists including Meraj Mohammad Khan, Tufail Abbas, and Mahmood Nawaz Babur would have had a serious chance of defeating the traditional leadership of feudal landowners and capitalists. Despite this avoidable possible mistake on the part of left leadership, the 1968–69 movement was a great emancipatory experience for many thousand of students and labour activists as well as for ordinary people who participated or witnessed it.

Conclusion

Student unrest against military dictator, Ayub Khan, culminating in the killings of 7 November 1968 soon converted into a huge and effective public protest that ultimately forced him to relinquish power in March, 1969. Despite the participation of a wide spectrum of people including intellectuals, professionals, industrial workers, and peasants, this movement failed to bring any fundamental change in the socio-economic structure or radical reforms. Major issues of national importance including provincial autonomy, regional imbalances, and ethnic and language issues remained unsettled. The traditional delaying tactics of the Pakistani establishment led to the rise of a nationalist movement in East Pakistan and to its ultimate independence as Bangladesh in December, 1971. In West Pakistan, Zulfiqar Ali Bhutto eventually took over as head of state from General Yahya Khan. Bhutto came under tremendous pressure to fulfill his election promise of 'Islamic Socialism', equality and social justice in the society.

Thus the raising of social consciousness during 1968–69 continued as a legacy to the early 1970s. Peasants' demands forced Bhutto to introduce land reforms in two phases, 1972 and 1977. Industrial workers also expected electoral promises to be fulfilled and that the new government to meet their demands. A major confrontation between workers and state authorities, took place in Karachi on June 7, 1972 when police fired on workers who had *gheraoed* (encircled) a textile mill on non-payment of their wages. The police fired on the workers, killing seven. In order to quell rising workers' unrest, Bhutto announced a policy of 'nationalization of industries', taking various private industries into government control. Simultaneously, several heavy industrial units were established with the help and assistance of the USSR, China, Romania and other socialist countries, thus creating substantial employment opportunities for industrial workers. Bhutto further fulfilled his election manifesto by announcing the nationalization of private educational institutions.

Bhutto's actions provided temporary relief and satisfaction to the ordinary people, but he was unable to bring the military under civilian control. Alleging electoral fraud, opposition political parties started agitation against his regime in March 1977. After initial hesitation, the army imposed martial law in July, 1977, which remained in force until military dictator general Zia-ul-Haq died in a plane crash on 17 August 17 1988. Zia-ul-Haq's martial law government reversed most of the developments in raised political consciousness, liberalism and social tolerance stimulated by the movements of 68/69. Zia also denationalized industries, banks and educational institutions. Finally, he promoted religious fundamentalism during the Afghan war, naming it a *jihad*, a holy war, against atheistic and communist Russia. His motive was to gain legitimacy in the eyes of the West. Thousands of *madrassas* (religious seminaries) were established across the country. Very soon, Pakistan became the hub of Islamist movements and the epicenter of the global Islamist movement.

References

Ahmed, F. 1973. Structure and Contradiction in Pakistan. In: K. Gough and H. Sharma eds. *Imperialism and Revolution in South Asia*. New York: Monthly Review Press: 221–243.

———— 1985. Pakistan's Problems of National Integration. In Asghar Khan ed. *Islam, Politics and the State; The Pakistan Experience*. 106–119. London: Zed Books Ltd:.

Ahmed, K. 1975. *A Socio Political History of Bengal and the Birth of Bangladesh*. Dhaka: Inside Library.

———— 1978. *Labour Movement in Bangladesh*. Dhaka: University Press Limited.

Ahmed, M. 1971. *Politics Without Social Change*. Karachi: Space Printers.

Ali, T. 1978. *1968 and After: Inside the Revolution*. London: Blond and Briggs.
———— 1987. *Street Fighting Years*. London: Collins.
Banuri, T. J. Khan, Shahrukh, R. and Mahmood, M. eds. 1997. *Just Development*. Karachi: Oxford University Press.
Burki, S. J. 1972. Ayub's Fall: A Socio-Economic Explanation. *Asian Survey*.12, 3 (March): 201–212.
———— 1988. A Historical Perspective on Development. In Shahid Javed Burki and Robert Laporte (eds.) *Pakistan's Development Priorities*. 15–41. Karachi: Oxford University Press
Choudhry, G.W. 1974. *The Last Days of United Pakistan*. Western Australia: University of Western Australia Press.
Cohen, S. P. 2005. *The Idea of Pakistan*. Lahore: Vanguard.
Dobell, W.M. 1969. Ayub Khan as President of Pakistan. *Pacific Affairs*. 42, 3: 294–310.
Feldman, H. 1967. *Revolution in Pakistan: A Study of the Martial Law Administration*. Karachi: Oxford University Press.
———— 1971. *From Crisis to Crisis: Pakistan 1962–69*. Karachi: Oxford University Press.
Haroon A. and Saleem A. 2008. Student Movement Revisited. *Dawn*, April 15. Karachi.
Hasan, S. ed., 2008. *Marx Aur Mashriq (Urdu) (Marx and the East)*. Karachi: Maktaba-e-Danyal.
Hussain, I. 1999. *Pakistan – The Economy of an Elitist State*. Karachi: Oxford University Press.
Inayatullah. 1970. *Bureaucracy and Development in Pakistan*. Peshawar: PRA.
Islam, N. M. 1990. *Pakistan - A Study in National Integration*. Lahore: Vanguard.
Jahan, R. 1972. *Pakistan: Failure in National Integration*. New York: Colombia University Press.
Khan, R. 1999. *The American Papers: Secret and Confidential India-Pakistan-Bangladesh Documents*. Dhaka: University Press Ltd.
Khan, L. 2008. *Pakistan's Other Story – The 1968–69 Revolution*. Lahore: The Struggle Publication.
Laporte, R. 1969. Succession in Pakistan: Continuity and Change in a Garrison State. *Asian Survey*. 9, 11 (November): 842–861.
Mazari, S. K. 1981. *Underdevelopment, Poverty and Inequality in Pakistan*. Lahore: Vanguard.
———— 1999. *A Journey to Disillusionment*. Karachi: Oxford University Press.
Naseem. S.M. 1981. *Underdevelopment, Poverty and Inequality in Pakistan*. Lahore: Vanguard.
Niazi. Z. 1998. *Press in Chains*. Karachi: Royal Book Company.
Papanek, G. 1967. *Pakistan's Development: Social Goals and Private Incentive*. Cambridge Massachusets: Harvard University Press.
Qureshi, A. 2003. *4th March Aein Aaj Jee Sindh* (Sindhi) (4th March and Today's Sindh). Dadu: Manchhar Publication.
Salauddin, G. www:geothe.de/ges/ztg/prg/akt/wlt/asa/pak/en2924280.htm (accessed on July 12, 2009).
Sayeed, K. B.1980. *The Politics in Pakistan. The Nature and Direction of Change*. New York: Praeger.
Shaheed, Z. 1983. The Role of the Government in the Development of the Labour Movement. In: Hasan Gardezi and Jamil R. eds., *Pakistan - The Unstable State*. Lahore: Vanguard: 216–236.
———— 2007. *The Labour Movement in Pakistan*. Karachi: Oxford University Press.
Siddiqui, K. 1972. *Conflict, Crisis and War in Pakistan*. London: The Macmillan Press Ltd.
Sobhan, R. 1969. Power Struggle in Pakistan. *New Statesman* (28 February).

Umar, B. 1974. *The Political Objectives of the Gherao Call.* Dhaka: Mowla Brothers.
―――― 2006. *The Emergence of Bangladesh.* Karachi: Oxford University Press.
Waseem, M. 1994. *Politics and the state in Pakistan.* Islamabad: NIHCR.
Wilcox W. 1970. 'Pakistan in 1969: Once again at the starting point'. *Asian Survey.* vol. 9, 2 (February): 73–81
Zaidi, A. 2000. *Transforming Urban Settlements.* Karachi: City Press.
Ziring, L. 1971. *The Ayub Era: Politics in Pakistan 1958–69.* Syracuse, N.Y: Syracuse University Press.

Part II
THEORETICAL & CULTURAL SIGNIFICANCE

Chapter 6

NINETEEN SIXTIES RADICALISM IN THE UNITED STATES: ITS RISE, DECLINE AND LEGACY

Mike O'Donnell

Introduction

The purpose of this chapter is to explain the rise, character and trajectory of radicalism in the United States during 'the long nineteen sixties' and to comment on its significance to some of today's related issues. For comparative purposes, I will also refer to nineteen sixties radicalism in Britain. My already smouldering interest in American radicalism was ignited in 1968 when as a student I attended the 'alternative' democratic convention in Chicago, if 'attended' is the right word to describe the heavily policed gatherings of assorted radicals in the parks and streets outside the official Convention Hall. Since then I have made three research visits to the United States when I interviewed several activists and accessed a wide literature. More recently I interviewed ten British men and women (five of each) who were at a minimum sympathetic to the radical mood of the period (for a fuller description of my research base see O'Donnell 2008; and 2010 forthcoming). If 1968 was the height of sixties radicalism, its decline was also becoming apparent and I will treat 1968 as an approximate turning point.

Nineteen sixties radicalism in the United States was extremely diverse and was expressed in intermingling political and cultural 'streams'. Accordingly, I will use the capitalised term 'Movement' to refer to the phenomenon as a whole. In so far as it is appropriate to separate the two streams, I use the term 'New Left' to refer to the various political groups of the Movement and the term 'counterculture' to refer to those who aspired to a radical and in some cases adopted an 'alternative' lifestyle. These three terms were the ones most used by radicals during the sixties and with good reason. The word 'Movement' was inclusive, eclectic and vague and therefore capable of embracing any who identified with the rising mood of progressive, if not radical change. It suited the open and exploratory characteristic of early and mid-sixties radicalism. The term 'New Left' indicated an intention to re-explore and reframe a radicalism of the left. In Britain the New Left was mainly a phenomenon within Marxism whereas in the United States traditional labels were initially 'suspended'. The term counterculture came into popular use later in the 1960s as the alternative culture gathered momentum (see Roszac 1968; Reich 1970). Divisions between political and cultural radicals developed in the second half of the sixties, but initially the focus was on the integration of culture and politics through a consistency of values and practice.

In the United States radical students played a prominent role within the Movement (the much smaller British student movement lacked comparable influence, see Marwick 2003, 140). I will argue below that they were a particularly powerful example of what Mannheim termed a generational unit whose actions had wider reverberations. Radical students, then, were at the core of a much broader movement.

The Movement in the Context of the Conservative Nineteen Fifties

The rise of radicalism in the United States can be understood in the context of a wider although by no means uncontested shift towards a more liberal social and political climate in the late 1950s and early 1960s. This was in part a response to the social and political conservatism of the 1950s. David Riesman's *The Lonely Crowd*, published in 1961, captured the prevailing social conformity while the relentless pursuit of suspected communists and fellow travellers by the House of Un-American Activities Committee (HUAC) and the aggressive 'witch-hunting' of Senator Joseph McCarthy put radicals of all kinds on the defensive. The mildest of mavericks could be socially ostracised or politically victimised and cut-off. However, the rise of a media-led hedonistic youth culture, the civil rights protests in the southern states and the election of a young and relatively progressive president in 1960 were signs of a weakening of the conservative grip.

In a still longer perspective stretching into the twenty-first century, the radical sixties can be interpreted as the cutting edge that opened up a freer space of social expression. As was widely appreciated at the time the potential for increasing cultural opportunities depended largely on the growing affluence that provided the material basis to sustain it (Marcuse 1969a (1955); Roszac 1968; Reich 1970). Although this was basically 'a space' of culture and lifestyle it also involved an increasing engagement in civil society rather than formal institutional political channels. Most widely conceived, it was a re-vitalisation of what Habermas terms the life-world (see chapters 1 and 9). Of course, there is no guarantee that expanded cultural opportunity and freedom will be expressed in radical or socially constructive ways – the opposite is always a possibility. However as the rest of this chapter illustrates, most nineteen sixties radicals did not interpret 'freedom' in exclusively individualistic terms but, as the civil rights and commune movements demonstrated, also as freedom for others.

In Britain the 1950s were also a conservative period although the Cold War did not generate repression comparable to the virulence of McCarthyism in the US. It is arguable that Britain in the nineteen fifties was still in many respects socially and culturally Victorian. Most working class adults aspired to and achieved a life of respectable conformity in which, as Richard Hoggart painstakingly described, attitudes of 'them' and 'us' still ran deep (1958). However, as in the Unites States, traditional mores and boundaries were being tested. Among the first to do so were working class youth, many of whom responded with uninhibited zest to the opportunities offered by new technology and the international media and entertainment industry (see, for instance, Mark Abrams *The Teenage Consumer* 1959). For the liberal middle and upper classes, the unsuccessful prosecution under the *Obscene Publications Act* of Penguin, the publishers of D. H. Lawrence's *Lady Chatterley's Lover* in 1960, symbolised a growing rejection of censorship and conventional morality and a desire for greater cultural freedom, not least, sexual freedom.

New Left intellectuals on both sides of the Atlantic sought to redefine radicalism partly in cultural terms. There was widespread revulsion at the brutal and inhumane turn that the communist revolution had taken in the USSR and journals such as *Studies on the Left* in the United States and *New Left Review* in Britain sought to re-root the left in more durable cultural values. Charles Wright Mills refers to the relationship between ideals and culture in his *Letter to the (British) New Left*:

> 'As for the articulation of ideals, there I think your magazines have done their best work so far. That is your meaning – is it not – of the emphasis upon cultural affairs.'
> (Reprinted in Horowitz ed., 1967, 252)

Breaking the Mould

The radicalism of the 1960s was more than a simply a reaction to the conservatism of the 1950s. While sixties radicalism was part of the upsurge of liberalisation of the 1960s it had distinctive origins and identity. Several factors account for the radical revival in the United States, some of which apply to the new radicalism elsewhere. These included the existence of both a number of serious issues and a body of people in a position to act on their concern about them. In the longer term the prospects of the Movement depended on the development of shared values and beliefs, if not necessarily an agreed ideology. How and to what extent the Movement should be organised became increasingly relevant as the decade wore on. This was a matter of greater concern to political rather than countercultural radicals, the latter of whom tended to believe that the kind of change they wanted was best achieved through personal communication and, in a more public context, dramatic performance and example.

Thus the first factor was the existence of a potential body of radical activists sufficiently well located to organise effectively. The higher education system in the United States had expanded rapidly to the point that, in 1960, there were approximately five million students – more than the population of many nation states. Just as the industrial working class was concentrated in and able to organise out of factories, the same was true of radical students in universities. Despite the size of the United States the telephone provided adequate means of communication across the country's campuses. In any case, the intense interest of the mass media in the radicals' activities informed students of events and facilitated and even stimulated their responses. Of course the majority of students were not activists. What mattered however was that there was a critical mass of activists able to make an impact and that some were organisationally effective (in the anti-elitist spirit of the Movement the word 'leader' tended to be avoided). In the early phases of the Movement, the experience of students involved in anti-segregation activities in the mid to late nineteen fifties was organisationally useful. In particular, 'the sit-in' used to disrupt segregated facilities in certain southern states was a ready example of direct action which became a favoured tactic particularly in the early days of the Movement (Haber in Brown ed., 1969).

The issues that motivated activists were broadly of two kinds: those that affected students directly and those relating to the wider domestic and international context. Especially in the early 1960s many campus protests focused on matters of specific concern to students such as visiting and stay-over rights for boy and girl friends to student hostels and representation on university committees. However, these issues of immediate self-interest inevitably raised questions about the way higher education was run, including bureaucratic dehumanisation and the links between higher education, corporations, the military and government, encapsulated in the term 'multi-university' (Spence in Brown ed., 1969). The Berkeley Free Speech Movement of 1964 challenged paternalist authority in pursuit of greater student autonomy but also raised wider issues of bureaucratic alienation and freedom of speech within the context of higher education. A similar case of local issues often challenging hierarchical control and matters of more general concern also characterised student actions at the London School of Economics and the University of Nanterre.

The main national and international issues of initial concern to Movement activists demonstrate its diversity and decentralised character. The most prominent were the Cold War, nuclear disarmament, racial segregation and civil rights and, slightly later, but crucially in terms of wider support and impact, opposition to the Vietnam War. From approximately the mid-1960s the Movement became enmeshed with a much more widely shared 'rights agenda' encompassing anti-racism and racial equality, feminism, and gay and lesbian rights. Whilst the Movement undoubtedly gave an early impetus to these movements this faded as they increasingly gained independent momentum.

The Identity of the Movement

The Movement was not an on-going organisation in any formal sense and the use of the term as an indicator of a broad collective identity needs further explanation. Three points can be made in this respect. The first is that, in fact, there were many organised groups within the Movement that to a greater or lesser extent coordinated for the purpose of collective action. Secondly, the term Movement primarily indicates a broad cultural and political orientation and shared mood rather than a complex of organisations. It is this rising spirit of political and cultural radicalism rather than any formal institutional framework that characterises the Movement in the early 1960s. Exclusivity and formality were precisely what the radicals wanted to avoid. Thirdly, the largely youthful generational base of the Movement intensified a sense of collective identity.

The Southern Nonviolent Coordinating Committee (SNCC) and the Student Peace Union (SPU) that respectively coordinated antisegregation and nuclear disarmament protest and action were among the more prominent organisations in the early days of the Movement. These and many other groups as well as individuals supported the March on Washington in 1963 and a rather different and even more eclectic gathering came together for the 'alternative convention' in Chicago in 1968. From the mid-sixties the Black Panther Party (BPP) challenged both the leadership and non-violent philosophy of Martin Luther King and had an influence beyond its immediate membership. The Panthers were instrumental in shifting some white as well as black radicals away from reformist towards revolutionary politics.

The most influential student organisation was Students for a Democratic Society (SDS). Founded in 1960, SDS was a non-sectarian student organisation specifically established to explore and express the new radicalism. This intent was impressively articulated in the founding document of SDS, *The Port Huron Statement*:

> 'We are people of this generation, bred in at least modest comfort, housed now in universities looking uncomfortably to the world we inherit ...

> As we grew …our comfort was penetrated by events too troubling to dismiss. First, the permeating and victimising fact of human degradation, symbolised by the Southern struggle against racial bigotry, compelled most of us from silence to activism. Second, the enclosing fact of the Cold War, symbolised by the presence of the Bomb, brought awareness that we ourselves, and our friends, and millions of abstract 'others' we knew more directly because of our common peril, might die at any time.'
> (Various Authors, *The Port Huron Statement* 1962, reprinted in Jacobs and Landau ed., 1969, 154)

SDS initiated and/or participated in many events and protests and also set up a number of community action projects – the *Economic Research and Action Project* (ERAP) – aimed at developing a grass-roots democracy of the poor. As I will discuss, SDS also generated significant ideological debate (Moody 1966).

Paradoxically, the flexible and open approach to organisation and ideology of the New Left initially helped in making it a focus of identification. Its lack of central organisation was, on balance an organisational strength. And the absence of a membership form and fee also helped to swell the ranks! It was the shared desire to produce new ideas and strategies for change rather than any specific programme or set of beliefs that provided a sense of cohesion and common purpose. The search itself presumed a rejection of any authority perceived as dogmatic, repressive or self-interested. In the United States the openness of the New Left to new political ideas was expressed in the search for 'a third way' (a term later used in a different context by Anthony Giddens 1998). A common theme was to avoid the worst and take the best from socialism and liberalism and, if possible, develop new ideas (Jacobs and Landau in Jacobs and Landau eds., 1966, 47). Perhaps the closest to a new or at least distinctive idea to emerge from the American New Left was participatory democracy concretely expressed in demands for the democratic reform of higher education and the ERAP.

The intellectual inspiration of the early New Left came from Charles Wright Mills, sometimes referred to as 'the big daddy of the New Left'. Mills's thinking, not least his celebrated advice to link personal troubles with public issues (Mills, 1970 (1959), 9–10), is strikingly apparent in *The Port Huron Statement*. Unlike many prominent British New Left intellectuals Mills was not a Marxist and despite his comprehensive critique of the American 'power elite' (1956) and scathing attack on its foreign policy (1958 and 1960) was pragmatic rather than programmatic. His death in 1962 deprived the emerging New Left of a potentially vital source of knowledge and experience.

The second point referred to above is that as far as the wider Movement was concerned identification was as much emotional and moral as rational. At its most inclusive the Movement was an expression of a new mood, a sense of cultural as well as political freedom and exploration. The strength and pervasiveness of the feeling that 'something' different, and perhaps profoundly authentic and significant, was happening is not easy to convey in more straightened and conventional times. However, as Frederic Jameson perceptively remarked the 'sense of freedom and possibility' experienced by those it touched was 'for the most part of the nineteen-sixties a momentarily objective reality, as well as from the hindsight of the eighties a historical illusion' (Jameson 1984, 408–9). Civil rights activist Jane Stembridge's remark that 'Love alone is radical' (quoted by Zinn in Frisch 1968, 36) expresses in the extremity of its idealism the spirit of the early Movement. The following comments were made retrospectively by British former sixties radicals but are typical of several made to me at different times by those involved on both sides of the Atlantic:

> 'In 1968 we absolutely thought we were going to change the world … we thought we could do anything.'
>
> 'In the sixties and seventies there was a collective sense of a whole generation being bound together.'
>
> (Field Interviews 2004–5)

The emerging wave of social engagement and cultural experimentation was powerfully expressed in popular youth culture. 'Cometh the hour, cometh the man', and in this case the inspirational genius who supplied the words and music to the mood was Bob Dylan. Some of his songs referred to specific social or political issue but others, such as *Blowin' in the Wind* and *The Times they are a Changin'*, transcended the specific, feeding back subliminally into the swell of popular feeling and engagement.

As the sixties progressed a radical vision and practice of a potentially different way of life to the mainstream began to take shape. Almost every area of lifestyle was re-interpreted and re-signified within the alternative culture. As the sources cited in this chapter show, at the time supporters and opponents of the counterculture felt it was a highly significant development and responded strongly to it – a sense of engagement that some recent general histories of the period fail to capture (see Sandford 2005; DeGroot 2008). The concept of homology, the holistic bringing together of a variety of symbols, objects and practices, is helpful in understanding what happened (see Hebdige 1979). In the space of a few years, expressive and often naturalistic styles in hair, clothes and music spread widely among young people. The Puritan ethic was turned on its head as young people began to find virtue in pleasure rather than in its repression. Hedonism took on the glow of morality as those who had 'turned on' urged other to do the same. A 'subterranean' culture previously more or less confined to West Coast and Greenwich Village beats suddenly surfaced across the nation, especially but not exclusively among the young. Perhaps the most radically different and challenging practice within the counterculture was the taking of psychedelic drugs. Psychedelics were claimed to induce profound experiences and insights that made the competition and conformity of work-regulated life appear superficial and boring ('alienating' is the word Marx might have used had he 'turned on'). The potential conflict with the American mainstream and the work ethic need not be laboured here. However, it should be acknowledged that it is possible that many, possibly a majority, of those who adopted the counter-cultural style were not deeply or knowledgeably committed to social transformation. At the margin of the Movement, particularly the counterculture, there were some whose participation was partial and tentative or who were just plain muddled. The bewigged weekend hippie was an extreme case (for two accounts that focus on the negative aspects of the radical nineteen sixties see Collier and Horowitz 1996; DeGroot 2009). However, this in no way detracts from the serious intent of others.

The term 'ideology' is too suggestive of consensual thinking to apply to the counterculture. However, there was a sense of a shared philosophy within the counterculture reflecting challenge to convention, openness to difference and hedonism. If the political New Left in the United States was initially notably tolerant and open, the counterculture can virtually be defined in those terms – at least in respect to mutual relations between participants However, tolerance was less readily extended to 'straights' – defined as unquestioning conformists. The extent to which both the politics and culture of the Movement sought to reject what was seen as repressive conformity is illustrated by the popularity of the terms 'anti-politics' and 'anti-psychiatry' and 'counter-culture' itself. However, the Movement was not locked into negative critique but highly focused on creating a more participatory politics and 'liberated' culture.

Thirdly, in terms of the identity of the Movement, its strong, though far from exclusively generational base, assisted both formal and especially informal contact and organisation. Hundreds of underground newspapers, notice boards in cafes and student unions, and simply the ease with which contacts were made among the leisure-rich and foot-loose young facilitated the creation of a vibrant national and even international network. Unsurprisingly, interpretations of the Movement have largely focused on its generational character (see pp.104–06). However, here I briefly introduce Mannheim's theory of generational identity which, presented some thirty years before the rise of the Movement, is robust enough to provide a point of reference with more recent interpretation.

Mannheim's key concepts are generation of *location*, generation of *actuality* and *generational units* (1952a). A generation of location is synonymous with generational cohorts and in itself does not connote a shared generational identity. In contrast a generation of actuality is one that because of a common experience develops some degree of shared identity. Generational units refer to groups within 'the same actual generation that work up the material of their common experience in different specific ways' (1952, 304). Mannheim's model allows for the variable interplay of historical and social context, including class, on generational identity. He developed it with reference to the political youth groups of interwar Germany but it is transferable to other contexts, including nineteen sixties student radicalism. The location of students in universities, their typically liberal upbringings and inclinations and the motivating effect of major political issues and rapid social change all stimulated them 'to work up their experience' in a specific way. Because the same often unusually dramatic political and social scenario was also experienced beyond the campuses and, partly inspired by the activities of students, other young people were drawn to various degrees to the new radicalism. To that extent a generation of actuality was in the making although it would overstate matters to claim that it ever became a reality.

More recent sociologists of youth have preferred terms such as 'neo-tribe' to refer to the often unstructured cultural drifting of post-war youth (Bennett 1999; Muggleton 2000; Muggleton and Weinzierl 2004). This characterisation has some purchase in terms of the cultural 'stream' of the Movement but less so to its activist core. These authors also tend to stress the individualist values of post-war youth cultures. My own view is that the growth of individualism that greater affluence and leisure facilitates was and is shaped within a search for sociality, if not community and, as today's anti-capitalist movement demonstrates, does not preclude collective action. Both individualism and community take various forms and change in relation to each other at different times. It is a mistake to disregard the collective endeavours and aspirations of the radical sixties. Given the relevance of Mannheim's analysis of the association of generational and collective identity, I agree with Jane Pilcher's comment that his legacy on the sociology of generations has been 'undervalued' (1994).

The Break-up of the Movement

The break-up of the Movement is best understood in the context of its relationship to the wider society, particularly government. Confrontation between radicals and law enforcement agencies escalated as the decade wore on. A second factor was that whilst the fundamental diversity of the Movement was helpful in the early stages, it became a weakness when a disciplined and coherent response was needed under the serious pressures of the late 1960s. These two factors combined disastrously and I will treat them together.

As activists and sympathisers became increasingly frustrated at the continuation of the Vietnam War and what they regarded as the slow pace of social reform, the underlying diversity of the Movement began to harden into philosophical and strategic disagreements. By the late nineteen sixties it was beginning to fragment into incompatible groups and tendencies. A contemporary commentator describes the problem without perhaps quite grasping its likely consequences:

> 'The fact is that the Movement is incredibly diverse – as multileveled and varied as American society itself. Its members have neither blueprint nor party line, neither national office nor secretariat. There is no unanimity among them about tactics or even appropriate ends except in the most general way. The 'window breakers' are only one element. The Movement also encompasses hippies and doctrinaire Leninists, anarchists and populists, the 'campus cong' and peaceful communards, militant confrontationalists and mystics, Bakuninists and humanists, power seekers, ego trippers, revolutionaries whose domain is the individual mind, Maoists, rock bands and cultural guerrillas.'
>
> (Burck 1969, 133-4)

Not specifically mentioned in the above list were social democrats who wanted to work with the Democratic Party; socialists who wanted to form a new party (see Lynd 1970); non-violent counter-cultural revolutionaries; various religious sects, among which the Jesus Movement and Divine Light Mission stood out; and the revolutionary Weather Underground.

The escalating tension and conflict between the Movement, particularly its revolutionary elements, and the government and forces of law enforcement were a major factor not only in its break-up but in the way it broke up. Partly in solidarity with 'third world' liberation movements, some individuals and groups shifted to more revolutionary, confrontational and, in a minority of cases, violent rhetoric, ideologies and strategies – a shift criticised in the European context by the German critical theorist, Jurgen Habermas (see chapter 9). An influential minority of black activists and some prominent members of SDS led this change of direction. In the mid-1960s the initiative in what radicals had begun to refer to as the black liberation movement had shifted from the coalition led by Martin Luther King to the much more confrontational Black Panther Party (BPP). The police and FBI crackdown on the BPP was severe and effective. The revolutionary group the Weather Underground (initially Weathermen) emerged out of SDS but attracted others angered at the continuation of the Vietnam War and at United States foreign policy generally. This group took their name from a line in a Bob Dylan song – *You don't have to be a Weatherman to see which way the wind is blowing*. Unlike the BPP the Weather Underground was not locally based in community chapters and so was less easily targeted by police or FBI action. As its name implies the group operated covertly; partly modelling itself on 'third world' guerrilla movements. Their target of attack was now specifically American liberal capitalism and imperialism and violent tactics against corporations and banks, considered particularly implicated in what was often referred to as the military industrial complex, were seen as legitimate. To put it mildly this was a fundamental change, if not a reversal, from the non-violent philosophy and tactics of the early Movement.

A sense of apprehension and that matters were getting out of control became pervasive as police and FBI pressure mounted and the Movement began to fragment. Disorientation was as characteristic of the counterculture as the New Left. A remark by Timothy Leary, 'the prophet of LSD', that it was 'a sacred act' to pre-emptively shoot 'genocidal' police drew the following comment from the novelist, Ken Kesey: 'In this battle, Timothy, we need every mind and every soul, but oh my doctor we don't need one more nut with a gun' (Kesey 1970, 31).

The other side of this dialectic of confrontation was that attempts to control activists became more repressive and in some instances violent. In 1970 members of the National Guard killed four protesting Kent State University students. However, following the shock of Kent State de-escalation, rather than increase in violent confrontation occurred. Crucially, the United States government increased the speed of troop withdrawal from Vietnam and serious confrontation subsided with the notable exception of the activities of the Weather Underground. In 1972 many young activists directed their efforts to supporting the presidential campaign of Senator George McGovern. His resounding defeat was a reminder that there was 'another America' little enamoured of the radical sixties. With the interlude of the one-term presidency of Jimmy Carter America entered a long period of conservative Republican ascendancy which, like Thatcherism in Britain, had a strong element of backlash about it.

Set against the Movement's highest aspirations its often-chaotic fragmentation has a tragic element as the following quotation from a book authored by two activists expresses:

'The experience of the 1960s, with all their pain and struggle, have not left one mass-based organisation which has the power to resist either repression or co-option; some of our friends are dead – too many; some of our friends are underground in a noble but spurious attempt to make classical terrorism the catalytic force for the creation of a viable revolutionary movement. We who tried most desperately to turn America-the-obscene into America-the- beautiful have failed...'

(Calvert and Nieman 1971, preface: x)

In retrospect this expression of failure seems an over-reaction to admittedly depressing immediate circumstances. 'The sixties' still resonate and I will discuss its longer-term influence later.

The fact that the Movement broke up in the way it did was avoidable. First, the significant minority that switched to a violent revolutionary approach were mistaken and with dire consequences. The United States was not a totalitarian society but a liberal democracy sufficiently open and responsive to render violent revolution unjustified. Further, public opinion, including most radical opinion, is deeply opposed to such a strategy. Second, and relatedly, while attacking the United States 'military-industrial' complex for oppressing and exploiting 'the third world' was arguably ideologically valid, imitating the methods of 'third world' revolutionaries was not. Apart from the view of the overwhelming majority of the country's population that the military and police power of the state was legitimate an armed revolution was most unlikely to succeed. Third, violent revolution contradicted the initial peaceful aims of the Movement and particularly the approach based on a moral and psychological consistency between means and ends.

The above points are not an argument against violent revolution *per se*. If there is such a thing as a just war, then there is such a thing as a just violent revolution. However, neither the practical conditions nor moral justification for a violent revolution applied in the United States at this time.

Having made the above points, it must be said that the atmosphere of heightened conflict and violence in the mid-to-late nineteen sixties was not primarily due to the activities of radicals. Domestically the murders of the Kennedy brothers and Martin Luther King provoked anger, anxiety and a pervasive mistrust. This was exacerbated as the explanations for the killings failed to convince. The Vietnam War provided a backdrop of relentless brutality and destruction. At the best of times the United States is a relatively violent society and the late 1960s were especially violent. Without being too apocalyptical, there is a sense in which the Movement was simply swept away by forces beyond its control.

Harbingers of the Future or Misguided Youth? Contemporary Interpretations of the Movement and Lessons Learnt

Nineteen sixties radicalism generated huge and often partisan response and the ideological underpinning of much of the commentary referred to below is quite apparent. The following review of contemporary interpretations of the Movement treats them as part of the broader phenomenon they seek to explain. As well as other sources, I draw particularly on two journals that consistently published contrasting interpretations of the radical sixties. The articles in *Social Problems* tended to be sympathetic to the radicals and those in *Encounter* highly critical.

In an article in *Social Problems* (1970) Richard Flacks argues that a specific social segment of students entering higher education, particularly 'elite' universities, during the late 1950s and 1960s came into conflict with the hierarchical and bureaucratic ethos and structure of large universities. Importantly, according to Flacks, they increasingly extended the same criticism to the organisations that most could expect to work for. Flacks states that student activists tended to come from relatively liberal and progressive middle class family backgrounds and their parents were openly critical of conformist and conventional values. Their offspring aspired to lives and careers underpinned by these liberal values. There is ample supporting evidence that the development of the New Left was informed by these ideas and values (Keniston 1971; Liebert 1971; Hampden-Turner 1971). A striking illustration is the consistently idealistic, anti-hierarchical albeit pragmatic tone of *The Port Huron Statement*. Alienation from bureaucracy was also a strong theme of the Berkeley Free Speech Movement. Among the paraphernalia of protest some students wore a badge inscribed with the ironic message 'Do not fold, staple or mutilate'. More dramatically, prominent activist Mario Savio urged protestors to 'put their bodies on the gears and upon the wheels' of the bureaucratic 'machine' (quoted by Spence in Brown ed., 1969, 40). He objected to the requirement that 'to become part of society, to become lawyers, ministers, businessmen (sic), people in government, that very often they (i.e. students, MO'D) must compromise those principles which were most dear to them' (Savio in Brown ed., 1969, 35)

In a later article in *Social Problems* (1973) Samuel Friedman framed a similar analysis to Flacks in more Marxist terms. He argued that the shift from a manufacturing to a service economy had created a 'new proletariat' of intellectual labour that was becoming alienated because of the requirement to work for the profit of capital rather than for intrinsic reasons. He considered that his approach 'subsumed' arguments pointing to the growth of the 'multiversity' and the emergence of what he termed a 'liberated generation'. However, publishing in 1973. Friedman observed that the student movement was in decline and that in order to contribute to future fundamental change student activists would need to link to 'working class radicalism'.

Both Flacks and Friedmann were inclined to optimism about the longer-term influence of the Movement and the consequences of underlying social structural change. Flacks anticipated an erosion of the culture of capitalism and the increasing emergence of critical attitudes to it within the expanding university system (355). Friedmann clearly felt there was an underlying logical dynamic to the development of solidarity between the 'new' and traditional 'working class (297–8). In contrast, leading liberal Daniel Bell assumed that what he described as the new service class should, like other groups, realistically accommodate to the work ethic and that in due course it would do so (1973, 1988 (1960)). Flacks quotes Bell as referring to the student revolutionaries as 'the guttering last gasps of a romanticism soured by rancour and impotence' (in Flacks 1970, 355).

Interestingly the business journal *Fortune* in a special publication, reviewing student dissent, *Youth in Turmoil* (1969), offered a more mixed assessment than Bell. This volume was a collection of interpretations of a survey carried out in 1968 by the Yankelovich organisation on behalf of *Fortune*. On the basis of a sample of nearly 23,000, the survey categorised three million out of a total of eight million 18 to 24 year olds with experience of higher education as 'forerunners'. Similar to Flacks and Friedman, this group was described as taking a high standard of living for granted and as motivated by moral idealism and a desire for intellectually fulfilling careers. However, predictably contributors to this volume had less sympathy than Flacks and Friedman with the radicals' criticisms of liberal capitalism. In a key contribution to the collection, Daniel Seligman assumes that 'the forerunners' will have to engage with the system though he expresses uncertainty as to how they would do so. He suggests that they 'seem quite capable of bringing the disorders that have beset the campuses into their parents' world – into business and government ...' but that they could also become 'the most productive generation in American history' (Seligman 1969, 30).

Mainstream liberals were generally more unambiguously critical than Seligman. Daniel Bell's comment quoted above may have been directed at more confrontational activists but by the mid- to late 1960s many liberals considered that the Movement in general, particularly the student core of it, was a juvenile rebellion that had got dangerously out of hand. The journal *Encounter* regularly published articles attacking student radicalism. Among the contributors were Bruno Bettelheim (1969), Edward Shils (1969) and Robert Nisbet (1970). Their common theme was that the radical students were reacting to a vacuum of authority by behaving in an uncontrolled and self-indulgent way. This interpretation was frequently couched in psychoanalytic language. Bettelheim explained the students' rebellion in terms of their over-permissive liberal middle-class childhoods and Lewis Feuer argued that the combined lack of parental guidance and the normal discipline of work left the students free to direct their energies to destructive generational conflict (1969). Seymour Martin Lipset's analysis in *Encounter* and elsewhere (Lipset 1967; Lipset 1972; Lipset and Raab 1971) was more political but also had a psychoanalytic dimension. He categorised the New Left as a 'monistic' movement characterised by 'populism, simplism, and moralism'.

The contrasting radical and liberal interpretations of the Movement reflect a decade of friction between the two groups. The radicals argued that the liberals were too willing to accept extremes of inequality in the United States and were insufficiently critical or even supportive of American foreign policy whilst the liberals argued that the radicals failed to understand the importance of civil liberties and of working within the law in a democracy. Any contemporary or future radical revival should consider both these perspectives.

Mannhiem's theory of generations provides a relatively objective framework for synthesising aspects of the above comments (1952a). I have already argued that the radical students formed, in his terms, a generational unit and, given the spread of the Movement well beyond the campuses that an incipient actual generation existed. Mannheim's emphasis on historical context can accommodate Flacks and Friedman analysis that certain students' were alienated from their circumstances but his model provides no particular insight into the direction the Movement later took. However, another of Mannheim's works, *Ideology and Utopia* (1952b) offers further potential for theorising the Movement including interpreting more sympathetically what Bell disparagingly refers to as 'romanticism' and which several other leading liberals clearly see as a collective psycho-behavioural problem. In *Ideology and Utopia* Mannheim distinguishes between ideology as concerned with group self-interest and utopia that realistically seeks a better society not only for the group that aspires to it but for others, particularly the oppressed. Crucially, Mannheim distinguished between attainable or realistic utopia and mere idealism remote from the possible. It is arguable that the radicals were realistically utopian in their goals if not in the methods that some employed. This is the view that Herbert Marcuse, another German émigré tentatively adopted in the late 1960s (1968b; 1969c) and to that extent his work is complementary to the perspective I have extrapolated from Mannheim.

More than any other thinker, Marcuse popularised the idea that material conditions of substantial and rising affluence in the United States made utopianism 'realistic' (1968; 1969a). Despite this, most of his writings are pessimistic about the possibility of what he conceived of as a genuinely liberated society in the United States because the psychological and cultural conditions were lacking (see especially, *One Dimensional Man*, 1968). He argued that a 'one dimensional' culture of robotic mass consumption was the necessary complement to a system of production driven by a repressive work ethic, competition and the accumulation of private wealth. However, he considered that student radicalism reflected a genuine potential for social liberation in material conditions that could sustain it and to that extent was realistically utopian (1969b; 1969c).

In the light of Mannheim and Marcuse's perspectives, the 'romanticism' and idealism of students takes on a realistically transcendent aspect. Had it been possible for the radicals' ideals to be put into practice they would have transformed American society, including the world of work. If leading liberals had acknowledged this potential and lent their experience towards its realisation matters might have developed differently. Admittedly this became less easy as the actions of some in the Movement appeared to justify their worse fears.

The Achievements of the Movement

Two problems stand out in assessing the impact of nineteen sixties radicalism. First, the radical sixties has become a deeply symbolic decade, demonised by some on the right and seen as an iconic reference point by many on the left. Among such commitment dispassionate interpretation is difficult. Second, as I have argued, the radical sixties were a part of a wider if milder movement of liberalisation both politically and personally and it is not easy to demonstrate the relative extent of its contribution.

In the broadest context, then, a major achievement of the Movement was to extend the boundaries of personal and cultural freedom and engagement and in so doing put down markers for the future. The title of Jeffrey Weeks' *The World We Have Won: the Remaking of Intimate and Erotic Life* (2007) refers to a pervasive shift in British society towards greater personal freedom that transcended any one group or movement. This was also the case in the United States but I would stress that sixties radicalism provided a particular cutting edge to processes of liberalisation, individuation and democratisation, including in personal life. Crucially, however, the Movement also attempted to achieve these developments in a collective way. In its distinctive emphasis on personal and cultural liberation, it was the first new social movement of the left and as such remains an inspiration and source of ideas for later social movements.

A second and related achievement of sixties radicalism was in helping to put minority rights firmly on the national and international agenda. Again, the extent of this contribution is difficult to establish given that the various rights movements had some roots distinct from sixties radicalism. However, the radicalism of the nineteen sixties greatly contributed to the momentum of rights movements and so helped to shape society in the later part of the twentieth century. Several former activists I interviewed on both sides of the Atlantic spoke positively about the extension of the rights movements to the global level although others on the left regard human rights as ideological window-dressing for liberal capitalist hegemony.

The struggle for racial equality and freedom in the United States long preceded the civil rights movement of the late 1950s and early 1960s but the involvement of students mainly from north eastern and western states during this period gave impetus to it. The student sit-ins and the brutal way they were sometimes dealt with compelled a public and eventually a political response to racism and repression in the South. Despite setbacks there since has been some momentum towards greater equality of opportunity between the races in the

United States. In particular the association of the Democratic Party with the civil rights movement has resulted in the greater representation of black people in public life. However, whether for reasons of class or racial discrimination or a convergence of the two, black people as a whole remain on most measures significantly poorer and more disadvantaged than white people.

The Movement accelerated the progress of the Women's Liberation movement albeit in a more paradoxical and even contradictory way. In the early days of the Movement women tended to fulfil traditionally gendered roles within it – generally supporting male activists. However the absurdity of advocating equality and practising patriarchy became too obvious to ignore. Women increasingly took part in political organisation and action on an equal basis to men. Discussion of the ideological and practical aspects of gender equality featured prominently among the various political factions of the late 1960s. At the level of social practice the Movement offered some women the possibility of more egalitarian and democratic relationships. In some cases this took the form of creating exclusively female networks and power bases (see chapters 11 and 12). My interviews with sixties radicals indicates that networking has survived and is more characteristic of the women I interviewed than the men.

A third, more political legacy of the Movement was to provide a reference point for future social movements of the left. The word 'political' here almost requires inverted commas because, as I have emphasised throughout this chapter, the political and cultural were seen as ideologically and morally indissoluble, even if practice sometimes fell short of aspiration. The idea that radical lifestyle is intrinsic to social transformation has attracted many twenty-first century radicals. Although their focus has become even more global than that of the nineteen sixties radicals, there is evident continuity between the two eras. Thus, concern for the environment has become a movement to conserve the planet; a relatively uncomplicated rejection of American imperialism has been replaced by a pervasive anxiety about Western economic and military hegemony against which there is no obvious lever of change; the struggle for minority rights has become a project for human rights.

The Movement also left a legacy of strategic and tactical political experience to later social movements. This tends to eschew immediate involvement in party and pressure group politics (though there is some overlap) in favour of direct action and diverse attempts to engage the moral conscience of civil society. This grassroots approach complements the consistency that social movements tend to seek between values and action. The use of the worldwide web by contemporary social movement activists has added a new technical dimension to the 'horizontal' and participatory forms of communication favoured by nineteen sixties radicals but it is too early to say to what extent it might enhance democratic practices among activists.

Conclusion: An Unfinished Movement

'Verdicts' on the Movement varied greatly at the time and have continued to do so. If anything they have become more impressionistic and stereotypical, tending to blend the radical sixties with the merely fashionable sixties (see Introduction). This denigrates the serious issues sixties radicals raised and the idealism with which they pursued them.

My own critique of the Movement is an immanent one and in my view the transformation it began to articulate and represent is even more urgently needed. However, necessity rather than desire is again the main driving force. The threat of environmental disaster is cumulative and there is a renewed awareness of the dangers inherent in the proliferation of nuclear weapons. Globally, absolute poverty may have decreased but inequality between the extremes has increased and in the global media 'goldfish bowl' is even more visible. If these matters are to be effectively addressed an even more fundamental change may be required than attempted by the radicals of the 1960s They focused on their own cultural revolution, many believing it would inexorably spread. When it did not, some over-reacted variously turning to violent revolution, cultural escapism, and religious cultism. None of these 'strategies' had the remotest chance of radically changing liberal capitalism. Today the complexity and interconnectedness of globalised liberal capitalism requires comparably sophisticated analysis and strategic response. The apparent reluctance of some leading financial and commercial capitalists to change their behaviour following the crisis of 2008–09 indicates that they are unlikely to do so unless legally coerced. This is unlikely to happen on a sufficient scale unless the democratic majority can be persuaded to ensure that 'the system' including now, the planet, is run in the public interest. To achieve this the current generation of youthful radicals will not only need to avoid the pitfalls of their predecessors but successfully negotiate the dangerous path from protest to power whilst retaining their ideals.

References

Abrams, M. 1959. *The Teenage Consumer*. London Press Exchange Papers: No. 5.

Bell, D. 1973. *The Coming of Post-Industrial Society: A Venture in Social Forecasting*. London: Heinemann.

────── 1988 (1960). *The End of Ideology: On the Exhaustion of Political Ideas in the Fifties*. Cambridge: Harvard University Press.

Bennet, A. 1999. Subcultures or Neo-tribes? Rethinking the Relationship between Youth, Style and Musical Taste. *Sociology*, 33, 3: 599–617.

Bettelheim, B. 1969. Obsolete Youth: Towards a Psychograph of Adolescent Rebellion. *Encounter*, vol. XXIII (September): 29–42.

Brown, M. ed., 1969. *The Politics and Anti-Politics of the Young*. Beverley Hills: Glencoe Press.

Burck, C. 1969. 'The Movement': Freeform Revolutionaries. In : *Youth in Turmoil: Adapted from a Special Issue of Fortune.* New York: Time Incorporated.

Calvert, G. and Nieman, C. 1971. *A Disrupted History: The New Left and the New Capitalism.* New York: Random House.

Collier, P. and Horowitz, D. 1996. *Destructive Generation: Second Thoughts About the 60s.* London: Free Press Paperbacks.

DeGroot, G. 2008. *The Sixties Unplugged.* London: Pan Macmillan.

Feuer, Lewis. S. 1969. *The Conflict of Generations: The Character and Significance of Student Movements.* London: Heinemann.

Flacks, R. 1970. Social and Cultural Meaning of Student Revolt: Some Informal Comparative Observations. *Social Problems*, 17, 3: 340–57.

Friedman, S. R. 1973. Perspectives on the American Student Movement. *Social Problems*, 20, 3: 283–99.

Giddens, A. 1998. *The Third Way: The Renewal of Social Democracy.* Cambridge: Polity.

Haber, R. 1969. From Protest to Radicalism: An Appraisal of the Student Movement (1960). In: M. Brown ed., *The Politics and Anti-Politics of the Young.* California: Glencoe Press: 25–36.

Hampden-Turner, C. 1971. *Radical Man: The Process of Psycho-social Development.* London: Anchor Books.

Hebdige, D. 1979. *Subculture: The Meaning of Style.* London: Methuen.

Hoggart, R. 1958. *The Uses of Literacy.* Harmondsworth. Penguin.

Horowitz, I. ed., 1967. *Power Politics and People: The Collected Essays of Charles Wright Mills.* Oxford: Oxford University Press.

Jameson, F. 1984. Periodizing the 60s. *In*: S, Sayres, A. Stephanson, S. Aronowitz, and F. Jameson eds., *The 60s Without Apology.* Minneapolis: The University of Minnesota Press: 178–209.

Jacobs, P. and Landau, S. eds., 1966. *The New Radicals.* Harmondsworth: Penguin Books.

Keniston, K. 1971. *Youth and Dissent: The Rise of a New Opposition.* New York: Harcourt, Brace Javonovich, Inc.

Kesey, K. 1970. 'An Open Letter to Timothy Leary'. *Rolling Stone*, November 12, 1970: 33.

Liebert, R. 1971. *Radical and Militant Youth: A Psychoanalytic Enquiry.* New York: Praeger.

Lipset, S. M. ed., 1967. *Student Politics.* New York: Basic Books.

Lipset, S. M. and Raab, E. 1971. *The Politics of Unreason: Right-wing Political Extremism in the United States.* London: Heinneman.

Lipset, S. M. 1972. Ideology and No End: The Controversy 'Till Now' in Encounter, vol. XXXIX (December): 17–22.

Lynd, S. 1971. Prospects for the New Left. *Liberation*. 15, 10: 13–33.

Mannheim, K. 1952a, The Problems of Generations. In *Essays on the Sociology of Knowledge.* London: Routledge and Kegan Paul.

Mannheim, K. 1952b. *Ideology and Utopia: An Introduction to the Sociology of Knowledge.* London: Routledge and Kegan Paul.

Marcuse, H. 1968 (1964). *One Dimensional Man.* London: Sphere Books.

―――― 1969a (1955). *Eros and Civilisation.* London: Sphere Books.

―――― 1969b. *Essay on Liberation.* Boston: Beacon Press.

―――― 1969c. Postscript 1968. In: Wolff, R. P., Moore, Jnr. B. and Marcuse, *A Critique of Pure Tolerance.* Boston: Beacon Press.

Marwick, A. 2003. *British Society Since 1945.* 4th ed. London: Penguin Books.

Mills, C.W. 1956. *The Power Elite.* Oxford University Press.

―――― 1958. *The Causes of World War Three.* New York: Ballantine Books.

———— 1960. *Listen Yankee: The Revolution in Cuba*. New York: Ballantine Books.
———— 1970 (1959). *The Sociological Imagination*. Harmondsworth: Penguin.
———— 1967 (1962). Letter to the New Left. *In:* I. Horowitz ed. *Power, Politics and People: The Collected Essays of C. Wright Mills*. Oxford: Oxford University Press: 247–259.
Moody, K. 1966. Can the Poor be Organised? In: Cohen, M. and Hale, D. eds., *The New Student Left*. Boston: Beacon Press: 153–9.
Muggleton, D. 2000. *Inside Subculture: The Postmodern Meaning of Style*. Oxford: Berg.
Muggleton, D. and Weinzierl, R. eds., 2004. *The Post-Subcultures Reader*. Oxford: Berg.
Nisbet, R. 1970. Who Killed the Student Revolution? *Encounter* vol. XX1 (February): 10–18.
O'Donnell, M. 2008. Nineteen-Sixties Radicalism and Its Critics: Radical Utopians, Liberal Realists and Postmodern Sceptics. *Psychoanalysis, Culture and Society* 13: 240–60.
———— 2010, forthcoming. Generation and Utopia: Using Mannheim's Concepts to Understand Nineteen Sixties Radicalism. *Young*.
Pilcher, J. 1994. Mannheim's Sociology of Generations: An Undervalued Legacy. *British Journal of Sociology* vol. 45: 481–95.
Reich, C, A. 1970. *The Greening of America*. London: Allen Lane, The Penguin Press.
Riesman, D., Glazer, N. and Denney, R. 1969 (1961). *The Lonely Crowd: A Study of the Changing American Character*, New Haven: Yale University Press.
Roszac, T. 1968. *The Makings of the Counter-Culture: Reflections on the Technocratic Society and Its Youthful Opposition*. New York: Doubleday.
Savio, M. 1968. An End to History. *In*: M. Brown. ed., *The Politics and Anti-Politics of the Young*. California: Glencoe Press: 32–36.
Sayres, S., Stephanson, A., Aronowitz, S., and Jameson, F. eds., 1984. *The 60s Without Apology*. Minneapolis: University of Minnesota Press.
Seligman, D. 1969. A Special Kind of Rebellion. *In: Youth in Turmoil: A Special Issue of Fortune*. New York: Time Incorporated.
Shils, E. 1969. Plenitude and Scarcity. *Encounter* vol. XX111 (May): 37–57.
Spence, D. 1969. Berkeley: What It Demonstrates (1965). *In:* M. Brown, ed., *The Politics and Anti-Politics of the Young*. London: Glencoe Press: 36–42.
Various Authors. 1967 (1962). The Port Huron Statement. *In*: P. Jacobs and S. Landau, eds., *The New Radicals*. Harmondsworth: Penguin Books: 154–167.
Various Authors. 1969. *Youth in Turmoil: Adapted from a Special Issue of Fortune*, New York: Time Incorporated.
Weeks, J. 2007. *The World We Have Won: The Remaking of Erotic and Intimate Life*. Oxford: Routledge.
Zinn, H. 1968. A Comparison of the Militant Left of the Thirties and Sixties. *In*: M. J. Frisch ed., *The Thirties*. Northern Illinois University Press: 34–52.

Chapter 7

STUDENTS, ARTISTS AND THE ICA: THE REVOLUTION WITHIN

Ben Cranfield

1968: Writing and Event

As the highpoint of sixties radicalism, 1968 was a year of action. This was certainly true for London's Institute of Contemporary Arts which moved that year from its small premises in Dover Street to its current grander location on the Mall. However, Roland Barthes comments that, 'every national shock produces a sudden flowering of written commentary' (1968, 149) and 1968 was also a year of prolific written documentation. The immediacy of 1968's historicization not only reveals its importance, but also its compromises and failures, as writers struggled to make sense of its disparate aims and ideological absences. America may have had some of the most famous chroniclers of that generation in the form of Susan Sontag, Norman Mailer and Paul Goodman (Sayres 1984, 217–219), but the UK also had its own acute observers such as Jeff Nuttall (1968), Australian born Richard Neville (1971) and Michael Kustow (1975). The confusion and frustration, as well as excitement, felt in these writers' voices may well have been a consequence of the newness of many of the movements that comprised the late 1960s.

Sayres sees Norman Mailer's alienation as stemming from his being left outside by 'women writers, blacks, gays, third world authors [who] presumed to speak for themselves about struggles he was barely privy to' (Sayres 1984, 218–219). However, in Britain in 1968, these movements were very much still emergent (although, far from non-existent, as attested by the activities of Anti-University (Elzy 1969) and Birmingham's Centre for Cultural Studies under the new direction of Stuart Hall). For example, Lisa Tickner identifies that, despite the presence of many female participants in the Hornsey College of Art student sit-in of that year, gender issues were not apparent, due to the fact that 'this was the nascent moment of 'second wave' feminism' (Tickner 2008, 93).

In British educational and cultural institutions, the initial battles were not those of the New Left, but were waged against a perceived hierarchical inertia, such as Perry Anderson diagnosed within the British intellectual establishment (Anderson 1968; and see also Jones, chapter 1 in this volume) and Tom Nairn identified at Hornsey College of Art (Nairn 1968). The ICA continued to battle against this inertia in its new larger premises, as it had done since its inception in 1947. However, its in-house magazine produced throughout 1968 reflected the broader narratives and dramas of that year as well as more parochial concerns.

Undoubtedly, the manner of 1968's instant historicization was also a consequence of the omnipotent witness of the period, television, and of the possibilities it had opened up for instant reflexivity. The conceptual and actual development of 'mass' television represents an important post-war development which by the 1960s was introducing new ways of relating to the world via new cultural forms (Williams 1974, 44–74). The spread of television, far from stemming the tide of other media, seemed to be accompanied by a swelling in radical broadsides, pamphlets and texts, cultural manuals, biographies and methodological declarations which proliferated during the period, along with amateur film and documentary (Nelson 1989; Barthes 1968, 149). Furthermore, the development of satellite technologies set expectations of a new standard in communication speed and distribution (Williams 1974, 138; Kurlansky 2004, xvii). As if in response to this, cheap gestetner reproduction and lino cuts proliferated too – speed, costs and the deluge of media demanding a return to crude, homemade iconography (Tickner 2008, 32, iii–iv); this was the dynamic of Marshall McLuhan's 'hot' and 'cold' media (McLuhan 1964, 22–32).

In reference to the suggested duality of 1968 as an historical moment and textual manifestation, this chapter considers two narratives which were the fallout of that most uncertain of years, in order to suggest the particularity and complexity of the, often neglected, British context and its avant-garde cultural institutions. The first is *The Hornsey Affair* (THA) (Students and Staff of Hornsey College of Art [HSS] 1969), the book written by the students and staff of the Hornsey College of Art following their six-week protest sit-in in the summer of 1968. The sit-in, originally sparked by a furore over the freezing of student union funds, soon turned into a major discussion about the entire future of art and design education (HSS 1969, 31). The second text is *TANK* (1975), Michael Kustow's 'autobiographical fiction' of his two and a half years as the ICA's director between 1968 and 1970. The ICA and Kustow were closely linked with the events at Hornsey: hosting *Hornsey Strikes Again*, an exhibition put on by the sit-in students and staff in July 1968 (ICA Bulletin July 1968; HSS 1969, 171), publishing documents from the sit-in in the *ICA Magazine* (July 1968) and staging a conference on the future of art education in 1973 entitled *After Hornsey* (Warren-Piper 1973). The ICA and Hornsey represent the progressive, but licensed face of experimental art and educational practice in Britain in 1968: Hornsey had a reputation for experimental excellence which preceded it (Tickner 2008, 16–17, 22–23), whilst the ICA, which had been one of the only avant-garde institutional voices in post-war Britain, was given a further license with the granting by the state of a long lease on larger premises, just metres from Buckingham Palace. The texts discussed here are examples of specific ways in which 1968 was digested in institutional and personal narratives. They resonate with the wider confluence of historic events which are understood to constitute the significant core of 1968 – student sit-ins, public protests and prolific artistic production. They are consistent with Mark Kurlansky's description of the activities of 1968 as broadly 'anti-authoritarian' and reflect his observation that 'ideologies were seldom clear' (Kurlansky 2004, xv).

Equally, *THA* and *TANK* demonstrate the typical manifestation of 1968 as posters, collage and sound-bite. However, as well as being shadows of 1968 as an historic generality, they reveal complexities and particularities that demand an understanding of more specific contexts and discourses. The ICA, as a locus for debates about changes in cultural climate in post-war Britain, will be used here to locate the activities discussed within such a specific context. The post-war role of the ICA, 'to encourage unity among all the arts, and to consider them in relation to contemporary life' (Gregory 1947), created a space in which the arts could examine themselves in relation to each other and in relation to changes in society, most notably in media and technology. Themes central to the discussions and programme of the ICA in its first twenty years can be seen to come problematically together in *THA* and *TANK* – the role of the arts in society and with each other, the relationship between art and politics, and the future of the arts and education in relation to technological change.

THA and *TANK* present two divergent, but related positions on radicality, protest and art in this period. Hornsey represents a possible future caught between technocracy and democratic participation, whereas Kustow's text reflects a more traditional lineage of an academically situated Romantic past inspired by Blake and Apollinaire, whilst simultaneously foreshadowing the radical performance practices of the 1970s and 1980s. It is to be argued here that the drama of 1968 is set in both arenas (Hornsey and the ICA) by a dialectic between an interest in technology, on one hand, and the desire for a 'refusal' predicated on 'liveness' and participation, on the other. By doing so, it is possible to explore these manifestations of 1968 as part of, but particular within, the general flow of that tumultuous year. The romantic idiom is often seen as extended into the 60s (Martin 1981, 80–84; Seago 1995, 12–17); this chapter aims to explore how this purported extension may be re-thought in terms of dialectical relationships with the languages and devices of media, technology and technocracy. Such a transformation of terms allows for a view of competing radical visions within the same societal moment, without negating a continuing relationship with hegemonic structures of consumption and production.

Towards 1968: Negotiating Change in Post-War Society at the ICA

1968 was exemplary of McLuhan's global shrinkage, where 'distant events of the day were immediate' (Kurlansky 2004, xvii). However, well before the events of 1968 realized the political potentialities of this shrinkage, the ICA had been contemplating such shifts in technology, media and society since its very inception. For example, in 1950 it hosted a discussion on the impact of television and from 1955 it staged a series of discussions and talks on communication media. Whilst the former was part of the ICA's early role in mediating changes in British cultural life, the latter series was due to the technological interests of the ICA-born, though frequently dissenting, Independent Group (IG). The IG, which comprised critics, artists, architects and musicians (many of whom were educators in Britain's art and architecture schools) with a broad and voracious interest in all aspects of contemporary culture, met in the ICA club room from 1952–1955, although different collaborations amongst members continued throughout the fifties.

Lawrence Alloway, ICA assistant director 1955–1960 and Independent Group member, provided the rhetoric for the group which connected it with the expansion of mass media (Alloway 1959). For Alloway, this connection was also a class based and educational issue: 'when we (that was the IG) might have gone to university and become predisposed to high culture, we didn't, so we were left free to keep our relish of the mass media' (Alloway quoted by Kalina 2006, 11). This engagement with mass media was one of the crucial parts of the IG's practice, leading to their later description as 'The Fathers of Pop' (Alloway 1990, 50). Beyond an interest in the popular image, members of the IG also put on exhibitions at the ICA that demonstrated a more particular concern with the scientific and technological representation of the world. In 1951, future IG member Richard Hamilton designed an exhibition incorporating biological images of human, animal and plant cells and structures and abstract drawings of pattern and developmental form. This installation, drawing comparison between organic and artistic development, was entitled *Growth and Form* (ICA 1951) and was accompanied by a symposium, *Aspects of Form*. Both the exhibition and the symposium demonstrated the impact of scientifically and technologically produced images on artistic production and a strong interest at the ICA in the relationship of artistic experimental practice to scientific and technological experiment, innovation and discovery. This relationship was further explored in Nigel Henderson and Alison and Peter Smithson's *Parallel of Life and Art* (ICA 1953) and Hamilton's 1955 ICA exhibition, *Man Machine and Motion*.

A number of years after the final IG meeting, former member John McHale produced an important essay on technological change and art, *The Plastic Parthenon* (1961). McHale, reflecting on the huge shifts that had taken place in post-war industrial culture, crucially identified the climate within which the work of the 'Fathers of Pop' had been formed. He suggested that:

> As the apparatus of cultural diffusion becomes increasingly technological, its 'products' became less viewable as discrete, individual events, but rather more as related elements in a continuous contextual flow, i.e., the book-novel as compared to TV. The artwork, as, for example, in Rauschenberg-type 'Combines', moves towards a continuous format, juxtaposing 'still' images with live radio and TV sets in the same piece, which characteristically spill out of the frame into the general environment (McHale 1961: 1952)

The Independent Group had attempted to make sense of this 'continual contextual flow' that Alloway had famously named the 'Long Front of Culture,' (Alloway 1959) by making exhibitions into installation experiences and collaged tableaux (Massey 1995).

The interest at the ICA and amongst the IG in technological change was accompanied by discussion about the future of arts education. Indeed, during the post-war period British arts education was a topic of constant debate and underwent significant alteration. In 1956, at the Society for Education through Art (SEA) conference, the proponents of an emerging arts education based on the principles of basic design, namely Harry Thurbon, Tom Hudson and Maurice de Sausmerez, challenged what Richard Yeomans calls the dominant values of 'intuition and expression' which were the 'bedrock of much liberal art educational thinking' (Yeomans 2005, 195). In Yeoman's account of the conference, the attack mounted against the establishment was formed from two key principles: firstly, the belief that 'art should address the modern world of science and technology' and secondly, that the art student should be orientated towards a more realistic professional training (Yeomans 2005, 195). Thurbon's suggested reforms were a direct attempt to shatter the illusion of the 'wooliness of thought which sustains the romantic isolation of the artist' (Lynton 1992, 172).

In 1959, Victor Pasmore, Richard Hamilton and Tom Hudson held a discussion at the ICA, entitled *The Developing Process*. David Thistlewood describes this process as one in which the single point can move from the two-dimensional artwork into the architectural realm and where intellect and intuition can work together to create work that relates to the realities of late industrial society (Thistlewood 1981, 8). The 'developing process' used the principles of basic design which Hamilton had taken from the Bauhaus model and applied to the creation of his innovative foundation degree at Newcastle. Art Education was, therefore, to be pulled away from a romantic model of expression towards an intellectual process that engaged with the technological realities of the post-war world.

In 1959, following the lead of the SEA conference, the National Advisory Committee on Art Education was set up under William Coldstream. The Committee recommended the replacement of the National Diploma with the Diploma in Art and Design (Dip AD). The arrival of the Dip AD meant that students had to come away from the art college with more than just a development of their skills in painting, drawing and sculpture. In addition they were supposed to have a broad educational grounding provided by 'general studies.' Over the next few years, via the Summerson Committee, set up in 1961, and the Robbins report of 1963, the art colleges underwent a process of professionalisation, with many being closed due to their failure to meet the new criteria, and, at the same time, a process of ostracism, with the remaining colleges failing to secure university status (the notable exception being the Royal College of Art). The art colleges fared badly in comparison to the Colleges of Advanced Technology, ten of which had university status conferred upon them that year (MacDonald 1970, 357). The art colleges overall had undergone a strange transformation in the post-war period: firstly, with their democratisation due to the influx of ex-service men, secondly, with their reformation from the romantic tradition via the Dip AD and finally, through a process of closure and belittlement.

In a 1966 issue of *Studio International*, three key figures from the ICA's first twenty years, its president, Herbert Read, Richard Hamilton and frequent ICA panel member, Misha Black, offered their views regarding the state of art education in an interview with Victor Willing. In Hamilton's opinion, the answer to the question posed by the article 'What Kind of Art Education?' was to create an environment 'producing people with good minds, who are capable of seeing society as a whole, trained to think constructively though not necessarily productively'(Willing 1966, 132). In sympathy with Hamilton's desire for social consciousness, Misha Black envisaged something along the lines of a school of 'human ecology' where 'architecture, landscape architecture, industrial design, and town planning' were 'natural bedfellows' (Willing 1966, 134). Herbert Read went even further, suggesting that the only thing to do with the art schools was to abolish them – proposing instead a multi-disciplinary school like the ground-breaking Black Mountain College (Willing 1966, 136), which had fostered experimental collaborations between key figures including Joseph Albers, Buckminster Fuller, Merce Cunningham, Robert Rauschenberg and John Cage, from the mid-1930s to the late-1950s.

By the mid 1960s the ICA had fostered a generation of thinkers, artists and educators in Britain who were disseminating a new interdisciplinary and developmental attitude towards art, education and design throughout the UK. In relation to the changing technological society discussed and debated at the ICA, the Dip AD had been created and with it its creators had, unintentionally, sown a radical seed at the heart of the art colleges in the form of the progressive logic of basic design and the challenge to the old values of aesthetic training through the inclusion of 'general studies' and a broader outlook. However, they failed to follow through with the logic of the reforms to realise truly radical solutions such as those suggested by Hamilton, Read and Black. It was this failure that made the Art Colleges ripe for protest.

The Hornsey Affair: Art Students and Technological Change

1968 is often seen as a year of student radicalisation and protest – where a previously apathetic body of young people came together nationally and internationally in a Marcusian 'Great Refusal' of the violence and injustice of the dominant 'system' (Cockburn 1969, 7). Britain was not without its student protests, with notable instances at LSE, Birmingham, Manchester, Leeds, Liverpool, Bristol, Keele, and Leicester (Thomas 2002, 278). The most prominent of these was, arguably, the LSE sit-in, where in June 1968 ten prominent New Left leaders were invited to take part in a debate entitled 'Students in Revolt' (Kurlansky 2004, 353). If, as a whole, student protest in Britain has been neglected as the poor cousin of protest elsewhere (Thomas 2002, 277), then the art school protests, most notably at Hornsey and Guildford, have been, until recently (Tickner 2008), particularly ignored. In fact, Hornsey and Guilford represent one of the most consistent and sustained attempts to reform not only the hierarchical environment of higher education, but also its curriculum; reflected in their establishment of a national movement, the Movement for the Rethinking of Art and Design Education, which held a major conference at the Roundhouse in London in July 1968 (Nairn and Singh-Sandu 1969, 113–114).

At Hornsey Art College in 1968, the disagreement over student union funds quickly escalated into a full scale sit-in. A year later, the rebelling students and staff produced *The Hornsey Affair* (THA), a Penguin Education Special detailing the proposals, narratives and views of the sit-in. Whilst *THA* is clearly a text of 1968, reflecting a desire for protest, democratic control and Marcusian 'refusal', it also makes evident its routes in the specific contradictions inherent in the partial reformation of the art colleges through the Dip AD (Tickner 2008, 14). Whilst, as Tickner comments, the arrival of 'general studies' can be seen to have radicalised the college (Tickner 2008, 72–73) with its imposition of left-wing tutors and new theories, the contrast between this suggested interdisciplinary freedom and the reality of the college system caused much consternation:

> But just how paper-thin were authority's gestures of deference towards 'culture' and 'stimulus' and a 'broader outlook' was quickly revealed in the situation which then developed. They soon made it very clear that culture is all right in its proper place, that stimuli are fine just as long as discipline is unaffected, and that the broader outlook is splendid when it is strictly confined to the College library. Otherwise, one is in trouble (HSS 1969, 211)

THA is an extraordinary piece of self-analysis. It is remarkable because it avoids creating a seamless narrative, through its use of multiple authors, only identified by initials, offering, instead, a de-centred and non-hierarchical historical account. The text was meant to be an extension of the 'revolution' and, as such, remains true to the democratic rhetoric and nature of the sit-in (HSS 1969, 117–118). In its opening statements and within the very manner of the project, we can see that the defiant wonder of the book is its ability to be non-violent even in its making of history, whilst, for perhaps the same reasons, we may see its potential futility. To what extent does it succeed in being revolutionary at all? Is it not simply a proposal for gentle reform, the natural fall-out of the Coldstream committee of 1959? If one is to examine the general findings of the documents which comprise pages 105–136 of *THA*, entitled 'the educational debate', it is possible to reassess *THA* not as a revolution but as a continuation and culmination of the educational debates of the 50s and early 60s and the dialectical confrontations with contemporary media and technology such as had been taking place at the immediate post-war ICA.

Document 11 outlined the 'basic demands' of the student's proposed education reforms – a result of many long meetings and open discussions. The main demands of the document focused around the elimination of the GCE entrance criteria, something they considered irrelevant to the required aptitudes of a potential art student. The paper also proposed the rejection of a 'linear' education path and the accompanying forms of traditional discipline and examination (HSS 1969, 117–118). The aims of Document 11 may seem almost embarrassingly modest. However, they broadly highlighted three crucial areas of change in contemporaneous British society: a) the democratization of higher education; b) a rejection of 'medieval' academic paths; and c) the rapid expansion of technology in fields of communication and image production (HSS 1969, 117–118, 130–131). Although the students appeared to reject the Coldstream measures and the attempt at professionalization through the Dip AD (MacDonald 1970, 355–360; Tickner 2008, 18–19), they wished their educational programme to have a relevance to the world at large. This is best seen in the students' proposal for the adoption of, what they term, the 'Network' approach to education. In document 70 the students explained further what was meant by the 'Network' system:

> The system will allow the students to acquire a range of skills and experience which they feel most suitable for their career. This range is in fact a number of ranges: a range of subjects (of course); a range from liberal design education to an intensive industrial one; a range from a craft to a production of education, and so on (HSS 1969, 119)

The 'Network' approach is intimately related to the perceived technological super advance of the 60s, from which the students stated clearly that they did not want to be excluded (HSS 1969, 130–131). Furthermore, the rationality of this method is posited in relation to new technologies and to media theorist Marshall McLuhan's concepts of technological interconnectedness. McLuhan was, in fact, one of the few external commentators to make it into the pages of THA. Quoted talking not about interconnected media, but about the need for a qualitative change in the technologies of the classroom, McLuhan advocated the teach-in as a method that would shift education 'from instruction, from imposing stencils, to discovery – to probing and exploration and to the recognition of the language of forms' (HSS 1969, 105). McLuhan's shift is remarkably similar to the change desired specifically in art education by the proponents of basic design, a change described by Yeomans as 'a distinct shift from technique-based courses, towards a more open-ended experimental approach which encouraged a critical attitude of mind' (Yeomans 2005, 209). Furthermore, the inclusion of McLuhan in *THA* suggests the relationship between new modes of pedagogy and new utopian technological configurations (McLuhan 1964).

The students used the sit-in to become fully engaged with the media of their zeitgeist: setting up a radio station and putting on film showings and experimental projections (Tickner 2008, 32). This use of home-made, ad-hoc technology was, however, in opposition to the idea of technology that had gripped the College until then, exemplified by Hornsey's pre-sit-in, flagship project of the electric car (discussed during post screening panel discussion of *The Hornsey Film*, Barbican, May 12th 2008). The documents of the sit-in themselves opted for technological languages of choice and hybridity, rather than those of industrial super-advance. This was not one giant leap for mankind, but the possibility of multiple leaps in multiple directions for any number of people. The 'Network' approach adopted the languages of general systems theory to construct new configurations of social and technological organisation and imagination.

By reconsidering their practice in relation to changes in technology and society at large, the rebelling students were not just opposing authority, but were becoming Hamilton's ideal of an art and design student capable of constructive and socially relevant thinking (Willing 1966, 132). One author of *THA* claimed that 'the Hornsey sit-in was the profoundest educative experience for those who participated, teaching them more about themselves, their relationships and their work than the normal four or five years of higher semi-education' (HSS 1969, 9). What are we led to understand constituted this profundity? What were the outcomes of this educative experience? Included among the student's creative 'artistic' outputs during the sit-in were:

> clothes for spastic children; the double page spread we had in International Times; utilization of waste products; fabric packaging; children's multiple-component play kits; an analysis of our canteen requirements; redesign of level crossings; the letterhead for the Association; industrial ceramics into sculpture for buildings; modular W.C.s for trains; mass-production sculpture; audio visual aids for sixth formers, telling them about art colleges; a high capacity water pump; applications of colour distortion through light projection; and a feasibility study on converting the Alexandra Palace into an art college (HSS 1069, 55)

Does this list of projects suggest a moment akin to what Herbert Marcuse (1968, 185) declared as his 'utopia' at the *Congress for the Dialectics of Liberation* (Roundhouse 1967), a micro 'society as a work of art'? This certainly seems to be the implied reasoning of *THA*. The list of 'artworks' produced during the sit-in suggests that the manner of creation, the *very act of creation*, makes, both in concrete and nominal terms, the artwork and that, by engaging in a radical reformation of the Hornsey micro-society, *all* that the students succeeded in producing should be considered as artistic. By internalizing the supposedly unique function of the artist as an autonomous, radical figure, the art student was able to, perhaps falsely, syllogise that an act of autonomy, or radical subversion, must therefore *be* an artwork. In a different register, one could also read *THA*'s list of profound successes as a claim for the utility and productivity of the art student.

The crowning glory of the sit-in was arguably the canteen. One THA chronicler writes:

> The canteen flourished. I had been very pessimistic about its survival, but never have I been more surprised to find that things can exist without

planned organization. Never before had I experienced such communal awareness, each person taking individual responsibility (HSS 1969, 41)

The students took over the canteen early on in the sit-in, perhaps realising that as a place of sustenance and sociability it was crucial for the sit-in's durability. They attended to every aspect, from a reformation of its menu, to its redecoration. The radicality of the canteen as an artistic project lay in its politicization of the art college as an experience of living in the broadest sense. The reformulation of the experience of everyday life at Hornsey and its assimilation into the artistic life of the college had moved the discussion of the 'Long Front of Culture' beyond the pop-art representations of the Independent Group towards the radical implication of everyday experience. To wake up and experience the canteen as art was to enter a kind of bizarre Eden:

> As the birds began their busy day on the trees outside, one could sit and relax in the gleaming clean canteen listening to the early morning raga being played over the p.a. The canteen was the vibrating heart of the revolution (HSS 1969, 41)

The canteen is described as place of ontogenetic rebirth, where the individual could be recreated as an organism related to the communal without the instruction of slavish rules and without the imposition of competitive desire. However, the characterisation of the canteen as an artwork is more than just an imaginative leap. In the exhibition held by the rebelling members of the college at the ICA in July 1968, *Hornsey Strikes Again*, the canteen formed the 'Nirvana' of the exhibition, with visitors arriving at it, like an oasis, at the end of the dramatically recreated Dip AD 'nightmare'. The canteen as recreated installation was detached from the main frame of the full sit-in experience and offered to the gallery as a dramatisation of utopian potential and the politicisation of everyday life. The installation suggested how the debate about art education and the students' understanding of what might constitute an artwork had become conflated:

> A huge 'Diploma in Art and Design' in a gilt frame on a silver easel, surrounded by hundreds of coloured flashing lights, beckoned the visitor into the first section – the 'Dip A.D. Course' – where a dark, narrow labyrinth of corridors provided the right oppressive atmosphere. It contained an interview room, wooden authority-figures, a display of forms, and an art-history nightmare. When one pushed out of this, there was by contrast a large open area where information of all sorts could be obtained, and a miniature replica of the Hornsey student canteen where one could get coffee and watch a continuous multi-screen projection

about what had been going on in the college. After this was a debating room, where discussions were arranged in the evenings with outside speakers from the art and design fields (HSS 1969, 171)

What can be seen in the translation of the values of Hornsey 1968 as a series of documents for reform into the description of Hornsey 1968 as an art installation, is that art and debate have become inseparable, impossibly entwined. The artwork and its frame, its conceptual apparatus, are one. Furthermore, a discussion held in the right place and in the right way may also constitute an artwork. This notion of art as self-referential debate was central to the emergence of conceptual art projects such as the collaboration *Art and Language*, founded in 1968 (Archer 1997, 79–81). Indeed, within the remit of conceptual art *THA*, itself, could certainly be claimed to be an artwork. As well as understanding Hornsey as an artwork, the debates in *THA* also reveal, as did the work of Hans Haacke and the other proponents of what has been latterly termed 'institutional critique,' the *artwork as a work of society* (Rosenthal 1974). As well as using the artwork to consider meta debates of art and design education, Tickner notes that active sit-in student Prue Bramwell Davies developed social design projects, concerned with 'humanitarian or inclusive design' (Tickner 2008: 88–89). For the students involved in the sit-in it was clear that the notion of an artwork had been exploded and that their world abounded with possibilities. Whilst some of the broader issues of 1968 – namely Vietnam, state violence and institutional democratisation – were in evidence at Hornsey (Tickner 2008, 33), it was arguably this substantive change in the thinking around the meaning and purpose of art that represented Hornsey's particular 'revolution'.

TANK and the Media

THA presents a confusing narrative of hope and failure – with contradictory pieces on the purpose of the sit-in and its revolutionary potential, or lack thereof. The airing of multiple voices and positions was itself a radical thing: a thing typical and exemplary of 1968. When Michael Kustow chose to write his account of his time as Director of the ICA in 1968, he created the fictional persona of 'K' and narrated in the third person, saving the first person for passages of free-flowing italicised confession. Kustow's third person voice creates a distance from his own narrative which is compounded by the cut-up and fractured manner of the text. His narrative detachment, battling like *THA* between ego and history, was something which appeared to be increasingly popular or even necessary in the 60s. As Mark Kurlansky notes, chronicler of 1968 par excellence Norman Mailer, 'often referred to himself in third person singular' (2005, 43). Whilst this created in Mailer's writing a distance from his contemporaneous subjects, providing a space for often startling confessional revelations, 'K' seems to hint at the reason for his own bemused narrative detachment by commenting on the back-blast caused by the acceleration of communication media. As 'K' breathlessly explains, any 'camera worthy drama' could carry 'across the airways of continents like wildfire, generating a fall-out of imitation, rituals preformed by style-conscious young people in cities across the world' (Kustow 1975, 79). This sense of visual 'wild-fire' may be seen as the radically unpredictable underbelly of the 'consensual', if extensive, news debate that was prevalent on British television (Williams 1974, 50–51). Indeed, the effect of media on one's ability to know, to produce, to narrate is clearly of uppermost importance to Kustow.

In his preface to *TANK*, deceptively entitled 'Artist and Model', Kustow creates a scene borrowing heavily from Samuel Beckett's meditation on the essence and consequence of the moving image, *Film* (1965). At the end of *Film*, an ageing Buster Keaton confronts himself in a conflation of observer and observed. The comic actor's now artistically-conditioned, rather than technologically imposed, silence centres the action on the eyes, which show horror and surprise in the confrontation with self. Kustow mirrors this moment of technological collapse in the final words of his preface, when the artist and model view each other, he writes: 'I open my eyes and look into his eyes. His face is mine. His face is mine. The two men in the room are one' (Kustow 1975, 10). Like Beckett, Kustow seems to suggest that the technological capturing of self creates an often disturbing and potentially altering dislocation within narrative and identity.

As if in response to the media wild-fire of 1968, which Kustow observes with caution, and the danger of the fractured self, reflexively reunited with horror, in filmic representation (the condition of the media age), *TANK* details a criticality predicated on 'liveness' and 'presentness'. This 'liveness' may be understood to be posited against what Paul Edwards has called the 'closed worlds' of cold-war technological methods and metaphors (1997, 2–7) and what Jeff Nuttall called at the time *Bomb Culture* (1968). Nuttall himself founded a theatre group, *The People Show*, in 1966, proving that there was still hope for forms of artistic communication despite his diagnosis of a solipsistic tendency within the avant-garde of the late 60s (Nuttall 1968, 251) and the present threat of nuclear annihilation (Nuttall 1968, 142). Similarly, Kustow turned to the theatre to provide connection in the face of the supposed alienation of late modernity and his fear of artistic impotence (Kustow 1975, 13). Prior to taking his role as ICA Director, he had travelled Europe with a theatre company, returning to London to organise a large satirical performance in Trafalgar Square, in 1967, using giant puppets of political figures (Kustow 1968). In 1968, 'K' believes that theatre is 'still the emblem of real, tigerish art' (Kustow 1975, 153), and that certain pieces were 'so perfect, so powerful, so holy, that [they] had to be shielded from his paternal governors...' (Kustow 1975, 153).

Theatre was, then, for Kustow a response to the media saturation and technological violence of the late 1960s. In 1968 Kustow himself was caught up in the media wild-fire as his own arrival at the ICA was celebrated in print, television and radio, in marked difference to the muted collection of articles and letters which followed the founding of the Institute in 1947 (ICA Press 1947–1968). This was due in part to the ICA gaining larger premises in 1968, but it was equally a consequence of the arrival of an omnipotent media and faster technologies of reproduction and communication. By 1968, Kustow had taken Alloway's 'Long Front' and had begun to fight on the performative end.

1968 and Simultaneity: Drowning in the Devices

It seemed that Kustow, like the rebelling students of 1968, yearned for something more immediate and embodied than the installations of the IG or the witty synecdoche of pop-art collage. He embraced the raw and crude lines of the lino cuts used to make posters at the Sorbonne and Hornsey and the physicality of sit-ins, be-ins and happenings. This was not to say that the dialogue with technology had been abandoned; far from it, it had instead become more dialectically extreme in its internal polarisation. For example, a performance at the ICA by Carolee Schneemann, renamed in *TANK* as Rosalee, is described by Kustow as an act of 'simultaneity', with 'Rosalee' literally divesting herself of all technologies of acculturation as she rolled naked, whilst flanked by two large projections (Kustow 1975, 46–7). The projectors showed images which accompanied Schneemann's *Nude Action Lecture*. After the 'action', Schneemann's *Fuses* was shown (ICA Bulletin: June 1968) (Schneemann 1997). This is a film which used the materially present particularity of the medium, its scratches and blurs, to bring the embodiment of experience to the embodiment of technology. Schneemann later commented, 'I wanted to put into that materiality of film the energies of the body, so that the film itself dissolves and recombines and is transparent and dense' (Schneemann n.d. accessed 1st October 2009).

'Simultaneity' was not only, as Kustow observed, *the* buzz-word of 1968 (Kustow, 46–47), but it was also an apt description of the world as re-presented as news broadcast, especially in 1968- a conflation of footage into a simultaneous cultural event, rather than a collage of column inches. Simultaneity, which had been the technological holy grail of early talkies, implying technological seamlessness and illusion, was re-appropriated as full body experience, technological immediacy and a breaking open of taboos.

'K's own attempts at radicalism also pulled between a poverty of performance and new technologies, as much as between a romantic tradition (Blake especially) and modernist classicism; seen in references to modernist heroes in the *ICA Magazine* April–November 1968. The exhibition arena, for Kustow, had seemingly become an unproductive space – a space which struggled to be more than a museum exhibit. When producing a season on Apollinaire, 'K' handed the space over to Roland Penrose, the last bastion of Parisian modernism at the ICA, and Simon Weston Taylor, whilst 'K' went away with painter and poet of the Liverpool cultural renaissance Adrian Henri to write a multi-media theatre piece entitled *I Wonder* (Kustow 1975, 79). The play embraced William Burroughs-style cut-up text, on the one hand, and media sound bite on the other, as they attempted to weave a play entirely out of Apollinaire's own words. 'K's 'kaleidoscope' of a play used, 'every conceivable theatrical device…transformable cubist scenery, film and slide projections, inflatable plastic globes, masks, dummies, quick-change subterfuges, slapstick routines.' The result was something which 'was often almost drowned by the devices' (Kustow 1975, 83–84).

As if to repent for this lack of purity in his own art, Kustow invited Polish theatre director Jerzy Grotowski to present his 'Theatre Laboratory' at the ICA in 1969. Grotowski's treatise 'Towards a Poor Theatre' (1965), available to buy from the ICA book stall in 1969, called for a particular type of poverty-of-means which constituted a significant break with methods of technological advance. For Grotowski, greatly influenced by Stanislavski, the key question was how to re-engage with theatre as a particular space of production. He asked, in his treatise, 'What is the theatre? What is unique about it? What can it do that film and television cannot?' Out of these questions Grotowski found that, 'Two concrete conceptions crystallised: the poor theatre, and performance as an act of transgression' (Grotowski 1965, 19–18). Grotowski's method was, therefore, a 'via negativa – not a collection of skills but an eradication of blocks', crucially formulated against the particularity of film and television.

In seeming contradiction to Kustow's desire for theatrical liveness, Schneemann's naked performance and the 'poverty' of Grotowski's method, the most popular event at the ICA in 1968 was *Cybernetic Serendipity*. The landmark exhibition was ICA assistant director Jasia Reichardt's attempt to:

> show creative forms engendered by technology. To present an area of activity which manifests artists' involvement with science, and the scientists' involvement with the arts. To show the links between the random systems employed by artists, composers, and poets, and those involved in the use of cybernetic devices (*ICA Magazine* August 1968)

Reichardt was returning to the original project of the early ICA to help unite the 'two cultures' (Snow 1993) of science and the arts but within the framework of a new, cybernetic rather than biological, organicism. Reichardt was not only interested in computer art and cybernetic experiments, but also those projects which embraced an idea of the automated spontaneity of the technological system (Reichardt 1966, 164–165) – what Jack Burnham was to see as the vitalism of the cybernetic sculpture (Burnham 1968, 76). The computer, as a place of autonomous action offered something similar to Grotowski's stark poor theatre; it stripped away the pretences of spectacular creation and denuded the artist of his/her aspirations towards uniqueness as the product of personal expression. Reichardt's interest in computer art went beyond the particular aesthetics of the cybernetic and entered into the political and social possibilities of digital image production. She asserted that 'the computer, as Abraham Moles points out, is not only a tool for making serial pictures, or transforming an image, but is above all an instrument of democracy' (Reichardt 1971, 16). Furthermore, the use of technological systems offered the potential for democratic access and choice evident in Hornsey's 'Network' approach.

Kustow, however, does not mention *Cybernetic Serendipity* in his narrative of that year. The fact was that Kustow's use of technology was purely as theatrical device – the special-effects of media wild-fire and filmic experimentation. Whilst Kustow put the artist/performer centre stage in full-embodied rapture, Reichardt's exhibition showed her scepticism of the artist as the main torch bearer of future creative practice with 87 out of the 120 participants being non-artists (Reichardt 1971, 11). As ICA director, Kustow's main concern was not with radical democracy or changing the nature of creative practice, but with attempting to find that which was radical in its dramatic 'sharpness' (Kustow 1975, 54). In 1968, the rebelling Hornsey Art College students and staff appeared to offer something of the sharpness of the European passion for political action that 'K' had experienced in his travels in the early 1960s. However, despite the fact that Kustow gave the Hornsey rebels a chance to exhibit at the ICA, he commented that:

> with the art school rebels, however, [K] was struck by what he felt to be an eminently British tone of common sense, very different from the inebriating atmosphere of poetic insurrection in the Sorbonne (1975, 74)

In 1968 the ICA was pulled between poetic inebriation and the utopian consideration of technological futures.

Conclusion: Change, Democracy and Technology

Marcuse, in an interview piece entitled 'On Revolution', outlined what he saw as the potentially important refusal witnessed amongst the student and youth movements of 1968:

> This opposition is free from ideology or permeated with a deep distrust of all ideology (including socialist ideology); it is sexual, moral, intellectual and political rebellion all in one. In this sense it is total, directed against the system as a whole… (Marcuse 1969, 372)

Marcuse tempered his enthusiasm with the assertion that 'if it remains isolated it runs the risk of falling victim to inoculation and thus to the system itself' (Marcuse 1969, 372). Marcuse's warning was re-published in another Penguin Special of 1969: *Student Power: Problems, Diagnosis, Action*. Alexander Cockburn, in his introduction to the volume, wished to save the student protests from charges of inoculation and incoherence, claiming that, in capitulation: 'it does not mean, once the enemy has returned, that control was useless, or that the confrontation of the system on their own ground by students has been a vain thing' (Cockburn 1969, 13).

On the specific question of the British art college sit-ins, Tom Nairn and Jim Singh-Sandhu argued that, through 'active discussions and demands for radical reform' realised in the Movement for Rethinking Art and Design Education (MORADE), the apathy of the art school had been challenged with potentially lasting effect. Furthermore, they asserted that 'by its very nature, art and design education militates against the authoritarianism of the old teacher-student relationship' (Nairn and Singh-Sandhu 1969, 115). Despite this affirmation of the radical role of the art student, Nairn and Singh-Sandhu made a less palatable observation, that the prevalent tendency was either towards a traditionally romantic idea of the genius artist who simply needs to be left to do their thing and a contrary, but equally damaging, tendency towards a 'violent new careerism in these design-arts' (Nairn and Singh-Sandhu 1969, 106).

The Hornsey Affair was both resistant to the above dualism and representative of the dichotomies that these different ideas about the role of the artist produced. It was openly confused in its aims, wanting to revolutionize artistic practice by making it more technologically flexible and applicable to a commercial sphere and, at the same time, to exalt further the freedom of the artist by suggesting his/her unique position for criticality and organic development. These contradictions were not simply a problem of 1968, but were embedded in post-war British experimental artistic practice from the Independent Group onwards, where hegemonic technologies of reproduction, commercialisation and communication dialectically confronted a removed aestheticism of the pre-war artistic elite.

Despite evidence that Hornsey's 'refusal' of the system was not quite as total as Marcuse may have wished, a radicality did exist in the manifestations of the Hornsey sit-in; its films, book and exhibition and in the students' ability to challenge not only hierarchies of educational exclusivity, but tendencies towards technological particularisation by a persistent articulation of a democratically run and socially engaged art school. Their use of technological metaphors in systems of choice and social design and in their ad-hoc use of media from lino cuts to radio and film projections offered an alternative to more industrial forms of technological white heat. In so doing, the sit-in attempted to offer an alternative constructive space without what Andrew Feenberg describes as the usual 'retreat from the technical sphere into art, religion, or nature' (Feenberg 1996, 50).

THA demonstrates not that Hornsey created the art of the seventies, or new modes of art education in Britain, but that situations *such as* Hornsey, despite apparent failure with the collapse of the sit-in in the face of authority, produced texts of such an intensely democratic and reflective nature that art and reflection on the processes which constituted and conditioned art became radically conflated. Furthermore, *THA* is the kind of open-ended discursive site that allowed for technological, political and aesthetic concerns to relate without the polarisation that is perhaps felt between Grotowski's purest 'Poor Theatre' and Riechardt's *Cybernetic Serendipity*. The debates at the ICA of the post-war period can be seen to coalesce at Hornsey in 1968. Yet the ICA in 1968, as a space of artistic display and as a public interface, can be seen to be more concerned with performing the styles of radical transgression and experiment than with educational and political reform. As such, Hornsey arrived at the ICA as no more and no less than an artwork – an installation conveying a conceptual provocation framed by and contained by the gallery space.

These differences can be summarised by the romantic attitude of 'K' towards 1968 in *TANK* and the pragmatism of the reforms suggested in *THA*. The radicality of the former was licensed and tamed by the sanctioned space of the art centre and the moderation of the latter was conditioned by the political realities of the Art College's confrontation with local government. However, despite these differences, both texts demonstrate the major shifts that were occurring in thought and practice within Britain's more avant-grade cultural institutions in relation to the educational, social and technological change of the post-war period. This specificity prevents the events of 1968 (especially within arenas away from the main action centres of 1968, such as Prague, Paris and New York) being reduced to a general historic moment of antithetical behaviour, or its gestures being dismissed as acts of romantic individualism, as suggested by certain accounts of the period; most notably Martin (1981).

A film of the Hornsey sit-in was entitled *Our Live Experiment is Worth More than Three Thousand Textbooks* (Goldschmidt 1969). However, it is the textbook of *THA* which is perhaps the most remarkable legacy of the sit-in. Can we imagine Penguin publishing the collective views of an art school protest today? Similarly, could a director of a major cultural institution today adopt such a confessional and urgent style, as Kustow does in *TANK*? Hornsey and the ICA did not resolve the problems facing art and art education in third wave industrial society. Indeed, John A. Walker has noted how battles over productivity, utility, liberality, tolerance and democratic participation continued at British Arts Schools right through the 1970s (Walker 2002). However, Walker also notes that the post-68 art schools had fostered a new conceptualism which 'questioned the very concept of art and its embodiment in physical objects such as paintings and sculptures addressed to the senses of sight and touch' (Walker 2002, 231). If the events of 1968 at Hornsey and the post-war activities of the ICA had not been solely responsible for creating this revolution within the thinking of the artist and the art student, then they were certainly central to its development.

The dramatic techniques of narrative fracturing and detachment, as if reeling from a bomb blast, employed in both books discussed here, reveal how the texts and events of 1968 cannot be separated – just as much as one cannot separate action and contemplation. As Paul Ricoeur notes of all significant action, in its moment of utterance (occurrence) it becomes 'text'. As 'text' the 'event' enters a world of symbolic order and myth (Ricoeur 1973, 91–117). It is this myth that we need to reanimate in the present in order to recapture the hunger for change inherent in these, at times flawed, historically particular actions.

References

Alloway, L. 1959. The Long Front of Culture. *Cambridge Opinion* 17: 24–6.
⸺ 2006 (1956). The Arts and Mass Media. In: Kalina R. ed., *Lawrence Alloway: Imagining the Present: Context, Content and the role of the Critic*. London and New York: Routledge: 55–59.
⸺ 1990. The Aesthetics of Plenty. In: Robbins, D. ed., *The Independent Group: Postwar Britain and the Aesthetics of Plenty*. Cambridge, Mass. and London: MIT Press: 49–53.
Anderson, P. 1968. Components of the National Culture. *New Left Review* 50: 3–58.
Archer, M. (1997). *Art Since 1960*. London: Thames and Hudson.
Barthes, R. 1986 (1968). Writing the Event. In: Barthes, R. *The Rustle of Language*. trans. Richard Howard. Oxford: Basil Blackwell: 149–154.
Beckett, S. 1965. *Film*, Dir. Alan Schneider.

Burnham, J. 1968. *Beyond Modern Sculpture*. London: Allen Lane and Penguin Book Press.
Cockburn, A. 1969. Introduction. In: Cockburn, A. and Blackburn, R. eds., *Student Power: Problems Diagnosis, Action*. Harmondsworth: Penguin: 7–21.
Edwards, P. N. 1997. *The Closed World: Computers and the politics of discourse in cold war America*. Cambridge Mass: MIT Press.
Elzy, R. 1969. Founding an Anti-University. In Berke, J. ed., *Counter Culture*. London: Peter Owen Limited.
Feenberg, A. 1996. Marcuse or Habermas: Two Critiques of Technology. *Inquiry* 39: 45–70.
Goldschmit, J. dir., 1969 *Our Live Experiment is Worth More than Three Thousand Textbooks*. London: ITN.
Gregory, E.C. 5th July, 1947. Letter to the Editor. *Times* London.
Grotowski, J. 1965. Towards a Poor Theatre. In: Barba, E. ed., preface by Brook, P. *Towards a Poor Theatre*. London: Methuen: 15–21.
Institute of Contemporary Arts (ICA). Bulletins 1947–68. Tate Gallery Archive: 955/14.
Institute of Contemporary Arts (ICA). Press Cuttings 1947–68. Tate Gallery Archive: TAM: 48.
Institute of Contemporary Arts (ICA). 1968 April-November. *ICA Magazine*. London: ICA.
Kalina, R. 2006. Introduction. In: Kalina R. ed. *Lawrence Alloway: Imagining the Present: Context, Content and the role of the Critic*. London and New York: Routledge: 1–22.
Kurlansky, M. 2004. *1968: The Year that Rocked the World*. London: Jonathan Cape.
Kustow, M. 1975. *TANK: An Autobiographical Fiction*. London: Jonathan Cape.
Kustow, M. 1968 (January). Statement. *ICA Bulletin*.
Lynton, N. 1992. Harry Thurbon: Teacher and Artist. In: Thistlewood, D. ed., *Histories of Art and Design Education: Cole to Coldstream*. Harlow: Longman: 169–179.
MacDonald, S. 1970. *The History and Philosophy of Art Education*. London: University of London Press.
Marcuse, H. 1968. Liberation from the Affluent Society. In: Cooper, D. ed., *Dialectics of Liberation*. Harmondsworth: Penguin: 175–192.
Marcuse, H. 1969. On Revolution. In: Cockburn, A. and Robin, B. eds., *Student Power: Problems Diagnosis, Action*. Harmondsworth: Penguin: 367–372.
Martin, B. 1981. *A Sociology of Contemporary Cultural Change*. Oxford: Basil Blackwell.
Massey, A. 1995. *The Independent Group: modernism and mass culture in Britain, 1945–59*. Manchester: Manchester University Press.
McHale, J. 1961. The Plastic Parthenon. In: Gablik, S. and Russell, J. eds., *Pop Art Redefined*. London: Thames and Hudson.
McLuhan, M. 1964. *Understanding Media: The Extensions of Man*. London and New York: Routledge.
Nairn, T. 1968. Hornsey. *New Left Review* 50: 65–70.
Nairn, T. and Singh-Sandu, J. 1969. Chaos in the Art Colleges. In: Cockburn, A. and Blackburn, R. eds., *Student Power: Problems Diagnosis, Action*. Harmondsworth: Penguin: 103–115.
Nelson, E. 1989. *The British Counter-Culture, 1966–73; a study of the underground press*. London: Macmillan.
Neville, R. 1971. *Play Power*. London: Jonathan Cape.
Nuttall, J. 1968. *Bomb Culture*. London: MacGibbon & Kee.
Reichardt, J. 1966 (September). On Chance and Mark Boyle. *Studio International*: 164–165.
Reichardt, J. ed., 1971. *Cybernetics, Art and Ideas*. London: Studio Vista.

Ricoeur, P. 1973. The Model of the Text: Meaningful Action Considered as Text. *New Literary History* 5, 1: 91–117.

Rosenthal, N. ed., 1974. *Art into Society, Society into Art*. London: ICA.

Sayres, S. 1984. Reading for What: Introduction. In: Sayres, S., Stephanson, A., Aronowitz, S. and Jameson, F. eds., *The 60s Without Apology*. Minneapolis: University of Minnesota and Social Text: 17–20.

Schneemann, C. No Date. Fuses. [Online] Available from: http://www.caroleeschneemann.com/works.html [accessed 1st October 2009].

Schneemann, C. 1997. *More Than Meat Joy: Performance Works and Selected Writings*. Bruce R. McPherson, ed., Kingston, NY: McPherson and Co.

Seago, A. 1995. *Burning the Box of Beautiful Things: the development of a postmodern sensibility*. Oxford: Oxford University Press.

Snow, C. P. 1993. *The Two Cultures* (Originally delivered as a Rede Lecture, 7th May 1959, as 'The Two Cultures and the Scientific Revolution'), introduction by Stefan Collini. Cambridge: Cambridge University Press.

Students and Staff of Hornsey College of Art. 1969. *The Hornsey Affair*. Harmondsworth: Penguin.

Thistlewood, D. 1981. *A Continuing Process*. London: ICA.

Thomas, N. 2002. Challenging Myths of the 1960s: The Case of Student Protest in Britain. *Twentieth Century British History*, 13, 3: 277–297.

Tickner, L. 2008. *Hornsey 1968: The Art School Revolution*. London: Francis Lincoln Ltd.

Walker, J.A. 2002. Radical Artists and Art Students versus Management and Bureaucracy during the 1970s. *Journal of Art and Design and Education*, 20, 2: 230–237.

Warren-Piper, D. 1973. *Readings in Art and Design Education: 1 After Hornsey*. London: Davis-Poynter.

Williams, R. 1974. *Television, Technology and Cultural Form*. London: Routledge.

Willing, V. 1966 (September). What Kind of Art Education? interviews with Richard Hamilton, Misha Black, and Herbert Read. *Studio International*: 131–144.

Yeomans, R. 2005. Basic Design and the Pedagogy of Richard Hamilton. In: Romans, M. ed., *Histories of Art and Design Education: Collected Essays*. Bristol: Intellect: 195–210.

Chapter 8

THE SITUATIONIST LEGACY: REVOLUTION AS CELEBRATION

Eloise Harding

Introduction

'And everybody wants to breathe, and nobody can breathe, and some people say "We can breathe later".' (Raoul Vaneigem 1968)

The above quotation to some extent encapsulates the Situationists' perspective on revolutionary theory. Put simply, the Situationists did not believe in either waiting for a revolution or deferring the living of life until after this possibly hypothetical point. The claim that 'everybody wants to breathe' describes the existence of a human spirit which can be truly revolutionary when brought to the surface. 'Nobody can breathe' depicts the 'spectacular' world in which we live, mired in the illusion of mainstream society and gasping for the 'air' of liberation. 'We can breathe later' refers to the outlook of many of Vaneigem's contemporaries who saw pleasure, desire and other such concepts – elements of the 'living of life' without 'dead time' – as somewhat trivial distractions which could wait until after a definitive social and political revolution had swept away the existing order. This approach – the Situationists and today's 'horizontals' alike would argue, and I would tend to agree with them – underestimates the value of creating spaces within the reality of one's current lived existence and, as such, chipping away at the nature of this reality to bring about wider changes.

The overall theme of this paper is what I perceive the legacy of the Situationists to be with regard to their impact on certain political movements today. Assertions about such movements are based in part on my own reflections on the organisation of summit mobilisations, and beyond that on the edited volumes which have arisen in the wake of many such actions. This legacy hinges to some extent on the Situationist conception of revolution: in particular the element of celebration which explicitly distances it from theoretical outlooks which regard revolution as an act of sacrifice. Much of the theoretical background of this piece is drawn from two of the most enduring Situationist texts, Guy Debord's *Society of the Spectacle* (1967) and Raoul Vaneigem's *The Revolution of Everyday Life* (1968).

Terminology (and a Point to be Made)

Before moving on to the Situationists' legacy, it is worth giving some attention to the terminology in use here. The following definitions are derived from the first issue of the *Internationale Situationniste*, published in 1958 and translated into English by Ken Knabb. It is quite possible that the idea of an 'official story' would be decried by at least some of those involved: however, these are possibly as close as one can get to such a thing. At any rate, the glossary provides background information to the ideas discussed here. Each term is related in some way to the Situationists' overall outlook, and hence to the main point of this chapter.

Firstly, the term 'Situationist' is defined as:

'Relating to the theory or practical activity of constructing situations. One who engages in the construction of situations. [or] A member of the Situationist International'. (Situationist International 1958a)

It can refer, therefore, to an individual or to a wider outlook – although not, as we shall see shortly, an ideology. This sets the baseline to some extent for what can be regarded as a 'situationist' idea or practice. A 'constructed situation' in this context is defined as 'a moment of life, concretely and deliberately constructed by the collective organization of unitary environment and the free play of events.' (Situationist International 1958a) It is a specific counterpoint to what is known as 'dead time', an antidote if such a word can be used to Spectacular mindless consumption. In particular, it should be noted that there are no intrinsic restrictions regarding who can engage in the construction of situations: this definition and the claim of membership of the SI are explicitly not synonymous.

The definitions given for 'culture' and 'détournement' also have some bearing here. Culture, in the aforementioned glossary, is described as follows:

'The reflection and prefiguration of the possibilities of organization of everyday life in a given historical moment; a complex of aesthetics, feelings and mores through which a collectivity reacts on the life that is objectively determined by its economy. (We are defining this term only in the perspective of creating values, not in that of teaching them.)' (Situationist International 1958a)

This demonstrates the level at which the Situationists wished to have an impact: specifically, through subverting and transgressing the values promoted by the Spectacle. A tactic to this end is 'détournement': 'Short for "détournement of preexisting aesthetic elements", the integration of present or past artistic productions into a superior construction of a milieu. In this sense there can be no situationist painting or music, but only a situationist use of those means. In a more elementary sense, détournement within the old cultural spheres is a method of propaganda, a method which reveals the wearing out and loss of importance of those spheres.' (Situationist International 1958a) It is, therefore, the artefacts of Spectacular culture which are being used as a tool of resistance. This is, among other notable features a, theoretically at least, egalitarian praxis in that it can be conducted and understood at the grassroots level. There is – again, at least in principle – a level of leeway in what qualifies as détournement: it is not a tightly-controlled process.

The Spectacle, the entity – for want of a better word – that the Situationists aim to resist, is incidentally not defined in the 1958 glossary. This task is left for Debord almost a decade later. He describes how:

'The spectacle grasped in its totality is both the result and the project of the existing mode of production. It is not a supplement to the real world, an additional decoration. It is the heart of the unrealism of the real society. In all its specific forms, as information or propaganda, as advertisement or direct entertainment consumption, the spectacle is the present model of socially dominant life. It is the omnipresent affirmation of the choice *already made* in production and its corollary consumption. The spectacle's form and content are identically the total justification of the existing system's conditions and goals. The spectacle is also the *permanent presence* of this justification, since it occupies the main part of the time lived outside of modern production.' (1967)

The Spectacle is composed of elements such as popular culture, social norms and the mass media, which interject between people and 'real' life. As such it is the origin of dead time.

This brings us to something of a non-definition, namely: 'Situation*ism*: A word totally devoid of meaning, improperly derived from the preceding term. There is no situationism, which would mean a theory of interpretation of existing facts.' (Situationist International 1958b) In other words, the Situationist outlook is not an 'ism', and is not intended to be a hard and fast ideology. It has been argued – both positively and negatively – that fears of the SI becoming such were the reason for its demise. What is clear here is that Situationists wish to avoid creating a 'higher good' for which individuals are able to sacrifice themselves. The author of the glossary concludes that the 'notion of situationism was obviously conceived by anti-situationists'; (Situationist International 1958b) critics who either fail to grasp the point or, alternatively, wish to smear the Situationist International (SI) in some way.

It can be deduced from these definitions that the Situationists rejected the idea of imposing an 'ism' or creating a grand scheme for acolytes to follow. Following on from this is the key principle of self-determination, more specifically of creating one's own revolution.

Thinking (and Daubing) for Yourself

The first Situationist concept which feeds into the redefinition of revolution is that of 'revolutionary self-theory'. The origins of this concept are, according to one pamphlet: 'The alienation felt as a result of having your thinking done for you by the ideologies of our day, can lead to the search for the pleasurable negation of that alienation: thinking for yourself'. (Law n.d.) This is in direct contrast to the instruction paraphrased by Vaneigem: 'Become as senseless and easily handled as a brick! That is what the social order benevolently asks you to do.' (Vaneigem 1968) Juxtaposing these two opposing ideas helps us understand what the Situationists were fighting for and what they were against. Also relevant here is the idea that human creativity is a force with which to resist this senselessness:

> 'Nobody, no matter how alienated, is without (or unaware of) an irreducible core of creativity, a camera obscura safe from intrusion from lies and constraints. If ever social organization extends its control to this stronghold of humanity, its domination will no longer be exercised over anything save robots, or corpses. And, in a sense, this is why consciousness of creative energy increases, paradoxically enough, as a function of consumer society's efforts to co-opt it.' (Vaneigem 1968)

This idea is essential to understanding the emphasis on the individual in Situationist thought: it is only through *unforced*, unimposed co-operation that humans can create conditions in which they are truly free.

The emphasis on self-determination in the Situationist outlook can be seen in the first instance in a popular piece of graffiti; the longevity of which arguably underscores the egalitarian nature of Situationist. A slogan daubed on the wall can in this context have as much impact as the major works. The line 'Don't beg for the right to live, take it' (anonymous graffiti circa 1968) highlights clearly the idea that there is no point asking those in charge for change. It can be taken, for example, as a critique of the idea that one can effect genuine change by lobbying the government. This idea is emphasised further by the declaration that 'We will have good masters as soon as everyone is their own'. (Anonymous graffiti circa 1968) This serves as a rejection of traditional hierarchy and in particular of the idea that this can be included in any truly changed world, as well as highlighting the need to take control of one's own lived existence.

The ideal which forms the heart of this paper can be summarised by another graffito – 'Don't liberate me. I'll take care of that' (anonymous graffiti circa 1968). While this has in itself become something of an empty slogan in the intervening years, it does arguably have a very real message. The task of liberation cannot, according to this view, be delegated to another. It cannot be reliably entrusted to a third party; and, furthermore, it is the territory of each ordinary person rather than a distinct group of leaders or specialists. The rejection of the specialists is the next step in the idea of revolution being advanced by the Situationists. This is the idea that, to use another bit of graffiti, 'The revolution doesn't belong to the committees, it's yours' (anonymous graffiti circa 1968). Again, the issue here is largely one of directing one's own life, and taking charge of one's own liberation. This is not necessarily done through grand revolutionary gestures, but also through small day-to-day conscious acts of revolt; including, it can be assumed, daubing graffiti.

Vaneigem elaborates on his objection to the role of the specialist when he states that 'If anyone says or writes that practical reason must henceforth be based upon the rights of the individual and the individual alone, he invalidates his own proposition if he doesn't invite his audience to make this statement true for themselves.' (Vaneigem 1968) Nobody, therefore, can or should set themselves up as the true voice of revolution or of an oppressed class: the most that can be done is to invite each individual within that group to discover their own voice, and – as the previous two sets of graffiti suggest – to take charge of their own liberation.

To put the matter in historical context, the Situationists regarded this as the problem posed by many of the revolution-seeking contemporaries from whom they were attempting to distance themselves (cf Vienet 1992). The Marxist groups which predominated tended, their critics argued, to cling to monolithic and deterministic ideas. Furthermore, they were often heavily invested in the concept of an intellectual vanguard. This, to Vaneigem, is 'The logic of Bolshevism' which, in the Russian revolution 'demanded the heads of the leaders of social-democracy; the latter hastily sold out, and they did so precisely because they were leaders.' (Vaneigem 1968) He continues: 'The logic of anarchism demanded the liquidation of Bolshevik power; the latter rapidly crushed them, and did so inasmuch as it was hierarchical power.' (Vaneigem 1968) This is, in his view, the problem with a revolution in which 'liberation' is delegated to others. In this argument it is possible to see echoes of the older ideas of *Socialisme ou Barbarie*, in particular Castoriadis when he refers to his surprise at the idea of 'betrayal' by revolutionary leaders (Castoriadis 1955). When decision-making power is invested in a specific group, this argument goes, one should not be surprised if the decisions made begin to veer away from wider opinion.

These ideas regarding leadership were a source of tension between the Situationists and other movements involved in the Paris uprising, particularly with regard to the occupation of the Sorbonne university in which the boundary between co-ordination and self-appointed authority appears to have become somewhat blurred. One document from the time describes how, within the occupied campus:

> 'the various specialized groupings that had set themselves up in the Sorbonne all followed the directives of a hidden 'Coordination Committee' composed of self-appointed organizers, responsible to no one, doing everything in their power to prevent any 'irresponsible' extremist actions. An hour after the re-election of the Occupation Committee one of these 'coordinators' privately tried to declare it dissolved. A direct appeal to the people in the courtyard of the Sorbonne aroused a movement of protests that forced the manipulator to retract himself.' (SI 1968)

It is evident from incidents such as this that the Situationist ideas regarding leadership were not unanimously shared in the wider movement. It is also clear, however, that the Situationists regarded such incidents as justification for their suspicion of leaders and specialists.

Self-determination, then, is tightly connected to the core of individual creativity mentioned above by Vaneigem. It is at this point that the relevance of the celebration angle comes into play, as the expression of this allegedly irrepressible revolutionary force.

Revolution as Celebration

The contention, therefore, hinges on one question: that of revolution as a sacrifice versus revolution as a celebration. The central concepts here are 'causes' and 'a higher good', for which revolutionaries sacrifice themselves; and, Vaneigem in particular argues, also sacrifice revolution itself. Specialists are widely perceived as the ones who define the 'best' cause and the higher good, ideas which are indicative of a hierarchy. The argument that in my view distinguishes the Situationists from other movements of their era is that there is no cause greater than the individual, and that therefore no greater good is sufficient for self-sacrifice. Furthermore, introducing the concept of self-sacrifice into a revolution undermines its liberatory potential, creating a hierarchy in which the individual is subsumed and transformed into a cog in the machinery: something which contains oppressive potential of its own.

One quotation in particular arguably highlights Vaneigem's attitude to the idea of revolution as a higher good. Young leftist radicals, he argues:

> 'enter the service of a Cause – the "best" of all Causes. The time they have for creative activity they squander handing out leaflets, putting up posters, demonstrating or heckling local politicians. They become militants, fetishising action because others are doing their thinking for them.' (Vaneigem 1968)

Here, again, we see the focus on self-determination: not allowing others to 'do your thinking for you'. This, along with the idea of a revolution transformed into a fetish, is a consistent trope in Vaneigem's argument. What happens next is, in simplistic terms, the dark side of the spirit of resistance through human creativity referred to previously. Vaneigem describes how the dominant order triumphs when sacrifice is perceived as necessary:

> 'Where people are not broken – and broken in – by force and fraud, they are seduced. What are Power's methods of seduction? Internalized constraints which ensure a good conscience based on a lie: the masochism of the *honnête homme*. Thus Power castrates but calls castration self-denial; it offers a choice of servitudes but calls this choice liberty. The feeling of having done one's duty is Power's reward for self-immolation with honour.' (Vaneigem 1968)

Duty and servitude to revolution, therefore, have the same overall impact as duty and servitude to power; that is to say, no impact on the Spectacle except to reinforce it.

The idea of fighting for a higher good can therefore be seen as a concept which is almost intrinsically authoritarian. As Vaneigem puts it:

> 'When the rebel believes that he is fighting for a higher good, the authoritarian principle gets a fillip. Humanity has never been short of justifications for giving up what is human. In fact some people possess a veritable reflex of submission, an irrational terror of freedom; this masochism is everywhere visible in everyday life.' (1968)

Here we see an idea central to this perspective on revolution: that 'what is human', far from being a frivolous distraction from revolution, is on the contrary its essence. This is highlighted to some extent when Vaneigem details the difference between revolutionary and reformist movements in terms of their traditional attitudes to sacrifice; while:

> 'the best cause is one in which the individual can lose himself body and soul. The principle of death is simply the denial of the principle of the will to live', 'our reformists of death in small doses and socialists of ennui cannot even claim the dubious honour of having an aesthetic of total destruction. All they can do is mitigate the passion for life, stunting it to the point where it turns against itself and changes into a passion for destruction and self-destruction.' (Vaneigem 1968)

At any rate, the call for sacrifice serves in both cases to denigrate 'passion for life'. It degrades what Situationists tend to regard as humans' greatest chance for genuine freedom. The idea that anybody should sacrifice themselves for something greater is therefore in itself authoritarian and reactionary. By contrast, what is truly revolutionary is the overcoming of this reflex of submission, and a developing excitement – rather than fear – at the idea of freedom.

The idea of sacrifice is, in Situationist terms, almost intrinsic to that of a higher good. Neither, as we have seen, is welcome in the conception of a revolution advanced here; in Vaneigem's words: 'The moment revolution calls for self-sacrifice it ceases to exist. The individual cannot give himself up for a revolution, only for a fetish.' (Vaneigem 1968) The existence of a higher purpose – or a purpose perceived to be higher than one's own lived existence – negates in his eyes the very concept of revolution, perpetuating instead the established order. Instead, Vaneigem argues, 'Revolutionary moments are carnivals in which the individual life celebrates its unification with a regenerated society.' (Vaneigem 1968)

So how might this idea be defined? A constant theme in the work of Vaneigem, Debord and other Situationist writers is the living of life 'without dead time', that is to say 'truly' (not to be pretentious!) living. 'Dead time' is time spent mindlessly consuming the Spectacle, being part of the illusion, living up to socially expected goals and acquiring symbols of status. The media and fashion have been cited as examples in this context. Everyday life can in this way be liberated from the Spectacle, the illusion at the surface of consumer culture. A revolution will thus, Vaneigem argues, 'spring' from 'lived experience' rather than ideology: it will be a 'poetic creation'. Central here is the idea expressed by another piece of graffiti: 'No replastering – the structure is rotten.' (Anonymous graffiti circa 1968)

What kind of actions, then, exemplified this style of revolution? It is surprisingly difficult to locate empirical details of detournement-style actions. This could be attributed to the possibility that those involved in the 1968 uprising were too busy creating actions to document them. Certainly, today's generation of activists is somewhat spoiled in terms of access to the means of distributing information with minimal fuss. A commentator in *Anarchy* puts a different slant on this issue, suggesting that the situationists never arrived at an adequate practice: 'Afraid to get their hands dirty in the confusion of radical activity (which they scorned as 'militantism') they confined their interventions to the theoretical level.' (*Anarchy* n.d. quoted in Knabb ed., 1981, 387) It is quite possible that this statement applies to certain participants in the movement who were largely active in generating theory; and in particular some whose ideas have lasted in printed form. I would, however, be inclined to regard the graffiti-daubers – whose words have also lived on! – as part of the movement, making such claims more complicated than they may first appear. It could also be argued that, even if the anonymous author in *Anarchy* is correct about the majority of the movement, it is still possible to see the usefulness of the ideas involved in terms of future legacies. At any rate, for the time being it will be necessary to refer to a less narrow range of movements to see the variety of action which may be consistent with Situationist ideas.

During the Paris occupation, the emphasis on subverting culture and confounding expectations is demonstrated by the fact that the 'first non-university territory to be occupied by students during the revolt was the 'Theatre de France' at the Odeon. The wardrobe department was raided and dozens of demonstrators came out to face the CS gas dressed as centurions, pirates and princesses.' (Beyond TV n.d.) This use of costume to appropriate something familiar – in this instance the cultural signifiers present in theatrical costume – and to alter the impact of something *un*familiar such as a protest was popular at the time and has remained so with certain movements to the present day. By turning a protest into carnival, it is often thought, the element of the absurd spreads beyond those who introduced it and infects bystanders and opponents. In particular, the police are made to appear ridiculous by threatening with batons and gas a group of people in flamboyant costume. Furthermore, through this appearance of ridiculousness, the forces of the state are themselves co-opted as part of the action. This tactic was used to great effect by the Situationists' Dutch forerunners, the Provos. Van Herpen describes how:

> 'The Provo movement started in 1965 as an absurdist movement around 'anti-smoke' rituals organised near 'het Lieverdje', a statue of an Amsterdam streetboy, offered by a cigarette company to the city. These 'happenings' on Saturday night on the Spui square attracted more and more spectators and began to make the police nervous. According to the Dutch novelist Harry Mulisch, the happenings started with the "marihuette play": "But marihuana didn't almost play a role, unlike hay that looked like it ("marihoe"), and the rules were not understood by anybody, what was also intended.' (Van Herpen 2008)

The police, summoned to the scene, became part of the happening: there was no grounds for action on their part since it would be ridiculous to arrest people for smoking hay. Their involvement, however, highlights the hypocrisy – and ridiculousness in a far less benign sense – of objecting to marijuana use in the vicinity of a statue promoting what many believe to be a more dangerous smokeable substance.

A further reason why the comment made in *Anarchy* can be taken with a pinch of salt is that in many cases the production of ideas could be said to constitute an action in some way. This is particularly the case with the pamphlets that were distributed in the vicinity of the occupations, which serve the same purpose as the graffiti and alterations to adverts in making a minor change to the familiar in order to turn 'accepted' ideas inside out. Plant describes how:

> 'The subversions of comic strips which the lettrists claimed as their own were perfect examples of such appropriation: in the pages of *Internationale Situationiste*, true love stories were confused with bubbles of political propaganda, and soft porn pin-ups declared "I love to sleep with Asturian miners, they're real men" or insisted that the "emancipation of the workers will be the work of the workers themselves".' (Plant 1992, 87)

Certainly this is not an action in the literal sense of getting participants' hands dirty, in the sense that those involved in tearing up paving stones to arm themselves at the barricades could be said to be doing. However, it is possible to argue that such material was integral to *inspiring* many actions which took place during this period. 'Beneath the paving stones, the beach' (reproduced at multiple sources) was after all a key slogan of the uprising.

The rationale of such actions is summed up in the argument that:

> 'People's creativity and participation can only be awakened by a collective project explicitly concerned with all aspects of lived experience. The only way to "arouse the masses" is to expose the appalling contrast between the potential constructions of life and the present poverty of life. Without a critique of everyday life, a revolutionary organization is a separated milieu, as conventional and ultimately as passive as those holiday camps that are the specialized terrain of modern leisure.' (SI 1961)

In other words, altering something that is familiar and taken for granted – a popular consumer product, maybe, or a teenage comic – and giving it a meaning which highlights the necessity to question the ideas contained in such artefacts; and wonder if there might not be more to life. It is this belief which leads initially to the advocacy and use of 'carnival' tactics. Debord, for example, argues that:

> 'The goal of the situationists is immediate participation in a passionate abundance of life by means of deliberately arranged variations of ephemeral moments. The success of these moments can reside in nothing other than their fleeting effect. The situationists consider cultural activity in its totality as an experimental method for constructing everyday life, a method that can and should be continually developed with the extension of leisure and the withering away of the division of labour (beginning with the division of artistic labour).' (Debord 1958)

In such moments of carnival, the Spectacle is at least temporarily subverted: however, even when the subversion is temporary, when the action itself may last for an objectively short period of time, a crack has still been opened through which an alternative can, if one looks from the right angle, still just about be glimpsed. Chasse regards this as a source of liberation, arguing that

> 'It is only when the nihilist – or activist – rediscovers play that he rediscovers himself as subject. Then the bourgeois world becomes the object of and for his play. He will play with cops as a guerrilla plays with columns sent against him (meet them on *his* terms), play with all the "forms" and manifestations of the bourgeois world, which is the equivalent of foiling them, doing a turnabout on them, for the purpose of his own liberation.' (Chasse 1968)

The police and bystanders both incredulous and disapproving can in such a context be turned into participants in the carnival, as in the actions described previously. Notes from Nowhere, a collective whose members have been involved in carnivalesque protests across the world in more recent years, describe how: 'Carnival works all over the world, as political actions, as festive celebration, as cathartic release, as wild abandonment of the status quo, as networking tool, as a way to create a new world.' (Notes from Nowhere 2003, 180) The emphasis here, although the term was not used by the Situationists, is on prefiguration: creating cracks in the world as we know it in order to demonstrate the possibilities for other worlds to grow within them.

The Legacy

What, then, is the legacy of the Situationists? Indeed, can they be said to have one? In the traditional sense of a direct family tree, this may not be the case.

However, the Situationist ethos does appear to be echoed in many cases by today's 'horizontal' political movements, and there are several areas in the practice of such movements where the ideas discussed above are clearly evident.

At the surface level, there is a strong tendency towards carnival: larger mobilisations have an element of street party about them, and there is an emphasis on creativity and spontaneity. For example, a mission statement on the website of the Clandestine Insurgent Rebel Clown Army (CIRCA) describes how 'Operation BROWN-NOSE will involve giving hugs to the needy, playing games with all our friends, and other similarly militant activities. We request full cooperation from the public for this operation.' (CIRCA n.d.) A frequent criticism of such actions is that they are frivolous, trivialising serious issues and losing the message in a somewhat self-indulgent medium. Such criticisms have, however, been fiercely countered. 'Cultural activist' Jennifer Verson provides one such defence:

> 'this isn't just about making things pretty, fluffy or fun. Cultural activists are taking direct action against war, ecological destruction, injustice and capitalism, but they are also constantly asking how we can act directly against their social and psychological effects. After all, who can really know what it is that really inspires an individual to care, or to turn away, to give up or to rise up? Cultural activism is where art, activism, performance and politics meet, mingle and interact.' (Verson n.d.)

There are a number of Situationist elements here. Firstly, there is the focus on inspiring individuals to take action, and on using creative means to stir humans' hidden reserves of 'creativity' in the sense in which the word is meant in Situationist literature. Secondly, the psychological landscape of resistance is a key factor for cultural activists, who make a priority of subverting the images which they perceive as mediating between humans and lived existence. It might not be too strong a phrase to argue that individuals are encouraged to reclaim their minds from a society viewed by activists in a way which would be familiar to Debord.

Here it might be worth referring to a couple of examples given by the Notes from Nowhere collective of carnivalesque actions which have in recent years arguably pursued or fulfilled the aims stated by the Situationists. The first refers to the arrest of an activist at Quebec City's Carnival Against Capital for alleged possession of a dangerous weapon:

> 'The weapon in question is a 25 by 10 foot catapult. It was smuggled into the most heavily fortified city in Canadian history by a group calling themselves the Medieval Bloc, who wear pots on their heads and carry the lids as shields. During the action they wheeled the wooden catapult

up to the fence that surrounded the summit and fired dozens of teddy bears over it.' (Notes from Nowhere 2003, 179)

In a similar action in Prague, meanwhile, the Tactical Frivolity bloc 'were dressed in outrageous pink dresses, wild bouffant wigs, and nine-foot-high fan tails, and danced towards lines of confused Czech police waving magic wands and dusting off the riot shields with feather dusters.' (*Ibid.*, 280) In such scenarios, it is the protestors who arguably appear reasonable and the forces of authority who appear somewhat ridiculous for using force against the catapulting of teddy bears or the improper use of cleaning equipment: in other words, it is an inversion of 'normality' and one which has the potential to confound expectations while drawing attention to the wider questions behind the protest.

This deeper meaning to carnivalesque tactics is one which is often referred to in activist literature. There has, to give one fairly obvious example, been no small amount of discussion regarding some of the more colourful elements of the protests against the 2005 G8 summit at Gleneagles, and in particular the actions of CIRCA. The editors of a volume on these protests suggest that 'The clowns, for instance, can be seen as a clever attempt to increase the flexibility of the protesters by moving beyond the dichotomous roles of "violent" and "legitimate" protester. From another angle, they can be understood as part of an attempt (...) to recognise our vulnerability as human beings and to meet the needs which spring from this.' (Harvie *et al* 2005, 13) Among other purposes, such tactics add a new dimension to what could be a strictly economically-based objection to the policies of the G8. The Free Association, for example, admit (if 'admit' is the word, implying as it does a level of wrongdoing) that:

'The whole idea of the counter-summit wasn't really about protesting against the G8. For us, it wasn't even directly about abolishing global poverty. It was about life. It was about becoming human. It was about our desire.' (Free Association 2005, 25)

Here, direct echoes of the Situationist ethos are clearly evident: most notably, the idea of humanity as a driving force. Furthermore, the term 'becoming human' suggests a conscious effort at *reclaiming* the humanity from which we are in general restrained. They repeat this sentiment, and defend it from the more obvious critics, arguing that

'This was living; this was being human. This "ragged and ecstatic joy of pure being". Of course, it's easy to dismiss is as if it's simply about a "feeling" or an obsession with "process". But doing stuff for ourselves, making decisions, running our own lives… this process of creation, invention and becoming isn't a "feeling", it's a material reality. The new capacities we experience at these events don't just disappear. They are there to be accessed during the rest of our lives… if we can work out how to reach them again.' (Free Association 2005, 25)

It is not, therefore, a matter of sidelining the very real and tangible issue of global poverty for the sake of holding a party, as has been alleged. Rather, the focus is the promotion of a form of liberation which goes beyond the economic questions and probes more deeply into issues of power and dignity. Furthermore, there is an emphasis here on what Juris and others call 'prefigurative politics': the idea of 'being the change you want to see' (Juris 2005) and creating this change in one's day-to-day life; a concept paralleled in other sixties movements (see O'Donnell chapter 6, Freely chapter 12 and Conclusion). This idea is posited in opposition to waiting until after a revolution before things can be changed. Revolution, according to these ideas, is not a grand one-off gesture but a series of small and autonomous eruptions.

In terms of the practicalities of organisation for such movements, the principle of self-determination can be seen clearly in modes of organisation which are based on autonomy and consensus. At the aforementioned protests, for example, the Hori-zone convergence site consisted of a number of mostly-autonomous neighbourhoods or 'barrios', which were largely able to make their own rules. Affinity groups were also considered to be autonomous with regard to how, when and where they organised and participated in actions against the G8. This principle can be said to have generated a number of advantages in blockading the Gleneagles complex, although this is not the time or place to go into such technical detail. Decisions made within barrios or site-wide came about using the consensus method, an explicitly non-hierarchical model. One collective which advocates the use of consensus is Seeds for Change who argue that:

'People are often inactive because they feel that they have no power in the system and that their voice won't be listened to anyway. In consensus every person has the power to make changes in the system, and to prevent changes that they find unacceptable. The right to veto a decision means that minorities cannot just be ignored, but creative solutions will have to be found to deal with their concerns.' (Seeds for Change n.d.)

Again, this statement echoes the Situationist ethos regarding the revolutionary potential of the individual. It can be tempting to dismiss the consensus process as time-consuming and somewhat self-indulgent, or indeed as a distraction from the real issues at hand. However, it is worth noting in response the statement made above regarding the capacities developed in such circumstances and their potential for future action. As in the Situationists' day, there is tension with other movements engaged in the same actions, particularly around a major summit mobilisation. Although, to a great extent a 'movement of movements' is able to absorb a certain level of diversity or else refrain from working directly with other entities where the disagreements may become insurmountable.

Putting these factors together, I would argue that there is a strong current in today's anticapitalist movements for a revolution which 'does not belong to the committees', (Anonymous graffiti circa 1968) and that the Situationists have played a part in the evolution of this attitude if only by situating – no pun intended – themselves in the public psyche and being available, consciously or not, for reference. This may not appear at first glance to be a convincing argument. However, when the same tactics and language are in use and similar defining principles underly these, it might be harder to convincingly argue for the absence of any such connection.

Conclusion

I will conclude with one last quote from Vaneigem, one which I believe sums up the Situationist view on revolution:

> 'The real demand of all insurrectionary movements is the transformation of the world and the reinvention of life. This is not a demand formulated by theorists: rather, it is the basis of poetic creation. Revolution is made everyday despite, and in opposition to, the specialists of revolution. This revolution is nameless, like everything springing from lived experience. Its explosive coherence is being forged constantly in the everyday clandestinity of acts and dreams.' (Vaneigem 1968)

This, if nothing else, is unlikely to be disputed by the protesters quoted above.

References

Anonymous. Circa 1968. Various graffiti collected at http://www.everything2.com/index.pl?node_id=760469 (accessed 03/03/08).

Beyond TV n.d. 'Détournement'. Online at: http://www.beyondtv.org/nato/detournement/detournement.htm (accessed 13/10/09).

Castoriadis, C. 1955. From the Critique of Bureaucracy to the Idea of the Proletariat's Autonomy. In: D. Curtis ed. 1997 *The Castoriadis Reader*. Oxford: Blackwell, 40–48.

Chasse, R. 1968. *The Power of Negative Thinking, or Robin Hood Rides Again*. Online at http://www.notbored.org/robin-hood.html (accessed 13/10/09).

Clandestine Insurgent Rebel Clown Army (CIRCA) n.d. 'Operation Brown-nose' online at http://www.clownarmy.org/operations/brownnose.html (accessed 24/07/08).
Debord, G. 1958. *Theses on Cultural Revolution* http://www.bopsecrets.org/SI/1.cultural-revolution.htm
Debord, G. 1967. *The Society of the Spectacle*. Online at http://library.nothingness.org/articles/SI/en/pub_contents/4 (accessed 03/03/08).
Free Association. 2005. On the Road in Harvie, D., Milburn, K., Trott, B. and Watts, D. eds. *Shut them Down! The G8, Gleneagles 2005 and the Movement of Movements*. Leeds: Dissent: 9–16, pp17–26.
Harvie, D., Milburn, K., Trott, B. and Watts, D. 2005 'Introduction' in Harvie *et al* (eds) *Shut them Down! The G8, Gleneagles 2005 and the Movement of Movements*. Leeds: Dissent: 9–16.
Juris, J. 2005. Social Forums and their Margins. *Ephemera* 5. 2. Online at http://www.ephemeraweb.org/journal/5-2/5-2juris.pdf (accessed 03/03/08).
Knabb, K. ed., 1981. *Situationist International Anthology*. Berkeley: Bureau of Public Secrets
Law, L. n.d. *Revolutionary Self-Theory*. Online at: http://www.burngreave.net/~aland/personal/spectaculartimes/cornersoul.com/revolutionary.html (accessed 24/07/08).
Notes from Nowhere. 2003. *We Are Everywhere*. London: Verso.
Plant, S. 1992. *The Most Radical Gesture*. London: Routledge.
Seeds for Change. n.d. *Consensus decision-making*. Online at http://www.seedsforchange.org.uk/free/consens (accessed 24/07/08).
Situationist International. 1958a. *Theses on Cultural Revolution*. Online at http://www.bopsecrets.org/SI/1.cultural-revolution.htm (accessed 13/10/09).
Situationist International. 1958b. Definitions, *Situationist International 1*. Online at http://www.bopsecrets.org/SI/1.definitions.htm (accessed 03/03/08).
Situationist International. 1961. *Instructions for an Insurrection*. Online at http://www.bopsecrets.org/SI/6.insurrection.htm (accessed 13/10/09).
Situationist International. 1968. *May 1968 Documents*. Online at http://libcom.org/book/export/html/2011 (accessed 13/10/09).
Van Herpen, M. 2008. *Paris May 68 and Provo Amsterdam 65: Trying to understand two postmodern youth revolts*. Online at http://www.cicerofoundation.org/lectures/Marcel_Van_Herpen_May_68_and_Provo_Amsterdam_65.pdf (accessed 13/10/09).
Vaneigem, R. 1968. *The Revolution of Everyday Life*. Online at http://library.nothingness.org/articles/SI/en/pub_contents/5 (accessed 03/03/08).
Verson, J. n.d., quoted at http://handbookforchange.org (accessed 24/07/08).
Vienet, R. 1992. *Situationists and Enrages in the Occupation Movement of 1968*. NY: Semiotext(E).

Chapter 9

HABERMAS ON SIXTIES STUDENT PROTESTS: REFLECTIONS ON COLLECTIVE ACTION AND COMMUNICATIVE POTENTIAL

James Driver

Introduction

As one of the greatest sociologists and social philosophers of the latter part of the twentieth century, Jürgen Habermas's interactions with, and theorising of the problems confronted by the sixties student movement are of both major historical and contemporary significance. Other chapters in this book (McDonald chapter 2; O'Donnell chapter 6, Cranfield chapter 7) describe the movements for protest and greater freedom of expression amongst the student generations in Europe and North America. More specific to inter-generational conflict in Germany was the awakening of the baby boomer generation to the country's National Socialist past. The *Wirtschaftwunder* had provided the country with a great deal of new found confidence in the decades since the Second World War, but with the Adolf Eichmann trial of 1961 and the Auschwitz trials of 1963–65, as well as explorations of collective moral culpability emerging in theatre and literature, prosperity alone was an unsatisfactory basis for national confidence amongst a new generation who had reached the age of political consciousness. With their awakening, they developed a barely concealed anger with their elders' misdeeds and considered their 'no questions asked' attitude not as a matter of discretion which allowed the resumption of everyday life, but as a complacent desire to forget, which could lead to the return of fascism. The sixties student movement became the highly politicised focus and catalyst for the radical expression of these sentiments. It was their ideological and political dynamics which became both a target for Habermas's intellectual critique and, also, part inspiration for his sociology of the social movements struggling against the illiberal and dominating tendencies of the political system.

Habermas and the SDS: From Empathy to Estrangement

An overtly political split between the younger and older generations resulted in the development of a highly activist student body with little confidence in the parliamentary politics of the Federal Republic. Concerns about the state's authoritarian tendencies remained fresh from the raid on the offices of Der Spiegel in 1962, after the magazine had criticized Konrad Adenauer's defence policy. Adenauer was forced to admit to a violation of press freedom when Axel Springer, the editor of the magazine, was charged with treason. The SDS (Socialist German Students) which had been demanding resistance to 'renazification' was expelled by the Social Democratic Party as an affiliate group in 1960 after the party had reconstructed itself on an explicitly non-Marxist basis and had declared that being a member of the SDS was no longer compatible with being a member of the SPD (Della Porta 2006, 96). The SDS consequently aligned itself with the extra-parliamentary opposition or APO (Die Außerparlamentarische Opposition) when the Social Democrats entered the Great Coalition with the Christian Democrats in December 1966, which had installed Kurt Georg Kiesinger, a former Nazi and Hitler Foreign Office official as Chancellor (Turk 1999, 155).

Habermas's reputation amongst the SDS at this time was high because of the positive reception within the SDS of his first major work, *The Structural Transformation of the Public Sphere* (1965). Habermas argued that the bourgeois civic sphere which had emerged in the eighteenth century had undergone a 'refeudalization' with the intertwining of society and state regulation in the late nineteenth and twentieth centuries (Habermas 2009, xii, 141–51). He considered the book to carry a contemporary warning about the fragile resilience of the Federal Republic's civic sphere, a thesis which gave succour to the SDS's belief in its increasing authoritarianism. The story of the relationship between Habermas and the SDS is one which began as a discourse but ended as a bitter falling out over the limits and legitimacy of direct action within a democracy. Habermas initially felt a great deal of affinity with the SDS after their expulsion from the SPD and showed solidarity by founding the Socialist League with several other university professors, which included his friend Wolfgang Abendroth (Dews 1986, 78). He hoped to provide a constructive critique of some of the tactics of the student movement, which he saw as misplaced and intended to provide a reorientation away from what he regarded as obsolete Marxist elements of its political philosophy. However, as events unfolded over the three years from 1967, it became clear that each side had irreconcilable views about the continuing relevance and influence of ideology within the capitalist system. Habermas's frustration climaxed as a 'look back in anger' with the publication of *Protestbewegung und Hochsculereform* (Protest Movement and University Reform) in 1969, by which time the SDS had disbanded.

The 'blue touch-paper' which ignited student activism and began the exchange between Habermas and the SDS was the fatal shooting of Benno Ohnesorg during the visit of the Shah of Iran to Berlin on 2 June 1967. The city had seen a series of angry street demonstrations in the preceding two years as President Johnson had expanded the Vietnam War, which stoked opposition to American imperialism in south-east Asia. This visit drew the largest demonstration of the time. Events reached crisis point in the evening when the Shah was at the German Opera House watching a performance of *The Magic Flute*. The police took the decision to disperse the demonstration after the Shah's security men responded to provocation from the crowd. Ohnesorg was fatally shot whilst running away from police lines. The photograph of his pregnant wife cradling his head as he lay dying in the street became the student movement's iconic image.

A week later Ohnesorg was buried in Hanover and Hanover University was selected as the appropriate place to hold a special commemorative congress entitled *Hochscule und Demokratie* ('University and Democracy') on 9 June. Habermas was one of seven plenary speakers (Holub 1991, 81). In his address Habermas condemned the press for promoting anti-intellectualism in their denigration of student agitation and the mainstream political parties for propagating an authoritarian attitude. Habermas stated his alarm at the force the police used in the demonstration and claimed 'For the first time since the days of fascism in Berlin we must recognize fascism again in the Federal Republic' (ibid, 81). He then praised the student movement for compensating for the lack of theoretical perspective in the Republic and for retaining the imagining of a radical alternative future.

It was his warning about the limits of the movement in this speech which was negatively received by the leader of the SDS, Rudi Dutschke. Habermas stated that there were objective and subjective dangers to the movement which formed its limits. Universities had an objective dilemma in choosing either to increase their productivity, which would also integrate them into the system of social labour and lead to the negation of their political identity, or they could assert their democratic potential by democratising themselves. If they chose the later, they would have to accept the integration of political enquiry into the educational process and agree to the democratic governance of the universities. The subjective dangers were of a more ideological nature and it was this aspect which was so badly received by Dutschke and the SDS. Habermas warned that the tension between theory and practice could lead to an arbitrarily conceived 'actionism'[1]. The tension between principled engagement with the body politic and a pragmatically driven pursuit of a career through examinations could have a negative outcome on each count: theoretical oversimplification or a positivistic reduction of life choices within the system. Habermas made it clear that although the state had demonstrated authoritarian aspects, the political context clearly remained democratic. This non-revolutionary situation excluded provocation and violence and required reason and argumentation (Holub 1991, 82–83, Habermas 1981, 213–15).

Dutschke stood up to make a 45 minute rebuttal. He claimed the student movement was a response to the economically determined restructuring of the educational system in capitalism. Enlightenment without action was meaningless as this would only lead to meaningless consumption. Students needed to be the central point of organization and co-ordination for demonstrations and mass protest to prevent the imposition of emergency laws, the advance of nationalist parties and to resist the Vietnam War. Dutschke stated that empiricism was conceptually deficient and prevented the development of an emancipated consciousness. Dutschke left for Berlin after he finished his speech so he did not hear Habermas accuse him and the SDS of 'left fascism' in response. Habermas wrecked his reputation with the student movement with this remark. The SDS was infuriated with the association with fascism, its political nemesis. Habermas privately sought to clarify what he meant in private correspondence with the poet Erich Fried in 1969 but publicly he continued to assert the SDS's justification of violence as the method of last resort to be wrong because they were acting against a legitimate democratic state (Holub 1991, 83–84, Habermas 1981, 213–15).

Tensions rose further in 1968 with the anti-Springer campaign and an assassination attempt on Rudi Dutschke in April. Nick Thomas in *Protest Movements in 1960s West Germany* (2003) says that 'Dutschke's shooting has to be seen in the context of what can only be described as mutual hatred between the protestors and the Springer Empire' (Thomas 2003, 168). The SDS and other left wing organizations had conducted a number of demonstrations outside the offices of Springer Group newspapers and magazines, which included Der Spiegel. The group owned 80 per cent of the print media in Germany and had consistently portrayed the SDS and 'Red Rudi' as communist insurgents (Katsiaficas 1987, 51). Some of these demonstrations turned into attacks on Springer premises, which prompted the group to accuse the SDS of using '*Sturmabteilung*' and '*Kristallnacht*' tactics. In response, the SDS pointed out that Axel Springer had been a Nazi from 1933 and that his group's near-monopoly level of control was trying to choke the democratic process by stoking up unjustified public hatred of radical politics.

Dutschke was the particular target of Springer's contempt and was represented as a demonic figure in the Springer press (Thomas 2003, 167). He was the public face of the student movement and embodied the new threat of communist revolution which frightened the right. Because of the intensity of the personal attacks which had been run on Dutschke in print, many SDS supporters suspected that his would-be assassin, the gunman Josef Bachmann, had been hired by the Springer Group. However, although Bachmann was a fanatical anticommunist, he was a loner. At 11 a.m. on 11 April, Dutschke was outside a pharmacy next to SDS headquarters on Kurfürstendamm, waiting for it to open so he could buy medicine for his daughter. Bachmann, who had set off from Munich earlier that morning with a revolver and ammunition, found him; having called at the headquarters and been told where he had gone. Upon seeing him sitting on his bicycle outside the pharmacy, Bachmann casually asked, "Are you Rudi Dutschke?" When Dutschke replied "Yes", Bachmann shot him in the head. Incredibly, Dutschke was not killed and managed to struggle with his assailant for a moment before being shot twice again. Bachmann then fled, eventually being cornered by the police in a cellar. He was convicted of the attack and sentenced to seven years imprisonment but committed suicide in 1970. Although Dutschke survived, he suffered significant brain damage which impaired his speech and caused frequent epileptic attacks. Epilepsy finally claimed his life in 1979.

In this climate, student radicalism received substantial impetus from the protests in Paris. The University of Frankfurt (where Habermas was Professor of Philosophy and Sociology) was the scene of the most high profile sit-in of the period when it was occupied and renamed 'Karl Marx University'. The registry was ransacked and records were destroyed, which led to the police being called and the protestors forcibly removed (Thomas 2003, 135). However, by 1969 the plethora of left wing views within the SDS had caused widespread internal disagreement, preventing it from being able to agree even the broadest goals. Its momentum slowed and it increasingly began to resemble an anarchist group. In 1970 the remaining 4000 members decided to dissolve the organization at the annual general meeting. Some of them went on to form Maoist or Leninist groups, but the force of the movement had been lost. Most were disorganised and had so few members they inevitably remained on the fringe. One group which left a small legacy was the Marxist K-Gruppen, which played a part in the emergence of the German Green Party (Doherty 2002, 41). However, the remnants of these ultra-radical groups eventually transmogrified into terrorist organizations like the Red Army Faction (a.k.a. Baader-Meinhof). Most former SDS members relinquished their radicalism and rejoined the SPD, which increased its membership in the under 35 age group by nearly 100,000 members by 1973 (Kolinsky 1984, 35).

Habermas claimed victory with the dissolution of the SDS and published *Protestbewegung und Hochschulreform* in 1969. These three essays were published in English with several other essays under the title *Towards a Rational Society* (1971).

The first essay, 'The University in a Democracy' (1969), is developed from a lecture he delivered at The Free University of Berlin in 1967 and also contains many of the views he expressed at Ohnesorg's commemoration. The second and third essays (which read like one essay in two parts) 'Student Protest in the Federal Republic of Germany' and 'The Movement in Germany: A Critical Analysis' collates and reviews his arguments with the SDS. The essays are heavy with accusations and a strident tone is almost audible beneath Habermas's routinely analytical language. He accuses the movement of having a myopic vision of a homogenous Marxist universalism, a perfect totality which is 'abstractly conceived' and contrasted to the demands of praxis in an unyieldingly deterministic manner.

Because this world-view rejects purposive rational action, it leads to a striving to create counter-worlds that disable competent action in the political sphere. Such a strongly-held counter-world view leads to an anti-authoritarian attitude which 'rejects the imperatives of achievement' because all moral value judgements outside of its own ideological framework are conceived of as not having any validity: all moral value systems other than the students' own are seen as part of the matrix of the dominant ideology. Habermas claims that this perspective can be explained sociologically. Students remain a privileged group in Western society and their conceived alliance with the Third World is naively misplaced. He claims that such an idealistic rejection of practical political norms is only possible because the new generation has been brought up in a social environment cushioned from the sphere of production and its everyday imperatives. Their world-view is predominantly formed by a reactive response to consumer relations and the mass media.

Protestbewegung und Hochschulreform is quite a peculiar piece. Habermas's style is not the most lucid at the best of times, but compared to his usual writing style it is even more awkward to read. In many respects it is a polemic made in clinical sociological language. Conjunctions tumble over one another as he makes a lengthy list of judgements and the anger he feels from his encounter with the student movement remains in evidence as vindictiveness occasionally rings out over his analysis. Words like 'naïve', 'juvenile' and 'slogan' are repeated, pushing the reader to the conclusion that whilst the political effects of the movement are acknowledged as significant, its thought had little substance.

Habermas' emphasis on the movement's shift from the class conflict of traditional Marxism to what he calls the 'politicization of private conflicts' is very important to understanding his critique. The student movement tried to target the psychological dimensions of conflict between the old and the young and the motivation of individuals who continued to conform to the imperatives of mass organizations. Habermas makes it clear that the focus on the individual as a subject who could be emancipated from a society of mass conformity does not imply that the movement has adopted a left-liberal perspective because in fact its ideology was an incoherent mix of social determinism and anarchism. However, student militancy was indicative of a more self-reflective generation because its emphasis on the perils of conformity signified a decrease in the influence of tradition.

For all the emphasis that was placed on changing social relations through a psychological transformation of intersubjectivity, Habermas says that the movement's fascination with psychology belies its own collective psychological problems. Towards the end of 'The Movement in Germany', he snidely notes that there have been other pseudo-revolutionary youth movements who were so disconnected with reality they were 'clinical potential' (Habermas 1971, 42). He conjectures that many members of the movement did not want to participate in society because of their own fear of failing in a competitive meritocratic system. This is the peculiar nature of Habermas's analysis: the explanation for all the sit-ins and demonstrations is little more than 'I didn't fail because I didn't try'. Habermas accepts, even defends, meritocracy on the grounds that successful social systems need to operate – in part at least – with purposive-rational action systems and functionally established imperatives. The psychological profile of many members of the movement could be attributed to the rise in the standard of living. Student militants had the liberty to reject the values of work and consumption *because* they had been raised in an environment free from scarcity. The affluence of Western societies was able to support a generation which was absorbed with a focus on 'aesthetic experience, instinctual gratification and expression to be realised in the here and now' (Habermas 1971, 33).

Habermas says the student movement operated with three broad justifications: the first comes from Marxism, the second from anarchist traditions; and the third from aspects of Cultural Revolution. The first justification is The Theory of Imperialism. Habermas says that 'Marxist slogans would not be credible if the liberation movements of the Third World had not given the theory of imperialism a new impetus' (Habermas 1971, 34). Militant students took up this theory and developed an ideology which perceived a global network of resistance. They believed in a world-historical unity of resistance to capitalism which extended 'from guerrilla struggles in South America and Asia through black revolts in North American cities and the Chinese Cultural Revolution'. It was an ideology which crudely amalgamated the differences between these struggles and obscured the fact that they had nothing to do with each other (ibid. 35).

The second justification is Neo-anarchism**,** which is also the psychologically orientated part of the student movement's ideology. Developed industrial society is viewed as an integrated whole which serves the needs of the system. All individuals are perceived as being heavily subjected to compulsive behavioural norms which produce conformity and enable social reproduction. Marx's idea of the material 'base' of society is adapted to mean all members of society. Neo-anarchism takes the view that a universally emancipated consciousness can be achieved by the mass disruption of the everyday life of the majority of people who have their identity invested in the comfort of petit-bourgeois society. Habermas says the lessons of structural functionalism show this to be a completely unrealistic analysis. Modern capitalism has developed over hundreds of years and formed functionally established imperatives which cannot be substituted with revolutionary symbolism. Existing relations of power and socio-economic interests which have formed from and adapted to historical conditions are capable of resistance and will be defended by social actors who carry these needs and interests. He wryly observes that if prosperity raises awareness of the neglected area of humane community life, then revolution in the most developed societies would not bring about the abolition of poverty but presuppose it (Habermas 1971).

The Third Justification was Cultural Revolution. Habermas is very dismissive again, opening his remarks by observing that Cultural Revolution in China is highly authoritarian and the mobilization of the youth there stopped when Mao ordered it to. The fascination with Red Books and Mao badges represents little more than a reawakening in the younger generation's consciousness of the original revolutionary situation (ibid 38). Students are not taking possession of the means of production when they occupy a university classroom. The Maoist idea of the abolition of history is a dangerous illusion because beliefs and judgements raised in the post-revolutionary society have no context against the collective rational achievements of the past. This would destroy society's capacity to test truth claims, making it vulnerable to totalitarianism. Habermas doesn't say 'as is the case in China' but the implication is there. The communist abolition of culture needs the repression of communicative discourse.

Habermas's accusation that the 'student militants' were exploiting the latitude granted by liberal institutions (Habermas 1971, 41) is quite telling, for it shows that for all his critique of them, he has a commitment to the achievements of liberal democratic societies. In labelling the protestors 'anti-authoritarian' he shows that he is no radical; he believes in formal channels of protest and legitimate power and authority. His later philosophical work was to be concerned with establishing exactly on what terms power and authority might be deemed accountable, transparent and consensual. So his reaction can be understood as one of dismay at futile social disruption that distracted attention from the real issues. The student protests represented a crass challenge to the problems of the capitalist order, a bad distraction from the philosophical enlightenment necessary to develop the communicative potentiality of democratic societies. However, for the leading critical theorist of his generation, some of Habermas' remarks sail close to conservatism. Claiming that the student protestors reject imperatives of achievement is the most conservative claim, for this implies that there are certain standards which distinguish excellence from mediocrity and below that, a place where failure is deserved if one does not meet a minimum standard. This resonates with Nietzsche's idea of *ressentiment*, the slave mentality in which defeat is turned into victory. In the same way, the student who does not have the nerve to face his exams is deluding himself in thinking that he is beating the system by dropping-out.

The protestors' rejection of self-regulating systems in favour of immediate self-gratification and their striving to create counter-worlds show an inability to take account of hard social facts. The influence of Weber and Durkheim is apparent here, as Habermas sees the students as naïve about the power of the state and the recalcitrance of reified systems to rapid change. The early signs of his adoption of Parsonian functionalism in *The Theory of Communicative Action* (1984/2004) are apparent as he argues that institutions and systems that have evolved historically cannot just be changed overnight. Political violence has no effective purpose and can only be explained as an emotional reaction to injustice which is unable to pressurize public opinion or those in power. Theory is not counterfactual fantasy. Even a theorist needs tactics and strategy.

In rejecting the activists' acceptance of neo-anarchism he reveals his own acceptance of the essential elements of liberalism; that one cannot arbitrarily upset public or private life or seek to smash the patterns of the everyday order on which capitalism depends. Within routine order is the private space of the individual, private consciousness is necessary to public enlightened consent: when private consciousness is dissolved in a collective society (as in Maoism) the result is totalitarianism. Social change must be achieved through agreement and consensus. He claims that the student movement failed to understand the inter-subjectivity which exists between persons. This is why they became monologically set within their own world view and incapable of juxtaposing their egos to society's alter. Their lack of ability to see the perspective of others enmeshed them in Marxism, Maoism and anarchism and is why they were unable to see the flaws of these ideologies.

Considering this level of criticism, it comes as a surprise that Habermas thought that the protests had any political merit at all. However, he did acknowledge one noteworthy aspect: they had at least raised the idea of a social alternative that had challenged the boundary limits within which capitalism defined itself:

> That protest has brought to consciousness the distinction between technical and practical problems, is, as I see it, a critical achievement. Attacking the ideology of the achieving society has made clear that today citizens' needs are recognized only within certain definitions [...] these

needs themselves are always already operationalised in categories of economically and administratively disposable rewards. Publicly tolerated definitions extend to what we need for life (income, leisure time and security) but not to how we should like to live if we could find out, in view of available potentials, how we could live. (Habermas 1971, 41)

Habermas's Later Reflections on Radical Politics

In 1979, Habermas gave an interview to Detlef Horster and Willem van Reijen, who asked him about his argument with the SDS. Habermas said that he 'clashed harder with the students than was perhaps politically necessary' (Dews 1986, 79) and that 'perhaps' [he reacted] 'a shade too much like a bourgeois intellectual' (ibid. 81). He said he responded in this way because he did not want the students' naïve conceptions of radical theory and change to gain wider support within the university generation. He also felt that the naïve radicalism of the students had presented a threat to the objectives and the success of his own conception of Critical Theory.

Habermas said that he was surprised to be called a neo-Marxist by Karl-Otto Apel[2] after the publication of *The Structural Transformation of the Public Sphere*, but he accepted this definition (ibid. 78). Marxism could no longer be viewed as a 'sure fire explanation' but it was important to preserve the essence of Marx, which is the idea that theoretical analysis can provide a critique which can lead to changes in life, open up possibilities and ward off the dominating effects of complex and expansive social systems which constrain people's lives. 'This is one tradition of the left which cannot be sacrificed' (ibid. 78).

Radical critique remained vital in the conservative Federal Republic, but the students had not recognized the country's new democratic potential. It was important for the progressive left to construct a critique which could accurately assess this potential and assist positive social change. The problem with the students' agenda was that it had continued using aspects of Marxism which were obsolete under the changed conditions of welfare state capitalism. This had an effect contrary to its intentions – unreconstructed Marxism had become ideological and now hindered democratic progress.

In spite of its errors, the protest movement was very significant because it 'brought about a rupture in the normative area and provided a reorientation of values in the cultural value system' (ibid. 81). He disagreed with the claim that contemporary students are more willing than ever to submit to all sorts of restrictions and this is where his argument has relevance for radicalism today. The 1960s saw an active distancing from the value orientations of the 1950s, which were privatized, instrumental values centred on career and family. The student movement marked the shift from an old to a new politics with more liberal values. Remembering that Habermas was speaking nearly a decade after the disbandment of the SDS, he said 'we are only beginning to see the effects of the protest movement' and the altered forms of socialization they have brought in' (ibid. 81).

The alternative value systems of the new politics can 'exercise a power of veto' over the worst effects of system-driven imperatives which run against them and try to overturn their potential. This means that radical politics can no longer determine the form of a future society with direct action because the scale of social systems in modern capitalism is beyond the full control of *all* individuals and groups, even those who exercise power. Complex and highly integrated 'steering' relationships exist between state, economy and society, which form a network of legitimations which do not respond to the political system alone (Habermas, 1971). These only become possible through increasingly reflexive attitudes to knowledge, which result in faster rates of learning and achievement in the sciences, which in turn contribute to further developments in the technical rationalization of society. Rationalization in the social domain leads to greater self-consciousness of norms and values, hence the emergence of the social sciences and the bourgeois civic sphere.

The outcome of these historical developments is that although there are now mass-scale, purposive-rational systems which have no central control, there is a high degree of awareness among many social actors about their negative effects. This is where protest groups exercise their veto: although they can no longer be certain about the outcome of their actions, or where the next movements in power and domination will come from, a high degree of legitimate resistance is possible which can bring about improvements to democracy. This is not to say such changes are secured without tension or conflict. What enables such democratic potentials to be eventually conceded by powerful groups is the bourgeois claim of the universality of its value system. Claims about the equality of men – and their equality to trade freely with one another – could not be maintained without contradiction if the claims of other groups, such as women and racially oppressed groups were not also conceded (Habermas 2001b, 329–87).

In the 1979 interview (Horster and van Reijen in Dews, 1986) Habermas says that the trends these values have instigated are hard to diagnose and that he doesn't want to make specific predictions. However, this remark was made only a few years before *The Theory of Communicative Action, Volume Two* was published in 1984, where his developed view of the direction of these alternative potentials can be found in the chapter 'The Thesis of Internal Colonization' (a key part of the conclusion). These comments can also be interpreted as the legacy of the generational changes of the 1960s and of what were ultimately the effects of the student protest movement.

The thesis of the internal colonization of the lifeworld can be understood as a reconstructed version of Marx's concept of alienation. Habermas rejects the labour theory of value which he claims results in Marx seeing worker-capitalist relations as the singularly important schism between objectively unjust social conditions and the subjective desire for an ethically reconciled society by those who are being exploited. Modern alienation reflects the complexity of contemporary capitalism because it can occur at the system level of economy and state and at the lifeworld level of private and public domains in each of the roles of employee and consumer, client of state bureaucracies and citizen of the state. Habermas combines a phenomenological concept of the lifeworld with the notion of communicative action. The lifeworld is understood as a stock of everyday knowledge about norms, traditions and customs which social actors use to navigate their everyday experience. Communicative action describes an intersubjective orientation to the truth between speakers about claims made in the objective, subjective and social worlds. In *The Theory of Communicative Action* and works such as *What is Universal Pragmatics?*, Habermas tries to show how truth claims are embedded in the lifeworld. Truth claims are tested in everyday contexts and while they may be distorted, they cannot ultimately be suppressed.

Habermas explains how rationalization leads to a greater degree of separation, or distancing of social systems from the everyday lifeworld of social actors as traditional societies develop into liberal-capitalist ones. Modern societies attain a degree of systemic differentiation which connects increasingly autonomous organizations to each other through the 'delinguistified' media of money and power. This differentiation results in social intercourse being disconnected from the moral and political will of actors (Habermas 2004b, 154). Thus the lifeworld becomes colonized by the system. Rationalizations in different domains such as law, culture and science result in a fragmentation of consciousness which dilutes ideological potency and 'blocks enlightenment by the mechanism of reification' (Habermas 2004b, 355). Thus the thesis of the internal colonization of the lifeworld, a theory of late-capitalist reification, has to exchange the Marxist theory of false consciousness for an analysis of cultural modernity. This brings the old form of radical social theory to an end:

> Rather than serving as a critique of ideology, this analysis would have to explain the cultural impoverishment and fragmentation of everyday consciousness. Rather than hunting after the scattered traces of revolutionary consciousness, it would have to examine the conditions for recoupling a rationalized culture with an everyday communication dependent upon vital traditions. (Habermas 2004b, 355–6)

However, it is simultaneous developments in law and moral thinking which lead to increases in the rationalization of the social or civic sphere. The effect is that communicative rationality gains more and more independence from normative contexts. Discourse about the lifeworld develops the potential to take place in a context which is autonomous of the system and the distortions it imposes on it. Habermas also points towards the new potentials for resistance to the colonization of the lifeworld in the 'Concluding Reflections' to *The Theory of Communicative Action*.

Habermas and Post-Sixties Movements

Habermas says that the two decades since the 1960s have seen conflict in advanced Western societies move away from the welfare state pattern of institutionalised conflict over distribution (Habermas 2004b, 392). Such conflicts no longer flare up in the domain of material reproduction and can no longer be alleviated by the compensations of the welfare state. This signals a move away from traditional class conflict, in which each class tries to gain power through political parties and promote its interests through trade unions or employers associations. The new conflicts occur in the realms of social and cultural production and which are not directly connected with traditional sites of power. Thus disaffection with the effects of the mass scale or 'reified' social systems, which have developed in modern capitalism, manifests itself as sub-institutional or extra-parliamentary protest so that these issues focus around 'defending and restoring endangered ways of life' (ibid. 392). A thesis explored in the UK context in Jones's chapter in this volume.

Habermas mentions a number of empirical studies (Inglehart 1979; Hildebrandt and Dalton 1977; Barnes and Kasse 1979) which provide evidence of the alternative values of the new politics. He says that there is a difference between protest movements with interests in traditional values and based on the defence of social rank (e.g. tax and school reform protests) and those which want to defend the space of the lifeworld, such as the antinuclear and environmental movements. The new politics is not a particular movement, but a diverse range of interest groups or issues which are focused on 'quality of life, equal rights, individual self realization, participation and human rights' as opposed to economic, social, internal and military security (Habermas 2004b, 392).

The Theory of Communicative Action was written about six or seven years before climate change was acknowledged in the wider scientific community as a serious problem and twelve to fifteen years before concerns about global sustainability became an issue in general public opinion. Somewhat prophetically, Habermas mentions 'green problems' and a reaction to 'problems of excessive complexity' such as nuclear power plants, genetic engineering and the storage of private data as being the main motivators of the opinion of the new politics. This has very much turned out to be the case. The Green movement and other groups motivated by environmental concerns are those who now hold the mantle of resistance to the capitalist system and its belief in its permanence and inevitability. Green movements specifically embody Habermas's claim of the alternative potential within the public sphere which resists its now global effects and which look to preserve and promote alternative, sustainable ways of living which are discordant with capitalism's emphasis on repetitive consumer consumption.

This is where the 'conceiving an alternative' and the 'how we *could* live' that Habermas mentioned in *Protestbewegung und Hochschulreform* now rests. It no longer means commitment to socialist revolutionary praxis, but promoting the sources of Green alternative potential and their capacity to continue to imagine what we need to do and what our course of action should be. The clearest immediate hope is in changing our patterns of consumption, as we are invoked to do so by the Green movement (Soper 2008). The purchasing of fair trade products, the boycotting of unethical products and an overall appetite for buying less 'stuff' would have the power to morph capitalism into a more ethical form if it were taken up on a mass scale. The need for sustainability and the increasing realization that there is a finite point to the environment as resources run low and the climate changes are more likely to be reasons which will induce substantial changes to the ways in which capitalism shapes our lives. As Habermas says in *The Theory of Communicative Action*, changes in action only occur when interests and motivation converge (Habermas, 2004a: 186–215). Green politics holds the kernel of a realistic alternative, which in comparison with anti-capitalism has a greater emphasis on nourishing transformation which will release further democratic potentials. Such transformations will have to be brought about by all of us because we see the need for it, rather than being taken to it by induced transformation.

The mantle of direct action for the purpose of socialist transformation is left to the anti-capitalist movement, which has been endorsed theoretically as well as pragmatically by Alex Callinicos (2003). Callinicos claims that the 'alternative potentials' that theorists like Habermas have identified as belonging to a post-socialist world in fact remain completely compatible with socialist analysis and objectives. Global capitalism has concentrated wealth and power on a greater scale and managed to fragment the working class and other excluded groups more successfully than before. Deeply entrenched global inequalities are testament to the continued power of capitalism and the injustice it causes. Class relationships have not disappeared, they have merely been reconstituted and it is vital that socialist groups continue their struggle. Protest remains an essential part of challenging the hegemony of capitalism and bringing about social justice because powerful elites have too much invested in the capitalist system to allow full democratization.

Global inequalities and injustice are manifest to anyone with a sociological imagination. However, from a Habermasian point of view, Callinicos's insistence that class conflict remains the cause of these inequalities fails to do justice to the problems the world's poor and exploited face today. Although not as crassly, Callinicos's argument makes the same error the student radicals made in wrapping a multitude of local struggles into a false unity of global resistance. Such an argument fails to move on from the totalizing errors of Marx's original analysis; as Habermas explains in 'Concluding Reflections' of *The Theory of Communicative Action*. The anti-capitalist perspective also does not learn from the two main lessons behind the legacy of 1960s radicalism and its failure.

The first is that it is not credible to maintain that false consciousness is the impediment to further social progress when there have been genuine achievements in the progression of democracy. Protest and disruption always invoke a response from the state (consider the notorious G8 summit in Genoa in 2001) but repression should not be confused with the state's legitimate defence of the rule of law. Direct action which goes beyond peaceful demonstration is a risky strategy because capitalism has at its disposal the liberal idea that violence or obstructionism has no place in the political process and this can always be used to delegitimise such forms of protest. They will always be checked by the argument that they are circumventing constitutional democracy. The second reason is that radicalism does not have widespread public support in the age of mass affluence. Affluence detracts from the convergence of interests and motivation that is necessary to make people demand change in their social circumstances. Anti-capitalism is the Left making claims it insists are compelling but which are not. The anti-capitalist justification retains an element of the Leninist idea of an ideological vanguard.

Conclusion: Habermas Bridging Sixties Radicalism and Today's Movements?

In the late 1960s, students thought China and Maoism was the model to follow. Today China is showing the world a new combination of autocracy and capitalism and is overtly pursuing exploitation of a greater share of the planet's diminishing resources. The USA has elected its first black president, but racial inequality in America remains widespread. The 'Third World' still has substantial levels of debt and governance in Africa remains problematic. The supposed sweep of leftist world revolution is gone, barring the anti-capitalists' fascination with the Zapatista movement (Callinicos, 2003: 81–82; 113–14).

Habermas's claim that he never saw himself as being outside of the student movement (Dews 1986, 80) is not a remark which stands up to scrutiny, however sincerely he believed, or continues to believe this. His emphasis on the crude nature of the students' position stands in contrast to his own highly developed analysis of the complexity of modern capitalism. The legacy of Habermas's rejection of naïve radicalism was the development of an analysis which accurately characterised the alternative democratic potentials which exist in the counter-cultures of today. The issues pertaining to a critique of global capitalism affect people the world over more than ever. In spite of failure of the student radicals' critique of capitalism, the problems of capitalism have taken on a new form with the more or less unrestricted nature of global capitalism. But with these problems, there is more or less greater potential than ever for resistance. The world has more states with democratic constitutions than ever and there are high levels of democratic aspiration, even where there is no democracy. These developments give cause for optimism that Habermas' alternative potentials are developing and diversifying beyond the boundaries of the West.

Notes

1 In the translator's preface to Towards a Rational Society, Jeremy J. Shapiro defines actionism (Aktionismus) as 'not activism but the policy of direct political action as a compulsive response to all conflict situations'.
2 Karl Otto-Apel, b. 15 March 1922. German philosopher whose work combines the traditions of analytic and continental philosophy; especially pragmatism and critical theory.

References

Barnes, S.H. and M. Kasse.1979. *Political Action: Mass Participation in Five Western Democracies*. Beverly Hills, CA: Sage

Callinicos, A. 2003. *An Anti-Capitalist Manifesto*. Oxford: Blackwell

Della Porta, D. 2006. *Social Movements, Political Violence and the State: A Comparative Analysis of Italy and Germany*. Cambridge: University Press

Dews, P (ed.) 1986. *Habermas: Autonomy and Solidarity: Interviews With Jürgen Habermas*. London: Verso

Doherty, B. 2002. *Ideas and Actions in the Green Movement*. London: Routledge

Habermas, J.1969.*Protestbewegung und Hochschulreform*. Frankfurt am Main: Suhrkamp

_____ 1971. *Towards a Rational Society*. London: Heinemann

_____ 1981. *Kleine Politische Schriften*. Frankfurt: Suhrkamp

_____ 1989. *Legitimation Crisis*. Cambridge: Polity Press

_____ 1990. *Moral Consciousness and Communicative Action*. Cambridge, Massachusetts: MIT Press

_____ 2001a. *The Postnational Constellation: Political Essays*. Cambridge, Massachusetts: MIT Press

_____ 2001b. *Between Facts and Norms: Contributions to a Discourse Theory of Law and Democracy*. Cambridge, Massachusetts: MIT Press

_____ 2004a. *Theory of Communicative Action Volume One: Reason and the Rationalization of Society*. Cambridge: Polity Press

———— 2004b. *Theory of Communicative Action Volume Two: The Critique of Functionalist Reason*. Cambridge: Polity Press

———— 2006. *Time of Transitions*. Cambridge: Polity Press

———— 2009. *The Structural Transformation of the Public Sphere*. Cambridge: Polity Press

Hildebrandt, K. and Dalton, R.J.1977. 'Die neue Politik'. *Politische Vierteljahreschrift* 18

Holub, R.C. 1991. *Jürgen Habermas: Critic in the Public Sphere*. London: Routledge

Inglehart, R. 1979. 'Wertwandel und politisches Verhalten', in Sozialer Wandel in Westeuropa. J. Matthes, ed. Frankfurt am Main: Campus Verlag

Katsiaficas, G. 1987. *The Imagination of the New Left: A Global Analysis of 1968*. Cambridge, MA: South End Press

Kolinsky, E. 1984. *Parties, Opposition and Society in West Germany*. Beckenham Croom Helm

Marwick, A.1999. *The Sixties: Cultural Revolution in Britain, France, Italy and the United States, c. 1958–1974*. Oxford University Press

Soper, K. 2008. Beyond Consumerism: Self-Interest, Pleasure and Sustainable Consumption. Online: http://www.sussex.ac.uk/Units/CCE/conferences0607/beyondconsumerism_katesoper (accessed 28 July 2008)

Thomas, N. 2003. *Protest Movements in 1960s West Germany: A Social History of Dissent and Democracy*. Oxford: Berg

Turk, E.L. 1999. *The History of Germany*. Westport: Greenwood Press

Part III
SOCIAL MOVEMENT LEGACIES

Chapter 10

SIXTIES MOVEMENTS, EDUCATIONAL EXPANSION AND COGNITIVE MOBILISATION: POSTMATERIALIST VALUES AND UNCONVENTIONAL POLITICAL PARTICIPATION IN WEST GERMANY

Andreas Hadjar and Florian Schlapbach

Introduction

This chapter will focus, from a quantitative and longitudinal perspective, on the cohorts who experienced and were involved in those sixties events often symbolized by reference to the climactic year 1968. It looks in particular at the connection between education and values and unconventional political participation. As education has been a major characteristic of the active sixties generation, educational level and educational expansion will be theorised to analyse social mechanisms behind the sixties movement and its development. We will compare the sixties generation – the birth cohorts 1946–53 at the core – to other earlier and later cohorts regarding their values, and political participation. As there are strong differences between different educational levels, three educational groups will be compared to each other (low educated, intermediate educated and more-highly educated people). As another issue the change in values, orientations and behaviour over time period or age will be analysed for different cohorts and educational levels. To follow the course of development of values and political participation of the sixties generation over time in comparison to other cohorts, longitudinal methods of analysis will be deployed – in particular A-P-C-Analysis (i.e. simultaneous analysis of age, period and cohort effects). The data base used is the German General

Social Survey (ALLBUS). To analyse these changes appropriately, we consider a time span of 20 years – beginning with 1986 and ending with 2006.

The core thesis of this article is that the sixties movement is connected to processes of educational expansion before and in the 1960s. On the one hand, members of the cohort of citizens born between 1946 and 1953 were among the first in West Germany to undergo the new programmes and who benefited from the educational expansion. Hence, they were the first which should have cultivated a stronger political interest and sensibility for political topics. On the other hand, the sixties movement is also an actor within the educational expansion as the sixties generation contributed to the new development by actively participating in the reforms, being just out of school at the time of the educational expansion and being part of a worldwide movement which began to challenge the decisions of the political elites, also by participating in unconventional political activities such as demonstrations and boycotts.

Whereas the main idea behind educational reforms all over Europe in the 20th Century was to extend education to produce more sophisticated people and to increase economic growth, social democratic and liberal thinkers like sociologist Ralf Dahrendorf aimed at an improvement of education among the citizens to increase civil liberty and to strengthen democracy (Dahrendorf 1965). In West Germany, another important idea behind the extension of the educational system was to improve people's ability to understand the political system and to contribute actively to it. Inglehart provided first evidence of such a *cognitive mobilization* that leads to a value change as well as a change in political behaviour and is strongly linked to education (Inglehart 1990). Analyses of cognitive mobilization mainly focus on cohort effects. What are needed are complex analyses that reconstruct social change by considering different temporal effects (age, period and cohort effects) simultaneously. As Hadjar and Schlapbach (2009a) have already demonstrated regarding political interest, only a complex A-P-C analysis allows the drawing of conclusions on temporal effects.

Our main thesis is that political activity, as unconventional forms of participation, increased and a change in values – people showing more postmaterialist values, i.e. environmental protection, tolerance of diversity, participation in decisions – has been consolidated through educational expansion in West Germany. The sixties generation may be affected by these changes in particular. We first develop a theoretical framework, including insights of current research. Then visual inspections regarding the cohort- and education-specific political activity and postmaterialism will be presented. Before we turn to the discussion, we use multivariate analyses to empirically analyse the impact of factors like education and cohort, as well as age, cohort and period, on the change in the level of political activity and the shift of values towards postmaterialism. Using an A-P-C model – including a surrogate for the metric cohort variable to prevent the common temporal fallacies – enables us to distinguish different temporal effects. Specifically, to show that political activity is highest among the young people but also increases in successive cohorts, and that, though postmaterialism decreases with age, it increases over cohort succession.

Educational Expansion, Political Activity and Postmaterialism

Before considering the impact of the educational expansion on postmaterialism and political activity in temporal perspective, we first focus on the links between education and these two traits at the individual level.

Education and Political Activity and Postmaterialism on the Individual Level

The link between education and political participation can be theorised by use of the Standard Socioeconomic Model of Participation (Verba et al. 1978) which suggests that people with more education, a higher income level and people who work in professional or white-collar jobs are more likely to participate in politics. Education turned out to be the best predictor for political participation. The Civic Voluntarism Model of Political Participation (Verba et al. 1995) shifts the perspective from the notion of education as a socioeconomic variable to the notion of education in terms of competences and skills: citizens not only have to be motivated to participate in political processes, they also have to be *able* to participate. This refers to political competences that may be greater in settings characterised by a higher educational level. Education also turned out to be a strong predictor of postmaterialist value preferences – since a higher education goes along with a cognitive mobilisation (Inglehart 1990).

More highly educated people have an easier access to politics and political issues (Verba & Nie 1972), as they are characterised by more advanced competences in recognising, understanding and reflecting political issues and by certain, rather postmaterialist, value systems (Inglehart 1977). A higher educational level also leads to a higher perception of 'internal political efficacy' (Becker 2004), that is higher individual behavioural control beliefs: more highly educated people perceive themselves as more competent to deal with political processes and to participate in orthodox and unorthodox political activities. A higher educational level also stands for lower costs of political participation, because higher information processing capacities and reflection skills reduce costs for information search and the costs that occur when reflecting political issues. All in all, a higher educational level means an easier access to politics. Education is also connected to individual values and attitudes, like postmaterialism, which are related to participation. According to Inglehart (1977) postmaterial values are positively associated with unconventional political participation rather than involvement in voting.

The first hypothesis is directly derived from the preceding reflections: education leads to a change in value preferences and increased abilities in the three mentioned fields:

Hypothesis 1: political activity and postmaterialism increase with educational level.

Educational Expansion and Cognitive Mobilisation

The link between education, values and participation on the individual level may be applied to the macro level: educational expansion should have caused an increase in political engagement and participation behaviour. Many scholars focus on the effect of a 'cognitive mobilisation' on the population (Dalton 1984; Inglehart 1990). Cognitive mobilisation may be regarded as an element of long-run societal change on the collective level (Baumert 1991; Deutsches PISA Konsortium 2003). Applying the assumed link between education and political values and behavioural pattern on the individual level to the cohort level or level of society, it may be assumed that a higher educational level goes along with an improved access to politics and are a higher political activity among cohorts or societies. Cognitive mobilisation means an increase in skills to deal with politics, i.e. a rise in genuine political competences (Dalton 1984; Hadjar and Schlapbach 2009a). Another consequence of the cognitive mobilisation may be a value change – the drift from materialist (wealth, security) to postmaterialist values (civil rights, self-realisation) – although this mainly links back to the rising level of economic wealth (Inglehart 1977, 1990).

As temporal change – in our view – has to be analysed by simultaneously considering three temporal effects – age (lifecycle), period (events) and cohort effects (socialisation) – we hypothesise several temporal assumptions. Due to the educational expansion, younger cohorts especially should show a higher level of postmaterialist values and political activity. The role of cohort-specific socialisation experiences may be also theorised by use of the Civic Voluntarism Model (Verba et al. 1995) according to which people develop capacities and motivation for political involvement in family and school early in life. Following the additional assumption that motivation and capacities are accumulated over lifetimes, political activity should increase with age.

Analyses on *cohort effects* will focus on 'abstracted cohort bundles' which represent particular generations and their formative socialisation experiences.

According to the concept of political generations, a cohort represents a generation that is characterised by shared socialisation experiences and therefore has a common general world view – although there may be differences. Following the socialisation thesis of Inglehart (1977) this world view is relatively stable over time. Regarding political generations, the cohort change should follow the same pattern as may be expected from the perspective of a cognitive mobilisation. Consequently, as economic problems disappeared and a student movement spread challenging prevailing ideas, a rapid political mobilisation may be expected for the people born after World War Two. However, the youngest generation should have the highest political activity level, as these people were confronted with problematic societal conditions (environmental problems, rising unemployment, etc.) early in their lives and may therefore be highly mobilised.

Table 1 shows the birth cohorts – bundled up according to Klein and Ohr (2004) – with a core time of political socialisation around the age of 15 and main events, including educational expansion. In both samples, the birth cohorts 1954 to 1971 benefited from the educational expansion most and therefore may have a higher level of cognitive mobilisation than previous birth cohorts.

According to the theoretical exploration of the link between educational level and politics, the cohort effect should reflect a 'cognitive mobilisation' (Deutsches PISA Konsortium 2003; Inglehart 1990; Dalton 1984):

Hypothesis 2: younger cohorts show more political activity and show more postmaterialist values.

*Table 10.1: **Generations in West Germany, Birth Cohorts 1924–1964***

Birth Cohort	Time of Political Socialisation	Events in West Germany
1924–1934	1939–1949	*War-Generation, After-War Generation* totalitarian dictatorship, World War Two, downfall, end of war, post-war (poverty)
1935–1945	1950–1960	*Adenauer Generation* Re-Democratisation, Reconstruction, economic miracle (Wirtschaftswunder), full employment
1946–1953	1961–1968	*APO Generation (Protest Generation, sixties generation)* period of prosperity, beginning students movement, initiation of educational reforms
1954–1964	1969–79	*Generation of increasing crisis* continuing protest movement, Brandt Era (socio-democratic government), economic crisis, educational expansion

Additionally, *period effects* seem to influence the societal level of political activity and postmaterialist values – and therefore change on the macro level – to a large extent. Period effects arise from societal events, political developments and societal conditions both on the structural and ideological levels that affect all birth cohorts. Nevertheless there will be cohort-specific variations in the perception of these context conditions and in how they deal with such period-specific circumstances. Strong period effects are likely to occur in the environment of elections, in times of severe societal problems (e.g. unemployment, environmental crisis or recession). This fits with the assumption of Klages (1984) who interprets political interest in terms of dissatisfaction with the political system and governmental policies. An increasing perception of problems leads to a decrease of 'apolitical trust' in the state – resulting in a higher political interest and eventually a higher activity level. Looking at the periods of the survey, in the former state of West Germany, political activity should have increased towards the end of the 20th century as the unemployment rate increased and people lost their trust in the conservative government of Chancellor Kohl. Regarding postmaterialist values, it may be assumed that times of prosperity may support a postmaterialist value climate on the societal level. As the proportion of people who prefer postmaterialist values increases, postmaterialist values may spread to the whole society. However, as period effects depend on various issues, it does not seem appropriate to postulate a linear period effect:

Hypothesis 3: effects of education and cohort are overlaid by period effects that are based on social events, socio-structural change and value climate.

The postulated cohort and period effects do not stand alone, there is also an age effect – as political orientations and behaviour develop and increase during the lifelong socialisation process. Although there may be a core phase of political socialisation during late adolescence, knowledge and reflection competences may increase over the lifecycle. The argument that the process of political socialisation and political learning stagnates at older ages does not seem very plausible regarding societal discourses on pensions and health care. However, since it cannot be assumed that political activity and postmaterialism develop linearly with age, age groups will be integrated into the empirical models to have a closer look at particular ages.

Political activity will increase with political socialisation and therefore with age. According to theoretical reflections and empirical evidence, people lose their postmaterialist values when growing older and tend to follow more materialist values. But this is more an effect of changing circumstances at different stages of the life cycle than a biological age effect:

Hypothesis 4: whereas political activity increases with age, postmaterialism decreases.

Social status and gender are integrated into the models of analysis as control variables. Social status is a meaningful control for the education effect, since education is to be interpreted both in terms of cognitive abilities and socio-economic status – more highly educated people reach higher positions in the social structure. The introduction of a status variable (occupational prestige) aims to separate the effect of cognitive abilities (education) from effects of a higher social status. Gender is introduced for three reasons. First, because empirical evidence suggests a gender gap in political participation: women participate to a lesser extent. However, regarding postmaterialism, no clear gender difference may be assumed. Second, women benefited most from the educational expansion; gender inequalities regarding educational opportunities declined. Third, the introduction of a gender variable into A-P-C-models is meaningful, since women have a higher life expectancy – which otherwise would lead to a biased age effect.

Research Design: Methods, Sample and Instruments

To analyse social change adequately social change will be understood as a composition of age, period and cohort effects and therefore analysed by using an *A-P-C design* — meaning a simultaneous modelling of age, period and cohort effects (*cf.* Hadjar and Schlapbach 2009a). This approach will also prevent a 'temporal fallacy' which means the drawing of wrong conclusions from findings on one or two temporal levels. For instance, value change is not just a cohort effect – as Inglehart (1990) has put it – but may be overlaid by age and period effects. Respectively, it may be assumed that change in political activity and postmaterialism is a composition outcome of effects of the cohort-specific socialisation and educational level, aging effects (position within the lifecycle) and effects of the time of survey (political and societal events and conditions or zeitgeist). Since age, period and cohort variables cannot be introduced simultaneously in a regression model (confounding problem: Glenn 2005; Tuma and Hannan 1984, 192), we use the cohort-specific heterogeneity of the student population as a surrogate for the cohort variable.

The *database* of this analysis is a cumulated data-set of ALLBUS, the German General Social Survey. Only the timeframe 1986–2006 and the West German citizens with a German citizenship are considered for this study. Furthermore, we restricted the sample to the cohorts 1924–1964 and people between the ages of 21 and 80. This reduction was made in order to take into account only people who already received their general school certificate and already passed the core period of political socialisation. In total, the sample consists of 20,815 valid cases.

As for the *measures*, the dependent variables will be considered first before introducing the measures for the independent variables. Regarding *political activity*, respondents had to answer four questions concerning their participation in the following four activities: citizen's initiatives, petitions, boycotts and demonstrations. Based on the respondent's replies, we constructed an additive index ranging between '0', for 'never participated in any of the mentioned activities' and '4', for 'participated in each one of the mentioned alternatives', We dichotomised this index for the graphical interpretations. Respondents who participated only in one activity were assigned a '0', the rest with participation in up to four activities got a '1', The second dependent variable concerns, respectively, materialist and *postmaterialist values*. We used the Ingehart-Index based on the answers to four questions regarding 'calm and order', 'citizen's influence', 'control of inflation' and 'free speech', People had to determine the importance of each topic. Depending on their decision they were assigned either to the category of citizens with a tendency to postmaterialism (postmaterialists) or citizens with a tendency to materialism (materialists) or people with ambivalent values (indifferent value type).

Education was measured via the general school leaving qualification and has three categories: low-educational level, including people with no or a low qualification, intermediate educational level and high educational level, people with an education equivalent to the UK A-levels. The *birth cohort* as one of three temporal variables was included in various ways in the following analyses. For a better interpretation of different socialisation periods, cohorts were bundled up into four dummy variables, each consisting of birth cohorts that represent particular times. To figure out a trend over all birth cohorts, the year of birth was included. A third way to analyse cohort effects – and a way that is necessary when modelling age, period and cohort effects simultaneously – is to substitute the conventional cohort variable 'year of birth' by a variable that represents an important cohort characteristic such as 'heterogeneity of student population'. Regarding educational expansion, cohort succession is not just characterised by a rising educational level, which is already included in the models, but by a rising heterogeneity that results from the opening of the higher school pathways to all classes.[1] *Age* was measured in years and transformed into dummy variables each comprising of ten years. The time period – that is the year of data gathering – was also included as dummy variables within the model, each standing for one year. The dichotomous *gender* variable refers to the male gender as '1' stands for males and '0' for females.

Figure 10.1: Educational Expansion in West Germany.

	1924–1934	1935–1945	1946–1953	1954–1964
High educational level	13.1	16	22	32.3
Intermediate educational level	15.7	22	26.4	30.4
Low educational level	71.2	62	51.6	37.3

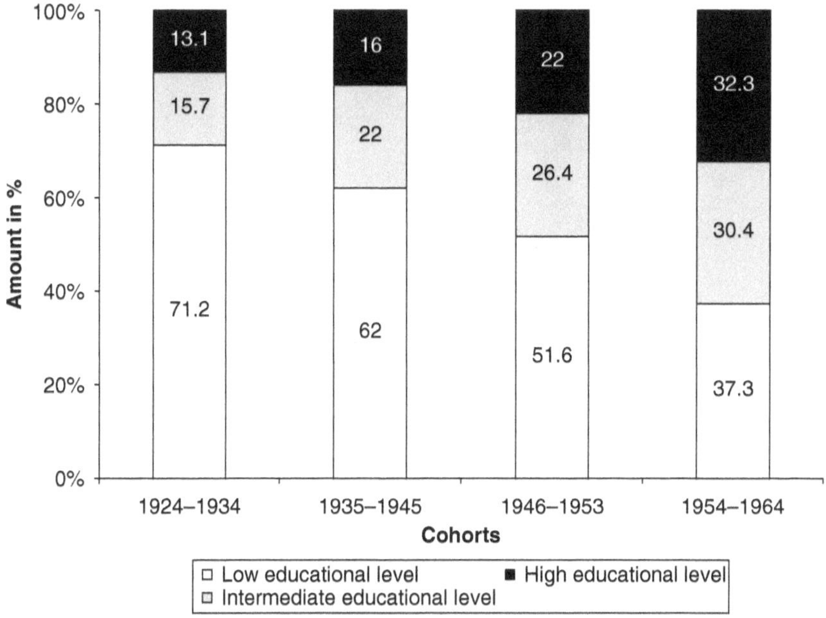

Data Source: ALLBUS 1980–2006; authors' own calculation.

Results of the Survey Analysis

First, we reconstruct the course of the educational expansion in West Germany in Figure 1. This figure shows cohort differences in education – the proportion of more highly educated people – and heterogeneity level regarding five cohorts. The average educational level rises gradually. In West Germany, only 13.1 per cent of the members of the 1924–34 birth cohorts attained an upper secondary school certificate, whereas the proportion rises to 32.3 per cent in the youngest cohort of people born between 1954 and 1964. The 'sixties generation', i.e. people born between 1946 and 1953, is characterised by an already raised educational level.

Secondly, the link between social origin and educational level decreases slightly during the educational expansion. This means that heterogeneity of the pupils in intermediate and higher educational institutions regarding social origin increases over cohort succession before reaching its highest level, i.e. the lowest level regarding educational inequalities, among the 'sixties generation'. A reversal of the heterogenisation process may be noted for the youngest cohort – as their parents already benefited from the educational expansion and reached a higher educational level (see Figure 2).

Figure 10.2: Association between Social Origin and Educational Level.

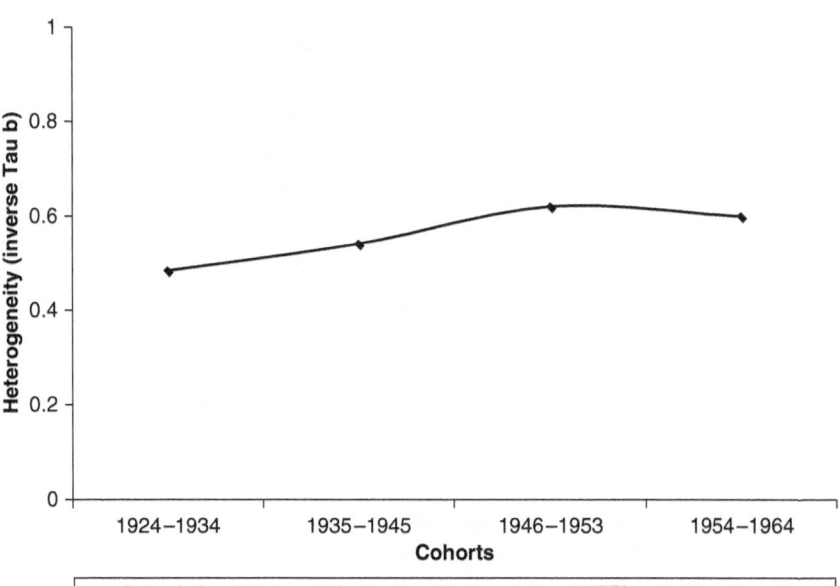

Data Source: ALLBUS 1980–2006; authors' own calculation.

Thirdly, the rise in political activity – in particular unconventional political participation – is explored in Figure 3. The rise in political activity during the educational expansion – expressed by the cohort succession – is much stronger among the more-highly educated than in the other educational groups. The political mobilisation and activation took place among the people with at least an upper secondary school degree. The 'sixties generation' has a higher activity level – the activity level does not increase further among the next cohort: the people born between 1954 and 1964.

Fourthly, differences in values are noticeable. In Figure 4, the percentage of materialist and postmaterialist people is indicated for each cohort and the different educational levels. Among the highest educational group the number of postmaterialists is much higher than among intermediate or low educated people. Regarding educational expansion, with respect to successive cohorts, the percentage of postmaterialists has risen much stronger in the highest educational group, whereas the increase in postmaterialism among intermediate and lower educated people took a much smoother course. The 'sixties generation' – the cohorts born between 1946 and 1953 – has a higher postmaterialism level than earlier cohorts. The increase in postmaterialism stagnates with the youngest cohorts (birth cohorts 1954–64).

Figure 10.3: Political Activity, Education and Cohort.

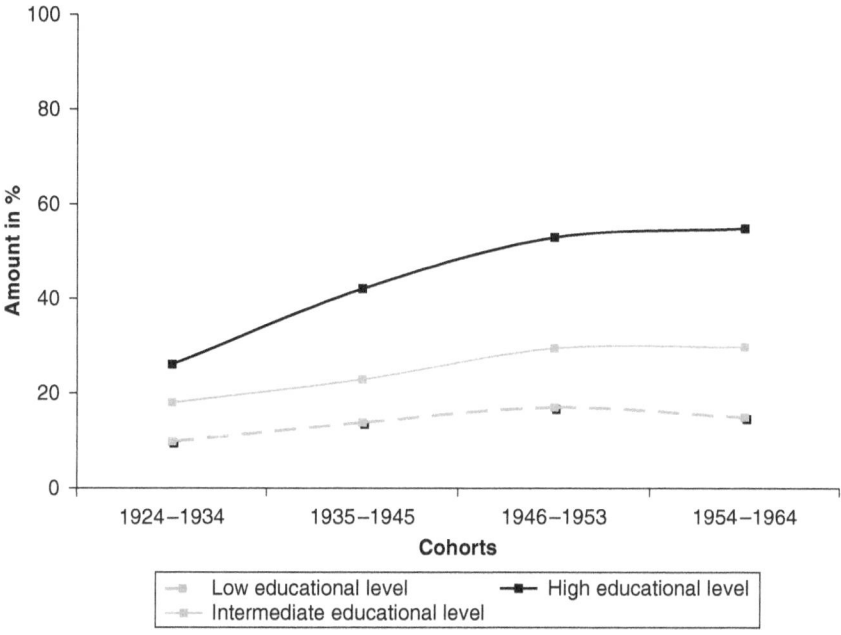

Data Source: ALLBUS 1988, 1990, 1991, 1992, 2000; authors' own calculation.

However, these descriptive results – in particular regarding cohort differences – are not interpretable without analysing age and period effect. Therefore in a further step, we use multivariate regression models.

Regarding unconventional political participation, we estimated ordinal regression models (Table 2). The coefficients may be interpreted in the same way as odds ratios – significant scores above 1 indicate positive effects, significant scores below 1 indicate negative effects. These results show that the higher the educational level, the higher the political participation. Women are less politically active than men. Political activity increases with social status (profession prestige). Both the cohorts born 1946–53 and the youngest cohort (born 1954–64) are characterised by a significantly higher level in political activity than earlier cohorts. But, again, we must look at the APC results in model 3 to interpret the change more correctly. In all of the APC models (models 3, table 2) including period effects, our reference category is the year 2000, since we only use four periods of data collection. All in all, there seems to be an increase in political activity between 1990 and 2000, although we have no data for every single year. And, the probability of being involved in unconventional political activity is highest for the youngest age group, decreasing slightly with age. Additional analyses (Hadjar and Schlapbach 2009b) of the interaction

Figure 10.4: Value Change, Education and Cohort.

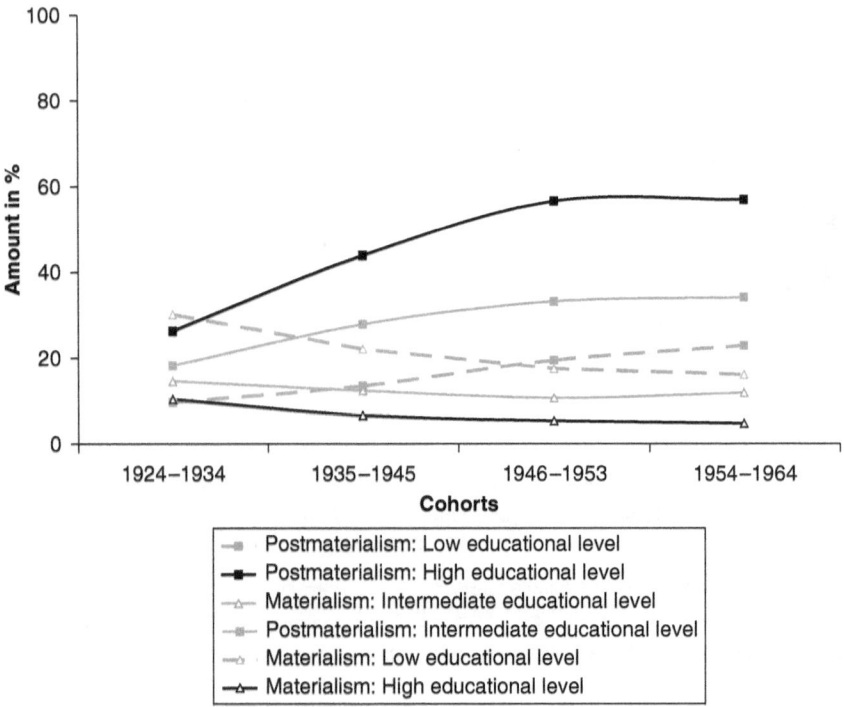

Data Source: ALLBUS 1986–2006; authors' own calculation.

effects of age and cohort show that the sixties generation and the previous generation (1935–45) cumulated political activity over lifecycle to a larger extent than the oldest did. Even the youngest cohorts did not accumulate as much political activity so far.

Regarding postmaterialism, we estimated multinomial regression models (see Table 3) in which significant odds ratio values of above 1 indicate a positive effect of the independent variable on postmaterialism while values below 1 indicate a negative effect. The results of model 1 suggest, in accordance to previous international findings of Inglehart (1990), that postmaterialism rises with the educational level and social status. Inglehart's (1990) socialisation and cohort thesis is also reproduced, since earlier born cohorts have a lower postmaterialism than the sixties generation and the later born (1954–1964) have a higher postmaterialism. Regarding materialism, the sixties generation is characterised by a lower materialism level compared to previous cohorts, but does not differ significantly from the later born cohorts (1954–64). There is only a slightly significant gender difference in postmaterialism. Women are less postmaterialist than men – which is not a common finding in values research.

Table 10.2: **Education and Political Activity in West Germany – Multivariate Analyses**

Ordinal Regression		Model I	Model II	Model III
Thresholds (Political Activity)				
	τ_1	.430***	.280**	−.257*
	τ_2	1.621***	1.496***	.959***
	τ_3	2.772***	2.664***	2.122***
	τ_4	4.058***	3.959***	3.416***
Variables				
Education				
Intermediate educational level		1.260***	1.270***	1.276***
High educational level		1.701***	1.639***	1.685***
Reference category: Low educational level				
Female Gender		.940***	.947*	.946*
Reference category: Male gender				
Occupational Prestige (MPS)		1.208***	1.007***	1.204***
Birth Cohort (Dummy Variables)				
Reference category: 1946–1953	1924–1934	.746***		
	1935–1945	.855***		
	1954–1964	1.028		
Birth Cohort (Year of Birth)			1.248***	
Interaction Education • Birth Cohort				
Intermediate educational level • Birth Cohort			1.023	
High educational level • Birth Cohort			1.129***	
Reference category: Low educational level • Birth Cohort				
Heterogeneity in Social Origin of Educational Groups (cohort substitute)				1.081†
Interaction Education • Heterogeneity (cohort substitute)				
Intermediate educational level • Heterogeneity				1.000
High educational level • Heterogeneity				1.088***
Reference category: Low educational level • Heterogeneity				
Period				
Reference category: 2000	1988		.669***	.611***
	1990		.867***	.805***
	1991		.924**	.880***
	1992		.885***	.840***

(Continued)

Table 10.2: (**Continued**)

Ordinal Regression		Model I	Model II	Model III
Age				
Reference category: 21–30	31–40			.890***
	41–50			.841***
	51–60			.814***
	61–70			.782***
	71–80			.916***
N		7'078	7'078	7'078
Nagelkerkes R²		.154	.176	.176

In model 3, we again follow an A-P-C design to analyse change adequately. The effect of heterogeneity, as substitute for the cohort effect, is not significant. This suggests that the cohort-specific change is based on the rise in education. The negative effect of heterogeneity regarding materialism indicates a significant decrease in materialism during educational expansion that goes beyond the changes caused by the increasing educational level itself. The significant interaction effect of high educational level and heterogeneity indicates that the increase in postmaterialism in the highest educational group has been much stronger than in the group of people with low or intermediate educational level. As can be seen looking at the period effects, there is no clear pattern regarding the postmaterialist value change between 1986 and 2006 on the societal level, although there are several significant period influences that may be rooted in political or societal events and the value climate. What is a new and important about these findings compared to Inglehart's (1990) argument is that the age effects follow a clear pattern: Whereas postmaterialism decreases with age, materialism increases with age: People seem to lose their postmaterialistic values as they become more established in work and family life.

Conclusions

We are now in a position to put the distinctiveness of the 'sixties generation' into a broader temporal and socio-cultural context. The results provide backing for several assumptions that have been derived from the theoretical framework. Firstly, and consistent with hypothesis 1, the findings indicate a robust *effect of education*: more highly educated people are rather postmaterialist and politically mobilised in terms of political (unorthodox) participation.

Table 10.3: Education and Postmaterialism in West Germany – Multivariate Analyses

Mixed Nominal Regression Ref.: Mixed Value Type	Model I Postmat.	Model I Mat.	Model II Postmat.	Model II Mat.	Model III Postmat.	Model III Mat.
Variables						
Education						
Intermediate educational level	1.653***	.753***	1.674***	.746***	1.664***	.750***
High educational level	2.933***	.635***	2.728***	.650***	2.781***	.636***
Reference category: Low educational level						
Female Gender	.931†	1.178***	.922*	1.165***	.925*	1.165***
Reference category: Male gender						
Occupational Prestige (MPS)	1.006***	.989***	1.007***	.989***	1.007***	.989***
Birth Cohort (Dummy Variables)						
Reference category: 1946–1953						
1924–1934	.436***	1.574***				
1935–1945	.686***	1.159***				
1954–1964	1.140**	.962				
Birth Cohort (Year of Birth)			1.030***	.980***		
Interaction Education • Birth Cohort						
Intermediate educational level • Birth Cohort			.996	1.017**		
High educational level • Birth Cohort			1.007	1.005		
Reference category: Low educational level • Birth Cohort						
Heterogeneity in Social Origin of Educational Groups (cohort substitute)					1.432	.244**
Interaction Education • Heterogeneity (cohort substitute)						
Intermediate educational level • Heterogeneity					.885	3.871†
High educational level • Heterogeneity					9.690**	3.098

(*Continued*)

Table 10.3: **(Continued)**

Mixed Nominal Regression Ref.: Mixed Value Type		Model I		Model II		Model III	
		Postmat.	Mat.	Postmat.	Mat.	Postmat.	Mat.
Reference category: Low educational level • Heterogeneity							
Period							
Reference category: 1986	1988			1.052	1.148	1.104	1.120
	1990			1.085	.915	1.189*	.867
	1991			.951	.758*	1.072	.700**
	1992			.740***	1.496***	.854†	1.375***
	1994			.710***	1.035	.859†	.936
	1996			.725***	.730**	.924	.637***
	1998			.555***	1.135	.742**	.967
	2000			.824*	.866	1.148	.711**
	2002			.766**	1.318**	1.125	1.054
	2004			.653***	1.076	1.009	.839
	2006			.646***	1.080	1.061	.828*
Age							
Reference category: 21-30	31–40					.810**	1.402**
	41–50					.648***	1.380**
	51–60					.464***	1.451***
	61–70					.389***	1.788***
	71–80					.283***	2.399***
N		17'958		17'958		17'958	
Nagelkerkes R²		.158		.172		.171	

*** p < .001, ** p < .01, * p < .05, † p < .10.
Data Source: ALLBUS 1988, 1990, 1991, 1992, 2000; authors' own calculation.

This is another successful test of the Socioeconomic Model of Participation as well as the Civic Voluntarism Model by Verba and colleagues. Secondly, the assumption that preference for *postmaterialist values*, as well as political activity, increases among younger cohorts (hypothesis 2), is also partially confirmed by the results. However, the complex A-P-C models show that most of these positive cohort effects may be linked to the increasing educational level over cohort succession and therefore to the educational expansion. Thirdly, however, *political mobilization* did not affect all educational groups in the same way: the gap between the highest educational level and the lowest educational level increases over cohort succession – very strongly regarding postmaterialism and to an intermediate extent regarding political activity. Therefore it can be stated that political mobilisation has been strongest among the more-highly educated people.

However, cross-cutting these general findings on education, values and political activity are findings related to hypothesis 3, postulating *'period effects'* from social events, socio-structural change and a different value climate: There are significant period effects, e.g. a high in political activity in 2000 and lows in postmaterialism during the 1990s. The 'de-radicalising' effects of ageing postulated in hypothesis 4 are of particular interest:

- as postulated, the likelihood of participating actively in politics clearly increases with age,
- postmaterialism decreases over the lifecycle, which may be linked to particular life stage differences,
- materialism seems to increase again when material wealth and security become more important; e.g. after family foundation.

On conventional indicators, women turned out to be less politically active and less postmaterialist than men. More generally, with a higher social status, in terms of profession prestige, political activity and postmaterialism increase. This finding provides backing for both the Socioeconomic Model of Participation (Verba et al. 1978) and the thesis of Inglehart (1977) that postmaterialism increases when materialist needs have been fulfilled.

What does this broader contextualisation tell us about the alleged distinctiveness of the sixties generation? This generation is certainly more highly educated and politically mobilised than earlier generations. However, the movement consisted mainly of the more highly-educated people. Amongst the '68 group, those who received A-level equivalent, or tertiary education are the most postmaterialist and most politically active. However, political mobilisation is recognisable also among younger cohorts. There has been a continuing increase in postmaterialism and political activity regarding the consecutive cohorts after the sixties generation. As these cohorts continued to experience high educational experience, educational expansion may be one root, along others, that supported the occurrence of the sixties movement.

Educational expansion may also be one root, among others, that has strengthened value change as well as the rise in unorthodox political activity. The cognitive mobilisation is indicated – although not in an optimal way, since we did no achievement tests – in the education effects. Since we included a status effect (profession prestige) in the models and modelled both education and status simultaneously, it may be assumed that the education variable is not an expression of status influences, but of cognitive abilities.

From a methodological point of view, a main outcome can be seen in the A-P-C results which allow us to differentiate clearly between age, period and cohort effects. Taking into account the three temporal effects simultaneously is an important necessity in analysing temporal change adequately. On the other hand, there are also several methodological limitations to be addressed. A rather short time period is covered, from 1986 to 2006, for political activity it is only from 1988–2000. Longitudinal data, covering longer time periods in particular panel data, are needed to separate age, period and cohort effects more adequately.

The sixties generation have, in a sense, passed on distinctive value shifts and political activities to subsequent cohorts. These did not fade away as the '68 cohort aged. However, their aims of spreading their values and political radicalism through the rest of German society have not succeeded. Postmaterialism and alternative political activities remain confined to similar, highly-educated strata of that society.

Note

1 Since a higher value of Tau b for the association between social origin (that is Magnitude prestige score of the father; Wegener 1988) and the educational level indicates homogeneity, the inverse Tau b is used as substitute for each year of birth or cohort to indicate increasing heterogeneity.

References

Baumert, J. 1991. Langfristige Auswirkungen der Bildungsexpansion. *Unterrichtswissenschaft*, 19: 333–349.
Becker, R. 2004. Voter Turnouts in East and West Germany. *German Politics*, 13: 1–19.
Dahrendorf, R. 1965. *Bildung ist Bürgerrecht*. Hamburg: Nannen.
Dalton, R. J. 1984. Cognitive Mobilization and Partisan Dealignment in Advanced Industrial Democracies. *The Journal of Politics*, 46: 264–284.
Deutsches PISA Konsortium. 2003. *Pisa 2000 – Ein differenzierter Blick auf die Länder der Bundesrepublik Deutschland*. Opladen: Leske and Budrich.

Glenn, N. D. 2005. *Cohort analysis.* Thousand Oaks: Sage.
Hadjar, A. and Schlapbach, F. 2009a. Educational Expansion and Interest in Politics in temporal and cross-cultural perspective: a comparison of West Germany and Switzerland. *European Sociological Review*, 25: 271–286.
Hadjar, A. and Schlapbach, F. 2009b. The 1968 Movement Revisited – Education and the Distinction in Values, Political Interest and Political Participation in West Germany. *German Politics*, 18: 180–200.
Inglehart, R. 1977. *The Silent Revolution. Changing Values and Political Styles among Western Publics.* Princeton, NJ: Princeton Univ. Press.
Inglehart, R. 1990. *Culture Shift in Advanced Industrial Society.* Princeton NJ: Princeton University Press.
Klages, H. 1984. *Wertorientierungen im Wandel.* Frankfurt am Main/New York: Campus.
Klein, M. and Ohr, D. 2004. Ändert der Wertewandel seine Richtung? Die Entwicklung gesellschaftlicher Wertorientierungen in der Bundesrepublik Deutschland zwischen 1980 und 2000. In: R. Schmitt-Beck, M. Wasmer and A. Koch, eds., *Sozialer und politischer Wandel in Deutschland. Analysen mit ALLBUS-Daten aus zwei Jahrzehnten,* Wiesbaden: VS Verlag für Sozialwissenschaften: 153–178.
Tuma, N. B. and Hannan, M. T. 1984. *Social Dynamics: Models and Methods.* Orlando: Academic Press.
Verba, S. and Nie, N. H. 1972. *Participation in America. Political Democracy and Social Equality.* New York, NY: Harper Row.
Verba, S., Nie, N. H. and Kim, J. 1978. *Participation and Political Equality.* Cambridge: Cambridge University Press.
Verba, S., Schlozman, K. L. and Brady, H. 1995. *Voice and Equality. Civic Voluntarism in American Politics.* Cambridge, MA: Harvard University Press.
Wegener, B. 1988. *Kritik des Prestiges.* Opladen: Westdeutscher Verlag.

Chapter 11

CARRYING THE FLAME FORWARD: ACTIVIST LEGACIES OF 1968 IN LIFE STORY REFLECTIONS

Barbara Körner and Rosemary McKechnie

> ...1968, we were sort of involved in all that... it was all very silly... I'm ashamed to think of it... well not exactly ashamed, but it was sort of cringeworthy you know? ... we had a sit-in outside a racist hairdresser... can you imagine... (laughs)... the classism of it! Some poor working class hairdresser that said that they couldn't cope with Afro hairstyles and we decided they were racist... (Interview K)

Introduction

Where have the revolutions gone? What happens with the passion of the day once movements are no longer publicly visible – what does it transform into? And what are the lessons learned? Our concern in this chapter is to critically examine the idealism of political movements following the moment of 1968, by listening to the voices of adults who have been engaged in a range of activist projects over their lifetime. Our discussion is founded on in-depth life story interviews with adults in the UK, however to contextualize and analyse this material we draw on theories about new social movements developed by European thinkers, as well as on feminist and post-colonialist criticism mainly from the US. We are interested to get beyond simple historical description and celebration and to trace the finer lines and subtle legacies of the spirit of '68 and its follow-on movements of the 1970s and 80s. The focus here is not on spectacular actions and major players, but rather on how adults make sense of participation in extraordinary actions and events within the context of 'ordinary' lives. In particular, we suggest that in order to fully grasp historical legacies of '68 as a key moment where cultural and political change seemed possible, it is necessary to consider the problematic aspects of social movements together with the promising and inspiring ones. The critical reflections about activist involvement we present here may serve as a useful contribution to such an appraisal.

The student protests of May 1968 have come to assume an iconic role as a historical watershed, yet the relationship between this moment of very visible and popular rebellion and subsequent activism is perhaps difficult to fathom. Touraine, for example, indicates difficulty in finding explanations for the disconnections between the diversity of cultural politics of the seventies, and the immediately preceding mainly class-based organization of the sixties and he argues that already 'an archaic form of ideology was masking new forms of protest.' (1995, 369–70) There are some accounts that look at political trajectories of activists from the sixties, but few highlight the significance of personal reflection.[1] One of these is by Whittier (1997) who has examined the history of the women's movement in Columbus, Ohio from 1969, regarding transformations resulting from ageing of participants and social relations between older and younger activists. This recognizes the complex relationship between personal maturation and engagement with a changing world. Nevertheless, much of the reflection on the significance of the sixties has focused on key figures, giving rise to somewhat hagiographical accounts (see Ross 2002). There has been a tendency to look at ideologies and ideas, at movements and leaders – and yet this does not really capture the continuing contribution of activism and activists, both in terms of different forms of activist involvement and passing on a 'legacy'.

Our research invited people to relate not just what they did, but more complex accounts of their social, emotional and intellectual engagement during periods of activism. This double narrative which relayed both external events and internal processes linked personal integrity, critical awareness of issues in the world, and motivation to act on this awareness. In addition, there are important strands of reflection that bring to the surface uncomfortable feelings such as guilt, uncertainty or anger that show being part of 'a movement' was less straightforward than is often assumed. More specifically, many of the critical self-reflections concern personal experiences with and key learning about social differences, privileges and hierarchies, relating to class, race, gender and sexuality. As part of her opening lecture to the *1968: Impact and Implications* conference in London, Juliet Mitchell (2008) noted her own concerns when she pointed out that women's activism tended to remain hidden from history, and that the 'masculinist' style of many anniversary posters contributed to such marginalization. It is of course feminist theorizing that from the start in the late 60s and throughout the 70s and 80s, consistently challenged the apparent homogeneity of movements, first by calling to task the male domination of 'class war', 'free love' and civil rights movements, and later, by questioning the idea of undifferentiated 'sisterhood' within the women's liberation movements. Feminist analysis of sixties radical movement culture such as Robin Morgan's *Demon Lover* (1989), and key contributions by Audre Lorde and other Black feminists on 'difference' can therefore help to clarify the particular complexities attached to the legacies of 1968.

We suggest that the crucial space for reflection, opened up in this case by life story research, throws new light on neglected dimensions of activist campaigns and movements. This area of 'complicating' reflection has normally remained muted within the everyday of movement culture, to enable 'the struggle' (against the state, injustice, capitalism and so on) to continue. One consequence of this has been that conflicts around social divisions are rarely given sufficient critical examination. We argue that less visible practices of inter-/ personal learning are often just as important as spectacular acts of heroism and collective action in ensuring that the 'fire at the heart of society' (Touraine 1995) gets passed on. Many of the movement theorists have themselves been involved in activism, and their theories partly arise from their own reflections.[2] Touraine for example is very honest about his own personal transformation from inflexible ideological stance of the sixties to a much more tolerant and broad-ranging orientation (1995, 370); he does not doubt that the loss of monolithic political perspectives has been necessary, and in his view such critical review has not dampened the fire of political engagement that contemporary movements mobilise.

Our analysis in this chapter will broadly follow three steps. First, drawing mainly on the work of cultural theorists Lefebvre, Melucci and Touraine, we will interrogate the notion that 'new social movements', starting from '1968', carry a special quality of authenticity and critical consciousness that is achieved through moments of disassociation from mainstream society. In a second step, we will make space for reflection on difficult experiences within movements and activist networks. By drawing on the work of Bourdieu, in conjunction with feminist critics including Morgan, Lorde and Reagon, we suggest that analytical critical consciousness in itself is not enough, and that social change needs to be worked for on a much deeper, personal level. In a concluding analysis, we make use of Melucci's concept of latency and the term 're-integration' to examine ways in which – sometimes despite of or precisely because of sceptical reflection on past action – revolutionary passions and values live on across the life course and perhaps are passed on between activist generations. Before expanding on these arguments, and exploring the activist accounts in some detail, we will first turn to a fuller description of our research project.

Activism and the Life Course: A Reflexive Life Story Project

The research we are reporting on here is based on 19 recent in-depth interviews, some of which are with interviewees of the '68 generation, though most belong to the follow-on generations active in the 1970s and 1980s. Having a personal background in activism ourselves, we set out to explore the biographical significance of periods of activism in the lives of adults who have been involved in a variety of forms of political engagement across their lifetime. Questions focused on activism as a way of relating to the world, and on in-depth personal reflection about selves as active in the world. Part of the interview process was the use of a time line where participants drew in their recollection of external events on one side and personal life experiences on the other, super-imposed by moments of activism. As a sociologist with a Women's Studies background and an anthropologist, we were interested to explore activism, not as an isolated phenomenon, but within the context of people's lives, and the life course. Themes included relationships and motivations, endings and continuity. We have aimed to capture the changing meanings of activism within participants' lives and were interested not only in how values and personal passions shape political engagement, but how life-experience matures and tempers standpoints and gives rise to nuanced reflection on past action. The interviews have thus resulted in a body of personal narrative that substantially illuminates how individual and group political responses have been influenced by the inheritance of, and sometimes reaction to, 1968.

Participants come from a range of backgrounds within the UK, and 11 of them are women, 8 men. The majority were in their 40s or 50s at time of interview (2006), although – except for the 30s – other age groups from 18 to 78 are also represented. There is pre-dominance of a 'classic' activist trajectory with heightened political activity in people's 20s and 30s, which coincided with participation in alternative and protest movements of the 1970s and 80s. We will mainly focus on this group here. However, some of our interviewees are younger and have only begun to get/ see themselves as actively involved recently, while others are older and began their activism later in life, or maintained a strong activist commitment and practice throughout their entire life.[3] Most who were not themselves active in '68 were nevertheless clearly influenced by the cultural and political strands of the movements that were begun in 1968. This sense of inheriting is what we refer to when we talk of 'follow-on generations/ movements'. For example, interviewee C, a woman in her 50s, reading the *Female Eunuch* when it came out in 1968, says that '*all that hippie stuff*' was enormously important and that she very much felt part of 1970s student movements. Recollection of those directly involved in '68 could however show enthusiastic, yet simultaneously uncertain commitment. The following quotation is from an activist who was in Paris and then also very active in Britain, without really feeling confidence or clarity about the choices he was making at the time:

> ...*the situation when I came back from France I didn't know anything about the groups in England, as I said when I was in France I'd been exposed to lots and lots of different strands of radical forms. So I recall that when I turned up, the first thing*

I did was to contact the Communist Party and someone from the young Communist Party came round and... we just didn't hit it off. You know... (laughs) So I dismissed the Communist Party. And when I was at college there was a pretty girl who was a Maoist so I almost joined the Reggie Burch's outfit, the Communist Party of Great Britain, they were Marxist Leninists and... for some reason I didn't join them either, and I can't remember what it was that turned me off them. I don't know what it was. I used to go up to, I was ... very close to the Students Union, and ... I used to go up there probably to have a drink and also they had some nice big study rooms, so I used to go up there. I must have gone up there and there were some kids from the Maoists and started talking to them. I think that was probably it. (Interview L)

It should perhaps also be noted that apart from the '1968' moment, there were other, earlier strands of activism that influenced the 1970s/80s protest generation – notably the much longer histories of pacifism, and the particular roots of CND and the 1980s peace movement in the UK, as marked, for example, by the milestone protests at Aldermaston in 1958.

The opportunity to reflect on life experience was valued by participants. While much of this reflection is intellectual, an emotional and dynamic process of recollection and self-interrogation was also apparent, for example in the struggle to communicate the sometimes uncertain choices of younger selves. Key theoretical models of contemporary society emphasize the reflexivity of social actors, in a social context where processes of individualisation make 'choice' an inevitable aspect of everyday life (Giddens 1991; Beck 1992; Beck and Beck-Gernsheim, 2001). There are some key differences between the reflexivity described by Giddens (1991) and the reflection of Beck, but both develop accounts which infer that reflexivity is essentially cognitive and rational (Welsh and McKechnie 1998; Lash 1994), and that it is a time specific activity, moving the actor along a trajectory through various life decisions that have to be negotiated. However, the activist reflections we are considering here did not follow an orderly progression through time or a series of rational choices: they were more readily characterized by a musing style, being long-term in nature, and combining emotionality and critical thinking in complex ways (McKechnie and Körner 2009).

Memory is impaired by time – the factual recall of events is likely to be weak over a period of decades. On the other hand, remembering can intensify our vision of the past highlighting key points which at the time might have seemed unimportant (see Jasper 1998). Much of the recounting of the past pushed the respondents to revisit events and find vignettes from their life which could convey the complexity of a moment, or the emotional intensity of a state of mind. We should not ignore the conceptual work that was necessary to rescue into language lost moments that had often never been shared before. The participants' own theories about their actions, their private narratives show intense engagement, and depth of critical thinking. Some described ongoing unease in campaigns or with the internal social relations of movements that eventually resulted in a change of direction or different kinds of engagement. This process could be prolonged, and the actions of younger selves were often a cause for laughter or exasperation. We go on to look at examples of such disquiet about intellectual analyses, or feeling patronised and silenced because of class, gender, 'race' or sexuality. This kind of deliberation often continued for long periods as individuals were unsure of how important their perceptions were, and were unable to find language at the time to express the problem. The full picture of activist engagement, available through in-depth reflection, indicates some important underlying processes shaping collective action.

Lighting the Flame: Authenticity and De-Integration

Critical social movements have been widely associated with a search for more 'authentic' ways of living or forms of social arrangements, away from the alienation of modern systems of rationality and consumption. One example is the celebration of 1968 'movements of contestation' as a symbol of an authentic challenge to the bourgeois culture of 'everyday life', found within the work of Henri Lefebvre (1971; 2008). While he saw them as rooted in everyday life, student activists were at the same time constructed as apart from the world, and capable of transcending its capitalist and bourgeois limitations – as special agents of 'permanent cultural revolution'. Following Lukacs and other Marxist thinkers, Lefebvre critiqued everyday life as ambivalent: on the one hand as a sphere from which alternative ideas, protest and creativity could emerge – but on the other, mainly, as the sphere of daily mundane repetition that has been taken over by what he calls the 'bureaucratic society of controlled consumption' (1971, 60).

A special note here is that women are seen as the archetypal consumers, least able to resist the oppressive side of everyday life, and least likely to grasp its more authentic possibilities. Needless to say, this aspect of Lefebvre's thought has been subjected to feminist criticism (Felski 1999–2000). It is important to keep in mind that at the time of writing *Everyday Life in the Modern World* (1968), ideas about revolution and social change were still dominated by masculinist class politics, with cultural politics only just emerging. While Lefebvre qualified his views on everyday life in later works, what stands out here is that the authenticity of protest action is posited in opposition to the banality of everyday life. What Lefebvre was looking for, according to Rob Shields (in Bennett 2002, 25) were '"moments of presence" – moments of intense emotion or heightened social involvement – that would transcend everyday life as individuals escaped its eviscerating structures to be more fully themselves.' In a similar vein, Jürgen Habermas' (1990) perhaps more optimistic theory of communicative action ascribes an important role to the 'new politics' of cultural and liberation movements in defending the 'lifeworld' from encroachment by the 'system' of economic/bureaucratic control imperatives. (McGuigan 1996) Liberation movements such as feminism are seen as having special importance in this project. (Habermas 1981) In the light of these theories, the 'flame' that is action for 'life', justice, equality, liberation is lit through passions that run deeper or are able to transcend the constraints and routines – the status quo – of everyday society.

On the surface Alain Touraine seems particularly insistent on the necessity of breaking with the everyday. Certainly he argues that individuals need to develop conceptual distance from the everyday roles, institutions and relations that constitute taken-for-granted reproduction of modern society. Only by breaking with the 'automata of the self' can individuals develop the critical view of their world necessary for political agency. He describes this potential for action as being dependent on what he calls 'deintegration', a process through which the self is transformed into the critical, self-determined subject (1995, 207). He claims that 'subjectivation' is always the antithesis of 'socialization': 'the I is revealed to itself only when it becomes detached from all personal and social bonds' and, elsewhere that …'the subject is burned in the flames that lit it up' (1995, 274). However, this apparent split that divides the unthinking self from the self-consciously critical subject is more ambiguous than it seems on the surface. Touraine is keen to emphasise that far from envisaging activist engagement as narrowly ideological, it must reflect the whole person and carry an emotional and personal significance to keep the flame alive: 'we must mobilise the total subject, the religious heritage, childhood memories, ideas and courage' (Touraine 1995, 207).

He notes that 'the emergence of the subject is closely bound up with relations with the other' (226). Far from being a narcissistic pursuit of self-knowledge,

> 'the love relationship does away with social determinisms and gives the individual a desire to be an actor … it results in commitment too absolute to be merely social… A militant commitment is of the same nature as a loving commitment.' (227)

King (2006) writes of how the movement she worked with used a co-counselling framework to develop emotional reflexivity. She argues this was strongly bound up with their effectiveness as movement, acting as subjects in Touraine's terms.

Concern with the relationship between the everyday and collective action is further developed by Alberto Melucci, in an attempt to understand the potential of social movements to engage with new, complex global processes since the late 1960s (1996, 114–115). He developed understanding of movements as processes which may oscillate between periods of heightened public visibility and what Melucci (1989) calls stages of 'latency'. While a movement may be apparently dormant during periods of latency, the shared and ongoing reflection of activists continues to cause ripples in their social relations, with persistent cultural impacts. This nexus between activism and everyday life is therefore blurred and the compartmentalisation of the activist from the everyday dissolved:

> '... we must distinguish between relatively permanent forms of network and specific moments of mobilization..... the former interweave closely with daily life, with the needs and identity of the movements members: the latter transform a potential which has prepared and nourished itself in latency into visible collective action.' (1996, 116)

The process of developing critical distance from 'the way things are' and becoming active subjects in Touraine's terms can be seen in interviewees' accounts. (McKechnie and Körner 2009; 2010) It is clear that activist motivations have a deep source akin to the metaphor of the 'flame' we have outlined above. If there is a constant in interviewees' reflections on what has motivated and sustained their action in the world, it is deeply held values about equality, social justice, freedom and non-violence. In most cases, the source of such values and motivations lies in early experiences with society, such as key moments of critical recognition in childhood or adolescence. One participant in her 40s for example reflects on how she became aware of injustice through an instance at school, and how this later led to activist involvement:

> *I grew up in almost an all White area. Um, and I had no real language for racism until the Anti-Nazi League. But I remember, I must have been 9 um, and at our school, ONE Black boy appeared... and I remember realizing that the teachers treated him differently... And I mean there WAS corporal punishment in the school... but nobody got treated like THAT... But I had absolutely no vocabulary – I couldn't go home and say, you know, this terrible thing happened because my parents... THEY wouldn't have been able to say 'that teacher is racist, and ...this is what you need to do about it.' ... Um, so then when the League started getting going it was obvious... So, obviously, the way to do it was to join this organisation and to go on marches.* (Interview E)

Another interviewee describes a more general coming to awareness about the world, both in terms of global inequalities and more personally, in terms of sexual identity.

> *...well a big political event for me was when I was at school in the sixth form, emm there was a famine in Ethiopia, it was pretty dreadful and it was one of many that had*

happened and at the time I was reading emmm... books about third world development and underdevelopment and emmm... I was involved in anti-apartheid, I think I had a growing awareness of my gay sexuality although it wasn't expressed. I felt different from other kids at school always. I always saw myself as an outsider I always felt that I was an outsider .... (Interview L)

It seems that the compulsion to act founded on critical distance from mainstream society, as hinted at in this latter quotation, can be bound up with feelings of separation or isolation from others. As we are reporting elsewhere (McKechnie and Körner 2010), there are indications in these activist reflections that activist values and motivations might clash with normative or 'everyday' adult identities. Interviewee G for example tends to keep his professional life quite separate from the rest of his life, as it doesn't seem safe airing his political views at work. Another participant (H) has left the church for ideological reasons. Critical consciousness about injustice can also be associated with feelings of guilt – and this woman in her 60s suggests that her guilt has lessened over time:

... I think I just feel less guilty, I think there were a lot of guilty motivations in my activism for the first sort of twenty years or so... I'm not... I probably do feel guilty but I'm not... emm you know I feel concerned about.. and I feel its difficult to live with the inequality in the world and so on... so to that extent I probably do feel guilty but I don't feel guilty in a personal sense, I feel trapped in a system that I hate and that I actually think damages all of us including the privileged... (Interview K)

These insights highlight that the activist search for authenticity is beset with complication. Activists' critical reflections on the world are woven into their relationships and self understanding or as Melucci notes, are 'submerged in the fabric of daily life' (1996, 114). The idea itself that it may be possible to 'de-integrate' or extricate from social contexts is problematic. A way forward, as indicated by this interviewee, is to come to an understanding of how the structures of privilege and inequality impact on activists' lives.

Critical Reflections on Activism

Talking about activist engagement over the lifecourse has involved deeply critical and self-critical forms of reflection for research participants. Not only are inhuman structures being interrogated, but in reflecting on their participation in a range of campaigns, interviewees also point to difficult dynamics within the movements themselves. In this emphasis on depth of reflection, involving the level of the personal and interpersonal, our approach differs from more unequivocally celebratory accounts of new social movement activity, where there is a focus on playful action and radical change through particular campaigns (see McKay 1990). There is a tendency in descriptive accounts of 'new movements' to posit activists in dichotomous opposition to 'normal' (oppressive) mainstream; as outside rather than part of a shared world in need of change.

Pierre Bourdieu, in contrast, emphasises a deep entanglement with cultures of domination, and, similarly to Touraine, does not take for granted an automatic link between activism and liberation. He suggests that:

> 'The effect of symbolic domination … is exerted not in the pure logic of knowing consciousnesses but in the obscurity of the dispositions of habitus… below the level of the decisions of the conscious mind and the controls of the will….' (2000, 170)

Hence, the social order is reproduced in dispositions and values which are infused in all aspects of life by primary socialisation, as well as inscribed on the body, and therefore not easily amenable to alteration. This means that Bourdieu can seem particularly harsh on the optimism of 1968 that social analysis coupled with effective action can change the world. He explicitly derides 'the Marxist tradition and feminist theorists who, giving way to habits of thought, expect political liberation to come from 'rising consciousness' (172). However, as Crossley (2001, 84) points out, Bourdieu is clarifying what predisposes agents to act in particular ways without reducing them to cultural dopes or inhibiting their strategic capacities. Bourdieu is not saying that liberation is impossible, only that it is not easy. In particular he is thoughtful about the ways that masculine domination permeates all aspects of social organization, so that the social order functions as a 'vast machine' and the 'harmonics' between different areas of this matrix serve to naturalise this form of symbolic domination and make it appear timeless (Bourdieu 2001, 8–9). In depicting the tasks facing activists as almost overwhelming, requiring analysis to make visible the processes responsible for 'the neutralisation of history' (2001, 34), to break the circle of mutual reinforcement across all regions of social space (88), Bourdieu is simply setting out the magnitude of symbolic domination. He advocates resistance on many fronts, combining reflexive analysis that makes visible the nature of domination with material change and what he calls 'countertraining' to transform habitus. This is a slow, painstaking process. 'Freedom is not something that is given – it is something that you conquer – collectively…' (Bourdieu 1990, 15)

Social movements by their nature foster critical reflection and analysis, unearth domination, but often in particularly focused ways that can prioritise some forms and expressions of domination. It is interesting that older activists, involved in the leftist activism of the sixties had strong memories of disquiet about this. Many of the critical reminiscences regard conflict between activists' loyalty to the vision of a movement, their belief in the ideas and the contradiction between those ideals and their real experience. Some silently put up with dynamics in activist networks they did not like. Learning to combine a critical view of the world, a critical view of the movement and fellow activists, with early values is a constant struggle. Many described situations where, far from feeling empowered they felt undermined, or where they acted in ways that seem incomprehensible to them in the present. There were some specific reflections on middle-class lack of understanding of class and classism within activist circles, for example in this eloquent narrative:

Right I think when I joined the International socialists and the SWP, this sort of middle-class people being in charge of me had come up again because ehh... though the IS and the SWP said they were for the workers... most of them were quite middle-class... and I had become aware quite early on that... [laughs] one of the reasons they had difficulty recruiting workers was because of their attitude towards them, they still had the ... what do you call it... I call it patterns, the middle-class patterns of talking down to people... emm so that was quite important. I thought that ... I think that I sussed that quite early on but I didn't actually move on it for quite a long time... (Interview Q)

In addition to reflections on classism (see first quotation at head of chapter), interviewee K reflects on an experience where she gave up an academic post as it was considered too bourgeois by her Marxist group. In retrospect, she realizes this to be discriminatory to women activists: '...*they didn't get it at all, they didn't get that women shouldn't give up jobs*'. This experience clearly echoes widespread concerns by women activists of the 1970s that issues of gender equality were put on the back burner until 'after the revolution'. Radical feminist Robin Morgan (1989) for example has critiqued late 60s revolutionary (including terrorist) and civil rights movements in the US as rife with sexism and male posturing. According to her analysis, there is a basic agreement between the (reactionary) men of the 'state-that-is' and the (revolutionary) men of the 'state-that-would-be' to pass on the myth of the hero –triumphant or martyred. But Morgan (1989, 217–42) also includes a piece of autobiographical reflection on her own involvement which is relevant here, as it conveys a strong sense of hard-earned self-critical awareness of her position as a woman in the movement and illustrates how she put up with self-doubt for the sake of the 'cause'. Any attempts at questioning the culture of violence or the sexual culture of the movement were silenced through the injunction that such questioning displayed 'bourgeois tendencies'.[4]

It is clear that political activism since '68 has been affected by dogma and dynamics of exclusion. In the case of feminist movements in particular, this has resulted in a bounty of critical work regarding divisions of class, sexuality, 'race'/ racism and later, disability.[5] Our research demonstrates some of these tensions. This woman in her 40s for example reflects on an uneasy experience with radical feminism, in regard to sexuality:

> *Issues around feminism... anti-porn... I remember that being very UNCOMFORTABLE actually... quite disapproving... I remember having this/ and I wasn't as assertive as I am now, I remember this woman saying to me 'oh all men use pornography'... and I was a bit awed by her certainty. So, there were various times in the women's movement when I felt it was quite difficult to be heterosexual, and even worse, to be... monogamous.... I was in AWE because there was like a STATUS thing, and I was very low DOWN, my status was very low, so I couldn't say 'well that's crap'[laughter] Whereas NOW I'd just raise my eyebrows.* (Interview E)

This woman realizes that she has 'moved on' from earlier activist dilemmas towards a more self-determined position. One of the key themes running through the narratives is about personal 'learning' in relation to anti-discriminatory values. We are talking here not of abstract ideas, but of real relationships and tangible emotions as they are affected by historical legacies of social division, inequality, discrimination, persecution. Learning to relate as equals 'across difference', Black US feminist Audre Lorde (1984) says, is a matter of survival and depends on our willingness to delve deep and examine our emotional responses. (Also see Jasper 1998) All experiences of discrimination such as sexism, racism, ableism – the 'isms' as interviewee J called them – are infused with emotions such as anger, fear, shame, guilt. Interviewees here recall instances where they faced issues around class and racism:

> *...story of a woman who scowled at me 'oh that's alright for you, you middle-class woman'... I was so shocked... that was quite a defining moment... learning about disadvantage and inequality and that whole area... For a while it did make me feel quite bad about being me... I had to really work through that to a point where I then knew that being me was fine, it was how you acted and what you did with that life position...* (Interview B)
>
> *I had anti-racist training in about 86... and that really made a big impact on me, because before that I hadn't – I mean yes, of COURSE I was aware of racism and I was into all the anti-Nazi staff but I suppose for me I hadn't really examined where I was, and that really changed things for me in terms of my activism.* (Interview C)

Learning about privilege and dynamics of oppression it seems tends to be the more painful, yet also the more worthwhile, the more 'personal' it is; when political awareness coincides with personal realization. In the work of Black feminists such as Lorde (1984, 131), anger in particular is claimed as a powerful tool with which to work towards clarity and transformation, while guilt and defensiveness are seen as key stumbling blocks:

> 'My response to racism is anger... It has served me as fire in the ice zone of uncomprehending eyes of white women who see in my experience and the experience of my people only new reasons for fear or guilt.'

Similar suggestions on the potentially constructive uses of anger can be found in the work of disabled women in the UK (Keith 1994). It is not just anger however, but any discomfort and difficult emotions that need acknowledgement and scrutiny if social divisions are to be overcome. As Bernice Reagon (1998) suggests, the comfort zones of our 'little barred rooms' of identity politics where we tend to surround ourselves with people just like ourselves, need to be left behind for real 'coalition politics' to take place.

This work towards changing social structures of inequality echoes the painstaking reflection and transforming of habitus that Bourdieu advocates. He warns that activism must not fall into other forms of fictitious universalism, but engage with all forms of domination, to challenge every principle of division (2001, 123).[6] The depth and ongoing intensity of reflection communicated in many of the narratives can be seen to support the idea that social change goes hand in with deep-level interpersonal learning. As Lorde (1984, 142) says in 'Learning from the 60s':

> 'If our history has taught us anything, it is that action for change directed only against the external conditions of our oppressions is not enough. In order to be whole, we must recognize the despair oppression plants within each of us – that thin persistent voice that says our efforts are useless... We must fight that inserted piece of self-destruction that lives and flourishes like a poison inside of us, unexamined until it makes us turn upon ourselves in each other... We can lessen its potency by the knowledge of our real connectedness, arcing across our differences.'

Activist engagement then seems to bring together conflicting experiences of enthusiasm and despair. Yet, a hopeful vision of social change may arise from critical reflection on activist relations; from the voices of difference and those willing to look at difficult feelings about social divisions.

Carrying the Flame Forward: Movement 'Latency' and Personal Re-Integration

We have looked at the recurrent theme in cultural theory that an essential aspect of becoming politically active is the taking of a stance of critical distance from society – or in the words of Touraine, de-integration. Activist involvement in the first place is fuelled by a sense of 'authentic' mission against in-human structures. We have begun to problematise the dualist tendency here to divide activism from everyday life, and argue that in reality the emotional involvement experienced in all spheres of life, for example caring respect for others experienced through everyday relationships also informs activist commitments. In a second step, we have further considered the complexity of this mission to change the world and shown how activists are also standing back from activism itself to reveal the pervasiveness of structures of inequality and their own involvement in these structures. In a third step, we would now like to briefly explore the importance of what could be called 're-integration' for the way in which legacies of '68 and ensuing social movements can be seen to be living on. As should be clear from the complexity of narratives quoted so far, the most critical reflections of activists concerning their early engagement with activisms should not be taken to indicate that they have rejected activism, that they have lost the flame. In Alberto Melucci's terms, we have observed both the power of cultural politics, and the ebbing of more exposed periods of activist visibility into less visible states of 'latency'. The narratives suggest that such movement between latency and visibility also has a parallel in different stages of the life course where passionate involvement with the world continuously transforms itself. In spite of or perhaps because of the critical reflections and more nuanced framing of activism, there is optimism here. In many of the interviews, reflections led participants to recognize how active they have been, and to what an extent activist values are in fact integrated into their lives. Struggling with guilt about 'stopping', one woman in her sixties for example (Interview H) realized through reflection that in fact, her activism just had taken a different turn – '*I haven't really stopped, have I?*'

Various routes of personal re-integration are discernable in our activist life stories. While more visible campaigning might have ended for a number of personal reasons such as work, parenthood, health and well-being, in several cases this only meant that efforts towards changing the world have changed shape and location and are more fully integrated into other areas of life, chiefly work or volunteering. This woman in her late 50s reflects on her own relationship with different forms of activism, and re-defines what activism means for her so that she can be 'counted':

> *I USED to define activism as kind of Greenham Common, peace action, going on demonstrations... campaigning type stuff. And I always felt a kind of SHAME that*

*I didn't do it. Um and now at the ripe old age of 56, my definition of activism is whatever goes against the grain. So, it is DOING things that actually SEEK to change the status quo.... So, it's anything that's subversive to existing structures... I realized that if I was properly true to myself, that I could do something that was worth doing. That if I stopped kicking myself for not being like other people... not living up to being an activist and joining committees and all that, if I did what **I** can do, that it was actually – it would have guts. ...So, I can be effective through subversion, through teaching, through example, through DOING... actually PRACTICALLY making a difference.* (Interview D)

It is clear here that these reflections centre around personal integrity, in the sense that activist motivations and values needed to find an outlet that was right for this person. Others, such as interviewee K, realized that re-integration into everyday life was actually a positive thing:

I think that my family commitments... I mean they've probably protected me from being one of these people who do nothing but activism. These serial activists who don't have a life. I mean I'm really glad I have a life and I think it's a total mistake to be nothing but an activist, but I could see that I might have done that if things had happened to be otherwise. (Interview K)

Adding to this sentiment, another participant emphasises the advantages of a more qualified, less dogmatic perspective that gradually evolved with the increasing distance to the heights of visible activism:

I felt very... close to some people and some people became almost enemies though... it was like very clear in those days, you are either for us or against us... I think I was very dogmatic for a long time... And in a way I think... it's better NOW where I'm starting to see other points of view as well... I don't think you CHANGE many people's views if you're too dogmatic, so it's great to have the enthusiasm you know that I had certainly in my 20s and 30s, but... it [activism] means different things at different times, I think, and I can see different ways and let other people do THAT bit now. (Interview C)

Several narratives included the idea of passing on activist responsibilities to a new generation, as can be seen in the quotation above. Here are two further examples:

I understood it more in a sense of it being you know like a RELAY – race or what I mean this isn't a race, but the fact that you know you actually RUN with something and you pass on – something to somebody else and then you / you hope that others will / because I was aware that I'd picked up things from meeting other people who I assumed weren't as involved as I then became. (Interview H)

...you change your life don't you, and things alter, maybe you think: well, actually I've done my bit, and there is another generation who haven't got all the responsibilities I've got, and who can maybe take some responsibility for attempting to change the world. (Interview G)

Making sense of the changing degrees and forms of activism across the lifecourse is of some significance when considering images such as carrying the flame forward in a kind of generational relay. As a concept, generation in this context can be taken to refer to the way in which the memories and predispositions of people born around the same time tend to be shaped by similar social and historical experiences, cultural influences or significant events – as for example in the war (or post-war) generation, the sixties generation, the Thatcher generation (Mannheim 1952; Pilcher 1995; also see O'Donnell, in this volume). As Burnett points out, the role of consciousness is paramount in generational theory... 'generations made by actors are the grit in the machine, prone to mobilisation, somnolence, deviance ... they change the social situation even as they live it' (2004, 44). Dividing lines between generations are of course not clear cut, and our analysis is meant to underline the particular fluidity of movement influences from the sixties across the 70s/80s follow-on generations and beyond, to the present. Mannheim's description leads itself to a conflict model of generational relationships.⁷ However, there was some evidence in the accounts of thoughtful management of relations with younger fellow activists by older interviewees, and an appreciation of changes in new forms of activism that seem to surpass older ideological intolerance and power plays. (Also see Whittier 1997) 'Passing on the flame' involved leaving some collective memories behind. Finally, some of those who had withdrawn from earlier activisms dismayed by themselves, by conflict or by aspects of the movement, have returned to re-enter activist circles with renewed enthusiasm and energy. The following quote from a working class activist in his 60s, veteran of a variety of left organisations and trade-union actions illustrates this.

'I think the other big effect was when I got involved with the anti-roads movement... what the Marxist left never caught on to was that there was a whole new vibrant movement out there with the anti-roads movement... I had been to these meetings for years with Marxists saying how can we get young people involved... and all these young people are involved in them things... and I find them more interesting and when I went on the demonstrations abroad... they were great because ... and you'd be going through streets in a crowd and there was... people would link hands ... and you could have a chat with a Swedish Christian who was sort of there because of world debt and then a Portuguese fisherman who was on about over-fishing ...and then if you were really lucky you would have somebody from the third world ... so the landless peasants

of Brazil or the Indian dam movement... so it's just ... you get the feel of this massive movement. And the other thing that affected me about that is they tried to work together on what they agreed on not what they disagreed on and that really was a complete difference ... if you've been on the Marxist left where there are so many small groups who would be like... its sort of like mediaeval sort of Christians who argue about how many angels you'd get on a needle... (Interview Q)

The activist reflections generally show a dynamic process of re-integration where world and self are viewed differently over time, and where activism and everyday life are revealed to be in a critical two-way relationship. The continuous process of reflecting on younger activist selves and on past and present activist involvement can be seen to have enabled activist participants to deal with greater complexity in their politics and to recognize themselves as actors shaped by multiple social legacies. As part of such review, activist commitment is frequently being renewed and reinvigorated.

Conclusion

The processes discussed above are often precisely concerned with the aspects of social hierarchy and dominance which Bourdieu describes as beneath the level of consciousness. The breach which was 1968 provided subjects with the possibility of action, but within these new movements that they brought their hope, optimism and idealism to, and even within themselves, they discovered obstacles, and unexpected constraints. The way the individuals we talked to struggled to recall experiences with different forms of conflict and with compromise indicates the invisible aspect of dynamic social change. These subjects appear to be working continuously against the dispositions they rub against within activism as in the real world. Rather than becoming fully active subjects through de-integration from the roles and expectations of the social world in Touraine's terms, these activists are oscillating between reflection and action in a complex way, where reflection on how they themselves respond in social relationships, where experiences of living with others provides catalysts for clearer understanding of being active and new experiments in finding ways of challenging constraint within the movement as well as outside it. The tolerance and flexibility of older activists which has been hard won plays an important role in the generation of new movements.

'68' is certainly a collective myth – a powerful symbol of a break or rupture, a new beginning, a new politics, new possibilities of action, new possibilities of personal freedom. It carries a tremendous weight. Here old certainties lost their grip on a world they could not make sense of. The title legacy presupposes inheritance, the passing on of something, a set of ideas, an ideology, a political orientation, a coherent package. However, this symbolic clarity obscures the real legacy of 1968 which has been the channelling of an 'ethics of conviction' into the development of new forms of organising, analysing and acting. As Melucci points out, new movements are born within the structures of pre-existing movements and 1968 burst through an inheritance of Marxist language, sectarianism and established militants (1996, 298). There has been a continuing need for the struggle to find new language and expressions which are sensitive to other forms of dominance and oppression. Foucault in reviewing a book written by a veteran of the left during the sixties praises his account for eschewing the metaphor of rupture for 'imperceptible moments of modification.' (2002, 444) He considers the present as a time when...

> The heroism of political identity has had its day. One asks what one is, moment by moment, of the problems with which one grapples: how to take part and take sides without letting oneself be taken in. (ibid)

Perhaps one of the most constructive actions available to us at this stage is to let go of the idealization of social movements and to embrace a hopeful, pragmatic disillusionment as one of the true legacies of 1968. The potential for emancipatory social change may lie less in the rupture of spectacular action than in the quiet work of grappling with internalized oppression within and amongst ourselves, and the long haul of continual effort of activism to reflect, consider.

Notes

1 While the life trajectories of those involved in the student movement of the sixties in the United States have been the subject of quite intense research, certainly in relation to their political views and affiliations (see Demartini 1985; Martin 1994; Sherkat and Blocker 1994), most of this research has been of a survey type.
2 Swartz (2003) points out that Bourdieu has followed an unusual trajectory becoming a highly visible public intellectual in France towards the end of his life. 'Bourdieu's relative silence during the May 1968 student uprising was conspicuous for virtually all other leading French sociologists at the time took public positions regarding the student movement'. (795)
3 Participants have been involved in: 1968 student revolts, communism, Socialist campaigns, Trade Union movement, miner strike, anti-nazi league, anti-racist campaigning and action, anti-apartheid movement, peace and anti-nuclear campaigns, CND, women's peace movement (Greenham), feminist campaigns (Reclaim the Street, women's centres, women's refuges, women's discos), lesbian and gay politics, Street Music, Welsh Language society, campaign to stop corporal punishment, anti-Poll Tax, Refugee support action, vegetarianism, Green politics, consumer boycotts, community politics, Coop movements, communal housing, anti-road and anti-globalization movements.

4 Melucci (1996a) saw the violent strands of sixties activism as a symptom of its inherent limitations. On violence in the break-up of movements see also O'Donnell in this volume.
5 For example Amos and Parmar (1984) and Spelman (1990) have critiqued structures of White domination in both feminist activism and theory. Others looked more generally at divisions within movements, in the UK (Segal 1987) and the US (Hirsch and Keller 1990). Also see Körner (1997) for a critical look at 1980s peace/ green and feminist movements.
6 Bourdieu also views feminism as having made the major contribution of the ...'considerable enlargement of what is political, or can be politicised, by making it possible to discuss or challenge politically objects and preoccupations excluded or ignored by the political domain because they seem to belong to the private domain' (2001 116). This clearly resonates with the famous slogan from the sixties Women's Liberation Movement that the 'personal is political'. A theme carefully examined in Freely's chapter in the present volume.
7 This conflict perspective has been developed by Turner (2002) in his discussion of the radical movements of the sixties. The very different kinds of data we are dealing with here yield a much less clear cut picture, with interviewees expressing a general will to work with younger people. This is not to be idealistic about whether this is the case in practice. Certainly accounts from research on activism that brings generations and cultures together show that there can be problems with older activists' assumptions (Chesters and Welsh 2006, 52). Melucci's optimism that old and young can work together, across the 'abyss of difference' (1996b) is of course attractive.

References

Amos, V. and Parmar, P. 1984. Challenging Imperial Feminism. *Feminist Review.* 17: 3–19
Beck, U. 1992. *Risk Society: Towards a new Modernity.* London: Sage
Beck, U. and Beck-Gernsheim, E. 2001. *Individualization.* London: Sage
Bennett, T. 2002. Home and Everyday Life, in Bennett, T. and Watson, D. (eds.) *Understanding Everyday Life.* Oxford: Blackwell/ The Open University
Bourdieu, P. 1990. *In Other Words: Essays Towards a Reflexive Sociology.* Cambridge: Polity
―――― 2000. *Pascalian Meditations.* Cambridge: Polity
―――― 2001. *Masculine Domination.* Cambridge: Polity
Burnett, J. 2004. *All About Thirtysomething: An Exploration of the Value of the Concept of Generation in Sociology.* Unpublished Ph.D. Thesis, Bath Spa University
Chesters G. and Welsh, I. 2006. *Complexity and Social Movements: Multitudes at the end of Chaos.* London: Routledge
Crossley, N. 2001. The Phenomenological Habitus and Its Construction. *Theory and Society,* 30, 1: 81–120
――――2002. Pierre Bourdieu (1930–2002). *Social Movement Studies,* 1, 2: 187–91
Demartini, J. R. 1985. Change Agents and Generational Relationships: A Re-evaluation of Mannheim's Problem of Generations. *Social Forces,* 64, 1: 1–16
Felski, R. 1999–2000. The invention of everyday life. *New Formations,* 39: 15–31
Foucault, M. 2002. *Power: Essential works of Foucault 1954–1984,* J. D. Faubion (ed.) London: Penguin
Giddens, A. 1991. *Modernity and Self Iden*tity. Cambridge: Polity
Habermas, J. 1981. New Social Movements. *Telos. A Quarterly Journal of Radical Thought,* 49: 33–37

_____ 1990. *Moral Consciousness and Communicative Action*. Cambridge: Polity
Hirsch, M. and Keller, E.F. eds., 1990. *Conflicts in Feminism*. New York, NY: Routledge
Jasper, J. M. 1998. The Emotions of Protest: Affective and Reactive Emotions in and around Social Movements. *Sociological Forum*, 13, 3: 397–424
Keith, L. (ed.) 1994. *Mustn't Grumble. Writing by Disabled Women*. London: Women's Press
King, D. 2006. Activists and Emotional Reflexivity: Toward Touraine's Subject as Social Movement. *Sociology*, 40, 5: 873–891
Körner, B. 1997. *Critical Passion: A feminist theory of non-violence and social change*. Unpublished PhD thesis, Lancaster University
Lash, S. 1994. Reflexivity and its Doubles: Structure, Aesthetics, Community. In Beck, U., Giddens, A. and Lash, S. (eds.) *Reflexive Modernization: Politics, Tradition and Aesthetics in the Modern Social Order*. Cambridge: Polity Press
Lefebvre, H. 1971. *Everyday Life in the Modern World*. [Transl. Rabinovitch. First published in France, 1968.] London: Penguin
_____ 2008. *Critique of Everyday Life, Volume 3. From Modernity to Modernism*. [Transl. Elliott. First published in France, 1981] London: Verso
Lorde, A. 1984. *Sister Outsider. Essays and Speeches*. Freedom, CA: Crossing Press
Mannheim, K. 1952. *Essays on the Sociology of Knowledge*. London: Routledge and Kegan Paul
Martin, B. 1994. Continuity and discontinuity in the politics of the sixties Generation: A Reassessment. *Sociological Forum*, 9, 3: 403–30
McGuigan, J. 1996. *Culture and the Public Sphere*. London, Routledge
McKay, G. 1990. *Senseless Acts of Beauty. Cultures of Resistance since the 60s*. London: Verso
McKechnie, R. and Körner, B. 2009. Unruly Narratives: Discovering the Active Self, in Robinson, D., Fisher, P., Yeadon-Lee, T., Robertson, S. and Woodcock, P (eds.) *Narrative, Memory and Identities*. Selected Papers from the 8th Annual Conference. Huddersfield: University of Huddersfield
McKechnie, R and Körner, B. 2010. Growing Up Through Activism: adult identities and the maturing of standpoints, in Burnett, J (ed.) *Contemporary Adulthood: Calendars, Cartographies and Constructions*. Houndmills: Palgrave Macmillan
McKechnie, R. and Welsh, I. 2002. When the Global meets the Local: Critical Reflections on Reflexive Modernization, in R. Dunlap et al. *Sociological Theory and the Environment*, New York and Oxford: Rowman and Littlefield
Melucci, A. 1989. *Nomads of the Present: Social Movements and Individual Needs in Contemporary Society*. London: Hutchinson
_____ 1996a. *Challenging Codes: collective action in the information age*. Cambridge: CUP
_____ 1996b. *The Playing Self: Persona and Meaning in the Planetary Society*, Cambridge: CUP
Mitchell, J. 2008. Women's Liberation; Feminism; Gender Studies – 1968 Lives On. Keynote address at *1968: Impact and Implications*. British Sociological Association Theory Study Group Conference 3–4 July 2008, Birkbeck, University of London
Morgan, R. 1989. *The Demon Lover. On the Sexuality of Terrorism*. London: Methuen
Pilcher, J. 1995. *Age and Generation in Modern Britain*. Oxford: Oxford University Press
Reagon, B. J. 1998. Coalition Politics: Turning the Century, in Phillips, A. (ed.) *Feminism and Politics*. Oxford: Oxford UP [Originally published in *Home Girls: A Black Feminist Anthology*, Kitchen Table Press, 1983]
Ross, K. 2002. Establishing Consensus: May '68 in France as Seen from the 1980s. *Critical Enquiry*, 28, 3: 650–76
Segal, L. 1987. *Is the Future Female? Troubled Thoughts on Contemporary Feminism*. London: Virago

Sherkat, D. and Blocker, J. 1994. The Political Development of Sixties Activists: Identifying the Influences of Class, Gender and Socialization on Protest Participation. *Social Forces*, 72, 3: 821–42

Spelman, E. 1990. *Inessential Woman. Problems of Exclusion in Feminist Thought*. London: Women's Press

Swartz, D. L. 2003. From Critical Sociology to Public Intellectual: Pierre Bourdieu and Politics. *Theory and Society*, 32, 5/6: 791–823

Touraine, A. 1995. *Critique of Modernity*. Oxford: Blackwell

Turner, B. S. 2002. Strategic Generations: Historical change, Literary Expression and Generational Politics, in J. Edmunds and B. S. Turner (eds.) *Generational Consciousness, Narrative and Politics*. Lanham: Rowmann & Littlefield

Whittier, N. 1997. Political Generations, Micro-Cohorts and the Transformation of Social Movements. *American Sociological Review*. 62, 5: 760–78

Chapter 12

WHEN THE PERSONAL BECAME POLITICAL: A REAPPRAISAL OF THE WOMEN'S LIBERATION MOVEMENT'S RADICAL IDEA

Maureen Freely

It began with a memo. Its original title ('Some Thoughts in Response to Dottie's Thoughts on a Women's Liberation Movement') suggests the spirit in which it was written. Carol Hanisch, a community organiser for the Southern Conference Educational Fund, was responding to a memo by another staff member. Like so many other activists in the civil rights movement, the anti-war movement, and the New Left, this colleague did not view the fledgling women's liberation movement as truly political. Dottie Zellner had been particularly scathing about the new vogue for consciousness-raising, which she dismissed as therapy.

Carol Hanisch was (in addition to being a civil rights activist) a member of New York Radical Women, credited with bringing consciousness-raising techniques into second wave feminism. The group was itself a response to what we would now view as a quite shocking array of sexist attitudes and practices that had, until then, gone unchallenged in radical circles. Early attempts to extend the logic of liberation to women had met with widespread derision, with opposition coming not just from men but women:

> ...they belittled us no end for trying to bring our so-called "personal problems" into the public arena—especially "all those body issues" like sex, appearance, and abortion. Our demands that men share the housework and childcare were likewise deemed a personal problem between a woman and her individual man. The opposition claimed if women would just "stand up for themselves" and take more responsibility for

their own lives, they wouldn't need to have an independent movement for women's liberation. What personal initiative wouldn't solve, they said, "the revolution" would take care of if we would just shut up and do our part. Heaven forbid that we should point out that men benefit from oppressing women. (Hanisch 2006, 1)

Hanisch and others would later recall being shocked and shaken by the emotive, abusive language used against them. When Ellen Willis stood up at one anti-war rally to propose a woman-led initiative, she was booed and heckled, with some in the audience calling for her to be pulled off the stage and fucked (Mitchell 1971. 85–86). But when Hanisch sat down in February 1969 to draft her memo – later anthologised under the title 'The Personal is Political' – her language was polite, her tone conciliatory. She did not even use the term 'consciousness-raising' to describe the groups she had set out to explain and defend. Instead she began by acknowledging that women who considered themselves 'more political' tended to dismiss them as 'therapy' or 'personal' groups. She then confessed to being 'greatly offended that I or any other woman is thought to need therapy in the first place. Women are messed over, not messed up!' (Hanisch 1969, 4)

She went on to assure her readers that, though the 'so-called therapy groups' encouraged women to speak from personal experience; the aim was never to solve their immediate problems. She, for one, felt uncomfortable even admitting to personal problems: 'As a movement woman, I've been pressured to be strong, selfless, other-oriented, sacrificing, and in general pretty much in control of my life. To admit to the problems in my life is to be deemed weak.' It was therefore 'a political action to tell it like it is, to say what I really believe about my life instead of what I've always been told to say....One of the first things we discover in these groups is that personal problems are political problems. There are no personal solutions at this time. There is only collective action for collective problems.' (Hanisch 1969, 4)

Comparing the early days of 'sixties' feminism with contemporary attitudes, I will argue that, despite persistent hostility and misrepresentation in media and establishment circles, the movement has established a successful and widespread ethic of practice. This ethic, based on Hanisch's credo and germinated by the early innovations in consciousness-raising groups, continues to sustain women's efforts to recast the private sphere and challenge the public understanding of it. This is a project that has not just transformed the homes and personal relationships of women in this phantom movement, but also made itself felt in the many disciplines, professions and centres of power that women have entered in significant numbers over the past forty years.

Origins of Politicisation and the Role of Consciousness Raising

Kathie Sarachild elaborated her ideas on a new mode of feminist collective action in a talk she gave on consciousness-raising to the First National Conference of Stewardesses for Women's Rights in New York City in 1973. This was a more sympathetic audience: flight attendants were amongst the first female workers to take legal action against sexist practices in the workplace. Sarachild had helped pioneer consciousness-raising in New York Radical Women and had outlined its principles at the First National Women's Liberation Conference five years earlier. At the flight attendants' conference she credited Hanisch with first proposing that consciousness-raising groups might move on to 'consciousness-raising actions'. These she defined as 'actions brought to the public for the specific purpose of challenging old ideas and raising new ones…' (Sarachild 1979, 147)

The first such action had been in Washington in 1968, during a march by a coalition of women's peace groups calling itself the Jeannette Rankin Brigade. Aiming to raise the consciousness of their older and more sedate sisters, New York Radical Women had staged a 'Burial of Traditional Womanhood'. It was during this action that the slogan 'Sisterhood is Powerful' was first used. (Carabillo et al, n.d.) Later that same year, NYRW (soon to regroup as the Redstockings) staged what would become its most famous action, the picketing of the Miss America Beauty Contest in Atlantic City. Sarachild later described this as 'an attempt to reach the masses with our ideas on one of those so-called petty topics: the issue of appearance….throwing high heels, girdles and other objects of female torture into a freedom trash can.' She went on to claim that it was this publicity stunt, with its Yippie and situationist echoes, that brought about the 'first widespread awareness of the new 'Women's Liberation Movement', capturing world interest and giving the movement its very name.' (Sarachild 1979, 149)

Though other participants and chroniclers of feminism generally do mark the protest as the movement's media baptism, they do not as often acknowledge that the Miss America protest also marks the moment when the media began churning out myths that continue to distort public perceptions of feminism to this day. In this instance it was the myth of the bra-burning feminist: the demonstrators had originally intended to burn the contents of their freedom trash can, but because there was an ordinance against fires on the Atlantic City Boardwalk, they dropped that part of the plan. It was a sympathetic female journalist working to the original brief who made a throwaway reference to burning bras in a preview story. The other commentators of the day seized on it, and through constant repetition, it became the WLM's defining metaphor. (Carabillo et al, n.d.; Collins 2009, 194)

The New York chapter of the liberal National Organisation of Women also participated in the Atlantic City protest, and this show of unity fed into a second key media myth about the women's movement: that it was organised, unified, and coherent. In fact, it never was, and though this has been a source of much hand-wringing (about which more later) it is important to note that, in sharp contrast to NOW, with its expanding reform agenda, the early proponents of consciousness-raising as a radical weapon had little faith in traditional political organisation. They did not want to operate in the name of a 'service' or 'membership' organisation. Instead they saw themselves operating 'zap action' (Sarachild 1979, 147), political agitation and education groups: 'We would be the first to dare to say and do the undareable [sic], what women really felt and wanted. The first job now was to raise awareness and understanding, our own and others—awareness that would prompt people to organize and to act on a mass scale.'(Ibid)

As pragmatists, they were willing to take inspiration wherever they found it, and the list of influences offered by Sarachild is eclectic in the extreme. She speaks of a debt to 17th century science: 'We were in effect repeating the… challenge…to scholasticism' by studying nature, not books, and putting 'all theories to the test of living practice and action'. (Sarachild 1979, 147) She acknowledges the importance of first wave feminism, quoting the nineteenth century suffragist Ernestine Rose: 'We had to describe to women their own position….and through these means, as a wholesome irritant, we roused public opinion….' (ibid). Sarachild credits the civil rights movement for informing much of their practice: 'We were applying to women and to ourselves as women's liberation organizers the practice a number of us had learned as organizers in the civil rights movement in the South in the early 1960's.'(Ibid) She quotes both Malcolm X and Stokely Carmichael – a generous gesture, if you bear in mind that it was Stokely Carmichael who made one of the most famous ripostes of the era: 'The position for women in the movement is prone.'[1]

Somewhat cagily, Sarachild acknowledges that consciousness-raising was also 'a method of radical organizing tested by other revolutions'. She goes on to offer wise words from Mao Tsetung and, more significantly, an excerpt from *Fanshen*, William Hinton's 1966 book on Communist China, which had greatly impressed Western radicals with its moving accounts of meetings at which young revolutionary cadres were tutored in the fundamentals of class relations and class consciousness 'so that they could, as they themselves said, 'get at the root of calamity.' (Sarachild 1979)

In *Women's Estate*, Juliet Mitchell would describe the importance of the Chinese example in greater detail:

> In fact, the concept of 'consciousness-raising' is the reinterpretation of a Chinese revolutionary practice of 'speaking bitterness'…These peasants,

subdued by violent coercion and abject poverty, took a step out of thinking their fate was natural by articulating it. (Mitchell 1971, 62)

Though Mitchell went on to stress that no one believed 'this revolutionary practice could be imported wholesale from…pre-revolutionary China to Women's Liberation Movements in the advanced capitalist countries', she insisted there was nevertheless 'a relevance which doesn't insult the plight of the Chinese peasant' which she described as follows.

In having been given for so long their own sphere, their 'other' world, women's oppression is hidden far from consciousness (this dilemma is expressed as 'women don't want liberating'); it is this acceptance of a situation as 'natural', or a misery as 'personal' that has first to be overcome. 'Consciousness-raising' is speaking the unspoken: the opposite, in fact, of nattering together'. (Ibid)

By 1971, when *Women's Estate* was published, consciousness-raising had gone international, with groups proliferating across Britain as well as North America. Most of those participating were middle-class women already in or bound for the professions. They would later recall the gatherings as exhilarating, eye-opening, and life-changing, and as 'seedbeds' for later action. In *Hyenas in Petticoats*, her account of the first two decades of second wave feminism in Britain, Angela Neustatter recalls that it was 'the friendship gained through these groups' that many women remembered with the greatest affection. 'A fundamental camaraderie emerged, and women found that they could enjoy supporting and being supported by each other. For many, this was exciting, startling, shocking even. It was a new phenomenon….' Neustatter 1989, 18)

Second Thoughts and the Media Massage

But not everyone approved, and again some of the most scathing criticisms came from women. In her famous essay on the women's movement, published in the *New York Times* in 1972, Joan Didion mocked the idea that 51% of the population of the nation could be seen as a 'potentially revolutionary class'. This, she claimed, 'was from the virtual beginning the 'idea' of the women's movement, and the tendency for popular discussion of the movement still to center around daycare centers is yet another instance of that studied resistance to the possibility of political ideas which characterizes our national life.' (Didion 1972)

It was this 'studied resistance' that, in Didion's opinion, doomed the women's movement from the outset, for 'it was precisely to the extent that there was this Marxist idea that the curious historical anomaly known as the women's movement would have seemed to have any interest at all.' To illustrate just how far it had moved away from its only interesting idea, Didion turned to consciousness-raising:

> Of course this litany of trivia was crucial to the movement in the beginning....but such discoveries could be of no use at all if one refused to perceive the larger point, failed to make that inductive leap from the personal to the political....More and more, as the literature of the movement began to reflect the thinking of women who did not really understand the movement's ideological base, one had the sense of this stall, this delusion, the sense that the drilling of the theorists had struck only some psychic hardpan dense with superstitions and little sophistries, wish-fulfilment, self-loathing and bitter fancies. To read even desultorily in this literature was to recognize instantly a certain dolorous phantasm, an imagined Everywoman with whom the authors seemed to identify all too entirely. This ubiquitous construct was everyone's victim but her own. (Ibid)

In her widely-read 1977 obituary, *The Rise and Demise of Feminism: A Class Analysis*, Marlene Dixon sees the movement as suffering the same fate as all the other mass movements of the era: internal differentiation along class and political lines' had led to the middle class dominating the leadership, thus 'reducing a vigorous and radical social movement to a politically and ideologically co-opted reformist lobby in the halls of Congress.' (Dixon 1977) She, too, sees consciousness-raising (CR) as the first wrong turning. Though it was meant to have been 'the path to sisterhood – that unity expressed in empathic identification with the suffering of all women – which would lead from the recognition of one's own oppression to identification with the sisterhood of all women, from sisterhood to radical politics, from radical politics to revolution' the early radical organisers 'talked much less about the fact that the common oppression of women *has different results in different social classes*.'(Ibid)

Focussed as it was on the informal pooling of common experience, and ill-equipped to allow for difference, consciousness-raising (CR) became a 'mechanism for social control and group therapy' controlled by middle-class women to serve a middle-class agenda: 'What radicals had not taken into account was the fact that middle class and wealthy women do not want to identify with their class inferiors; do not care, by and large, what happens to women who have problems different from their own; greatly dislike being reminded that they are richer, better educated, healthier and have more life chances than most people.' (Ibid)

What Dixon herself does not take into account is the part the media played in all this. They were already interested in attracting female audiences, especially the middle-class consumers advertisers most craved. But in the first years of the movement, the industry was still very much a male domain, and it is clear just from the language and artwork of early coverage that those in charge had been knocked sideways by this sudden revival of the woman question and were uncertain how best to respond. A classic example is *Time Magazine*'s famous cover story in 1972. Entitled 'American Woman, a Special Report: Where She Is and Where She is Going', it came with a cover featuring a sculpture by Stanley Glaubach: a see-through plastic head, female in shape and hairstyle, stuffed with female trivia – a curler, a doll's head, a key ring with a miniature globe, a contraceptive pill dispenser, a stick of lipstick, a credit card, a couple of necklaces, a toy spatula, a tiny bride with a tiny groom, a pair of ballet shoes, two feminist buttons, three paperbacks, and a tape measure. The article inside began with a quote from Byron's *Don Juan* ('There is a tide in the affairs of women/Which, taken at the flood, leads —God knows where). Though the article itself strained for balance, the tone was distant, mystified, and perplexed: 'By all rights, the American woman today should be the happiest in history. She is healthier than U.S. women have ever been, better educated, more affluent, better dressed, more comfortable, wooed by advertisers, pampered by gadgets. But there is a worm in the apple. She is restless in her familiar familial role, no longer quite content with the homemaker-wife-mother part in which her society has cast her.' (*Time Magazine*, 20 March 1972)

It goes on to describe a nationwide conversation, conducted without male supervision in 'rap session and kaffeeklatsch, in the radical-chic salons of Manhattan and the ladies auxiliaries of Red Oak, Iowa', as women with no formal connection to any movement whispered about nifty new ways to escape domesticity. Time Magazine's first concern, though, was for the worried men whose comforts were now at risk. 'The New Feminism has increasingly influenced young women to stay single,' it said darkly, 'and it has transformed – and sometimes wrecked – marriages by ending once automatic assumptions about woman's place.' There is no mention of consciousness-raising groups, perhaps because by 1972 the corporate authors of *Time* saw no need for women to worry their little heads too much. The radical weapon had been stream-lined and repackaged. It took only a second now to become a bra-burning feminist. All you needed was what Jane O'Reilly had described, in the first issue of *Ms Magazine*, as 'click of recognition…that parenthesis of truth around a little thing that completes the puzzle of reality in women's minds.' (in Collins 2009, 188) and which Time Magazine, struggling to translate the concept into manspeak, called 'a blinding click….a moment of truth that shows men's pre-emption of a superior role.' (Ibid)

Sadly, the blinding click seemed to be for women only. Where feminists saw parentheses of truth, the men of *Time* saw only ill-conceived ideas: 'If the feminist revolution simply wanted to exchange one ruling class for another, if it aimed at outright female domination (a situation that has occurred in science fiction and other fantasies), the goal would be easier to visualize.' The demand for equality was, by contrast, 'immensely complicated,' as 'true equality between autonomous partners is hard to achieve even if both partners are of the same sex. The careful balancing of roles and obligations and privileges, without the traditional patterns to fall back on, sometimes seems like an almost Utopian vision.' (Ibid)

In any event, *Time* was more worried about the dystopias. What if women were expected to take combat roles? What if 'protective legislation' was repealed, thereby forcing wives and mothers into full-time work? This sort of random fretting was very much in keeping with middle-aged dinner party conversation at the time. There was, I recall, much talk about female brain surgeons, and widespread agreement that it would be foolish to put one's life in their hands. To help the confused establishment grapple with the immense complications of equality, the media of the age depended heavily on its small coterie of femstars. And because this is my own term, let me offer a definition: A femstar is a feminist who presumes (or is presumed) to have insider knowledge of the women's movement: sometimes because she heads an organisation or department that represents or acts on behalf of women, sometimes because she has done serious scholarly work on women and gender, sometimes because she has name value as a journalist and/or has written a feminist best-seller, and sometimes because what she has to say is newsworthy on account of being rather extreme and frightening.

The first femstar of second wave feminism was Betty Friedan, whose 1963 bestseller, *The Feminine Mystique*, tapped into the silent despair of post World War II suburban housewives. She was one of the founder members of the liberal feminist National Organization of Women (NOW), and for five years she served as its head, fronting for the organisation, and publicising its list of desired reforms, while others of no profile did the legwork. The most charismatic femstar was Gloria Steinem, best known at the time as the founder of *Ms Magazine*, but best remembered now for her decades of work as a (liberal feminist) activist who built bridges with feminists of all persuasions, and who, through *Ms Magazine*, helped many issues first marked 'radical' into NOW's reforming agenda. By and large Friedan and Steinem were presented in the media as the voices of reason; the reformers who just wanted to make sure women could function as fully fledged citizens. But from the early 70s, they were competing for airtime (and arguing fiercely) with a whole slew of radical femstars, and it is interesting to note how many of them – Shulamith Firestone (*The Dialectic of Sex*), Anne Koedt ('The Myth of the Vaginal Orgasm') Pat Mainardi ('The Politics of Housework,'), Kate Millett (*Sexual Politics*), Susan

Brownmiller (*Against our Will*) and Robin Morgan (*Sisterhood is Powerful*) – came out of New York Radical Women and the Redstockings.

It was not just the liberal wing of the women's movement that took issue with their vast, wild generalisations about men, women, patriarchy, childrearing and sexual oppression. Marxist and socialist feminists in both Britain and the US were quick to locate the holes in their totalising, class and race-blind, 'atemporal' arguments, and so, too, would feminist theorists over the decades to come, most especially those aiming to recapture feminism's radical potential. But in the popular media that continued to be feminism's main messenger, we see that 'studied resistance' coming into play. There was little interest in this strand of the discussion, possibly because it came from the left, but also, perhaps, because it was conducted largely in academese – a language regarded as too complicated for female readers; or at least the female readers they saw as bringing in the biggest advertising revenues. What they offered instead was an arena where femstars of differing persuasions could fight it out, not just amongst themselves, but with a growing band of anti femstars (led in the US by Phyllis Shafly and Anita Bryant) and the more vicious that fight became, the higher the ratings. Audiences fearful of feminism could watch with fascination while declaring a pox on all its houses.

It is worth considering what those audiences might have found so fascinating, and also so worrying. It is generally agreed now that what one might call the post-war settlement for women was falling apart. A service sector eager to employ women was rapidly expanding. By 1960, almost a third of married women were in employment, partly to finance their family's consumer aspirations, but also, significantly, to pay for their daughters as well as their sons to go to university. These women were earning a great deal less than men for equal work. They were aware of being barred from many types of work and aware, too, that the sorts of work they could do were undervalued. When they went home at the end of the day, they began what Arlie Hochschild would later call the second shift. There was increasing tension between the daily experiences of working women and the then prevailing views of femininity. It was because liberal feminists were able to articulate this 'bad fit' that NOW was able to grow so rapidly during the late sixties. But it was the radical feminists who spoke most powerfully to women still studying at, or only recently emerged from universities. Crude as the terms of the debate were during the early years of second wave feminism, they nevertheless offered these younger women a new way of understanding the male-dominated institutions to which they were slowly gaining admittance. Where women just a few years older might have seen themselves as lacking when excluded or harshly judged, these younger women were more likely to begin from the premise that problem was institutional sexism. I should perhaps say 'we younger women' as I was one of them, and I should perhaps point out here that by 1970, the year I started university in the USA, there were no consciousness-raising groups on offer. The matter had been decided. On the nation's campuses, consciousness had been well and truly raised. What mattered now was the larger project, which was, by and large, making the personal political.

I am very glad now that no one was taping us. But I can remember that, for all our arrogant pronouncements, we shared an optimism that rarely figures in public accounts of early feminism. What made our conversations exciting was that they drew from personal experience to challenge expert knowledge. As such we were continuing the CR challenge to scholasticism ('putting all theories to the test of living practice and action') and reflecting its wide remit ('studying the whole gamut of women's lives, starting with the full reality of one's own'). We were particularly interested in changing the way in which the public realm defined and controlled the private, the personal, and the female. The (mostly male) politicians, doctors, sociologists, teachers, employers, philosophers, psychologists, childcare gurus, poets and novelists who had together defined the female condition were no longer to have the last word. Instead, there was to be a two-way conversation, allowing women to bring their own expert knowledge into play. For many of us (and this is echoed in this volume by the accounts in Körner and McKechnie's chapter and the Conclusion), this was to become a lifelong pursuit, a way of positioning ourselves in the professions we joined. It was also a way of pushing for radical change inside tiny spaces, and hoping that over time we might erode just one patch of the fabric of traditional society, while remaining forever mindful that we were powerless to challenge economic and political structures as we might have done, had we belonged to an organised and coherent movement.

We see an early manifestation of this strategy – this slow, collective subversion from within – in the Boston Women's Health Collective, a group that first came together at a women's liberation conference at Emmanuel College, Boston, in 1969. Most of the group's members were studying or practicing medicine. Their original idea was to compile a list of doctors they could recommend to other women. But as they talked, they found that one woman's recommendation was another woman's horror story. They decided that what women needed most was good evidence-based information that would allow them to enter into a conversation about their treatment instead of just accepting what the doctor decreed to be best. The result was *Our Bodies, Ourselves*. This is the manual, which is still selling well, still under the control of the collective, and now in its fifth edition, that did so much to transform our current approach to women's health. It developed along classic CR principles: a group of women gathers together in a safe space, initially just to talk and give each other support. But as they bring personal experience to bear on their shared concerns, they begin to define a problem and explore ways to resolve it (Wells 2009).

At no point do they refer to a feminist version of Moscow Centre to ensure that they are following a party line. Because there is no party line. By the mid-seventies, the movement that has always refused the traditional trappings of movements has expanded so far and morphed so often that it exists not as a movement, but as an idea, a click of recognition, a vocabulary, a series of questions, a narrative, and a way of challenging tradition. Only in the mainstream media does the women's liberation movement live on in the phantom plural, as an army of hairy-legged hags who must always be having a field day.

During the twenty-five years I have spent as a freelance journalist in Britain – often writing on what were originally known as women's issues – I have, along with many like-minded journalists, been in almost daily combat with the purveyors of that myth. It is, perhaps, to keep frustration and fury at bay that we have often taken the trouble to look for the patterns in their narratives, and in the shapes of their stock plots. We have tried to use that knowledge to challenge, amongst many other things, the hard/soft divide, and we have noticed that, in the end, the catalyst is almost always an important politician announcing that a matter formerly marked private is now a matter for public debate, as Gordon Brown did, when he announced in the mid-nineties, that childcare was an economic issue (!!!) and as Jack Straw did after the Labour victory, when he briefly upgraded family policy, while ensuring that his particular take on family policy had media prominence. We've seen that, despite their claim to speak truth to power, the media are hugely sensitive to the view from the top.

At the same time, we have seen how our media masters have, however inadvertently, kept the issues first explored in consciousness-raising groups at the forefront of the public imagination. Mostly these are consigned to the soft side of the 'hard news-soft news' divide that so often keeps 'soft' women's issues locked in the features sections of the mainstream media, that are targeted at the 'AB' women who bring in the most lucrative advertising revenues. They exist, by and large, in strictly policed, advertiser-friendly formats. There must be a body or bedroom or family issue and, unless they come in the form of an eye-catching and highly emotional confession, they must offer three case studies, doctored if necessary to fit the class aspirations of the desired reader, and decorated with the wise words of several experts to whom the writer of the feature must always defer; and from whom she is to glean seven bullet points with helpful hints. Only when there is a scandal does the issue jump the divide to enter television's Newsnight and the comments pages. But there is a never-ending string of these, and with them the desire to milk them for all they're worth. So whenever the scandal has cast a ghastly light on motherhood, fatherhood, marriage, sexual mores, childrearing, child abuse, fertility, pregnancy, sexual violence, the sex industries, or the state of modern womanhood, it is all hands on deck. The mediated cacophony that follows will contain many strong warnings about the threat that is feminism. But also in the mix are feminist voices. On rare occasions, and with the help of enlightened editors, it has been possible for feminist columnists, novelists, scholars, and activists to challenge or at least expose the ways in which politicians and media moguls have framed a particular debate. Even more rarely, it has been possible to change the frame itself. But even when the usual rules apply, it is possible to challenge received wisdom about the subject to hand – be it child abuse or marriage, working mothers or family courts – by drawing from personal experience, or speaking from a perspective not commonly believed to exist. I offer one telling example: at one newspaper where I had a column year ago, I made a point of writing weekly about politics from the perspective of a working mother: this was in response to a comment from my editors; insistent that I must be making it all up, as 'mothers never discuss politics.'

Conclusion: Personal Practice and the Sixties Heritage

The authentic voices are not all female. But almost always they come out of the same tradition, which has its roots in the social movements of the late sixties and early seventies. At its heart are the central tenets of CR: the rejection of prevailing demarcations of public and private, the assertion that women were 'messed over, not messed up'; the interest in the invisible and the unspoken; the linking of political analysis with personal experience; and the insistence that collective solutions rise out of sustained, collective analysis and reflective debate. Call it an ethic, if you will. Working mother that I am, moving as I do between many different houses, debates and disciplines, all in the line of work, I have had the privilege to see that ethic in action, if not in ascendance, at every level of education and in almost every area of women's health, from sex education, pregnancy and childbirth to the menopause and old age. I have seen it in academic practice across the disciplines, in social and particularly family policy, in government and in humanitarian and development work, and in grassroots organisations throughout the world, and I have seen its insights feed back into feminist theory. During 31 years as a mother, I have seen it in most families of my acquaintance, and in most families I have met as a journalist, even amongst those who define themselves as traditional. I have seen it in the so-called Muslim world as in the so-called West. And, perhaps most important, I have seen it passed on, usually without identifying labels, to the next generation.

When I look back at the experiment from which this ethic came, it seems deliciously naïve. Imagine thinking that a total revolution was only a few blinding clicks away. Imagine believing that the women of the world would be willing or able to set aside their differences. Imagine thinking that a message you made no effort to control could travel though the smoke and mirrors of the media and still retain its original radical intent! But in a way, what did happen is even more amazing. Somehow, and with both the help and hindrance of the media, the inventors of CR managed to convert an extraordinary number of women and a fair number of men to feminist practice. That's how I see it, anyway. You might think otherwise. But if we argue about it, we'll still be observing a central tenet of CR: which is to advance the argument through direct engagement with one's fiercest critics. The most interesting arguments continue to take place in the spaces that remain safe from the distorting glare of the media. But it is the media that have kept our concerns in the public domain, and the personal political, and it is the feminists in the media who have helped to keep the central insights of feminism alive in the public mind – if not always wisely, and never often enough, and rarely under conditions of our own making.

Note

1 Casey Hayden, a field secretary on the SNCC staff in the Atlanta office wrote an anonymous paper with Mary King on the treatment of women in the movement. She recalls a conversation during a break at a staff meeting: 'Our paper on the position of women came up, and Stokely in his hipster rap comedic way joked that "the proper position of women in SNCC is prone". I laughed, he laughed, we all laughed....' http://www.crmvet.org/mem/stokely1.htm

References

Carabillo,.T., Meulii, J. and Csida, J. B. '1968'. In *Feminist Chronicles* 1953–1993. http://www.feminist.org/research/chronicles/fc1968.html (accessed 2 January 2010)
Collins, G. 2009. *When Everything Changed*. New York: Little, Brown and Company
Didion, J. 1972. The Women's Movement, *New York Times*, 30th July
Dixon, M. 1977. The Rise and Demise of Feminism: A Class Analysis. http://www.cwluherstory.org/newsite/the-rise-and-demise-of-womens-liberation.html
Hanisch, Carol, 1969, *The Personal is Political*, pp. 3–5. http://www.carolhanisch.org/CHwritings/PIP.html (accessed 9.5.2010)
Mitchell, J. 1971. *Women's Estate*. London: Penguin
Neustatter, A. 1989. *Hyenas in Petticoats: A Look at Twenty Years of Feminism*. London: Harrap
Sarachild, K.1979. Consciousness-Raising: A Radical Weapon. In Redstockings. *Feminist Revolution*. New York: Random House, pp. 144–150
Wells, S. 2009. Our Bodies, Ourselves: Reading the Written Female Body University of Virginia lecture. March 11, 2009. http://www.youtube.com/watch?v=Ny3rSULs8eg (accessed 10th January 2010)

Conclusion

RESURGENCE? THE LEGACY OF THE SIXTIES TO CONTEMPORARY SOCIAL MOVEMENTS

Bryn Jones and Mike O'Donnell

Introduction

This book began by contrasting polarised interpretations of the longer term impact of sixties radicalism. One cluster sees cultural, social and political rebellion as ephemeral, politically inconsequential or absorbed into the mainstream. Others see legacies and practices from sixties radicalism as established and still influential in contemporary radical protest. This divergence is illustrated by the views of two Americans: Noam Chomsky (2009) and Gerard DeGroot (2008). On the BBC world news programme *Hardtalk* (November 3 2009) Chomsky consistently attributed what he sees as an increase in freedom of expression in American public life to the long-term impact of the radical actions of the nineteen sixties and particularly emphasised the role of young people. He cited the protests against the Iraq War as subject to less harassment than the anti-Vietnam War protests. A life-long 'sceptic' of the corrupting effects of power, Chomsky upholds protest as a continuous part of democratic life – a view once expressed even more forcefully by Thomas Jefferson in the phrase 'God forbid that we should ever be twenty years without … a rebellion' (quoted in Rosen 1969, 2). But is it possible to maintain such a perception of protest as process, a necessary and continuous part of a free society in an age when the great meta-narratives of the left are said by some to be 'exhausted' (Bell, 1988; Lyotard, 1984)?

Despite some intemperate commentary the substance of Gerard DeGroot's recent critique of the radical sixties nevertheless typifies the negative pole of assessment. Commenting on the founding document of the American Students for a Democratic Society, *The Port Huron Statement*, he derides 'the high-octave self-importance of young people who have just discovered 'eternal truths' and a confidence which 'came from their egos, all of which were extraordinarily large' (DeGroot 2008, 95). What DeGroot's evidence for the universally 'large size' of 'all' the activists' egos is not stated. His analysis of the counterculture is limited to repeating the now clichéd criticism that 'it relied on the established culture to give it voice' (444): an assertion that flies in the face of the evidence (see pp 96–8; 127–9; 142–3; 157–8; 211–2). DeGroot's an overstatement of a more generalised scepticism discussed elsewhere in this book (*cf* Jones chapter 1; O'Donnell chapter 6). The more complex analyses in the present book provide a strong counterpoint to the verdict of one sympathetic review of DeGroot's text as 'a strong case that the '60s counterculture achieved almost nothing, that the era was a brief, trivial and weird spasm that left only fragments in its wake (Kamiya 2008).

Even some who are broadly sympathetic to the radical sixties, like Gerd-Rainer Horn, consider that its impact has waned in the face of the long hegemony of neo-liberalism. As will become apparent, we offer a more optimistic interpretation which allows us to evaluate Chomsky's contrary interpretation of ongoing and possibly resurgent sixties-style radicalism capable of combating the renewed militarism and socially-destructive economies of the contemporary world. In the rest of this Conclusion we examine firstly the case against the evanescent-irrelevance thesis of commentators such as DeGroot by identifying the practices, institutions and ideas that have been established as a result of sixties radicalism. In the second part we probe the possibilities of a stronger renewal of radicalism advancing from these enclaves. To carry out this analysis we utilise two additional theoretical constructs and unpublished evidence of continuing commitment to sixties radical values. The theoretical constructs consists of an application of Foucault's distinction between utopias and heteretopias; plus an adaptation of classical Weberian sociology.

Weber identified a specific normative-behavioural complex, which he associated with the Protestant Ethic of early-modern capitalism, as the 'spirit' of capitalist economic motivation. We argue that the innovative Sixties' emphasis on social transformation through voluntary action – which contemporary Marxists exalted as 'praxis' – constituted an analogous behavioural disposition focussed, in both 'revolutionary' and reformist ways, on the sphere of civil society; creating a new 'spirit of community'. Ironically, the new radicals arrived at this pragmatic approach by the same route as the 'end of ideology' liberals with whom they had such an uneasy relationship. Both drew the conclusion from the example of the totalitarian ideologies that the human cost of imposing 'universal utopia' was unacceptably high. Nevertheless, for the radicals this dystopic conclusion entailed a need to act on a range of issues, both internationally and within the Western democracies. This logic led them into issue-oriented protest but also into life style politics, or what Foucault calls 'heterotopias'. Since the 1960s much radical action has been inspired by similar views and sentiments. Additional evidence of continuing commitment to sixties radical values comes from a targeted sample of male and female sixties veterans. It traces the extent of, and ways in which they sustained their values in the inhospitable political and social climates since their initial radicalisation. But first we examine the ways in which sixties utopias evolved into multiple enclaves, or heterotopias of commitment and activism, by contrasting the 1960s' societal context with today's world, in order to establish the extent to which such radicalism survived.

Institutionalisation of Sixties Innovations: From Utopia to Heterotopias

In his 1967 lectures on 'Other Spaces' (*Des Espace Autres*) Michel Foucault drew attention to modernity's tendency to supplant all-encompassing utopias with havens of specialised reverence, amusement and knowledge. In these physical locations, such as museums, fun-fairs, cemeteries, populations could explore and enjoy phenomena and feelings beyond everyday life in modernity (Foucault 1984). Foucault's binary concept can be extended, we would argue, to the cultural explosion of the sixties. As McDonald has pointed out, in chapter 2, much of the esoteric and extravagant ideologising of the sixties period can be attributed to the participants' search for ideas and philosophies that were expressive of novel experiences and situations. In their different, but often overlapping, discourses both the counter-culture and the Marxisant-Left were striving to define and then pursue societal transformation: utopias.

With the internal breakdown and external hammering of these utopian aspirations, some of the energy and idealism diverted into the burgeoning rights movements: the wider feminist, anti-racist and anti-gay 'identity' movements. The radical sixties had opened up space for these identities to be shaped, not by moralists and authoritarians, nor by DeGroot's sanctimonious egoists, but by those who lived them. Idealism then diverged from recipes and crusades for societal transformation to more localised, specialised and material projects. The various rights, cultural and life-style movements gradually established new social spaces with 'feminised' sexual and family relations, music festivals and, later, internet enclaves. These institutionalised practices and arenas had no grand project for societal revolution but they provided heterotopic alternatives to the mainstream ways of living. It is beyond our present scope to analyse these developments in more detail. Suffice to note that even the most utopian of contemporary social movements, that of anti-globalisation/'anti-capitalism' largely eschews definition of a monolithic alternative social order. Yet it has established protest traditions in the heterotopias of carnivalesque anti-globalisation demonstrations and 'global social forums' (see Harding chapter 8).

Radicalism – Then and Now: Continuities and Differences

An understanding of the main similarities and differences between sixties radicalism and the comparable contemporary social movements requires an appreciation of their respective historical contexts. As we outlined in the Introduction, increasing social opportunity and personal expression in the West emerged against the dominant international phenomenon of the Cold War. This was the decade of liberal higher education expansion and free rock concerts; but also of threats of nuclear war, such as the Cuban Missile Crisis, and of recurrent crises over a divided Berlin. Sixties radicalism was a response to serious issues and to considerable institutional conservatism and authoritarianism – much of it linked to the moral rigidity and cultural conservatism fostered by Cold War paranoia – that no longer seemed necessary or meaningful to a younger better educated and media savvy generation.

What might have remained a limited protest movement took fire politically largely in response to the Vietnam War – perhaps the first genuine 'media war' – and, culturally, because the available time, the technology, the social issues and the creativity coincided. Gerard DeGroot (2008) and the now 'penitent' Peter Collier and David Horowitz (1996) condemn sixties radicals for their extremism but there is surely some justification in regarding racial segregation and the Vietnam War as the radicals themselves did: as extreme and justifying extra-ordinary levels of response. As the scale of the militarism and racism became apparent the initial forms of non-violent civil disobedience came to be seen as inadequate.

Sceptics of the viability of sixties radicalism tend to see this turn to violence (Black Panthers and Weathermen in the USA, Red Army Faction, Angry Brigade and Red Brigades in Europe) as an inevitable and negative consequence of the immaturity and irrelevance of its philosophies and aspirations. Of course, it is undeniable that the violence of a minority of radicals in the late 1960s and early 1970s is part of the history of sixties radicalism and reflects a debate within the movement about 'the means of change'. However, the evidence of this book is that what was most distinctive and original about sixties radicalism was its attempt to create a 'lived radicalism', with consistency between its ends and means, within the womb of civil society rather than through violent revolution or conventional party politics. Reflecting this influential theme in radical sixties thinking, several contributors to this book have argued that a strategy of violent revolution in the context of Western democracies presents enormous moral and practical difficulties (McDonald, chapter 2; O'Donnell, chapter 6; Driver, chapter 9). However, as was indicated in the Introduction, the arguments in relation to violent revolution are very different in the context of authoritarian and severely repressive regimes of a type still common in the 1960s in the developing world (see Lunn, chapter 4; and Shaikh, chapter 5).

The allegation that nineteen sixties radicals were pre-occupied with superficial and self-indulgent concerns is belied by the gravity of the many causes that were pursued. Starting with the mid-sixties campaigns for black civil rights in the USA, the activism extended into, partially successful, attempts at democratisation. These ranged from reforms to university bureaucracies, for more participatory democracy elsewhere to movements against inequality and exploitation generated by capitalist corporations. The effectiveness of the campaigns to end the Vietnam War are debatable but the broader peace movement, to which they contributed, formed a persistent and, some would argue, successful opposition to establishment arms policies in Europe and North America in the 1970s and '80s. Sixties ideas were also influential in the birth of campaigning environmental organisations, Friends of the Earth in 1969, Greenpeace – originally an anti-nuclear campaign – in 1971. Even the much-maligned counterculture/alternative consciousness movement can claim to have contributed to important debates and changes in the fields of mental and physical health and nutrition. In the late 1960s and early 1970s other tendencies, baulked by Establishment intransigence and the limitations of mass protest, redirected some of the energy and idealism of nineteen sixties radicalism into the burgeoning rights movements: the wider feminist, anti-racist and gay 'identity' movements.

If the over-riding international spectre that constrained and stimulated 1960s radicalism was the Cold War and its conflicts, today's supra-national dimension lies in two consequences of capitalist economic globalisation. These are the material and political implications of environmental catastrophe – anthropogenic climate change; and the igniting of Islamic fundamentalism – prompting militarised, 'war on terror' counter-campaigns – as the principal ideological challenge to western liberal-capitalism. After 9/11 it became much more difficult for many Western radicals to see the global context simply in terms of the exploitative West and the exploited rest. The methods of combat used by militant jihadist, particularly, suicide attacks clash with the still predominantly pacifistic values of anti-capitalist and anti-globalisation sensibilities. However, key strands of Islamic culture, given prominence or exaggerated by its radicals, also conflict with values of personal rights and freedoms institutionalised by the women's and other rights movements in the global North.

As several of our contributors observe, the discourse of sixties radicalism – especially in its later phases – drew upon the rhetoric and vocabulary of what was sometimes, patronisingly, referred to as 'third world' alternatives to Western capitalism and Soviet-bloc Communism. As McDonald, Shaikh and Cardina observe in their chapters, contemporary cultural and linguistic overlaps made it easier for sixties radicals to identify with what were perceived as revolutionary movements from Cuba to Vietnam. The transposition of the term 'liberation' between national-revolutionary discourses in the colonial and neo-colonial countries and the emerging gender movements being the most obvious example. Similarly, in chapter 12, Freely traces the adoption and translation of the even-more influential concept of 'consciousness-raising'; from the radicalisation of peasants in China, to its major impact on the style and ethos of the women's movement in the West.

Yet in the context of the early twenty-first century, despite some inspiration from indigenous movements, including the Mexican Zapatistas, it is difficult for 'Northern' radicals to empathise with other major non-Western challenges, such as the Islamist ideologies which pose the main revolutionary alternative to global capitalism today. Radical rights activists have suddenly been required to relate to people who have experienced evident historical oppression, but also with cultural leitmotivs alien and, in some respects, antipathetic to, principles of moral relativism and autonomy integral to their own concepts of emancipation. This may be one reason why protest against the war in Afghanistan has, to this point, been much more muted than protest against the war in Iraq and the Vietnam War. Yet, as we elaborate below, the increasingly global web of capitalism enables social movements from the developed North and the impoverished South to find common cause and use information technologies to mobilise together against it. There is also a certain historical symmetry between Western radicalism's attitude to the contending blocs in both the sixties period and today's international situation. Sixties movements were guardedly sympathetic to Communist nations' rejection of capitalism but also vehemently critical of Communism's authoritarianism. Similarly today's social movements show some sympathy for their rejection of, and resistance to capitalist imperialism, but also antipathy to the violent tactics and limited human rights practices of radical Islamists.

Despite the proliferation of heterotopias for alternative life-styles and social movement campaigns, there are also signs of a more assertive and unified revival of sixties-style radicalism in the emerging synthesis of human rights, global justice and environmental movements. The complexities of the post 9/11 world have not prevented or stymied intellectual developments that have led to an integrated critique of climate change and global development/underdevelopment (e.g., inter-alia: Beck 1992; Monbiot 2003). For example, the Transition Towns movement, seeded in 77 UK towns and villages and another 24 localities world-wide, marries an ethic of sustainable energy and resource use with norms of self-help and sharing communities (Transition Towns 2009). If there is a new, kinder, more human universalism, it lies in this direction and has significant roots in the rights movements of the sixties. This is illustrated by the scope of the main targets of contemporary radicalism: the impoverishment of human rights in developing countries; environmental devastation; the global institutionalisation of the deregulated markets of hyper-consumerism; and the inequalities created by transnational corporate business.

Starting with the 1992 Rio Conference on the environment and then the 1999 protests in Seattle at the meeting of the World Trade Organisation (WTO) to negotiate tariff and trade regulation, in the last decade there have been regular major protests against related policies of neo-liberal capitalist expansion at the forums of inter-governmental organisations. At the 1999 WTO meetings, over 1000 groups and organisations came to protest against the policies of the WTO (which had replaced the General Agreement on Tariffs and Trade). Starting with this event many 'green' groups have successfully linked environmental damage with the progressive liberalisation of world trade (read: markets and capital accumulation). These protest campaigns have also helped stimulate and publicise a wide range of alternative policies; such as the licensing of companies significantly involved in world trade to require adherence environmental standards, and taxation of international capital flows to fund poverty alleviation (cf. ATTAC n.d.) which are now receiving support from mainstream international political figures.

More generally these various descendants of sixties social movements are now starting to achieve the integration of ideas and campaigns which divided their predecessors politically and ideologically. Academic commentators have begun to speak of a 'civil society regulation' of some business and market sectors (Gereffi et al 2001; Gunningham 2008, 19). Although some are sceptical of this 'incorporation' of sometime radical campaigning organisations, these can claim that they still operate a twin-track strategy; negotiating and collaborating where progress is feasible but also reverting to external opposition and protest where necessary (Rootes 1999; Naidoo 2003). A principle, accepted even by established world politicians such as Al Gore, who has argued that if a moral threshold of culpability is crossed in failing to deal adequately with climate change, then civil disobedience is justified in attempting to increase pressure for accelerated inter-governmental response (Gore 2009). Civil disobedience has a long-standing place in the tradition of particularly American and British protest and has been adopted by some contemporary social movement groups and activists. So some of the classic protest tactics of sixties radicalism have not only survived and been legitimated; but also co-exist with the more pragmatic politics which their original practitioners were accused – as with Habermas in Driver's chapter – of neglecting.

The role of the global human rights movement in contemporary radicalism is contested. On the one hand it can be seen as a logical extension of the rights movements of the 1960s and, although associated with the Western Enlightenment, has some support from within the developing and underdeveloped world. On the other hand, the human rights movement does not command the same now virtually universal support on the left as the 'identity' movements. Supporters of the human rights movement see one of its main purposes as extending the freedoms won in the West, many in the not so distant past, to the rest of the world (Delanty 2000; Kaldor 2003; O'Donnell 2007). Increasingly this perspective emphasises material as well as political and civil equality. Others on the left consider human rights as too tainted by liberalism and imperialism to provide a sufficiently radical ideology to underpin the fundamental changes they consider needed. In both the nineteen sixties and among today's radicals more systemic critiques of world capitalism are made than is typical of human rights activists (see Oglesby and Shaull 1967; Sklair, 2002). Nevertheless, formerly distinct and specialised civil society organisations and NGOs are extending their scope to overlap with campaigns in other spheres. Human rights campaigns such as Amnesty International are broadening their concerns to deal with the social, cultural and economic dimensions of civil rights (Naidoo 2003; Amnesty International 2009).

In particular, the focus of the contemporary anti-capitalist movement is on the systemic inequality produced by capitalism itself. Since the financial crisis of 2008–9 there has been wide support, even beyond the anti-capitalists, for the view that a more egalitarian and less volatile world requires an intellectual confrontation with contemporary capitalism and a systemic solution to the extremes of inequalities that it creates. 'Abolishing capitalism' is too glib a phrase but for the first time for several generations the proposals for significant reforms are being discussed outside the social movements dedicated to system changes. A wide range of thinkers and a large section of the public are sufficiently disillusioned and in many cases damaged by financially-driven globalisation and its near-collapse to want substantial change. Whether this opposition will persist and cohere into political programmes, based on principles such as the ATTAC programme, or diffuse with economic stabilisation, remains an open question.

Evaluation: Survival *and* Resurgence?

The preceding argument and much of the evidence in this book confirms a broad continuity in the concerns of sixties and contemporary radicals as well as in their underlying values; despite a shift in the relative importance and articulation of the issues. However, it is in the area of strategy and tactics that continuity is most obvious and more successful achievements are plausible. The social movements of both periods operate outside party politics and often independently of pressure groups. Activists target particular issues and events and tend to appear only intermittently in the media and public awareness. However, despite appearances, the various groups that make up social movements are not necessarily fragmented or disorganised. Mario Diani has drawn on the work of Rokan and Simmel to demonstrate that social movements can achieve sustained coherent action. From Rokkan he takes the observation that citizens are often members of multiple groups and associations 'below' the level of political parties and from Simmel that, among like-minded people, memberships may overlap (Diani 2000). Much common membership and therefore sharing of ideas and joint-organisation can develop between apparently separate groups. A point which is amplified by some of the convergence on issues between different campaigning organisations highlighted above. Because of the proliferation of voluntary sector groups and foundations since the nineteen sixties radical activists have more capacity to make common cause when their aims are complementary.

It has been one of the historic roles of social movements of the left to persuade wider publics and ultimately governments to implement progressive change. The slow extension of democracy in the West was partly a response to sustained protest and the securing of minority rights in the later part of the twentieth century owes much to the activities of nineteen sixties radicals. If anything, the agenda of today's social movements is even more important. Securing the planet and ensuring that its resources are used for the welfare of all is a big task for a generation. However, it represents both an advance upon, as well as a more meaningful crystallisation of the founding sentiments and rudimentary values which exploded in the 1960s. Several of the contributions to this book have highlighted the values of equality and freedom from hierarchical authority – in short the need for 'community' – which distinguished much sixties radicalism from both social-democratic welfarism and state-centred Communism as an alternative to free-market capitalism. Our contention is that this 'spirit of community' has survived and, through the arenas of global activism, expanded its scope whilst still allied to the other distinctive sixties values of personal commitment and activism. To illustrate practical embodiments and continuities in this 'praxis ethic and spirit of community' we offer, finally, personal case material from sixties radicals who have helped carry these sentiments and values into the globalised society of the present.

Now They're 64: Still Taking Radicalism Personally

One test of the broader resilience of sixties' values and practices is to assess their persistence at the individual level. While sceptic historians, such as Marwick, can portray the sixties as an evanescent phenomenon which left the broad mass of the population unaffected, the point is that much socio-cultural change arises from the activities of minorities. So, have sixties radicals maintained their values and practices or have they regressed to the demographic norm? Hadjar and Schlapbach's evidence from Germany in chapter 10 presents a mixed picture, with some persistence of political attitudes but also some retrenchment. Korner and McKechnie's qualitative interviews with British former radicals, suggests a continuing assertiveness together with some links to contemporary movements.

O'Donnell also conducted interviews with the radicals referred to in chapter 6. An aspect of Mannheim's theory of generations is that if a generational 'unit' shares a particularly formative experience or series of experiences it is likely to retain a sense of collective identification throughout the life-course (Mannheim 1952). The interviews summarised below give some support for this view and also substantiate the continuing resilience of an ethic of praxis. The interviews with the five women and five men, referred to in O'Donnell's chapter, focused partly on their life-courses since the nineteen sixties (detailed in chapter 6). In the absence of change on the scale they had envisaged, they necessarily had to engage with liberal capitalism and follow life-courses permissible within that system: employment and careers, personal relationships or children rearing. Far from, in Marcuse's terms, creating a new reality based on the pleasure principle they encountered the tougher realities of Thatcherism or Reaganism, neo-liberal economic strictures and, in the USA, moral agendas set by the religious right. How, then did the former sixties radicals respond to 'hard times'? If they have not changed 'the system', has it – as sixties sceptics would infer – changed them? Despite understandable variations between individuals the answer is that a clear trend to prioritise integrity rather than compromise emerged.

All ten chose careers that they felt were compatible with their principles. Eight took up careers in education and two in other public service sectors. However, for a radical working within 'the system', even employment in the pubic sector can present certain ethical and practical problems. Conventional career goals may seem self-centred and promotion may require a degree of organisational conformity that limits rather than enhances capacity to change things. These tensions have been made more testing in higher education because organisational changes have accentuated both bureaucratic hierarchy and market competition. No participant welcomed these changes. Several found that they conflicted with their educational values. Most have preferred to teach and/or research rather than pursue managerial careers.

In ways that have been more fully explored in Freely's account of informal women's movement networks in chapter 12, all five women participants in the interviews had found feminism to be a continuous formative influence. The feminist movement facilitated the combination of careers and a way of life for two research practitioners, one free-lancer and one academic although their feminism was seen as a break with the male chauvinism of some sixties radicalism. For these women feminist networks provide support for both personal lives and their research work; with the substantial legitimacy feminism has achieved allowing public funding of feminist inspired projects. One remarked that she has found it easier to make progress with her feminism than her socialism. An alternative strategy for a third academic respondent ('never very ambitious in career terms') was to focus on consistent and time-consuming involvement in radical causes and rearing of three children in ways consistent with her ideals.

Feminist values also shaped the work roles of the other two women respondents. In a classic sixties' diagnosis, one abandoned school teaching for adult education because she 'did not like what schools were doing to children ... inducting them into their place'. The other women respondent echoes the solidaristic sentiments about networking referred to above: contrasting the very, individualised work pattern of her first job as a lecturer ('for obvious structural reasons') with the 'collaborative' pattern of work of her subsequent research jobs, mainly with other women, on labour market issues. Preferring to work in a team and critical of 'managerial technicians', after thirty years she still works with some of these colleagues, describing these relationships as a defining feature of her working life.

Lacking the wider base of gender solidarity offered by feminism the men in the survey nevertheless sought life courses and practices consistent with their beliefs and values. Two did so through teaching and writing; another through teaching and a broad range of media engagement; another through publishing and one through public service. Perhaps marginally more conventionally 'successful' than the women, they also seem to have experienced more professional conflict. Two believe that their radical principles impeded their career progress; one claiming that his radical views and activities denied him promotion several times. The second attributes the slow progress of his academic career to his prioritisation of political and trade union work.

For several of the respondents teaching and/or research was seen as less likely to involve compromise of principle than a career in management. As a result, some have probably abjured conventional rewards of status and income but, on the whole, they show less concern about justifying their career choices than a number of 1960s ex-radicals interviewed for the *Times Higher Education Supplement* who took the career route to senior management (North *et al.*: 2004). Whether this latter group have gained the power and opportunity, or retained the intention, to effect sixties-sympathic change, is of course debatable.

In this context the life courses of these ten 'sixties survivors' make interesting comparison with a number of their contemporaries who pursued the path of orthodox political power. The younger roles of British politicians Gordon Brown, Jack Straw, Mo Mowlam and Claire Short could all be described as those of sixties radicals. In political careers personal principle and conviction famously conflict with pragmatics in circumstances such as the convention of collective

Cabinet responsibility. It could be argued, of course, that the academics studied had taken softer options surrendering opportunities to effect change which other sixties values prioritised. However, it could be equally argued that in different ways the initially radical politicians abandoned, or at least drastically scaled-down, the goal of serious social transformation – Mowlam and Short finally resigning but Brown and Straw hanging onto and climbing up Cabinet posts through three Labour administrations. For sixties radicalism means and ends are inseparable. By contrast New Labour politicians believed that they could achieve what they considered socially radical outcomes through the decidedly non-sixties means of bureaucratic power and capitalist markets. The near collapse of the financial and economic systems in 2008–9, the subsequent retrenchment of public services to accommodate the resulting government debt, the widening of class inequalities and the rampant commercialism of many areas of social life, all suggest that closer adherence to the diagnoses, and even some of the prescriptions, derivable from sixties radicalism might have provided better political guidelines than New Labour's flawed reliance on market-generated opportunities and gratuities.

By contrast the participants in O'Donnell's research, summarised above, individually and in co-operation with others have maintained the belief and practice that radical change must be holistic, personal as well as political. In so doing they corroborate the similar sentiments of Körner and McKechnie's interviewees as well as principles of lifeworld integrity diagnosed by Habermas and analysed in the chapters by Jones and Driver. Social movement theorists have observed that campaigning activities tend not to follow a linear path. More often they falter and become dormant before bursting once more into life when stimulated by propitious or provocative social and political conditions (McAdam 1994, 43). The flame of the nineteen sixties may often have flickered but the efforts of our sixties veterans and those like them have kept it alight, even if their achievements have fallen short of their aspirations. As well as taking their beliefs seriously at the personal level, of necessity they have had to pursue change through 'the long, hard march through the institutions' but have done so with a healthy scepticism of power and its capacity to corrupt. So, is the legacy of such individuals to contemporary radicalism likely to contribute to a resurgence that will counteract the generally unsympathetic public mood and political climate of the intervening three to four decades?

Conclusion: Is Another World Possible?

In the nineteen sixties the phrase 'you're either part of the solution or part of the problem' was popular. Though always too confrontational and divisive, this proposition contains a crucial kernel of truth: viz. that to be effective radical values have to be lived and not merely advocated. Those sixties radicals that tried to live their ideals have left a vital legacy to the today's generation of activists. An ethic of commitment (Martin 2009) to social causes, or 'praxis', has lived on; and, with complex implications, become institutionalised in broad swaths of the advanced societies (Chandler 2009). This praxis is sometimes individualistic, as in concerns with 'ethical' – less exploitative and environmentally harmful – life-styles. But it is still, like 60s radicalism, aimed at a more general community which embraces disadvantaged or excluded others. The question is whether this 'spirit of community' is remaining as a residual or latent ethic, or whether it is flowering into more potent forces for change in politics and civil society. There are a number of reasons for a tentative affirmative to this question.

Firstly, at the most obvious level, radicals gain credibility if what they do matches what they say. Secondly, to practise radical values is at least a start to reconstruct key societal institutions. Doing so also tests whether their values are as practical and morally sound as radicals believe. Thirdly, consistency of values and behaviour is a protection against the classic flaw of the Soviet and some other communist-inspired revolutions – the deferral of 'the good society' including decent human relations until 'after the revolution'. Taking power too often involved a high level of casualties and post-revolutionary repression – often indefinitely sustained. If an extreme divergence exists between means and ends it is likely that the former will substantially influence the outcome. This is a logical tendency rather than a law but history suggests it is a strong one and that those who aspire to change society need to be aware of it. It can be a short journey from adopting violent or coercive methods to implementing authoritarianism and repression. In contrast, a holistic radicalism is necessarily democratic – avoiding the treacherous 'short-cut' of enforcing conformity. Paradoxically it is also committed to compromise because that is what democracy invariably requires. The basic point that Habermas made to the German radical students and the American liberals to Movement radicals (see Driver chapter 9 and O'Donnell chapter 6) is apt: you cannot have all you want, at least not without argument and debate.

The fact that there is a 'cap' on freedom in the form of recognition of the (similarly constrained) freedom of others does not imply a retreat from utopian values and aspirations. However, as Mannheim (1952), Marcuse (1964) and Mills (1967) all argued, utopian ideals must reflect what is practically possible, otherwise they are mere 'ideology'. On that basis contemporary radicals can take heart. The world's resources are potentially adequate for all and modern communications have enormously enhanced cultural and educational opportunities. Of course the previous sentence implies a huge 'if' – it refers to a real potential rather than actual, certainly not guaranteed, outcomes. It would be facile to pretend that progress will be easily achieved from here. The 2008 global financial crisis and ensuing socio-economic recession has demonstrated both the complexity and concentration of power and wealth of contemporary capitalism and the variety and uncertainty of responses to dealing with it. In appreciating the functioning and consequences of capitalism 'the old left' was to that extent better informed than many 'new' radicals.

However, the basic answer of this book to the questions posed at the beginning of this chapter is an optimistic one; more so than the rather bleak assessment of Gerd-Rainer Horn in his generally sympathetic account of sixties radicalism (2007). The values and sensibilities of the radical sixties, as well as many of its organisational techniques and strategies, have survived into a new era. Increasingly, in the revelatory light of the current financial and economic crisis, there has been a resurgence of radical analysis and action. Some of the issues, such as what was termed the dominance of 'the military-industrial complex' and now as 'the warfare state', remain substantially similar; whereas other concerns, such as environmental crisis, have become more urgent. It is too early to say whether these campaigns will simply moderate state and market disruptions of civil society and the natural environment. Or, whether the relationship between political power and these spheres will be transformed. However, there is increasing intellectual appreciation of the systemic linkage between major issues and a growing tendency for concerned groups and individuals to act with reference to a larger if not yet fully articulated vision of change (Pugh 2009). Just as the radicals of the 1960s were in many respects 'ahead of their time', yet saw much of their agenda later adopted, so today's radical activists of civil society are defining and pursuing agendas that could, on an optimistic view, be expected to be adopted into the mainstream. In many respects, they have to be.

References

Amnesty International. 2009. *Economic, Social and Cultural Rights*. http://www.amnesty.org/en/economic-social-and-cultural-rights (Accessed 11th January 2010).
ATTAC (Association for the Taxation of Financial Transactions for the Aid of Citizens) n.d. http://www.attac.org/en/whatisattac/international-platform (Accessed 11th January 2010).
Beck, U. 1992. *The Risk Society*. London: Sage.
Bell, D. 1988 (1960). *The End of Ideology: On the Exhaustion of Political Ideas in the Fifties*. Cambridge: Harvard University Press.
Chandler, D. 2009. Questioning Global Political Activism. In *What Is Radical Politics Today?* Jonathan Pugh, ed. London: Palgrave Macmillan
Chomsky, N. *Hardtalk*. BBC2: November 3, 2009.
Collier, P., and Horowitz, D. 1989. *Second Thoughts: Former Radicals Look Back at the Sixties*. Lanham, MD: Madison Books
DeGroot, G. 2008. *The Sixties Unplugged*. London: MacMillan.
Delanty, G. 2000. *Citizenship in a Global Age: Society, culture, politics*. Buckingham: Open University Press.

Diani, M. 2000. Simmel to Rokkan and Beyond: Towards a Network Theory of (New) Social Movements. *European Journal of Social Theory*, 3 (4): 387–406.

Foucault, M. 1967. Des espaces autres, hétérotopies. In Michel Foucault, *Dits et écrits* 1984. (conférence au Cercle d'études architecturales, 14 mars 1967), in *Architecture, Mouvement, Continuité*, n°5, octobre 1984, pp. 46–49. (English version at: http://foucault.info/documents/heteroTopia/foucault.heteroTopia.en.html [Accessed 10th January 2010]

Gereffi, G., Garcia-Johnson, R. and Sasser, E. 2001. The NGO-Industrial Complex. *Foreign Policy*, 125 (July/August).

Gore, A. 2009. *Our Choice; a Plan to Solve the Climate Crisis*. London: Bloomsbury Publishing PLC.

Gunningham, N. 2009. Environment, Law, Regulation and Governance: Shifting Architectures. *Journal of Environmental Law* 21. 2:179–212.

Horn, G-R. 2007. *The Spirit of '68 Rebellion in Western Europe and North America*. Oxford: Oxford University Press

Kaldor, M. 2003. *Global Civil Society*. Cambridge: Polity.

Kamiya, G. 2008. *Through a bong, darkly*, April 9th, Salonstore.com. (http://www.salon.com/books/review/2008/04/09/sixties/index.html) (Accessed 11th January 2010).

Lyotard, J-F. 1984 (1979). *The Postmodern Condition*. Manchester University Press

Mannheim, K. 1952. *Ideology and Utopia: An Introduction to the Sociology of Knowledge*. London: Routledge and Kegan Paul.

Marcuse, H. 1964. *One Dimensional Man*. London: Sphere Books.

Martin, J. 2009. A Politics of Commitment. *In: What Is Radical Politics Today?* Jonathan Pugh, ed. London: Palgrave Macmillan.

McAdam, D. 1994. Culture and Social Movements. In E. Larana ed., *New Social Movements: From Ideology to Identity*. Philadelphia: Temple University Press

Mills, C.W. 1967 (1962). Letter to the New Left. In I. Horowitz ed., *Power, Politics and People: The Collected Essays of Charles Wright Mills*. Oxford: Oxford University Press: 247–59.

Monbiot, G. 2003. *The Age of Consent: Manifesto for a New World Order*. London: HarperCollins.

Naidoo, K. 2003. Civil Society, Governance and Globalisation World Bank Presidential Fellows Lecture http://web.worldbank.org/WBSITE/EXTERNAL/TOPICS/CSO/0,,contentMDK:20095848~pagePK:220503~piPK:220476~theSitePK:228717,00.html (Accessed 11th January 2010).

North, M., Levene, M. and Hugh-Williams, S. Does a radical past leave Its Marx? *Times Higher Educational Supplement*, 23.09.2007

O'Donnell, M. 2007. We Need Human Rights Not Nationalism 'Lite': Globalization and British Solidarity. *Ethnicities* 7 (2): 248–269.

Oglesby, C. and Shaull, R. 1967. *Containment and Change: Two Dissenting Views of American Society and Foreign Policy in the New Revolutionary Age*. New York: The Macmillan Company.

Pugh D. 2009. What *Is* Radical Politics Today? In: *What is Radical Politics Today?* Jonathan Pugh ed. London: MacMillan

Rootes, C. 1999. The Transformation of Environmental Activism: activists, organisations and policy-making. *Innovation: the European Journal of Social Sciences*. 12 (2): 155–73

Rosen, J. A. 1969. *The Little Red, White and Blue Book*. New York: Grove Press Inc.

Sklair, L. 2002 (3rd Edition). *Globalization, Capitalism and Its Alternatives*. Oxford: Oxford University Press.

Transition Towns. 2009. Transition Network: Tackling Peak Oil and Climate Change Together. http://transitiontowns.org/TransitionNetwork/TransitionNetwork (Accessed 20th January 2010)

NOTES ON CONTRIBUTORS

Miguel Cardina is a researcher at the Centre of Social Studies at the University of Coimbra. He studied Philosophy and Contemporary History and is now finishing his PhD thesis on Maoism in Portugal during the 'long sixties'. He has published a history of students' movements in Portugal from 1956 to 1974 (*A Tradição da Contestação. Resistência Estudantil durante o marcelismo.* Coimbra: Angelus Novus, 2008); as well as a didactical book on the radical left in the sixties and seventies (*A Esquerda Radical.* Coimbra: Angelus Novus, 2010).

Dr **Ben Cranfield** is a Lecturer in Arts Policy and Management in the Department of Media and Cultural Studies, Birkbeck College, University of London. His main research interests are in the development of the arts in post-war Britain, focusing on the rise of experimental, curatorial and archival artistic practices during this period, in relation to dialogues with technology, science and education. His PhD thesis was an archival analysis of the Institute of Contemporary Arts, London, from inception in 1947 to 1970. In 2007/8 Ben coordinated a year long programme of discussions on issues of contemporary curating with the ICA and was contributing editor of the ICA's 60th birthday publication, *How Soon is Now*. He has also led conferences and seminars on interdisciplinarity and creative practice. He has previously worked in the contemporary arts sector as a writer, consultant and as a director of a commercial art gallery.

James Driver is an independent academic and PhD graduate of The School of Politics and Sociology, Birkbeck College. He has an interdisciplinary perspective encompassing philosophy, sociology, politics and political theory. His particular interests are Wittgenstein, ordinary language philosophy, Habermas and communicative action, deliberative democracy and normative theories of ethics and discourse. His general interest is in the normative development of political and societal rationality, including constraints or blocks on rationality as well as reasons for its failure or lack of development in political and social contexts.

Maureen Freely was born in the US but grew up in Turkey, where her family still lives. She was educated at Radcliffe College (Harvard University) and has made her home in England for the past twenty-five years. She has been a regular contributor to the *Guardian*, the *Observer*, the *Independent* and the *Sunday Times* for two decades, writing on feminism, family and social policy, Turkish culture and politics, and contemporary fiction. She is perhaps best known for her translations of the Turkish novelist and Nobel laureate Orhan Pamuk. Now a Professor at the University of Warwick, she is the author of six novels and three works of nonfiction, all of which include aspects of feminism.

Andreas Hadjar, PhD/habil., became a professor at the University of Luxembourg in September 2010. His main research interests include sociology of education, political sociology, methods of empirical research and gender aspects. He studied sociology and journalism at Leipzig University (Germany) and received his MA degree in 1998. He was a visiting student at Glasgow University (UK) in 1995–1996. From 2000 to 2004, he worked as a research scientist in the Sociology Department, Chemnitz University of Technology (Germany), receiving his PhD in 2003 (PhD thesis "Elbow Mentality and Xenophobia among Adolescents"). He has been a lecturer in the Sociology of Education Department, University of Berne (Switzerland) from 2004–2010, receiving his habilitation degree in 2008 (habil. thesis "Meritocracy as a Legitimizing Principle"). He is currently co-leader of a project on the gender-gap in educational success at Swiss secondary schools (University of Bern, Bern School of Teacher Education, 2008–2011).

Eloise Harding is in the final stages of a PhD in Politics at the Centre for the Study of Social and Global Justice, University of Nottingham. Her research focuses on the conceptual morphology of 'horizontal' political movements. Her chapter in this book originates from a paper presented in July 2008 at the BSA *1968* conference. She thanks CSSGJ for funding her attendance. Also thanks to: her colleagues including Gulshan Khan, Sara Motta, Andrew Robinson, Matthew Rendall and Tony Burns for helpful comments in the early stages of this article; CSSGJ MA students for their engagement with this topic when Harding taught it as a class; Andreas Bieler for including an earlier draft on the Centre website; Ben Saunders for practical assistance; and Harding's supervisor Mathew Humphrey for tolerating the time taken out of thesis-writing to prepare this chapter.

Bryn Jones, PhD, is Senior Lecturer in Sociology at University of Bath and serial member of various social movements. After degrees in sociology from

London School of Economics and the University of Liverpool in the 1970s, his teaching and research in economic and political sociology has included periods as visiting researcher at the Universities of Wisconsin, M.I.T. and Bologna; and visiting lecturer at the Universities of Ljubliana and Calabria, Cosenza. A former (founding) co-editor of the BSA journal, *Work, Employment & Society*, he was scientific adviser to the European Centre for the Development of Vocational Training (CEDEFOP) and is an overseas 'corrispondento' for Italy's *Sociologia del Lavoro*. Publications, besides those cited in this book, include: *Work & Employment in Europe: A New Convergence?* London: Routledge (joint editor); 'Left-wing Political Activism in A Changing Political Culture' (*Sociology* 1996); and *Forcing the Factory of the Future: Cybernation and Societal Institutions*, Cambridge University Press, 1997.

Barbara Körner has a first degree in Philosophy and German Literature from the Free University of Berlin, and is a sociologist with a wide-ranging interdisciplinary background including Peace Studies and Women's Studies. Her PhD thesis on non-violence (Lancaster 1997) arose from her active involvement in peace/ green and feminist movements of the 1980s in Canada and the UK. She has published on non-violence, critical pedagogy and anti-racist teaching, with current publications emerging from research collaboration with Rosemary McKechnie on activism and the lifecourse. She is a passionate Open University tutor in the social sciences.

Helen Lunn is a music PhD student at UKZN. Her current work focuses on Anglophone students in South Africa in the 1960s and '70s. She edited anthologies of DRUM magazine, taught at UCT and Wits and works in television production when not involved in academe.

Kevin McDonald is a sociologist of social movements and collective action based at Goldsmiths, University of London, where he recently completed a Marie Curie International Fellowship. He holds a doctorate from the Ecole des Hautes Etudes en Sciences Sociales in Paris, where he is a member of the Centre for Sociological Analysis and Intervention founded by Alain Touraine. His recent publications include *Global Movements: Action and Culture* (2006) and *Our Violent World: Terrorism in Society* (2010). He is currently writing *Social Movements in the 21st Century* to be published in 2011.

Rosemary McKechnie is a graduate of the University of Edinburgh and senior lecturer in sociology at Bath Spa University. Her research interests cover biography and activism, Western European Identities, community responses to environmental issues; and reproductive health. She has also researched

Corsican Nationalism, local responses to Chernobyl-fallout and restrictions on the Isle of Man, and the management of peri-menopausal changes. Recent publications include: McKechnie, R. and Kohn, T. (eds) (1999) *Extending the Boundaries of Care: Medical Ethics and Caring Practice*, Oxford: Berg; McKechnie, R. and Welsh I (2002); 'Environmental issues through the looking glass. Whose Reflections can we see in Reflexive Modernization', in R. Dunlap and F. Buttel (eds) *Sociological Theory and the Environment*, New York: Rowman and Littlefield.; McKechnie, R. & Körner, B. (2010); and 'Growing Up Through Activism: Adult Identities and the Maturing of Standpoints' in J. Burnett, (ed.) *Contemporary Adulthoods Calendars, Cartographies and Constructions*, Basingstoke: Palgrave Macmillan.

Mike O'Donnell is Emeritus Professor of Sociology at Westminster University where he has taught since 1994. His publications include *Uncertain Masculinities: Youth, Ethnicity and Class in Contemporary Britain* (with Sue Sharpe, Routledge, 2000) and a four-volume edited collection, *Structure and Agency* (Sage, 2010). Among his articles are: 'Radically Reconstituting the Subject: Social Theory and Human Nature' (*Sociology*, vol. 37, no. 4, 2003); 'We Need Human Rights: Not Nationalism "Lite": Globalisation and British Solidarity' (*Ethnicities*, vol. 7, no. 2 (2007); 34, 38, 40; and 'Nineteen Sixties Radicalism and Its Critics: Radical Utopians, Liberal Realists and Postmodern Sceptics' *(Psychoanalysis, Culture and Society)*, vol. 13, no.2008).

Florian Schlapbach graduated in sociology from the University of Berne, Switzerland, in 2009. His research interests are online communities, network analysis, and methods of empirical research.

Riaz Ahmed Shaikh, PhD, is an Associate Professor of sociology at Institute of Business & Technology, Karachi, Pakistan. He is editor of the peer-reviewed international research journal, Journal of Management & Social Sciences- *JMSS*, and Managing Editor of Asia Journal of Global Studies- *AJGS*, Osaka, Japan. His several research papers have been published in journals of international repute. He is author of three books; the latest, *Pakistan: Democracy and Military Dictatorship*, being published in March, 2010. His fields of interest are religious extremism, fundamentalism and civil-military relationship. His research paper *Pakistani Military Role in Asian Context* has been chosen by Emerald Publishers as an *Outstanding Author Contribution Award Winner* at the Literati Network Awards for Excellence 2010.

AUTHOR INDEX

Abrams, M. 93, 108
Adelstein, D. 10, 19
Ahmed, F. 77, 86
Ahmed, K. 75, 79, 80, 86
Ahmed, M. 80, 86
Akhtar, M. and Humphries, S. 11, 19
Alexander, R. J. 43, 56
Ali, T. xii, xiii, xix, 75, 87
Alinsky, S. 14, 19
Alloway, L. 114, 129
Amnesty International 232, 238
Amos, V. and Palmer, P. 207n5
Anderson, P. 9–10, 11, 12, 19, 112, 129
Anonymous Graffiti (circa 1968) 137, 140, 147
Archer, M. 122, 129
Aron, R. 40, 56
Atack, M. 34–5, 37
ATTAC 231, 232, 238
Avakian, B. 42, 56

Badiou, A. 40, 56
Baldock, P. 15, 19
Banuri, T., Khan, J., Sharukh, R. and Mahmood, R. 75, 87
Barnes, S.H. and Kasse, M. 161, 164
Barreto, A. 45, 56
Barthes, R. 111, 129
Bassett, K., Griffith, R. and Smith, I. 17, 19
Baumert, J. 172, 186
Beck, U. 193, 207, 230, 238
Beck, U. and Beck-Gernsheim, E. 193, 207
Becker, R. 171, 186
Bebiano, P. 46, 56
Bell, D. 103–4, 105, 108, 225, 238
Bennett, A. 99, 108
Bennett, T. 194, 207

Bernan, P. 41, 56
Bettelheim, B. 104, 108
Beyond TV 141, 147
Bleiker, R. 36, 37
Bloom, A. 40, 56
Bocock, R. 11, 19
Boltanski, L., and Chiapolo, E. 25, 37
Bourdieu, P. xvi, 191, 198, 201, 205, 207n6
Boynton, G. 65, 71
Breines, W. 3, 19
Brick, H. viii, xix
Brown, M. 94, 108
Bubb, S. 17, 19
Burck, C. 100, 109
Burnett, J. 204, 207
Burnham, J. 126, 130
Burki, S.J. 76, 83, 87

Callinicos, A. 162–3, 164
Calvert, G. and Nieman, C. 101–2, 109
Carabillo, T., Meuli, J. and Csida, J.B. 213, 223
Cardina, M. xv, 229
Castoriadis, C. 137–8, 147
Castells, M. 36, 37
Cento-Bull, A. and Jones, B. 16, 19
Chandler, D. 237, 238
Charrière, C. 29, 37
Chasse, R. 143, 147
Chesters, G. and Welsh, I. 207n7
Chomsky, N. 225, 226, 238
Choudhry, G.W. 77, 87
Churchill, W. and Vander Wall, J. xiv, xix
Claire, H. 60, 71
Clandestine Insurgent Rebel Army (CIRCA) 144, 145, 148
Climaco, C. 53, 56

Coates, K. and Silburn, R. 13, 19
Cockburn, A. 117, 127, 130
Cockburn, C. 14, 19
Cockett, R. 4, 7, 19
Cohen, J.L. 11, 19
Cohen, S.P. 85, 87
Cohn-Bendit, D. 4, 19, 24, 37
Cohn-Bendit, D., Dubieu, J-P., Gerard, B. and Granautier, B. 27, 28, 37
Collier, P. and Horowitz, D. viii, ix, xix, 98, 109, 228, 238
Collins, G. 213, 217–8, 223
Craig, G., Derricourt, N. and Loney, M. 14, 20
Cranfield, B. viii, xvi, xvii, 149
Crossley, N. 198, 207
Crowson, N., Hilton, M. and McKay, J. xiii, xix

Dacosta, F. 49, 56
Dahrendorf, R. 170, 186
Dalton, R.J. 172, 173, 186
Dearden-Phillips, C. 17, 20
Debord, G. 134, 143, 148; – *The Spectacle* 135
Debray, R. ix, xix, 25, 37
DeGroot, G. viii, ix, 97, 98, 109, 225–6, 226, 227, 228, 238
Delanty, G. 232, 238
Della Porta, D. 150, 164
Demartini, J.R. 206n1, 207
Deutches PISA Konsortium 172, 173, 186
Dews, P. 150, 158, 159, 163, 164
Diani, M. 232–3, 239
Didion, J. 215–6, 223
Dixon, M. 216–7, 223
Dobell, W.M 73, 87
Doherty, B. 153, 164
Dome (newspaper) 64, 66, 70, 71
Dressen, M. 44, 56
Driver, J. viii, xvi, xvii, xviii, 10, 228, 231, 236, 237
Dubois, M. 68, 71
Duteuil, J-P. 26, 37

Edwards, P.N. 123, 130
Elbaum, M. 40, 56
Elzy, R. 111, 130

Feenberg, A. 128, 130
Feldman, H. 74, 79, 87
Felski, R. 194, 207
Fernandes, A. 50, 56
Feuer, L. 56, 109; – *The Conflict of Generations* 40, 104
Fields, B. 43–4, 56
Flacks, R. 103–04, 109
Follett, B. 62, 71
Foucault, M. 206, 226, 227, 239
Frank, R. 39, 49, 56
Frank, T. ix, xi, xix
Frederickse, J. 68, 71
Free Association 145, 146, 148
Freely, M. xviii, 146, 207n6, 230, 234
Freitas, E. 46, 56
Friedman, S. 65, 71
Friedman, S. R. 103–04, 105, 109
Frisch, M.J. 97, 110
Fukuyama, F. 25, 37
Fyfe, N. R.16, 20

Geismar, A., July, S. and Morane, E. 32, 37
Gereffi, G., Garcia-Johnson, R. and Sasser, E. 231, 239
Giddens, A. 96, 109, 193, 207
Gilbert, N. and Specht, G. 14, 20
Gitlin, T. 40, 56
Gleason, P. 36, 37
Glenn, N.D. 175, 187
Goldshmit, J. 129, 130
Goodman, P. 111, 130
Gore, A. 231, 239
Gosling, R. 12, 20
Greaves, D. 62, 71
Green, J. 14, 20
Gregory, E.C. 113, 130
Grotowski, J. 125, 126, 130
Grunenburg, C. and Harris, J. viii, xix
Gunningham, N. 231, 239

Haber, R. 94, 109
Habermas, J. 4, 5, 10–11, 20, 93, 100, 109, 150, 152, 164, 164–5, 194–5, 207–8; his critique of the German student movement 153–7; later reflections on radical politics 158–161; and post-sixties movements 161–3

Hadjar, A. and Sclapback, F. viii, xi, xii, xviii, 170, 172, 175, 179–180, 187, 233–4
Hampden-Turner, C. 103, 109
Hanisch, C. 212, 223
Harding, L. xii, xvii, 32, 227
Hardisty, J. and Furdon, E. xiv, xix
Haroon, A. and Saleem, A. 77, 87
Harvie, D. Milburn, K., Trott, B. and Watts, D. 145, 148
Hasan, S. 75, 87
Heath, J. and Potter, A. x, xix
Hebdige, D. 97, 109
Hildebrandt, K. and Dalton, R. 161, 165
Hitlin, S. and Piliavin, J. A. 5, 17, 20
Hobsbawn, E. 4, 25, 31, 34, 37
Hodgson, L. 16, 20
Hoggart, R. 93, 109
Holub, R.C. 151, 152, 165,
Hood, C. 15, 20
Horn, G-R. viii, xvi, xix, 7, 8, 20, 226, 238, 239
Hornsey Staff and Students (HSS) 112, 117–122
Horowitz, I. 93, 109
Horrell, M. 66, 71
Hussain, I. 74, 75, 87

Inayatullah 76, 87
Inglehart, R. 6, 20, 161, 165, 170, 171, 172, 173, 175, 180, 182, 185, 187
Institute of Contemporary Arts (ICA): *ICA Magazine* 114–5, 124, 130
Islam, N.M. 83, 87

Jacobs, P. and Landau, S. 96, 109
Jahan, R. 74, 87
Jameson, F. 39, 57, 97, 109
Jarausch, K. H. 8, 20
Jasper, J.M. 193, 200, 208
Johns, G. xi, xix
Jones, B. and Cento-Bull, A. 17, 20
Jones, B. xi, xii, xiv, xv, xvi, xvii, xviii, 16, 20, 112, 226, 236
Jones, P. S. 16, 20
Juris, J. 146, 148

Kaldor, M. 232, 239
Kalina, R. 114, 130

Kamiya, G. 226, 239
Katsiaficas, G. 41, 57, 152, 165
Keith, L. 201, 208
Kellner, D. 11, 20
Kendall, J. and Knapp, N. 15, 20
Keniston, K, 103, 109
Kesey, K. 101, 109
King, D. 195, 208
Khan, L. 75, 77, 78, 79, 85, 87
Khan, R. 83, 87
Klages, H. 174, 187
Klein, M. and Ohr, D. 173, 187
Knabb, K. 134, 141, 148
Kolinsky, E. 153, 165
Körner, B. 207, 208
Körner, B. and McKechnie, R. viii, xiv, xviii, 220, 234, 236,
Krivine, A. 32, 37
Kurlansky, M. 112, 113, 114, 117. 122–3, 130
Kustow, M. xvii, 111, 112, 122–7; – *I Wonder* (play written with Adrian Henri) 125

Lancelin, A. 37
Lapping, A. 12, 20
Lash, S. 193, 208
Law, L. 136, 148
Lawrence, D.H. 93, 109
Lawrence, R. 63, 71
Leat, D, 15, 20
Lefebvre, H. 191, 194, 208
Liebert, R. 103, 109
Lipset, S.M. and Raab, E. 104, 109
Loney, M. 13, 14, 20
Lorde, A. 191, 200, 201, 208
Lunn, H. xv, 228
Lynd, S. 100, 109
Lynton, N. 115, 130
Lyon, D. xiv, xix
Lyotard, J-F, 225, 239

McAdam, D. Tarrow, S. and Tilly, C. 34, 37,
McAdam, D. 236, 239
MacDonald, I. vii, xix, 4, 5, 8, 11, 21
MacDonald, S. 116, 119, 130
McDonald, K. viii, xi, xii, xv, xvi, 5, 36, 37, 149, 227, 228, 229
McGuigan, J. 195, 208
McHale, J. 115, 130

McKay, G. 198, 208
McKechnie, R. and Korner, B. 193, 196, 197, 208
McKechnie, R. and Welsh, I. 193, 208
McKie, D. 12, 13, 21
McLuhan, M. 130; hot and cold media 112; global village 114; on teaching 119
Mailer, N. 111, 122–3
Majima, S. and Savage, M. 6, 20
Mannheim, K. 92, 105, 109, 208, 237, 239; on generation 98–9, 204, 234
Marcuse, H. 92, 105, 109, 120, 130, 234, 237, 239; 'Great Refusal' 117, 127–8; 'On Revolution' 127, 26,
Marinetto, M. 16, 20
Martel, F. 35, 38
Martín, B. 113, 129, 130, 206n1, 208
Martin, J. 237,239
Marwick, A. viii, ix, 3, 4, 5, 11, 20, 39, 40, 57, 92, 109, 233, 239
Marx, Karl xiv, 75
Massey, A. 115, 130
Mazari, S.K 76, 87
Melucci, A. 191, 195–6,197, 202, 206, 208
Miller, C. and Bryant, R. 15, 17, 21
Mills, C.W. 93, 96, 109, 110, 237, 239
Mitchell, J. 190, 208, 212, 214–5, 223
Monbiot, G. 230, 239
Morgan, K., Rees, G. and Garmise, S. 16, 20
Morgan, R. 191, 199, 208
Morin, E. 30–1, 37
Morison, J. 15, 21
Morris-Suzuki, T. xi, xix
Muggleton, D. 99, 110
Muggleton, D. and Weinzierl, R. 99, 110

Naidoo, K. 231, 232, 239
Nairn, T. 127, 130
Nairn, T and Singh-Sandu, J. 117, 127, 130
Naseem, S. M. 84, 87
Nelson, E. 7, 8, 13, 21, 112, 130
Neustadter, A. 215, 223
Neves, J. 55, 57
Neville, R. 111, 130
Newman, J. 16, 21

Niazi. Z. 81, 87
Nisbet, R. 104, 109
North, M., Levene, M. and Hugh-Williams, S. 235, 239
Notes From Nowhere 143, 144–5, 148
Nunes, A. 45, 57
Nupen, C. 69, 71
Nuttall, J. 111, 130; – *Bomb Culture* 123,

O'Donnell, M. viii, xi, xii, xvi, 5, 17, 33, 91, 110, 146, 149, 204, 207, 226, 228, 232, 234, 236, 237, 239
Office of the Deputy Prime Minister (ODPM) 16, 21
Oglesby, K. and Shaull, R. 232, 239
O'Malley, J. 12, 14, 21

Papanek, G. 76, 87
Perrot, J-C., Perrot, M., Rebérioux, M. and Maitron, J. 30, 38
Pereira, J.P. 45, 57
Piltcher, J. 99, 110, 204, 208
Plant, S. 142, 148
Pugh, J. 238, 239

Qureshi, A. 78, 87

Radford, J. 12, 14, 21
Reagan, B. 201, 207, 208
Reich, C. 92, 110
Reichardt, J. 125–6, 128, 130; *see also Cybernetic Serendipity*
Resende, J. and Vieira, M. 46, 57
Rex, J. and Moore, R. 13, 21
Ricoeur, P. 129, 131
Ribeiro, M. 49, 57
Riesman, D. 92, 110
Rodrigues, M. 48, 54, 57
Rootes, C. xi, xix, 231, 239
Rosas, F. and Oliveira, P. R. 47, 57
Rosen, J. 225, 239
Rosenthal, N. 122, 131
Rosetti, F. 12, 21
Ross, K. 190, 208
Roszac, T. 7, 21, 92, 110

Salauddin, G. 80, 87
Salazar, A. 44, 57

AUTHOR INDEX

Sams, C. xiv, xx
Sandbrook, D. viii, ix, 3, 4, 5, 7, 21, 97, 110
Sarachild, K. 213, 214, 223
Saunders, C. C. 61, 71
Savio, M. 103, 110
Sayeed, K.B. 76, 87
Sayres, S., Stephenson, A., Aronowitz, S. and Jameson, F. viii, xx, 110, 111, 131
Schlebusch Commission Report 65, 71
Schneeman, C. 124, 131
Seago, A. 113, 131
Seeds for Change 146, 148
Segal, L. 207n4, 208
Seidman, M. 26, 32, 34, 38
Seligman, D. 104, 110
Shaheed, Z. 75, 76, 87
Shaikh, R. xiii, xv, 228, 229
Shapiro, J.J. 164n1
Sherkat, D. and Blocker, A. 206n1, 209
Shils, E. 104, 110
Short, C. xi, xx
Siddiqui, K. 74, 87
Situationist International 134, 135, 136, 138, 142
Skelcher, C. 16, 21
Sklair, L. 232, 239
Smith Wilson, D. 11, 21
Snow, C.P. 131
Sobhan, R. 83, 87
Soper, K. 162, 165
Spelman, E. 207n4, 208
Spence, D. 94, 110
Students and Staff of Hornsey College of Art (*SSH*) 112, 131
Swartz, D.L. 206 n2, 209

Tarrow, S. 34, 38
Telo, A. 45, 46, 57
Thistlewood, D. 116, 131
Thomas, N. 117, 131, 152, 153, 165
Tickner, L. 111–2, 113, 118, 119, 122, 131
Tilly, C. 34, 38
Touraine, A. vii, xx, 33, 34, 35, 36, 38, 190, 191, 196, 198, 202, 205, 209
Transition Towns 230, 239
Tuma, N.B. and Hannan, M.T. 175, 187
Turk, E.L. 150, 165,
Turner, B.S. 207, n7, 209

Turner, J. 62, 71
Turner, R. 61, 63–4, 69, 71

Umar, B. 82, 83, 88
Union Nationale des Etudiants de France 33, 38

Vaneigem, R. 133, 134, 136, 137, 148; *Revolution as Celebration* 139–40
Van Herpen, M. 141, 148
Various Authors The Port Huron Statement 95–6, 110, 225–6
Varon, J. 34, 38, 40, 57
Varon, J., Foley, M.S., and McMillian, J. ix, x, xii, xiv, xx
Verba, S. and Nie, N. H. 171, 187
Verba, S., Nie, N. H. and Kim, J. 185, 187
Verba, S., Scloman, K.L. and Brady, H. 172, 187
Vereker, C., Mays, J.B., Broady, M. and Gittus, E. 13, 21
Verson, J. 144, 148
Viansson-Ponté, P. 23, 38
Vienet, R. 137, 148

Wainwright, H. 8, 21
Warren-Piper, D 113, 131
Wasseem, M. 84, 88
Weber, M. 226–7
Webster, E. 61, 69, 70, 71
Weeks, J. viii, 106,110
Wegener, B. 186 n1, 187
Wells, S. 220–1, 223
Whittier, N. 190, 204, 209
Wickberg, D. 6–7, 8, 21,
Wilcox, W. 83, 88
Wilby, P. vii, xx
Williams, R. 10, 21, 112, 131
Willing, V. 116–7, 120, 131
Wilson, B. 6, 21

Yeomans, R. 115, 119, 131
Young, H. 7, 8, 21
Young, M. and Willmott, P. 13, 21

Zaidi, A. 75, 88
Zinn, H. 97, 110
Ziring, L. 74, 88

SUBJECT INDEX

1968 x, 8, 23–34, 60, 76–84, 111, 117, 127,128, 129, 190, 191, 205
1984 11
9/11 229
Abbas, Tufail 85
Abendroth, Wolfgang 150
Aberfan 12
ableism 200
abortion 24, 211
accountability xi, xii, 17
actionism 151, 164n
activism 41, 96, 164n1, 189–90, 191, 192, 195, 196, 197, 198, 199, 200, 201–6, 233
Adenauer, Konrad 150; generation 173
adolescence ix, 174, 196
adulthood ix
affluence xi, xiii, 155, 163
Afghanistan 230
Africa 47, 49, 55, 163
African National Congress (ANC) 60, 61
African Resistance Movement (ARM) 60
age effect 174, 175, 176, 179, 182, 186
Albania 43, 48
Albers, Joseph 117
Aldermaston 193
Alexandra Palace 120
Algeria 31
Ali, Mazhar 80
Ali, Tariq xv, 78
alienation xiv, 33, 41, 63, 123, 136, 160, 194
Alinsky, Saul 14
ALLBUS (General Social Survey; Germany) 169, 175, 177, 178, 179, 180, 181–3
Alloway, Lawrence 114, 115, 124
alter-globalisation xii, 25, 36
alter-Marxism xiv
Althusser, Louis 25, 28

America, Miss 213
Amin Jute Mills 79
American Express 28
Amnesty International 232
anarchism 43, 137, 155, 157
Anarchy 141
Anderson, Perry 9–10, 11, 12, 18, 112
Angola 45, 49, 55
Angry Brigade 228
anti-apartheid 197
anti-authoritarianism 7, 14, 41, 113, 154, 156
anti-capitalists xii, 162, 163, 227, 229, 232
Anti-Colonial Struggle Committees 52
anti-colonialism 44
anti-elitism 94
anti-fascism 46
anti-globalisation xii, xiv, 36, 227, 229
Anti-Nazi League 196
anti-nuclear 7, 11, 24, 161, 229
anti-politics 98
anti-psychiatry 98
anti-racism 200, 227, 229
anti-roads movement 204
anti-segregation protests 94
anti-slavery 6
anti-University 111
anti-war demonstrations and protests 7, 212, 225; movements x, xii, 211; *see also* Vietnam War
apartheid xv, 59, 60, 61, 63, 64
Apel, Karl-Otto 158, 164n2
APO (Extra-parliamentary opposition), Germany 150
Apollinaire, G. 113, 125–6
apolitical trust 174
architecture 26, 116
Area Partnerships 16

Armed Revolutionary Action 48
Army viii; Pakistan 79, 85; Portuguese 50–1, 55
art/arts ix, 5, 7, 9, 37, 144
Art and Language 17
art education xvii: changes in the 1950s and 1960s 115–7; Hornsey 117–22; impact of 1968 122, 128; art school protests: general character of 128–9
artistic expression viii
Asia 43
Asia Shurk Hai (Asia Is Red) 84
ASP (Portuguese Social Action) 45
Association of Community Workers 15
Association of Social Workers 15
Atlanta 223n
Atlantic City 213, 214
ATTAC (Association pour la taxation des transactions pour l'aide aux citoyens) 231, 232
Auschwitz 149
Authoritarianism viii, xiii, xiv, xvii, 11, 24, 127, 139–40, 150, 151, 228, 230, 237
autogestion (self management) 24
Ayaz, Shaikh 81
Azad 80

Babur, Mahmood Nawaz 85
Bachmann, Josef 153
Baader-Meinhof gang 153
baigar (wageless labour) 84
Bakunin, 41
Baloch, Shaista 84
Bandung Conference 44
Bangladesh 73, 85
barricades 30
Barthes, Roland 111
Basic Democrats 83
Bauhaus 116
BBC (British Broadcasting Corporation) 77
Beatles 8
Beckett, Samuel 123
Berkeley Free Speech Movement 94
Berlin 151, 152, 228
Bettelheim, Charles 42
Beveridge, William 12

Bhai, Munno 81
Bhashani, Abdul Hamid 82, 83, 85
Bhutto, Zulfiqar Ali 77, 84, 85, 86
Big Bang, metaphor xviii, 8, 18
Big Brother 13
Biko, Steve 64, 65
Birch, Reg 193
Birmingham 13
Birmingham, University of 111, 117
Black Consciousness (BC), 59–60, 65, 70
Black liberation movement 100, 106
Black, Misha 116, 117
Black Mountain College 117
Black Panthers 42, 95, 228
black power x, 33
Blake, William 113, 125
Bolshevism 137
Bolton, Harriet 66, 67, 69
Boston Womens Health Collective 220
Bourdieu, Pierre 191, 198, 201, 205
Bové, José 36
boycotts 176
bra-burning, myth of 213
Bramwell-Davies, Pru 122
Brazil 205
Bristol 17
Bristol, University of 117
Britain 5–18, 101, 215, 219, 221
Brown, Gordon 221, 235–6
Brownmiller, Susan 219
Bryant. Anita 219
Bukhari, Ustad 81
Buckingham Palace 113
bureaucracy/bureaucracies x, xvii, 10, 11, 34, 42, 76, 77, 94, 194, 195, 229, 234, 236
bureaucratisation 12, 14, 16
Burnham, Jack 126
Burroughs, William 125
Butt, Nawaz 77
Byron, Lord George Gordon Noel 217

Caetano, Marcello 47
Cage, John 117
Callinicos, Alex 162–3
campus protests 7
capitalism/capitalists 28, 29, 34, 63, 151, 156, 157, 158, 159, 160, 161, 162,

SUBJECT INDEX 253

164, 226, 229, 230, 232, 233n, 236, 238; consumer xi, 162; liberal 108, 160, 234
Carmichael, Stokely 214, 223
Carnation Revolution 55
Carnival 142-3, 144-5
careers 234, 235
Carol, K.S. 42
Carter, Jimmy 101
Castoriadis 138
Castro, Fidel 41
Catholicism 46, 48
Centre for Cultural Studies 111
centre-right, parties xi
Chandpur 82
Charsadda 84
Charonne Metro 31
Chataan 80
Chatelet, Francoise 52
chauvinism, male 234
Cheadle, Halton 64, 65
Chicago 91, 95
child-rearing 222, 234, 235
China 31, 43, 44, 48, 76-7, 86, 156, 163, 214-5, 230
Chitagong 79
Chomsky, Noam 225-6
Christian Democratic Party, Germany 150
cinema 46
citizenship 24
City Challenge 15
Civic Voluntarism Model of Political Participation 171, 172, 185
civil disobedience 228, 231
civil liberties 105
civil rights x, xi, 14, 40, 95, 97; movement 93, 106, 190, 199, 211, 214, 229
civil society xiii, 4, 10, 18, 226, 228, 237, 238; organisations xi, 15, 16, 17; regulation (of business and markets) 231
civil war xiii, 31
Clandestine Insurgent Rebel Clown Army (CIRCA) 144, 145
class 7, 14, 18, 176, 190, 194, 199, 200, 215, 216, 219, 221, 236; conflict xiv, 84, 154, 161-2; middle 216; ruling

218; war 190; working 13, 61, 93, 94, 162, 204
Cleaver, Eldridge 42
climate change 229, 230
Clinton, Hilary 19
clothing 46
CND (Campaign for Nuclear Disarmament) 193
co-counselling 195
Coca Cola 33
Cockburn, Alexander 127
cognitive mobilization 170, 171, 172, 173, 186
Cohn-Bendit, Daniel 23, 24, 26, 27, 28, 30
cohort(s) xviii, 5, 15, 169, 170, 173, 174, 176, 177, 178, 180-1, 183, 185; analysis 170-1, 172, 175, 176
Coimbra 50
Coldstream, William 116; Committee (National Advisory Committee on Art Education) 116, 118
Cold War 93, 95, 96, 228, 229
Colleges of Advanced Technology 116
colonialism xv, 44-45, 229
colonisation (see also: lifeworld) 10, 159-160, 161
Columbus, Ohio 190
comics 46, 142
commoditisation ix
Commune, Paris 30
communes 7, 11, 83; movement 93
communicative action 160-1, 194
communism 43, 156, 229, 230, 233
Communist Party of Great Britain 193
Communist Party of Pakistan 78, 79, 85
Communist Revolutionary Action 54
Communist Party of India 79
Communist Party of India (Marxist-Leninist) 82
Communist-Party of Pakistan (CPP) 81
communitarianism 15, 18
community/ies 12-13, 36, 37, 156, 230, 233; activism xv, 12-13, 18; groups 4, 15, 16; spirit of 226, 233, 237; studies 13; urban 12; work/workers 13-15, 17
Community Development Project (CDP) 13, 14, 16, 18

254   SIXTIES RADICALISM AND SOCIAL MOVEMENT ACTIVISM

Community Action Programme (USA) 14
compartmentalisation/
    decompartmentalisation 7, 195
computers 12, 13, 126
Confédération française démocratique du
    travail (CFDT) 24
Congress (US) 216
consciousness 160, 163, 197, 198, 204,
    205; raising 211, 212, 214–5, 216,
    217, 220, 221, 222, 223, 230
Conservative Party, Britain 11, 15
Conservatism x, xi, 9, 10, 46, 156, 174,
    228
consumer(s) 217, 219; culture x, 140;
    society 42, 136
consumerism xvii, 8, 11, 18, 25, 162, 231
consumption 25, 162,194
cooperation 8, 17
cooptation 17
corporate management 12
corporate social responsibility xii
corporations 229, 231
Coronation Brick and Tile Works 65
councils (local government) 12, 14–15, 17
council estates 13
counter cultures vii, x, xii, xiii, 4, 7, 8, 13,
    14, 18, 32, 41, 94, 97–8, 164, 226,
    227, 229; definition of, 91
coup 55
critical theory 158, 164n
Cronin, Jeremy 62
CRS (Compagnie Républicaine de
    Sécurité) 31
Cuba 32, 42, 53, 54, 229
Cuban Missile Crisis 228
Cultural Revolution 25, 43, 44, 52, 54,
    155, 156
culture 134, 141, 143, 144, 156, 160,
    161, 194, 226, 237; 'movement'
    191, 200; musical xvi; popular 135;
    youth xvi 25
Cunningham, Merce 117
Cunhal, Álvaro 52
Czechoslovakia 42

Daily Pakistan Times 80
Davies, Robert 65, 70
Davis, David 64, 65

De Sausmerez, Maurice 115
Dean, James 31
Debord, Guy 134, 135, 143, 144
Debray, Regis 25
decolonialisation 55
DeGroot, Gerard 225–6, 227
Dehqan Qalam (Peasant's Pen) 84
de-integration 195, 202
Delgado, Humberto 45
democracy, xvii, 6, 8, 13, 16, 32, 74, 113,
    118, 126, 128, 150, 159, 162, 163,
    164, 170, 226, 228, 229, 233, 237;
    participative/participatory, xiv, 15,
    16, 18, 42, 96,129, 229
Democratic Party 100, 107
Democratic Student Federation (DSF)
    (Pakistan) 77
demonstrations 176, 204
deprivation, 14, 18
Der Spiegel 150, 152
Dera Ismail Khan 84
deregulation 231
detournement 32, 34–35, 134, 140;
    definition 135
Developing Process, The 115–6
development, economic 73, 74, 75, 76,
    83, 230
DGS 52, 54
Dhaka 80, 82
dictatorship, xiii, xv, 39, 55, 73, 81, 173
Diploma in Art and Design 116, 118,
    119, 121
direct action 14, 162
disability 200
discourse, 10, 14, 25, 39, 44, 46, 49; in
    France xvi; radical, xiv
discrimination 200
Divine Light Mission 100
divinity ix
dockworkers 65
Don Juan 217
draft (military) 50
drugs, 8, 11
dualism (economic) 45
Duras, Marguerite 52
Durban 64, 65, 66, 67, 68, 69
Durkheim, Emile 157
Dutschke, Rudi 151–3

SUBJECT INDEX 255

Dylan, Bob 5, 97, 100
dystopia 218, 226

Eastern Europe 29, 42
East Pakistan Communist Party (Marxist-Leninist) 80
Ecole Normale 23, 28
ecology, human 116
economic development, viii (see also: development)
economic growth 18, 45, 73–5, 170
Economic Research and Action Project (ERAP) 96
economy, UK, 9 – 10, 11
education ix, 9, 14, 170, 176, 177, 181–3, 234; art 119–20; expansion 170, 172, 173, 176, 177, 186, 237; higher, 5, 8, 94, 171, 177, 183, 185–6, 228, 234
Edwards, Paul 123
egalitarianism, 6, 17, 18, 232
Egypt 78
Eichmann, Adolf 149
elderly, 11
elections, general, xiii, 9, 24, 84, 174
electoral systems, xiii
elites, political 170
emigration/emigrants 46, 51, 52–53, 61
Emmanuel College, Boston 220
employment 234
Encounter, journal 104
end of ideology 226
England 14, 78
Enlightenment 231
environment, and disasters, xv, 173, 174, 229, 238
environmentalism, 6, 11, 161, 229, 230, 231; protest xiv
equal rights vii, viii, 159, 161
equality 8, 9, 15, 17, 159, 195, 196, 218, 232, 233; gender 107, 159, 199; *see also* sexual rights, sexuality; racial 106, 159
Erwin, Alec 68, 70
Establishment, British 9, 12, 18
ethic(s) 230; of commitment 237; conviction 206; feminist 222; praxis 226, 234, 237; Protestant 226

Ethiopia 196
exploitation, xv
ethnicity, 7
European Union 16
evenements (France), 13

factories, 30, 32, 51, 79, 80
Fair trade 162
Faiz, Faiz Ahmed 80, 81
family ix, 12, 172, 182, 185, 203, 219, 221, 227
Fanshen 214
farmers 76
fascism 149, 151
Fathe, Tarek 77
Fatima, Kaniz 79
Federal Bureau of Investigation (FBI) 101
Federation of South African Trade Unions (FOSATU) 68
Female Eunuch 192
feminism x, xviii, 35, 95, 111, 190–1, 194, 199, 200, 211, 212, 217, 218, 219, 222, 223, 229, 230, 234–5
femstars 218, 219
feudal/ism 76, 82
Firestone, Shulamith 218
financial crisis (2008–9) 108, 236, 237, 238
fishing 204
Follet, B. 62
Foucault 206, 226, 227
Fouque, Monique 35
Fortune (journal) 104
France xv–xvi, 6, 8, 13, 23–37, 78
Frankfurt, University of 153
Frankfurt School 41
Frayn, Michael 11
Free Association 145–6
freedom 233
French Communist Party 25, 29, 31
Friedan, Betty 218
Fried, Erich 152
Friends magazine 13
Friends of the Earth 229
Front Homosexuel d'Action Révolutionaire 35
'Fronts' 35–36

Fuller, Buckminster 117
fundamentalism, Islamic 78, 87, 229

G8 summit 145, 146, 163
G20 36
Gandapur, Haq Nawaz 84
Gandhi, Mahatma 64
Garment Workers Union 66
Gauche Prolétarienne 32, 44, 52
gay, issues and rights (see also homosexuality) 11, 95, 111, 197, 229; Liberation x, 35–36
Gemeinschaft 13
gender (see also women) xi, 7, 10, 175, 176, 180, 181, 183, 190, 194, 199
General Agreement on Trade and Tariffs (GATT) 231
General Factory Workers Benefit Fund 68
generation(s) 98, 99, 149, 158, 172, 173, 191, 203–4, 233, 234, 237
generational attitudes viii, xviii
Genoa 163
Germany (Federal Republic) 8, 10, 78, 99, 149–64, 169–86, 233, 237
Gesellschaft 13
gestalt psychology, 7
Gherao 79, 80, 82, 86
gigantism, xi
Glaubach, Stanley 217
GLC (Greater London Council) 15
Gleneagles 145, 146
global justice (movement) 230
globalisation 59, 164, 195, 229, 230, 232
Godard, Jean-Luc 33
Gomez, Antonio Fereira 47
Goodman, Paul 111
Gordon College 77
Gore, Al 231
governance 4, 15–16
Gramsci, Antonio 9
green revolution 83
green, movements xiii, 161–2
Green Party, Germany 153
Greenham Common 202
Greenpeace 229
Greenwich Village 97
Grotowski, Jerzy 125, 128
guerilla tactics 54, 155

Guevara, Che 28, 41, 49, 54
Guildford College of Art 117
Guinea-Bisseau 49, 55
Gulbenkian Foundation 13

Haacke, Hans 122
Habermas 4, 5, 10–11, 12, 149–164, 194, 231, 237
habitus 198, 201
Hall, Stuart 111
Hamilton, Richard 114, 115, 116, 117
handicapped 11
Hanisch, Carol 211, 212
Hanover, University of 151
Hari Committees 84
Harvard academics 76
Hasan, Mehdi 81
Hasan, Saeed 77
Hassan, Mubashir 77
Hatirdia 82
Hayden, Casey 223n
health 12, 202, 220, 222, 229; care 174
hedonism x, 8, 11, 43, 46
hegemony 9, 12, 114, 226
Hemson, David 64
Henderson, Nigel 115
Henri, Adrian 125
heterotopias 226–7, 230
hierarchy xvii, 43, 112, 205, 233, 234
higher education see: 'education, higher'
Hinton, William 214
hippies 46, 96, 100, 192
Ho Chi Min 41, 49, 55
Home Office 14
homelessness 14
homology 97
homosexuality (see also gay issues/rights) 35
Horn, Gerd-Rainer 8, 226, 238
Hornsey Affair, the 110, 111, 112, 113, 121, 122–128
Hornsey College of Art 111, 117–122, 128
Horster, Detlef 158
Hochschild, Arlie 219
House (of Representatives) Un-American Activities Committee (HUAC) 92
housing 12, 14
Hudson, Tom 115
Huizinga, Johan 6

human rights xii, 23, 161, 230, 231, 232
Hungary 42
Hyderabad 78, 84

Ibrat 80
identity/identities 11, 12, 36, 37, 95, 196, 206, 227, 229, 232
ideology 9, 14, 32, 41, 94, 96, 98, 127, 141, 151, 154, 157, 158, 160, 163, 190, 195, 197, 204, 205, 216, 227, 229, 230, 231, 232, 237
Iftikharuddin Mian 80
imaginary 28, 29, 34, 36, 37, 41, 43
imperialism 28, 29, 42, 44, 51, 230, 232; American 107, 151
Imroze 80
Independent Group 114, 121, 128
India 74, 87, 205
individualisation 193
individualism xvii, 25, 99, 128
Industrial Conciliation Act 67
industrialism 18
industrialisation 45, 74–5
inequality 10, 162, 197, 202, 231, 236
Inglehart, R. 6
Ingelhart-Index 176
Institute of Contemporary Arts (ICA) 111, 121, 122, 124, 125, 128, 129
Institute of Labour Education 69
Internationale Situationniste 134, 142
International Socialists (IS) 199
International Times 120
Internet xiv, 227
Intersindical (Portugal) 48
interviews, qualitative xviii, 234
Isipongo 67
Iraq War 225, 230
Islam 86, 229
Islamism 229, 230
Israel 50, 78
Italy 8

Jalib, Habib 81
Jamalpur 82
Jamiat-i-Islami 78, 81
Jamiat Tulba-e-Islam (JIT Organisation of Islamic Students) 78

Jatoi, Hider Baksh 84
Jeannette Rankin Brigade 213
Jefferson, Thomas 225
Jesus Movement, 100
Jihad 86, 229
jotadrs (land owners) 82
Joplin, Janis 31
Johnson, Lyndon B. 151
journalists 80–81, 221
July, Serge 31–2
justice 195, 196

Karachi 76, 80, 86
'Karl Marx University', Germany 153
Karachi Municipal Corporation 79
Kazmi, Ameer Ahmed 77
Keaton, Buster 123
Keele, University of 117
Kennedy brothers 102
Kent (UK) 14
Kent State University 101
Kesey, Ken 101
Keynes/Keynesiansm 18, 75
Khairpur 84
Khakwani, Hameed 84
Khan, Ayub 73, 76, 77, 78, 80, 81, 83, 84, 85
Khan, Dera Ismail 84
Khan, Fatehyab Ali 77
Khan, Meraj Muhammad 77, 85
Khan, Rashid Hassan 77
Khan, Yahya 85
Khulna 79
Kiesinger, Kurt Georg 150
King, Martin Luther 95, 100, 102
King, Mary 223
Kneale, Nigel 11
Koedt, Anne 218
Kohl, Helmut 174
Krishak Samity 83
Krivine, Alain 32
Kristallnacht 152
Kristeva, Juila 42
Kropotkin, Prince 41
Kruschev, Nikita 43
Kubrick, Stanley 12
Kustow, Michael 111, 112, 122–5, 129

labour, domestic 11; markets 235; movement 24
Labour Party (Britain) 10, 15, 221, 236
Lahore 77, 78, 80, 81
Lail-o-Nahar 80
land reform 86
landlords 76
Langlade, Xavier 28
latency 191, 196, 202
Latin America 43
(see also 'South America')
Lawrence, Ralph 63
Leary, T. 101
Leeds, University of 117
Lefebvre, Henri 191, 194
Leftwich, Adrian 60
legacies, vii–viii, 190, 202, 205
legitimation 159
Leicester, University of 117
leisure-time 11
Leninism/ists 32, 41, 43, 48, 53, 153, 163
Lennon, John i, 5, 8
lesbian rights (see also sexual rights) 95
L'Humanité 29
Liaquat Park 81
liberalisation, of trade and markets 231
liberalism 102, 104, 157, 226, 232, 237
liberation (see also womens liberation) 7, 8, 18, 137, 143, 146, 195, 198, 229
Libération 31
libertarianism x, xv, 4, 8, 12, 14, 18, 32, 41
life expectancy 175
life course 192, 197, 202, 204, 234, 235 (see also 'lifecycle')
life stories 189, 192–4
life styles 3, 8, 11, 227; ethical, xi; materialistic xi
lifecycle 185
lifeworld xiv, xvi, 4, 12, 16, 18, 195, 236; colonisation, 10, 11, 18, 159–60, 161
literature 46
Liverpool 13, 125; University of 117
local authorities 12, 14–16
Local Strategic Partnerships 16
localism xi
London 12, 13, 117, 123
longitudinal data 186
Lorde, Audre 191, 200, 201

LSE (London School of Economics and Political Science) 94, 117
LSD 101
Lukacs, Georg 194

Macchiocchi, Maria Antonietta 42
McCarthy, Senator Joe 92
McCarthyism 93
McGovern, Senator George 101
McHale, John 115
McLuhan, Marshall 114, 119
MacMillan, Harold 11
McWillaw Iron and Steel Foundry 67
madrassas 86
Mafeje, Archie 62
mahajans (money lenders) 82
Mailer, Norman 111, 122
Mainardi, Pat 218
Majumdar, Charu 82
Malakand 84
Malcolm X 215
management 235
Manchester 15
Manchester, University of 117
Manhattan 217
Mannheim, Karl 98, 204, 234, 237
Maoism/ists 28, 29, 31, 32, 39, 41, 42, 43, 50, 52, 53–5, 77, 153, 156, 157, 163, 193
Mao Zedong (Mao Tsetung) 42, 49, 214
Marchais, Georges 25
Marcuse, Herbert 16, 63, 64, 65, 117, 120, 127, 234, 237
March on Washington (1963) 95
Mardan 84
marihuana (marijuana) 141–2
market(s), 10, 11, 18, 231, 234, 236, 238
martial law 86
Marwick, Arthur 5, 11, 233
Marx/Marxism x, 8, 9, 14, 32, 41, 42, 61, 63, 64, 75, 92, 98, 150, 154, 155, 156, 158, 160, 163, 199, 204, 205, 206, 215, 219, 226; libertarian xv
Marxist-K Gruppen 153
Marxist Leninist Communist Party of Portugal 51
Marxist Leninist Revolutionary Unit 51

SUBJECT INDEX 259

Marxist Leninist Revolutionary Committee(s) 52, 53
mass culture, 18
mass consumption 11, 46
mass media (see also 'media') 17, 94, 154
mass production 11
materialism 6, 172, 176, 178, 180, 182
means-testing 12
media viii, xvii, 12, 18, 46, 114, 123, 124, 216, 218, 219, 221, 223, 232
Medieval Bloc 144
Melucci, Alberto 191, 195, 202, 206
meritocracy 10, 155
Merseyside 16
Millett, Kate 218
militarism xv, 226, 228
military 73, 78, 86
military–industrial complex 102, 238
Mills, C.W. 96, 237
minorities xi, 11
Miss America (beauty contest) 213
modernisation 10, 11, 12, 18; urban 13, 46
modernity 160, 227
mahajans 82
Mohini Textile Mill 79
Moles, Abraham 126
Moravia, Alberto 42
Morgan, Robin 191, 199, 218
Morrell, Derek 14
motherhood 222
Mouvement de Libération des Femmes (MLF) 35
Movement for Rethinking Art and Design Education (MORADE) 127
Movement of 22 March 23, 30
Movement, The xii, xvi, 91, 92, 95, 108, 237; definition of 91–2; achievements of 106–8; break up of 99–102
MRPP 49, 52
Mowlam, Mo 235–6
Mozambique 49, 55
Ms Magazine 217, 218
Mujeeb-ur-Rehman, Shaikh 73
Munich 153
music, popular 5–6, 7, 46, 227
Muslim women 222

Nadeem, Shahid Mahmood 77
Nairn, Tom 9, 12, 18, 112, 127
Najmi, Baba 81
Nanterrre, University of 23, 28, 32, 36, 94
Narsingdi 82
Nasser, Jamal Abdul 78
Natal 65
National Advisory Committee on Art Education 116
National Assistance 12
National Committee for Liberation 60
National Diploma 116
National Guard (USA) 101
National Organisation of Women (NOW) 214, 218, 219
National Press Trust (Pakistan) 80
National Student Federation (NSF) (Pakistan) 76, 77, 84
National Union of South African Students (NUSAS) 60, 65, 68
nationalization 82, 86
nature ix
Nawa-e-Waqt 80
Nawabshah 84
Naxalbari line 82
Nazism 41, 149, 150, 152
neo-anarchism 155, 156, 157
neo-colonialism 73
neo-liberalism 226, 234
neo-Marxism 158
neo-tribe 99
'network' approach to education 119–20, 126
Neustatter, Angela 215
Neville, Richard 111
New Deal for Communities 15
Newman, Thunderclap 5
New Age philosophy 14
New Labour 15, 18, 236
New Left 10, 41, 60, 70, 91, 92, 93, 96, 104–5, 112, 117, 211; definition of 91
New Left Review (journal) 9, 93
New Right x
New York 35, 129
New York Radical Women 211, 213, 219

new social movements; see: social movements, new
Newcastle 116
Newsnight 221
NGOs xi, xii, 4, 232
Nietszche 157
Nihilism 40, 143
North West Frontier Province 84
Notes from Nowhere 143, 144
Nottingham 13
nuclear power 161
nuclear disarmament 95
Nupen, C. 65
nutrition 229
Nuttall, Jeff 123

O Communista 48, 50, 54
Obama, Barack xiii
Odeon (Paris) xii,141
O Grito do Povo 48
Occident 28
Ohensorg, Benno 151, 154
organic food xiii
'Old Left' 238
Orwell, George 11
Our Bodies, Our Selves 220
Oz trial xiv

Pakistan 73–86
Pakistan Communist Party (Communist Party of Pakistan) 78, 79
Pakistan Observer 80
Pakistan Times 80
Pakistan Federal Union of Journalists (PFUJ) 80
Pakistan Peoples Party (PPP) 77, 84
Palestine 78, 81
Pan African Congress 60
Papanek, G. 75–6
Paris 28–30, 129, 141, 153, 192
participation 8, 12, 14, 16, 17, 18, 96, 113, 142–3, 161, 170, 171,172, 175, 176, 178–9, 182, 185, 189
parties, political xiii, 8, 33, 62, 233; and the Movement 107
partnerships 17
Parsons, Talcot 157
Pasmore, V. 115

pass laws 60, 66
patriarchy 219
peace movement 11, 229; see also: anti-war
peasants 44, 74, 76, 78, 80, 82–85, 86, 204, 214
Penguin (publisher) 93
Peniche, prison 55
Penrose, R. 125
pensions 174
People Show, The 122
People's Jute Mills 79
period effects 174–5, 185
personal is political xvi, 17, 212, 220
personal life styles 11, 25
Peshawar 76, 87
petitions 176
Phoenix settlement 64
Piao, Lin 28, 31
Pietermaritzburg 67
Plastic Parthenon, The 115
planners 12
planning; civic/urban 11, 13, 116; economic 11
pleasure ix; principle 234
pluralism 14
Poland 42
police 13, 30, 41, 47, 48, 77, 79, 82, 84, 86, 141–143,145, 151; powers xiv
political culture, conservative xii
Political Economy Collective 14
political mobilization 185
political participation (see also 'participation')170–1
pollution 12
pop-art 124
Popular Action Front 48
Popular War Committees 52
Port Huron Statement 95–96, 103, 223–6
Portuguese Marxist Leninist Committee (CMLP) 48, 54
Portuguese Communist Party 45, 47, 50, 52, 53, 55
Portuguese Marxist-Leninist Communist Organisation (OCMLP) 48, 51
Portuguese National Union/National Action Party 47
post industrial xiii

postmaterialism 6, 18, 170–1, 172, 174, 175, 176, 178, 180, 182, 185, 186
Post-War Settlement 18
poverty 12, 79, 156, 173, 231
power 36
Prague 129, 145
pragmatism 164n
praxis 67, 70, 162, 226, 237; ethic 226
President, France 24; Portugal 45; USA xi
pressure group politics (and the Movement) 107
prestige, occupational 185–6
professions/professionalisation 5, 16, 17, 80, 85, 118, 212, 215, 220, 235
proletariat 41, 51, 61, 65, 75
protest 37, 39, 173, 190, 192, 194, 225, 226, 229, 231, 233 ; cycle of 34
Protestant Ethic 226
Provos 141
psychedelic drugs 98
public service 234, 235, 236
Punjab University 77

Qadri, Sibghatullah 77
Qasimi, Ahmed Nadeem 80
Quebec City's Carnival Against Capital 144
Quran, Holy 81

race 190, 194, 200, 219
race relations 10
racial equality 95
racial segregation 95, 228
racism xiii, 96, 106, 196, 200, 201, 228
radicalism 158, 186, 226, 228, 229, 230, 231, 233, 235–8
Rahim, J.A. 77
Rasheed, Shaikh Abdul 77
rationality 160, 194; instrumental 11
rationalisation 159, 160
Rauschenberg, R. 115, 117
Rawalpindi 76, 77, 81
Read, H. 116, 117
Reagan, Bernice 191
Reaganism 234
reality, nature of ix
recession xv, 174, 238
Red Army Faction (Rote Armee Fraktion) 40, 153, 228

Red Brigades 228
Red Oak, Iowa 217
Redstockings 213, 219
reflexivity 193
refeudalisation 150
regeneration, urban, 18; programmes, 16, 17
regression models 179–80
Reich, Wilhelm 27
Reichart, Jasia 125–6, 128
reification 160, 161
Reorganising Movement of the Party of the Proletariat 49
repressive tolerance 16
ressentiment 157
revolution/ary 3, 28, 30, 32, 41, 42, 75, 100, 102, 118, 127, 129, 133, 135, 138, 139–40, 142, 146, 147, 160, 162, 194, 199, 212, 215, 218, 226, 227, 229, 230, 237; action xviii, 30, 53; 'in the head' 18
Revolutionary Brigades 48, 54
Revolutionary Party of the Proletariat 54
Revolutionary Unity and Action League 48
Revolutionary Youth Movement 33
revolutionism 8, 42
Rhodes University 67
Ricoeur, Paul 129
Rio conference on environment and development 231
rights movements 106, 230, 231, 232
Robbins Report 116
rock, festivals 7
Rodrigues, Francisco Martins 48, 53
Rokan, Stein 233
Romania 86
romantic (idiom of) 116; tradition 125, 127
Ronan Point 12
Rose, Ernestine 214
Roundhouse Congress for the Dialectics of Liberation 117, 120
Royal College of Art 116
Rudd, Mark 33
ruling bloc 9, 11, 18
rural farming 83
Russell, Bertrand 78
Rustam 84

Salazar, Antonio de Oliveira 44, 47
Sandbrook, D. 5
Sanghar 84
Santos dos Ribeiro 52
Sarachild, Kathie 213, 214
Sarkozy, Nicolas 24, 40
Satire 123
Sartre, Jean-Paul 31, 52, 62, 63, 65
Saqi, Jam 78
Savio, M. 103
Sayres, S. 111
Schneemann, C. 124
schools 172, 235
Scilly Isles 12
Scotland 14
SDS (Socialist German Students) 150, 151,152, 153, 154, 159
Seattle 36
Seebohm Committee 13
Seeds for Change 146
sensibilities, 8, 18, 238 (see also: sentiments)
sentiments 4, 5, 6, 15, 18, 235
sex 7, 33, 34, 41, 211, 218, 222
sexism 199, 200, 211, 219
sexual relations vii, 11, 33
sexual rights xi
sexuality ix, 27–28, 34, 127, 190, 194, 196, 200
Shafly, Phyllis 219
Shah of Iran 151
Shahid, Riaz 81
Sharpeville 60
Short, Claire 235–6
Simmel, Georg 233
Sindh 84
Sindh Hari (Peasants) Committee 84
Singh-Sandhu, J. 127
Single Regeneration Budgets 15
sisterhood 216
sit-ins 106, 112, 117, 119–21, 155
Situationists/Situationism 32, 33, 41, 133–147, 213; definition 134
Slater Walker 68
Smithson, Alison and Peter 115
SNCC 223
Snow, C. P. 126
Soares, Mario 47
Social Democratic Party (SPD), Germany 150, 153

social democracy 233
social development 94
Social Forums xii, 227
social historians ix
social justice 196
social movements xi, 11, 33, 106, 107, 147, 195, 222, 232, 233; and party politics and pressure groups 232–3; New 4, 36, 191, 198; theory 34, 150, 206
social policy 13
Social Problems (journal) 103–4
social services, 12, 13, 14
social status 175, 178, 180, 186
social workers 12, 15
socialisation 5, 172–3, 174, 175, 176, 195, 198
socialism 8, 41, 76, 162, 219; Islamic 86
Socialisme ou Barbarie 137
Socialist League 150
Socialist Workers Party (SWP) 199
Society for Education through Art 115
Socioeconomic Model of Participation 171, 185
Sociology 13, 27, 28, 34
solidarity 17, 18, 235
Sontag, Susan 111
Sorbonne University 23, 29, 30, 32, 35, 62, 126, 138
South African Communist Party 62
South African Labour Bulletin 69
South African Students Organisation (SASO) 65, 68
Southern Conference Educational Fund 211
Southern Nonviolent Co-ordinating Committee (SNCC) 95, 223
spaces, social vii, viii, xi, xii, 46, 48, 198, 227
spectacle 137, 140, 143; definition 135
Springer, Axel 150, 152, 153
squatters 11,13
stagflation xi
stagnation thesis, UK 9, 12
Stalinism 42
Socioeconomic Model of Participation 171
Stanislavski, C. 125
state 10, 12, 13, 14, 15, 17, 152, 163, 238
Steinem, Gloria 218

Stellenbosch 64
stevedores 68
Stonewall 35
Straw, Jack 221, 235–6
street theatre xii
strikes xi, 48, 65–6, 79, 82
structural functionalism 156, 157
Student Action Committee (SAC) (Pakistan) 77
student radicalism xiii, 48, 70, 77, 94, 117–122, 127, 158, 163, 190
students, as social movement x, 33–34, 94,127, 173; in France xv, 33; in Germany 149, 150, 152–5, 158; in Pakistan 74, 76, 77, 81; in UK 111–3, 117,192
Students for a Democratic Society (SDS) 33, 65, 95–6, 100, 225
Student Peace Union (SPU) 95
Studies on the Left (journal) 93
Studio International 116
Sturmabteilung 152
subjectivation 195
Summerson Committee 116
surveillance, technologies xiii, 12
sustainability, environmental xii, 17, 161–2, 230
Swat 84
system, the 11, 14, 16, 18, 159, 161, 195

Tactical Frivolity bloc 144
Tangail 82
Tank 112–3, 122–4, 128, 129
taxation 231
Taylor, Simon Weston 125
technology xvii, 12, 75, 112, 113, 114, 116, 119–20,123, 124, 125, 126, 127–8, 230
technocrats/technocratic 11–12, 14, 18, 113, 114
television/telecommunications xv, 46, 112, 115, 123, 124,129, 131
temporal fallacy 175
terror 'war' on xiii
terrorism x
Thalidomide 12
Tharparkar 84
Thatcher, Margaret 204
Thatcherism 15, 101, 234

theatre 9, 46, 123, 124, 125–6, 128, 141, 149
Theatre Laboratory 125
Third Sector 15, 17
third way 96
'Third World' 42, 43, 73,100, 154, 155, 163, 229
Thistlewood, D. 115–6
Thurbon, H. 115, 116
Tickner, L. 111–2
Tilly, Charles 34
Time Magazine 217–8
Tip, K. 65
Tocquevillian 25
Tongi (Pakistan) 79
Torrey Canyon 12
totalitarianism 102, 157, 173, 226
Touraine, Alain 33, 35, 191, 195, 202, 205
Towards a Poor Theatre 125
tower blocks 12
trade unions xiii, 14, 47, 62, 66, 69, 75, 161, 204, 235
Trafalgar Square 123
traffic 12
Transition Towns 230
transport, air xv
Trotskyism/ists 28, 43, 60
trade 231
'two cultures debate' 126
Turner, Rick 62, 66, 68, 69, 70
Two Cultures 126

ul Haq, Mahbub 76
ul-Haq, Zia 86
UND (University of Natal Durban) 63, 65, 69, 70
undergraduate studies 13
underground press 7, 8, 13, 98
unemployment 173, 174
United Kingdom 16, 78, 111, 192
United Nations 44
United States of America (USA) xi, 5, 7, 14, 50, 59, 76, 78, 91–108, 111, 163, 211–222
Universities 13, 28, 30, 60, 151, 154 (see also 'higher education'); closures xi
University of Capetown 60, 62, 67
University of Pietermarizburg 67

264 SIXTIES RADICALISM AND SOCIAL MOVEMENT ACTIVISM

University of Witwatersrand 62, 67
University of Punjab 77
URML 53
urban environment 9, 12
USSR 42, 43, 44, 49, 86, 229, 237
utopia/nism xii, 32, 105, 120, 121,126, 218, 226–7, 237

values: cognitive 6; formation 5, 134, 170, 186, 196; political xviii, 159, 161; radical 227, 232, 235, 236–8; revolutionary 191; rights and freedoms 229; social viii, 4, 6, 11, 13, 14, 16, 154, 158, 161, 178, 197, 202, 233, 235
Van Reijen, Willem 158
Vaneigem, Raoul 133, 134, 136, 137, 138, 139, 140, 147
Vietnam 30, 118, 122, 229; War 8, 28, 31, 32, 40, 41, 50, 78, 95, 99, 100, 101, 102, 151, 152, 225, 228, 229, 230
violence, imaginary of 28, 29, 34, 200; as political tactics viii, xiii, 25, 31, 39, 40, 53, 54, 100, 102, 108, 145, 151, 151, 157, 163, 228, 230, 237; State 122, 163
Vive la Revolution 44
voluntary organisations 15, 16, 17, 233
Vorster, B.J. 68
VOSCUR (Voluntary Organisations Council for Urban Regeneration) 17

wages 11, 66, 67, 73
Wages Act 67
Wages Board 67
Wages and Economics Commission 65, 66, 69, 70
Wales 12, 14
Walker, J. A. 129
war xi, xv, 39, 74, 79
'war on terror' 229
warfare state 238

Washington 213
Water and Power Development Authority (WAPDA) 79
Weather Underground (Weathermen) 33, 40, 100–101, 228
Weber, Max 157, 226
Webster, Eddie 70
welfare 10; State 11, 158, 161
welfarism xiii, 18, 233
well-being 202
Weston-Taylor, S. 125
Willing, V. 116
Willis, Ellen 212
Willmott, Peter 13
Wilson, Harold 10
Wirtschaftswunder 173
Wittig, Monique 35
Witwatersrand 66
women (see also gender) 175, 179, 185, 194, 199, 212, 214, 215, 217, 219, 220, 222, 223, 234; and employment 219, 234
womens movement (see also feminism) xviii, 11, 190, 211–223, 230, 235; as Womens Liberation 107, 191, 211, 212, 213, 214, 220, 221, 229–30
work ix, 182, 202, 218, 235
workers 29, 30, 65, 66, 67, 68, 69, 142, 160; black xv, 61, 65–9; councils 32, 33; Pakistani 78, 79, 81, 85
World Trade Organisation 231
World War II 173

Yippies 213
Young, Michael 13
youth, cultures xiii, 18, 25, 31, 39, 43, 46, 97–8, 99; movements x, 33, 41

Zapatistas 163, 230
Zeitgeist 175
Zellner, Dottie 211
Zulu 69

www.ingramcontent.com/pod-product-compliance
Lightning Source LLC
Chambersburg PA
CBHW021821300426
44114CB00009BA/266